MENC Handbook of Musical Cognition
and Development

MENC HANDBOOK OF MUSICAL COGNITION AND DEVELOPMENT

Edited by

Richard Colwell

OXFORD
UNIVERSITY PRESS

2006

OXFORD
UNIVERSITY PRESS

Oxford University Press, Inc., publishes works that further
Oxford University's objective of excellence
in research, scholarship, and education.

Oxford   New York
Auckland   Cape Town   Dar es Salaam   Hong Kong   Karachi
Kuala Lumpur   Madrid   Melbourne   Mexico City   Nairobi
New Delhi   Shanghai   Taipei   Toronto

With offices in
Argentina   Austria   Brazil   Chile   Czech Republic   France   Greece
Guatemala   Hungary   Italy   Japan   Poland   Portugal   Singapore
South Korea   Switzerland   Thailand   Turkey   Ukraine   Vietnam

Copyright © 2002 by MENC: The National Association for Music Education,
2006 by Oxford University Press, Inc.

Published by Oxford University Press, Inc.
198 Madison Avenue, New York, New York 10016

www.oup.com

Oxford is a registered trademark of Oxford University Press

Library of Congress Cataloging-in-Publication Data
MENC Handbook of musical cognition and development / edited by Richard Colwell.
    p. cm.
  Includes bibliographical references and index.
  ISBN-13 978-0-19-518923-0; 978-0-19-530456-5 (pbk.)
  ISBN 0-19-518923-X; 0-19-530456-X (pbk.)
  1. Music—Instruction and study.   I. Colwell, Richard.
  II. Music Educators National Conference (U.S.)
MT1.M98736 2006
780'.71—dc22   2005048092

9 8 7 6 5 4 3 2 1

Printed in the United States of America
on acid-free paper

Preface

The use of research findings is critical to the success of music teaching and learning. There is probably no area of greater importance in the 21st century than research involving music and its impact on the development and use by the human brain. The popular press has reported partial findings of research indicating the importance of music in human development. It is important that teachers and researchers have a full understanding of the findings of valid studies in order that our knowledge not be misused. Andreas Lehmann, a German scholar, assembled an outstanding team that wrote chapters on our knowledge of perception and cognition for the *New Handbook of Research on Music Teaching and Learning* published by Oxford University Press in 2002. In this text, we provide an up-date of that material with the addition of a chapter on Music and Neuroscience by John W. Flohr and Donald A. Hodges.

This up-date is the result of the efforts of Ms. Kim Robinson and Ms. Eve Bachrach of Oxford University Press and Mike Blakeslee of the National Association for Music Education—MENC, believers in the importance of disseminating research findings to the profession. It is our hope that the publication of separate, small, economical, books on specialized research topics will make the material more accessible to users in a variety of fields. Music cognition is a vital topic for scholars in medicine, psychology, in educational psychology, and in music theory, as well as for music educators. One will note that we have selected authors from all of these fields and authors from continental Europe, Great Britain, Canada, and the United States. It has been my pleasure to work through with them with the assistance of Professor Lehmann issues of language, definitions, and concepts to make the material clear to not only English speakers but those who use English as a research tool. Accurate definitions apply to the topic of each chapter although the authors have coordinated their writing to avoid duplication and to cover the material of music perception and cognition as succinctly as possible in only seven chapters. Although the chapters stand alone as a research resource, they have also been organized to be read in the normal textbook fashion, from the introduction to the end of chapter 7.

It has been my pleasure to work with not only the authors but with the National Association for Music Education and Oxford University Press in this exemplary cooperative project. As one who does not normally think about how music works within the human, I have found these chapters enlightening as I'm sure will both sophisticated and those of us who are less sophisticated in brain functioning and its responses.

Contents

Contributors

JANE W. DAVIDSON is professor of performance studies in the Department of Music at the University of Sheffield and specializes in research on performance skills acquisition, expression, and social dynamics. Her recent edited volume, *The Music Practitioner*, explores the uses of research for the practicing musician. A former editor of *Psychology of Music*, she is currently vice-president of the European Society for the Cognitive Sciences of Music. She also holds a visiting professorial post at the University of Western Australia. Besides her academic career, as an ex-professional opera singer, she specializes in directing. She has more than thirty productions in her repertoire, having worked on the wildly contemporary (*Death and the Madman*, for Drama per musica in Portugal) to the pastoral and lyrical, including Mozart's rarely performed *Betulia Liberata*. Over the years, she has worked with the Hong Kong Cultural Centre, London International Opera Festival, the Edinburgh Festival, Wigmore Hall, Extemporary Dance Theatre, Théâtre de Complicité, Opera North, and Drama per Musica on a range of music theatre projects.

JOHN W. FLOHR received his doctorate in music education from the University of Illinois-Urbana. He has performed as a professional musician and taught at the college, public school, and preschool level. He is professor of music at Texas Woman's University–Denton, serves as current president of the Texas Music Educators Conference, and recently was faculty fellow at the national Arts Eduction Partnership. He specializes in early childhood music education and has authored research papers, books, videos, audio recordings, and computer programs in music and music education. His most recent book is *Musical Lives of Young Children*.

HEINER GEMBRIS holds a degree in music education from the Academy of Music Detmold and in musicology from the Technische Universität Berlin. He worked as a music teacher in secondary public schools for several years. In 1985, he earned his doctorate with a study on music listening and relaxation. After an employment at the University of Augsburg, he was appointed professor for systematic musicology at the University of Münster (1991), and later at the University of Halle/Wittenberg (1998). Since 2001 he has been head of music education and Music Psychology at the University of Paderborn and has directed the Institute for Research on Musical Ability (IBFM). Heiner Gembris has occupied numerous leading positions in scientific organisations and is member of the scientific board of national and international journals. His main research interests concern the effects of music listening, music preferences, and the nature and development of music abilities across the lifespan. In 1998, he published a textbook in German on musical talent and development (2nd edition 2002).

WILFRIED GRUHN is professor emeritus of music education at the University of Music (Musikhochschule), Freiburg, Germany. He served as chair of the Music Education Department, and worked as co-editor of several German journals for music education. His research areas include musicology, music education, and psychology. He specialized in the neurobiology of music learning, perception, and cognition and collaborates with neurologists in interdisciplinary projects. Currently he is director of the Gordon-Institute for Early Childhood Music Learning in Freiburg, Germany.

DONALD A. HODGES is Covington Distinguished Professor of Music Education and director of the Music Research Institute at the University of North Carolina at Greensboro. He is contributing editor of the *Handbook of Music Psychology* and the accompanying *Multimedia Companion* (CD-ROMs vols. 1 & 2). Recent research includes a series of brain imaging studies of musicians.

REINHARD KOPIEZ has been professor of music psychology at the School of Music and Drama in Hannover, Germany since 1998. He earned his PhD in 1990 from the Technical University of Berlin. After appointments as assistant professor for musicology at the Technical University of Berlin and later for systematic musicology at the school of music in Wuerzburg. Since 1998 he has been vice president of the German Society for Music Psychology (DGM) and since 2002 its president. He is also a member of the executive council of the European Society for the Cognitive Sciences of Music (ESCOM). Kopiez has written several books and numerous chapters and articles for national and international publications. His main areas of research interest are performance research, rhythm perception, and music in everyday-life. Some recent publications include: (1998) *Fussball-Fangesaenge* [Singing at soccer games], Wuerzburg: Koenigshausen; (2003a) Intonation of harmonic intervals: adaptibility of expert musicians to equal temperament and just intonation, *Music Perception*, 20(4), 383–410; (2003b) Tempo and loudness analysis of a continuous 28-hour performance of Erik Satie's composition "Vexations," *Journal of New Music Research*, 32(3), 243–258; (2003c) Stability of motor programs during a state of meditation: electrocortical activity in a pianist playing 'Vexations' by Erik Satie continuously for 28 hours, *Psychology of Music*, 31(2), 173–186.

ANDREAS C. LEHMANN is currently professor of systematic musicology and music psychology at the *Hochschule für Musik Würzburg*, Germany. He earned a degree in music education and a Ph.D. in musicology, both from the *Hochschule für Musik und Theater* in Hannover, Germany, from 1998 to 2000 he worked as a junior faculty ("Wissenschaftlicher Assistent") with Heiner Gembris in the musicology department at the *Martin-Luther University* in Halle. Between 1993 and 1998 he was a postdoctoral fellow in the Department of Psychology at the *Florida State University*, Tallahassee, Florida, where he worked with K. Anders Ericsson in the area of cognitive psychology. Andreas Lehmann received in 1997 a Young Researcher Merit Award from the *European Society for the Cognitive Sciences of Music (ESCOM)*, and he has co-edited a book on practice and published a number of chapters and journal articles. Currently, Andreas Lehmann is also associate editor of the journal *Musicae Scientiae* and vice-president of the German music education research organization *(AmpF)*. In his research, he is mainly interested in studying the structure and acquisition of high levels of instrumental music performance skills such as those displayed by advanced music students and professional performers. This research on practice and performance has real-life applications for music education and is of theoretical importance for many other domains of expertise.

FRANCES RAUSCHER is an associate professor in the Department of Psychology at the University of Wisconsin Oshkosh. She holds degrees in cello performance and experimental psychology. Her research focuses on the relationship between music exposure and cognitive performance in adults, humans, and rats. She has publications in music cognition, cognitive neuroscience, developmental psychology, and social psychology, and has given presentations in North America, Europe, and Australia.

E. GLENN SCHELLENBERG is a professor in the Department of Psychology at the University of Toronto at Mississauga with a cross-appointment in the graduate faculty in the Department of Human Development and Applied Psychology at the Ontario Institute for Studies in Education at the University in Toronto. He received his doctorate from Cornell University in 1994 in human experimental psychology. His primary research area focuses on cognitive developmental issues in the auditory domain with a special interest in music perception and cognition particularly on reciprocal influences between basic psychological processes and musical structure. He is also interested in the cognitive (nonmusical) consequences of formal music lessons. Ongoing research projects are investigations of how one becomes an enculturated listener, the development of children's memory for familiar songs, effects of aging and musical training on pitch perception, developmental perspectives of absolute pitch, and the impact of music lessons on cognitive development. His extensive record of publications not only in developmental and cognitive psychology but in social psychology has recently earned him the Premier's Research Excellent Award for 2002–2007.

WILLIAM FORDE THOMPSON is director of the CCIT and a professor in the Department of Psychology at the University of Toronto at Mississauga. He is also an associate member of the Unit for the Study of Musical Skill and Development. After receiving his doctorate in psychology from Queen's University, he began an exemplary career in music perception and cognition. He is an accomplished composer, writing music for the theater that has been staged throughout Canada and on CBS Radio. He is an officer in the Society for Music Perception and Cognition and heads Experiment Creator, which tests and teaches concepts related to audio-visual content. His research interests are in decoding speech prosody, acoustic cues and speech, visual influences on perception, and recognition of emotion in cross cultural situations. His most recent book is *Music Thought and Feeling: The Psychology of Music*, Oxford University Press, 2006.

BRUCE TORFF is associate professor of curriculum and teaching at Hofstra University in Hempstead, New York. An educational psychologist, Torff has published numerous books and articles on topics in cognitive-developmental psychology, teacher education, and musical cognition. His books include *Understanding and Teaching the Intuitive Mind* and *Multiple Intelligences and Assessment*. Torff earned a doctorate and two masters degrees at Harvard University, where he worked with Howard Gardner and served as a project director at Project Zero, Gardner's research organization. Torff also held a postdoctoral appointment at Yale University in collaboration with Robert J. Sternberg. Torff is active as a leader of professional-development workshops for educators and is also a jazz pianist and songwriter.

MENC Handbook of Musical Cognition
and Development

Introduction

Music Perception and Cognition

ANDREAS C. LEHMANN

Research in perception and cognition in music has seen tremendous growth over the last two decades (see Levitin, 1999). The reason for this expansion is not that music research has emerged only recently as a new discipline; instead, it appears that whoever had been interested in music years ago but did not dare to do music research can now freely admit to his or her "vice." As a result, the field has become extremely diversified and includes psychologists, sociologists, and anthropologists as well as AI researchers, physiologists, and acousticians. Many of them are active musicians with varying degrees of firsthand experience, while other scientists simply think that music is a convenient domain for their purposes. There are also artists who use their working environment to undertake new types of action research (see J. W. Davidson, 2004, e.g., chapters 11 and 22). Common to all is the desire to find out more about how our brain processes the auditory input we then experience as music. Unfortunately, the issues that entice researchers are not always identical to those that appeal to music educators, who, after successful mastery of the scientific jargon, are often disappointed to discover how difficult it is to apply the findings to the classroom. Admittedly, some research done today might only prove its usefulness many years from now in the context of future research.

In the wake of recent advances in neurobiology, trying to separate perception and cognition has become less appropriate and useful. Where, for example, does music cognition actually begin? Does it start in the cochlea or right after the cochlea, or does it emerge out of the simultaneous firing of neurons in different cortical areas? And how does our individual genetic makeup influence music perception and cognition? Where do our memories

3

and feelings enter into the perception and cognition game? As a result, and in order to be of maximal use for music educators, here we did not adhere to a strong division of perception and cognition but rather understood cognition in its broader sense, namely, how it applies in the context of experience, training, development, and culture.

This book with its seven chapters does not purport to cover the whole range of topics relevant to music perception and cognition. We have tried to capitalize on emergent issues and research done since the publication of the first Handbook (Colwell, 1992). In our experience, music educators as a group are likely to look at the research presented in the following 7 chapters. We should keep in mind, however, there is probably not *the* music educator, as there is not *the* music psychologist. Any choice of issues discussed, references cited, or references omitted (due to space limitations) will have to be the result of subjective decisions. A review of the literature is never objective, because the writer has an agenda, which is to introduce a personal view on a topic. With the help of the many reviewers who made thoughtful suggestions to improve the draft chapters, the printed chapters should now match the needs of aspiring or in-service music educators and music education researchers.

The chapters follow a certain logic in that the first five chapters proceed from the basic neurological and cognitive processes to a panoramic view of musical development and the theories behind research on learning. The last two chapters concentrate on music performance skills, musical expression, and the audience. A chapter that was not originally part of the *Musical Cognition and Development* part of the 2002 Handbook is the one by Flohr and Hodges on Music and Neuroscience. Here the authors circumscribe the research methods and results currently available in the area of neuroscience. It is obvious that we are starting to better understand how music is processed in the brain, and how nature and nurture interact. This chapter in fact provides the necessary backdrop to some of the others presented in this volume. Wilfried Gruhn and Frances Rauscher introduce neuropsychological and neurophysiological research as it relates to learning. They also introduce some learning theories that essentially can be viewed as theories of cognition, and they clarify one hotly debated topic in music education, namely, the question of transfer of learning, which sometimes serves as a justification for music education in schools. William Forde Thompson and E. Glenn Schellenberg are experts in basic music cognition with all its developmental and cultural implications. Their chapter abounds with pointers to current research methodology and brings to our attention the processes in music perception we often take for granted (e.g., melody perception, timbre, rhythm). Heiner Gembris gives a more panoramic survey of topics and issues in developmental psychology. While emphasizing cognitive aspects, he also incorporates sociological and cultural aspects. This chapter is closely tailored to the questions frequently asked by music educators. Bruce Torff comes from the general area of educational psychology. His chapter places research on music perception and cognition into the larger context of research on music learning and development with its changing epistemological facets. The contextualist perspective presented by Torff is today an accepted and important position for music education. Reinhard Kopiez reviews the area of performance research in which great progress has been made internationally. Most interestingly, researchers are no longer interested solely in motor programming and internal clocks (although these topics are still under scrutiny) but also interested in knowing how we communicate and understand musical expression. As a trained musicologist, the author is able to bring modern research into contact with its historical roots. Jane W. Davidson and I sum up some of the research in skill acquisition, which stresses the environmental aspects of music learning, especially in learning to play an instrument. In some ways, this chapter acts as a counterweight to the chapter by Gruhn and Rauscher, which emphasizes the "hardware" aspects of musical learning.

For those readers looking for an update in one of the areas mentioned earlier, each chapter should provide a suitable point of entry. For the novice reader the chapters offer a thorough introduction into the topics of music psychology that are relevant to music educators.

REFERENCES

Levitin, D. (1999). [Review of the book *The psychology of music* (2nd ed.), edited by Diana Deutsch]. *Music Perception, 16,* 495–505.

Colwell, R., & Richardson, C. (Eds.) (2002). *The new handbook of research on music teaching and learning.* New York: Oxford University Press.

Davidson, J. W. (Ed.) 2004. *The music practitioner: Research for the music performer, teacher and listener.* Aldershot, UK: Ashgate.

Music and Neuroscience

1

JOHN W. FLOHR
DONALD A. HODGES

Relationships among the brain, music, and musical abilities are of interest to musicians, psychologists, and neuroscientists. The purpose of this chapter is to provide a detailed and critical overview of the neuroscientific research dealing with music and music education. Unfortunately, a direct translation from neuroscience research into music education at this time is very problematic. Although our understanding of brain and behavior has increased at an exponential rate over the past 10 years, theories of brain functioning and our understanding of the neurobiological forces that shape musical behavior are still in their infancy. The focus will be on ideas helpful to music education from what is known about music and the brain. The chapter is organized into three sections.

1. *Strategies for conducting neuromusical research.* A review of the methodological approaches to conducting neuroscientific research in music. The neuroscience tools reviewed in this section have in many ways revolutionized our ability to examine both the function and structure of the brain. (For a more complete review, see Hodges, 1996b.)
2. *Overall development.* A review of findings relating to overall development, selected topics, and theories and theoretical areas.
3. *Future directions.* A generalized summary of findings and recommendations and considerations for future research directions.

Strategies for Conducting Neuromusical Research

How does one go about studying the phenomenon of music in the brain? The brain's immense complexity, in combination with the subtleties and intricacies of human musical behavior, means that conducting neuromusical research is difficult at best. Although there have been tremendous advancements in research tools, no single strategy is able to provide comprehensive answers. Rather, information from every approach possible must be combined to create a more complete understanding. The purpose of this section is to review current strategies, giving for each a rationale for its appropriateness and a critique of its strengths and weaknesses. Only minimal attention is paid to results, as that information is covered more thoroughly in the section on findings.

Throughout this chapter the reader should keep in mind two points. First, the brain is only part of a much larger system that includes the central nervous system (brain and spinal cord) and peripheral nerves (afferent nerve fibers and their receptors, which send messages to the brain, and efferent nerve fibers and their muscles and glands, which take messages from the brain). In addition, the brain regulates the release of hormones into the bloodstream, so that, in effect, the brain extends throughout the body. The second point has to do with mind-brain disagreements. Are the mind and brain one and the same, or are mind and brain separate entities? Untangling such a Gordian knot is beyond the scope of this chapter. Some researchers work from a more purely neurological viewpoint, concerned mainly with physiological processes. Others work from a more cognitive or mental approach. The reader should be aware that modern cognitive neuroscience is beginning to bridge this gap. The concept of psychoneuroimmunology is one that recognizes interconnections among the mind, brain, and body. Music, of course, is a phenomenon that arises out of interactions among all three.

This section is based on six categories: animal research, fetal and infant research, research on brain-damaged individuals, hemispheric asymmetry research, brain imaging research, neuromotor research, and affective research. These categories are based on a combination of methodologies and subject groupings. They appear to fit most closely with the way the literature is organized and reported. From animals we can learn about antecedents to human musical behavior. From infants we can learn about the brain's wiring for music, relatively independent of the influence of experience. Studying brain-damaged individuals provides the opportunity to isolate areas of the brain involved in musical processing. Hemispheric asymmetry research seeks to reveal how the brain is organized. Brain imaging research provides a window into the working brain. Neuromotor research is concerned with how the brain monitors both expressive (i.e., musical performance) and receptive (i.e., music listening) experiences. Finally, affective research looks into the brain's involvement in emotional responses to music.

Animal Research

Although studying animals may seem like an unusual place to begin, this has been a standard approach in psychology (e.g., Pavlov's dog) and continues in cognitive neuroscience. Investigating the ways animals process sounds gives neuroscientists useful information about human sound processing. Most animals have devices for detecting, analyzing, and responding to sounds. Once a sound has been detected, the animal analyzes it for "meaning," and this meaning shapes behavior. A housecat demonstrates this when it comes running into the kitchen at the sound of the can opener. When humans listen to music, the process is similar in that we analyze the sound for meaning and that meaning shapes our responses.

Significant insights into human musicality can be gained particularly by investigating sound-making and responding behaviors in such species as birds, whales, dolphins, monkeys, and apes (D'Amato, 1988; Geissman, 2000; Marler, 2000; Payne, 2000; Warren, 1993; Whaling, 2000). Sight (e.g., seen in displays of aggression or mating behavior) or smell (e.g., marking territory) are ways animals can communicate. But sound has certain advantages in that it can travel long distances rapidly, operate during day or night, and encode complex and changing messages (Slater, 2000). Therefore, many species have developed sophisticated sound-making behaviors (not only vocalizations but also other noises, such as chest-thumping among gorillas). To assume that animal sounds have nothing to do with human music would be to ignore a significant amount of information and would be counter to linkages found in other types of behavior (e.g., language and social organization).

The opposite is equally true; one cannot automatically assume that there is a direct correlation between animal sounds and human music. Thus, one of the first issues to be dealt with is whether or not animals actually create music. This is a difficult question and one that may elude a definitive answer. It is tempting to anthropomorphize animal sounds; after all, we call it bird-*song* because that is what it sounds like to us. But is it music to the animals? Certainly most animal sounds have to do with territoriality, courtship and mating rituals, and signaling (e.g., alarm calls) (Brody, 1991). Slater (2000) remarks that with more than 4,000 species of songbirds alone, and all the varied forms and patterns of their songs, it would not be difficult to find many seemingly musical characteristics embedded in their songs, but that this would most likely be coincidental. Even where birdsongs are more complex, varied, or elaborate than is strictly necessary for biological function, they may be so to achieve distinctiveness. If the point of sound-making is to communicate, it will do no good if the message is lost in a sonic environment rife with many voices. In a cacophonous habitat where many sounds are competing for "airspace," distinctiveness is an advantage. Krause's (1987) niche hypothesis is that each species produces sounds that occupy a particular bandwidth in the overall acoustic spectrum, along with unique rhythm patterns, tonal qualities, and so on. This ensures that the message will not get lost among all the other sounds. Having said that, however, does not preclude an animal deriving pleasure from the act of making sounds. Until we can gain access to their inner worlds, the most we can do is speculate.

In the meantime, this research strategy informs two concerns of music psychologists: What are the evolutionary antecedents of human musicality? What "extra" cognitive structures and processes do humans possess beyond those of other animals that allow for the degree of musicality expressed in all cultures? In the first instance, the sounds of nature (what Krause [1987] terms "biophony") most likely exerted strong influences on early hominid sound-making. It would be quite natural for us to mimic the sounds around us. Of course, with our sophisticated brains, it would not take long for us to move beyond mere mimicry to elaboration, extension, synthesis, and eventually the creation of novel sounds. In time, we would develop our own niche in the biophony. This line of research is important in developing a theory of an evolutionary basis for music (Hodges 1989, 1996a, 2000; Wallin, Merker, & Brown, 2000).

The second concern feeds more directly into the larger question of neuromusicology. For example, animals rely on absolute frequency analysis (D'Amato, 1988) rather than on relative pitch as we do (Trehub, Bull, & Thorpe, 1984). Thus, while various animals can be trained to choose between two songs, they fail miserably if those songs are transposed. By contrast, our adult musicality is possible, in large part, because we deal with pitch relationships. "Yankee Doodle," for instance, is recognizable to us at any pitch center.

There are other cognitive limitations among animals as well. For example, musical forms ranging from simple verse-chorus alternations to lengthy symphonic movements are possible because of our ability to retain musical information for long periods of time. Yet dolphins represent the best animals can do, and they can only recognize the second A section of a simple ABA form if each section is no more than 2 seconds long (Warren, 1993). Once again, however, it must be recognized that testing animals on their capacity for processing human music seems patently unfair. Nevertheless, this line of research does provide evidence of some of the neural mechanisms humans possess that allow for our musicality.

Fetal and Infant Research

In order to understand how the brain is predisposed to music, it would be ideal to look at the brain in a "pure" state, that is, without the influence of the environment. Since this is impossible, studying fetal and infant responses to music allows us to approach a "pure" state with minimal environmental influence. The limitations and difficulties of using babies as subjects seem apparent, but there is much useful information to be gained from this approach. A growing body of literature is focusing on fetal responses to music because in the last trimester before birth, the fetus is capable of responding to sounds in the womb. Researchers can gauge fetal responses by monitoring heart rate and through bodily movements (Abrams & Gerhardt, 1997; Deliège & Sloboda, 1996; Flohr, 2004a).

Almost immediately after birth, babies can orient toward sounds and soon after that can pick out the sounds of the mother's voice (Trehub, Schellenberg, & Hill, 1997; Trehub & Trainor, 1993). A significant amount of the interactions between a newborn and its caretakers is based on two-way sound manipulations. The caretakers sing lullabies and talk "baby talk," and there are musical crib mobiles and toys. "Motherese," a term psychologists have coined to refer to the type of baby talk typically spoken to infants, emphasizes pitch, timbre, dynamic inflections, and rhythm patterns in order to convey meaning (Dissayanake, 2000). Clearly, the baby cannot interpret the meaning of words but does learn to interpret the emotional content. Likewise, the baby learns early on to communicate by manipulating the same sonic elements to express mood states such as hunger, pain, fear, happiness, love, and so on. From this line of research, it is clear that infant musical behaviors are exhibited primarily because of inherited mechanisms (Imberty, 2000; Trehub, 2004). While learning takes place from the outset, babies do not need systematic, formal instruction in order to respond to music, speech, and other sounds.

Research on Brain-Damaged Individuals

Another approach that has a long history in neuroscience is to look at individuals who suffer from some form of brain damage, either from trauma, genetic defect, or aging. Studying persons who have suffered a tumor, stroke, or lesion indicates that some individuals suffer from aphasia (loss of language) but not amusia (loss of music) or vice versa. This lends support to the notion that music and language are dissociated; that is, that music and language are represented, at least to a large degree, by separate neural systems (Hodges, 1996b; Marin & Perry, 1999). Both are umbrella terms, in that there are many different forms of aphasia (e.g., loss of speech, comprehension, or the ability to read or write) and amusia (e.g., loss of ability to track pitch, or rhythm, or timbre or loss of familiar tune recognition). Because of the complexity and modularity of both systems, it is also possible that many brain regions are implicated in both language and music (Falk, 2000). (For more details on modularity see hereafter.)

A common research paradigm is to ask brain-damaged subjects to do a variety of music-related tasks. Their inability to do a task successfully (when compared to a person with an undamaged brain) is then linked to anatomical lesion sites. Several notes of caution must be inserted. First, a damaged brain is different from a normal brain, and the assumption that it is operating like the normal brain with the exception of the damaged portion is not necessarily warranted. Second, for older studies in the literature, anatomical lesion sites are not given very precisely; sometimes reports are as vague as "damage on the left side." Third, the case with music is somewhat different from the case with language. While one can reasonably assume that an adult has language competency, adult musical skills may vary all the way from minimal (even including "tone deafness") to highly professional. Thus, if, for example, a brain-damaged person cannot do a given musical task—such as match pitches, recognize familiar tunes, or read music—care must be taken to determine whether he or she had such skills prior to the trauma. (For a detailed review of the effects of brain damage on musical behaviors, see Hodges [1996b, pp. 212–216].)

A second class of subjects is those with inherited cognitive limitations. Musical savants are cognitively impaired but capable of amazing musical feats (Miller, 1989). Individuals with Williams syndrome often have cognitive "peaks" and "valleys," and music appears to be something many of them can do quite well (Levitin & Bellugi, 1998). Musical behaviors are only possible in such individuals because of the presence of specific neural structures. Williams syndrome, in particular, is a fertile area for research in that it may ultimately be possible to link research on genetics (Williams syndrome results from a microdeletion on chromosome 7) with neuroscientific and behavioral data. In contrast, some individuals may be born with musical limitations (e.g., deficits in pitch or rhythm processing) in what Peretz (2001) calls congenital amusia.

A third class of subjects involves those suffering from cognitive dementias due to aging (especially Alzheimer's). Individuals with prior musical backgrounds may retain procedural skills (e.g., singing or playing an instrument) in spite of declining linguistic fluency (Crystal, Grober, & Masur, 1989). In at least one case, an Alzheimer's patient was able to sing the words to familiar songs even though she could no longer communicate via language (Johnson & Ulatowska, 1995). Interestingly, music (among other things) is being recommended to elders as a means of staving off the ravages of Alzheimer's (Golden, 1994). The presence of musical skills, in the absence of linguistic and other skills, once again denotes neural structures devoted to musical processing.

Hemispheric Asymmetry Research

Hemispheric asymmetry, sometimes referred to as cerebral dominance, is concerned with possible differences between the two hemispheres, both in type of processing (e.g., sequential versus holistic) or in responsibility (i.e., which side is more responsible for particular tasks). Although a variety of strategies can be employed—most notably studying brain damaged individuals (discussed previously) and brain imaging (discussed subsequently)—the focus of this brief discussion will be on dichotic listening tasks.

Dichotic listening tasks have been widely used as a means of comparing one side of the brain's performance with the other. Basically, the technique is to present conflicting signals to the right and left ears via headphones. Approximately 70% of the fibers in the auditory pathway are contralateral, meaning that they go from the inner ear to the auditory cortex in the opposite hemisphere. Thus, although both sides receive all the information from each ear, signals from the right ear are more strongly represented in the left hemisphere, and vice versa (Kimura, 1961; Robinson & Solomon, 1974). Contralateral response times are faster than ipsilateral (from one inner ear to the auditory cortex on the same side) (Majkowski, Bochenek, Bochenek, Knapik-Fijalkowska, & Kopec, 1971) and can occlude impulses arriving along ipsilateral pathways (Kimura, 1967). In a typical experiment, subjects might hear a nonsense syllable such as "bleh" in the right ear and "teh" in the left ear (stimuli must be nonsensical, as real words would be immediately recognized). They are then presented with four foils and asked to identify the one they heard. Over a number of trials, consistency in picking out the right ear signal would indicate processing dominance by the left hemisphere and vice versa.

A major limitation of this technique for music research is that the stimuli can be no longer than 2 seconds. If they are longer, the brain can go back and forth, picking up enough information from each ear to make recognition of both stimuli possible. Obviously, only limited musical meaning can be found in 2-second fragments. Also, stimulus variables (the type of sound/music being used), task variables (whether subjects are asked to make global or local decisions), and subject variables (amount of training, gender, handedness, etc.) can make dramatic differences in the results. Sergent was highly critical of this line of research and felt that all such data could be discarded (Sergent, 1993; for an extended review of this literature and discussion, see Hodges [1996b, pp. 222–232]).

For a period of time, primarily during the 1970s, much was made of music being in the right side of the brain. This oversimplification has since been modified. Music is *not* in the right side of the brain alone; both sides are involved. In fact, sophisticated musical processing most likely involves the front-back, top-bottom, and left and right sides of the brain in widely distributed but locally specialized neural networks. Furthermore, selectively changing the focus of attention radically alters brain activation patterns (Platel et al., 1997). Further implications of this line of research are discussed subsequently.

Brain Imaging Research

Modern neuroscientists have a broad range of highly sophisticated research tools at their disposal. These include electroencephalography (EEG), event-related potentials (ERP) derived from EEG, magnetoencephalography (MEG), superconducting quantum interference device (SQUID), magnetic resonance imaging (MRI), functional magnetic resonance imaging (fMRI), positron emission tomography (PET), and transcranial magnetic stimulation (TMS, discussed in the section on neuromotor responses). Space does not allow for much more than a brief description of each of these technologies (see figure 1.1). Because of limited access to equipment, costs involved, and related issues, typical neuroimaging experiments are conducted with a very small number of subjects.

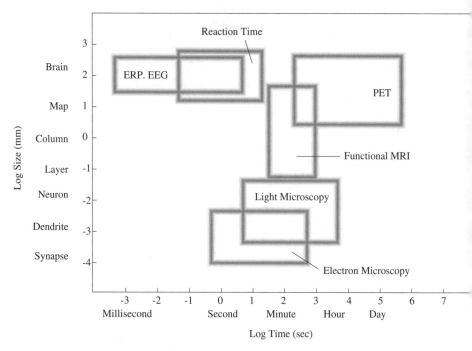

Figure 1.1. Schematic illustration of the spatial (vertical axis) and temporal (horizontal axis) resolution of techniques used to study brain function in humans. The hazy edges of each box suggest that these are approximations and that these techniques may not be limited to these boundaries in the future. This figure emphasizes the different spatial and temporal characteristics of methods used to study the neurobiology of behaviors, none of which alone is sufficient to understand the neural basis of a behavior or its development. (From Janowsky & Carper in Sameroff & Haith, eds., 1996.)

EEG and ERP.   Due to neural activity, the brain constantly produces a small amount of electrical current that can be measured; EEG measures the summed activity of millions of brain cells under electrodes placed in various places around the skull (Gur & Gur, 1994). Data are interpreted in terms of frequency (Hz), amplitude (microvolts), form, and distribution (sometimes converted into a brain map). Most often reported are frequency components, including delta (0.5–4.0 Hz), theta (4.5–8.0 Hz), alpha (8.5–12.0 Hz), and beta waves (12.5–32.0 Hz). Electroencephalography has been used for some time to study different levels of arousal and is now being employed to study cognitive processes in general and music processing specifically (Altenmüller, 1993; Barber, 1999; Faita & Besson, 1994).

While EEG tracks the brain's electrical activity over time, ERP examines the brain's immediate response to a stimulus in millisecond (ms) intervals. A computer averages EEG readings following multiple presentations of a stimulus. This allows extraneous aspects of the EEG to be canceled out, while electrical activity occurring in time-locked response to the stimulus is revealed (Brown, Marsh, & Ponsford, 1985). Data are evaluated for directional changes in the wave pattern (either positive or negative), intensity level (amplitude), and latency (time lapse). A P300 wave indicates a positive wave whose maximum amplitude occurred approximately 300 ms after the stimulus, while a N400 wave is a negative wave form occurring approximately 400 ms after the stimulus. The P300 has been more frequently studied in relation to music. It is hypothesized to be an indicator of "working" memory, comparing incoming stimuli to stored memories, and has been linked to the detection of musical events (Cohen & Erez, 1991; Frisina, Walton, & Crummer, 1988; Hantz & Crummer, 1988; Paller, McCarthy, & Wood, 1992; Paulus, 1988; Schwent, Snyder, & Hillyard, 1976).

MEG and SQUID.   The brain's electrical activity produces a magnetic field that can be measured just outside the skull through MEG, giving location information about neural activity. SQUID provides refined spatial information, in millimeters, and precise temporal resolution, in milliseconds (Hari, 1990). This approach has been used in only a few studies related to music (Kaufmann, Curtis, Wang, & Williamson, 1991; Williamson & Kaufmann, 1988).

MRI and fMRI.   MRI provides very precise information about anatomical structures under the skin but does not provide information about function (Ackerman, 1992). It has been used to show structural features of musician's brains (Amunts et al., 1997; Pantev et al., 1998; Schlaug, Jancke, Huang, & Steinmetz, 1994, 1995). A newer development, fMRI does provide data about both location and function. Currently, there is considerable interest in finding a way to use fMRI to study music. The difficulty is that both MRI and fMRI are very noisy environments for the subjects. The camera's motion within the scanner generates rhythmical noise that competes with musical perception. While it is possible to extract speech or other nonmusical sounds from the ambient noise, it is not so easily done with music. Regular headphones cannot be used, because of the strong magnet. Researchers are attempting to deliver musical stimuli through pneumatic tubes or to develop better antinoise cancellation devices. A recently developed technique causes the cameras to pause for up to 10 seconds, which allows stimuli to be presented during the resulting silent period; staggering the camera start time allows for full acquisition of the hemodynamic response. If these problems are solved, fMRI should prove to be a very valuable approach for studying music cognition.

PET.   In PET, radioactively tagged oxygen, water, or glucose is inhaled or injected into the bloodstream; PET scans then detect brain metabolism or regional cerebral blood flow (rCBF) while the subject engages in an assigned task (Raichle, 1994). By means of paired-image subtraction (subtracting the activations of one task from another), areas of the brain most active during a specific task are identified (Posner & Raichle, 1994). Areas of deactivation (i.e., less active than during rest) also provide useful information. Because PET provides information about function but not location, it is mapped onto MRI data. The combination of the two tells neuroscientists "what" is going on "where." PET is a powerful technique that is revealing important information about music processing (Fox et al., 1995; Parsons, Fox, & Hodges, 1998; Zatorre, 1994; Zatorre, Evans, & Myer, 1994).

Taken collectively, these various brain imaging techniques are opening up new understandings about the brain in general and about music cognition specifically. The most rapid advancements are being made in this field, and music psychologists, music educators, and music therapists should be aware of findings as they are reported (see Avanzini et al., 2003, Avanzini, Lopez, Koelsch, & Majno, 2005, and Zatorre & Peretz, 2001, for recent compilations).

Neuromotor Research

Musical responses are both expressive (i.e., performing) and receptive (i.e., listening). Musical performance activates motor control areas in the brain to such a high degree that musicians may be considered small-muscle athletes (Wilson, 1986). A PET study of eight professional pianists confirmed this as motor systems in the brain were strongly activated during performance (Fox et al., 1995; Parsons, 2001). Transcranial magnetic stimulation (TMS), a technique for mapping neuromotor pathways, was used with 15 subjects to show that the motor cortex controlling the fingers increased in response to piano exercises, both actual and imagined (Pascual-Leone et al., 1995). Researchers used magnetic source imaging to compare 9 string players with 6 nonmusicians; the main finding was that the string players had greater neuronal activity and a larger area in the right primary somatosensory cortex that controls the fingers of the left hand than controls (Elbert, Pantev, Wienbruch, Rockstrub, & Taub, 1995). These effects were greater for those who started playing at a young age.

Highly precise and rhythmically coordinated movements are critical for musical performance, and investigators are beginning to identify timing mechanisms in the brain (Freund & Hefter, 1990; Miller, Thaut, & Aunon, 1995; Moore, 1992; Wilson, 1991, 1998). A related issue is focal dystonia, a neuromotor problem in which the brain and hands (or other body parts, such as mouth structures used in embouchure formation) fail to communicate properly (Wilson, 1988, 1992; Wilson & Roehmann, 1992). Several concert pianists have had major careers curtailed by a focal dystonia in one hand. Highly practiced movements seem to be most affected, while other uses of the hand remain functional.

In the receptive mode, Thaut and colleagues have produced an impressive body of work on how Parkinsonian and stroke patients can regain motor function (e.g., walking or grasping) through rhythmic entrainment (McIntosh, Thaut, & Rice, 1996; Thaut, Brown, Benjamin, & Cooke, 1995; Thaut, McIntosh, Prassas, & Rice, 1993). Rhythmic timing embedded in music serves as a cue to motor system timing mechanisms in the brain.

Affective Research

Data-gathering techniques for studying affective responses to music fall into three categories: verbal reports, behavioral observations, and physiological responses (Abeles & Chung, 1996). In terms of finding out the brain's role in emotional responses to music, current strategies are quite limited. Recently, PET scans of 10 amateur musicians indicated that different brain regions were activated in response to positive and negative music listening experiences (Blood, Zatorre, Bermudez, & Evans, 1999). Another avenue of approach is found in biochemical analyses of blood samples (for a review see Bartlett, 1996). Music can elicit changes in such biochemicals as endorphins, cortisol, adrenocorticotropic hormone (ACTH), interleukin-1, and secretory immunoglobin A. The brain-music-biochemical relationship is not yet well understood but does hold some promise. In particular, studies in psychoneuroimmunology are being used in music medicine to document the physiological effects (e.g., changes in blood chemistry) that music has on the body (Pratt & Spingte, 1996; Reilly, 1999; Spingte & Droh, 1992). Fear and anxiety can be reduced in many clinical situations through the use of music.

Each of these research strategies has advantages and disadvantages. It is important to integrate findings from the various approaches into a more coherent whole. Where data from different techniques are in disagreement, efforts must be undertaken to resolve discrepancies. Wherever possible, it would be helpful to attack the same problem with more than one strategy. Particularly in the area of neuroimaging, it is important to keep up with new technologies and possibilities (e.g., with development of better sound delivery systems in fMRI).

Overall Development

To what extent do genes specify the intricate working of the human brain? To what extent are the intricate workings of the brain acquired as a result of experiences? New advances in neuroscience have addressed the ancient "nature versus nurture" debate. In general, neuroscience research has shown that neither nature nor nurture alone determines brain development. Human brains at the prenatal stages are already interacting with the environment (Standley, 1998). The brain appears to be more plastic and malleable during the first decade of life than in adulthood. According to Thatcher studies have shown that 40% of short term and 70% of long term connections in the brain are influenced by heredity. Therefore, 30% to 60% of the brain's connections come from environmental influences or an interaction of heredity and environmental influences (Thatcher, 1998). Nelson and Bloom (1997) cite numerous demonstrations that show how positive or negative early experiences can alter both the structure and function of the brain. It is also important to remember that a child's brain is not the same as an adult brain. There is agreement that during the first decade of life a child typically has up to twice as much neural activity and connections as an adult (Bates, Thal, & Janowsky, 1992; Chugani, 1998; Chugani, Phelps, & Mazziotta, 1987). The brain makes connections during the prenatal period and throughout life (Gopnik, Meltzoff, & Kuhl, 1999; Janowsky & Carper, 1996). Some connections are found to be predetermined genetically, and others develop from environmental influences (Cossu, Faienza, & Capone, 1994; Drayna, et al., 2001; Flohr, 2004a; Ibatoullina, Vardaris, & Thompson, 1994; Schlaug, et al., 2004; van Baal, de Geus, & Boomsma, 1998), Ibatoullina, Vardaris, & Thompson, 1994; van Baal, de Geus, & Boomsma, 1998).

   Children as young as 1 day old are able to make cognitive choices about their environment (Atkins & Flohr, 2000; Flohr, Atkins, Bower, & Aldridge, 2000; Woodward, Fresen, Harrison, & Coley, 1996). There are clear additive and regressive events in brain development. As shown in figure 1.2, a child at birth may have the largest number of neurons that she or he will ever have. After the age of 2 years, the number of neurons remains nearly the same until 65 years of age. Synapses, the connection between neurons, form in the brain and change as the child develops. (For an explanation directed to educators see Sylwester, 1995.) During early childhood the percent of adult cortical levels of myelin and glia are increasing and may be

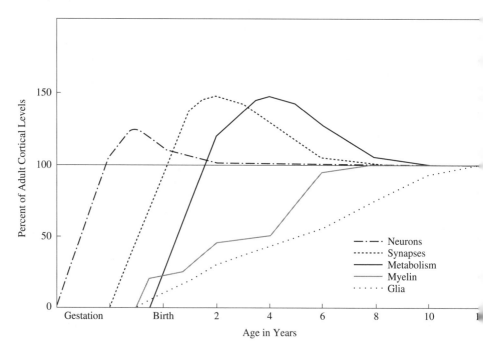

Figure 1.2. Approximation of the time course of additive and regressive events in brain development. (From Janowsky & Carper in Sameroff & Haith, eds., 1996.)

influenced by the environment. Myelination of the nerve axons increases the efficiency of neural transmission. The glial cell is a major cell type in the brain that nourishes neurons. Interestingly, a study of Einstein's brain showed his brain had significantly more glial cells than the brain of the average human (Diamond, Scheibel, Murphy, & Harvey, 1985). There are several glia subtypes, but there is not yet enough information to consider an active role for the glial cells in behavioral development (Janowsky & Carper, 1996). Note also that figure 1.2 illustrates a decrease in the level of synapses between the approximate ages of 2 and 8 years. This decrease, theorized to be a type of "synaptic pruning," may occur because networks atrophy over time because of unused or less used connections. Brains do not make more connections and stop. It appears the brain makes more connections than it needs and then deletes unused or less used connections by the process of synaptic pruning. Also, what is learned imposes restrictions on what can be learned. Although there is much growth and activity during the young years, there is evidence that there is room for change in the later years, and recent research indicates that the adult brain is able to produce new cells (e.g., in the hippocampus of adult humans) (Eriksson et al., 1998; Gibbs, 1998; Nelson & Bloom, 1997). The complex interaction of innate abilities and environment will continue to be a viable mode of research. The complexity of the interaction between innate abilities and environment may also depend on the variability inherent in individual differences (Barber, McKenzie, & Helme, 1997). Possible individual differences include emotional traits, temperament, and cognitive and intellectual propensities.

Four concepts central to brain development are addressed in this section: critical periods, optimal periods, windows of opportunity, and plasticity. Critical period refers to the idea that there are time frames in which there will be no development or stunted development if certain stimulation is not present. The brain may be open to experience of a particular kind only during narrow periods of time. Missing a critical period in learning would be as if you were playing the solo triangle part in a symphony and didn't play your quarter note after the 30 measures rest. You missed your chance and the triangle is no longer needed or useful. There are many examples from animals in which experience must be timed very precisely to have an impact. A classic research example investigated the vision of 23 kittens (Hubel & Wiesel, 1970). Nobel Prize–winners Hubel and Wiesel covered one eye of newborn kittens. The kittens grew up with only one eye in use. A few months later the covered eye was opened, but it was in effect not connected to the brain. What makes this a "critical" period is the finding that if the cats are later given visual stimulation, they are unable to use the stimulation to see. When deprived of visual stimulation in the covered eye until after the critical period, the part of their brain dealing with optical sensory data does not develop. One way of looking at critical periods is to imagine a sort of biological clock that only works during a certain period of development. An alternate view may be that experience has changed the brain so that the animal or person perceives and interprets the world in a different way. The experiences influence neural wiring, and the neural wiring has an effect on recognition or interpretation of new sensory data. It is presently unknown if the critical period is due to biological clock mechanisms, the brain structures that have developed, or an interaction of the two. There may be critical periods in musical development, and the search for these periods provides a fertile ground for research.

Authors often write about optimal periods as if they were critical periods, although presently there are no identified critical periods in musical development. An optimal period is used to refer to those periods in which development will be faster or easier. For example, it is easier to learn to sing in tune during the ages of 3–6 years than at 25–28 years of age. It may also be easier or more efficient to learn the language of classical, jazz, or any style of music before the age of 6. The period in all these cases is optimal rather than critical. There is no evidence to support the notion that a child cannot learn to sing if she or he does not have music experiences before, for example, 6 years of age.

There are indications of possible critical periods in music. For example, the music educator Gordon advanced the idea of developmental music aptitude (Gordon, 1979, 1990). He has found that children's scores on measures of musical aptitude do not change significantly after the age of approximately 9 years. A few studies indicate optimal periods and point toward possible critical periods for music training. A group of adults with a history of violin training and a group of adults without violin training had their brains mapped using MEG (Elbert et al., 1995). The area of the somatosensory cortex representing the fingers of the left fingering hand was larger than that in the contralateral hemisphere representing the right bow hand and also larger than the corresponding area in nonmusicians. This finding was consistent with reports of adult human amputees (Nelson & Bloom, 1997). A possible critical period was indicated by a trend for the effect to be larger for individuals who had begun music training before the age of 10. Another optimal period and possible critical period was seen in a study of violin training, where in a sample of 60 musicians and nonmusicians, those who started training before the age of 7 years exhibited increased corpus callosum size (Schlaug, Jänke, Huang, Steiger, & Steinmetz, 1995).

"Windows of opportunity" refers to the idea that there are general time frames in which optimal or critical development will take place. The fact that writers often do not specify the window of opportunity as critical or optimal leads to much confusion. It is important to underline the difference between optimal and critical periods when talking about windows of opportunity for brain development. For example, it is an overstatement of neuroscientific research to say that there is a window of opportunity for music during the ages of 3–7 years and if a parent does not give the child a chance during those ages, the child will not be musical. Bruer writes: "For most learning, particularly learning culturally transmitted skills and knowledge such as reading, mathematics, and music, the windows of experience-dependent opportunity never close" (1999, p. 187). On the other hand, there are indications of how early experience changes the way the brain works. Language research demonstrates how the 6-month to 12-month window of development is important and is an optimal period for sound organization (Gopnik et al., 1999, p. 108). One study of 18 very young babies showed no brain activity differences while listening to native language and foreign language sounds. After a few months native and foreign language stimuli produced a difference in left hemisphere activity (Cheour et al., 1998). The finding may mean that changes in the way a baby hears the sound produce changes in the brain. Are music sounds in general and music sounds of the culture processed in the same way as language sounds during the second 6 months of life? If so, that period in an infant's life would be an optimal window of opportunity that may help children learn music faster or more efficiently than music education later in life.

Work with older populations has shown that there are further chances for the brain to adapt or rewire itself. It is prudent to question the simplistic view that the brain becomes increasingly difficult to modify beyond early childhood. Much brain development occurs in early childhood, but the brain is far from completed even at the end of adolescence. After accidental brain damage, for example, the brain may reassign function from the damaged part of the brain to an uninjured area (Thulborn, Carpenter, & Just, 1999). This idea of how the physical structure of the brain changes as a result of experience is referred to as brain plasticity (Caine & Caine, 1994). "Plasticity" refers to the notion that the brain is very adaptable, fluid, or plastic in the way in which it can adapt. Involvement in music may help keep the brain fluid, or more fluid, as opposed to no musical involvement throughout the human lifespan. A study of 678 nuns has indicated that rich experiences, including music, in older age will help keep the brain pliable and adaptable (Snowdon, 1997, 2001). The study with nuns suggests that the adult brain can reorganize in response to positive experiences in the environment as well as negative experiences in the case of injury.

Theories and Theoretical Frameworks

A theory, or at least a conjecture of what may happen when an idea is applied to a situation, usually drives research. Neuroscience research is not different in this sense, although neuroscientists are not at a stage of precisely unified theories of music and the brain. There are several current theories that warrant attention. Students and scientists are able to use the experimental theories in their own research by testing a theory in new situations or previously studied situations. Various models of brain function and architecture have been proposed over the past century. (For an educator's view of several theories see Sylwester [1995, pp. 14–24, 39–46]. For models of brain functioning see Hodges [1996b, pp. 201–205].) An examination of current theories and studies that support them reveals that while some emphasize brain structure, others emphasize function. Many of these theories will undoubtedly be proven incorrect with time, some may be combined with others or new theories, many will be modified, and a few may even stand the test of time. The following theories have been selected from among many in the field because each has possible application to music education. (The theories and theoretical areas are presented in alphabetical order of keyword.)

Developmental Shifts

The theory concerning development shift refers to the idea that at certain times of significant changes, shifts, or "brain spurts," occur in brain development (Epstein, 1978, 1986). These changes are thought to be part of the human biological development program. The shifts can be modified by the environment but are part of a normal developmental sequence. The notion finds its roots in cognitive theory (e.g., Piaget, 1950), and the neurological basis for at least one developmental shift from the ages of 5 to 7 has been related to cognitive theory. Sameroff and Haith compiled several articles that point to the efficacy of the idea that a child's brain chemistry and electrical activity inherently change in significant ways between the ages of 5 and 7 (Janowsky & Carper, 1996). Flohr and Miller (1993, 1995) lend support to this idea in relation to music with a series of EEG studies with 13 young children. One finding was that children at age 7 exhibited significant EEG brain alpha activity differences in response to contrasting styles of music that were not present when the same children were 5 years of age. Music by Vivaldi stimulated different brain responses from the children from Irish folk song music while the children listened to the music and tapped rhythm sticks. These differences occurred in the motor strip and the temporal areas. The differences lend support to the idea of a developmental shift in music processing. Barber et al. (1997) also found brain activity differences in response to different styles of music. Subjects in their study were 21 adult musicians and 25 nonmusicians.

Future research investigating the theory of developmental shift will probably have much to say to music educators and educators in general. For example, when are the neurological attributes of a child best able to process sounds from music or language? Are most 7-year-old children ready (in the neurological sense) for abstract symbols in music, or is it more appropriate at an earlier or later age? Developmental research since Zimmerman's pioneering cognitive research (1971) has affected music education. Developmental "shift" and development research are fertile fields for music education and neurological researchers to collaborate in.

Expert or Habituation

Another theory, "expert" or "habituation" (or even "efficiency") theory, seeks to explain observed decreases in brain activity during certain tasks. One might expect to observe an increase in "thinking" brain activity of a subject during a cognitive task. The opposite phenomenon has been found; experts and students after training show decreases in brain activity as opposed to novices engaged in the same cognitive task. Some studies have supported the idea that less energy or brain electrical activity may be used to perform a task in an expert's brain than in a novice's brain (Languis & Miller, 1992; Miller & Flohr, 1995). The idea is that the brain of a novice learner is less efficient and expends more energy when confronted with a challenging task than the brain of an expert learner (Jensen, 1998). Thus, music instruction should enable children to expend less energy during musical tasks.

There is, however, an alternative idea of why the decreases in activity are observed. Petsche and colleagues suggested that the reduced temporal lobe activity in the beta frequency bands of 75 healthy college students was related to habituation from listening to music (Petsche, Lindner, Rappelsberger, & Gruber, 1988). It can be posited that the subjects developed a habituated type of cortical activity in their listening to music after they were involved in a period of music training. Habituation in an expert musician can also be thought of as the musician going on "automatic pilot" while performing the music. She or he has learned the piece so well that the motor systems and cerebellum take over the performance, and other areas in the cerebral cortex are deactivated, thereby producing less electrical or chemical activity. Parsons and colleagues have found a similar result in their PET scan studies with musicians (Parsons, 2000, 2001; Parsons et al., 1998). Cerebral blood flow in a musician's frontal cortex decreased as the musician performed music on a keyboard as opposed to rest. The reduction in PET scan activity may lend support to the idea that the expert (or a person with training) uses less energy in a well-learned task. However, the expert performer also exhibits greater activation in other areas during performance, and the current data do not show if there is less energy expended in the motor cortex among expert performers, which is what the expert theory would predict. The identified decreases in the research are clearly linked to expert musicians and students involved in music instruction. Future research will help determine the mechanisms involved.

Emotion or Affective Response

Research combining affective response and music may provide theories and research findings that explain aspects of cognition. Emotions in general (or, more broadly, affective responses) are difficult to study, and much less emotion research has been done than cognition research. Nevertheless, progress is being made in the understanding of relationships between emotion and musical behavior (Juslin & Sloboda, 2001). The emotional import of music experience is a strong component of music and music instruction (Leonhard & House, 1972). Reimer reminds us that "[t]eaching and learning music, then, have been understood to be valuable because they improve people's abilities to gain meaningful, gratifying musical experiences" (1999, p. 37).

Neuroscientists today have learned much about the organizing and structuring processes of neural connections and emotional response systems that influence higher thought processes (see Krumhansl, 2002 for a review). The way in which cognition is affected may occur through a complex web of processing among cortical and subcortical brain structures, neurochemicals and hormones, and through communication between central nervous system processing and the peripheral systems (including the autonomic nervous system and the somatic system). A significant area of progress is in the brain's effect on the body and emotions through the release of hormones, the area of neurochemistry (Panksepp, 1998; see also the discussion of affective research earlier).

Investigators used PET to examine cerebral blood flow (CBF) changes related to affective responses to music (Blood et al., 1999). Ten participants were scanned while listening to six versions of a novel musical passage varying systematically in degree of dissonance; CBF was observed in paralimbic and neocortical regions as a function of dissonance and of perceived pleasantness/unpleasantness of the music. The authors suggest that music may recruit neural mechanisms similar to those previously associated with pleasant/unpleasant emotional states but different from those underlying other components of music perception and emotions such as fear.

Modularity and Connectionism

Many theories have elements of modularity or connectionism. The theory of "modules" in neuropsychological research refers to the idea that processes relating to music or language, for example, are carried out in distinct brain structures. Extreme modular theory would argue that these regions or modules are largely autonomous. On the other hand, connectionism is a theoretical approach that takes a holistic view of the brain, arguing that the brain functions as a whole and that a part of the brain can be recruited for multiple tasks. Either viewpoint in its extreme form may fail to explain research results, and these two theories may not be mutually exclusive.

Current neuroimaging data suggest that the neural mechanisms supporting music are distributed throughout the brain (Parsons, 2000; Parsons & Fox, 1997). The modular idea is combined with a "connection" idea of interplay among modules. A module of music engages several different brain areas in a coordinated activity and is composed of submodules (e.g., musical syntax operators, timbre operators, and rhythm operators). (For further explanation of modular theory see Restak [1994] and Sylwester [1995].) The submodules are distributed in various regions throughout the brain. At this point of the theory, each submodule appears to be a specialized piece of neural machinery. For a music task, such as playing a C major scale on the piano, the musical brain would have to integrate several submodules in a coordinated activity. There may be modules or supermodules or mechanisms that coordinate among different modules.

Research findings about hemispheric differences and localization can be explained with modular theory in the sense that modular theory regards different submodules each to be a specialized piece of neural machinery. For example, there is a neural network for language and another for music; in each case the neural networks link together locally specialized modules. These modules are largely autonomous, each doing its own work, although it is possible that some modules may be recruited for differing tasks (e.g., prosody for language and certain musical functions may be subserved by the same systems). Increasing evidence is pointing to modularity in music processing, and the data support what is already known about language (Parsons et al., 1998). In addition, anatomical variances are a consideration in modular theory. Perhaps music training affects the actual size of brain areas that are important modules in music-making. For example, the left planum temporale is larger among musicians with absolute pitch, musicians who started serious study before the age of 7, and those with Williams syndrome (Levitin & Bellugi, 1998; Schlaug et al., 1995). Extensive musical experiences may cause an enlargement of the corpus callosum (Lee, Chen & Schlaug, 2003; Schlaug et al., 1995) and of the cerebellum (Hutchinson et al., 2003), as well as increased gray matter (Gaser & Schlaug, 2003; Sluming et al., 2002).

In his work on the effect of music on spatial reasoning, Parsons found that the cerebellum is activated in a coordinated effort with areas of the cortex in music activity (Parsons & Fox, 1997). Hetland (2000b) has used the term "rhythm theory" to describe Parsons's module theory of music and spatial tasks. The rhythmic elements of music (hence rhythm theory) operating in the cerebellum coordinated with areas in the cortex may be responsible for increasing ability to perform spatial-temporal mental rotation tasks. The rhythm theory is a module theory in the way that it explains how different areas of the brain work together.

Altenmüller and others attempted to demonstrate changes in cortical activity patterns with 9 participants (average age 13.8 years) after a 5-week period of music training (Altenmüller, Gruhn, Parlitz, & Kahrs, 1996). The results suggested that musical training produced certain cortical brain activity patterns in different areas of the brain and that these activity patterns may depend on the applied teaching strategies. Flohr, Perscllin, and Miller (1996) also reported EEG activity changes in different areas of the brain after a 7-week period with 22 preschool children (average age 5.25 years) receiving music instruction versus children receiving regular classroom instruction. The module theory supports the results of both studies in that different areas of the brain containing submodules operate in a coordinated activity. However, in the second study by Flohr and others, results showed an increase in some areas of the brain in contrast to a decrease in other areas. The module theory does not specify whether the submodules produce increased or decreased electrical activity. In addition, an increase in one module along with a decrease in another part of the brain may represent the way the brain relegates processing resources.

The term "coherence" may be viewed within the modular theory, although coherence has been used to support connectionism. Connectionist models postulate that "cognition occurs through a network of linked nodes. The nodes integrate activation through their excitatory and inhibitory links" (Carpenter, Akira, & Just, 1995, p. 92). Coherence reflects the number and strength of coordination between different brain locations. Some authors believe that coherence demonstrates evidence of anatomical connections and information exchange between two brain locations (Fein, Raz, & Merrin, 1988). Brain imaging studies have shown a relationship between music listening or music instruction and increased coherence activities in children (deBeus, 1999; Malyarenko et al., 1996; Sarnthein et al., 1997).

Coherence studies lend support to the idea that music instruction for children at an early age will promote more profuse and efficient connections. For example, Malyrenko et al. (1996) found that an exposure to music of 1 hour per day over a 6 month period had an effect on the brain electrical activity in a sample of 43 4-year-old preschool children. Brain bioelectric activity parameters indicated that listening to music resulted in an enhancement of the coherence function. DeBeus (1999) ran a coherence analysis on 20 preschool children's EEG data. In a baseline, resting condition and while listening to music, deBeus found increased connectivity for a music-training group versus a no-music-training group. Coherence patterns differentiated children with and without music training during a resting condition, and showed patterns similar to those identified by other researchers comparing trained to untrained musicians. The listening-to-music condition identified connections that included a topographical pattern of auditory analysis, increased working memory activity, increased activity among musically sensitive areas, and increased activity between hemispheres. Two limiting points about coherence are important to note. First, coherence values are not well accepted by all neuroscientists; second, skilled performers in comparison with low-level performers in other fields (e.g., a high-level chess player with a non–chess player, a high-level mathematician with a mathematically unskilled person) would presumably show differences.

Multiple Intelligences

In *Frames of Mind* (1985) and later in *Intelligence Reframed* (1999), Gardner describes the concept of multiple intelligences. Performing, listening to music, improvising, or composing music may require the use of at least eight intelligences. The eight types of intelligence used in music activities may include: music; visual-spatial (in the sense that instruments, e.g., cello, per-cussion, or piano, have a visual-spatial element); bodily kinesthetic (the way in which fine and gross movement functions in the perception of musical motion and is used in performing music); interpersonal (e.g., conductor and orchestral member); intrapersonal (e.g., expression of feelings through mu-sic); language, as in singing; spiritual (e.g., in performance of sacred music, deriving spiritual meaning and interpretation in music); and logical-mathematical (e.g., rhythm durations). Neurological research has indicated that many parts of the brain are utilized as children are engaged in music-making activities. The multiple intelligences idea may help explain why other types of intelligence are apparently affected by music instruction. The theory that several kinds of thinking are required to learn and make music has been called a "near" transfer theory (Hetland, 2000a). The quality of music in-struction (Elliott, 1995) or combination of activities used in music instruc-tion could help facilitate the transfer. One should not expect transfer from music to other skills unless significant learning has occurred in music. The idea of multiple intelligences and "near" transfer may help explain the ways brain activity is affected by music instruction (Flohr, Miller, & deBeus, 2000).

Trion Theory

Shaw (2000) proposed a "trion" cortical model for the "coding of certain aspects of musical structure and perception" and defines the trion model as "a highly structured mathematical realization of the Mountcastle organiza-tion principle in which the cortical column is the basic neural network of the cortex and is comprised of sub-unit minicolumns, our idealized trions" (p. 229; for more information on this theory see Leng & Shaw, 1991, 2000). The cortex is to a large extent organized into a vertical column of neurons. Shaw proposed that when the brain patterns predicted by his theoretical model were mapped onto pitches and instruments, recognizable human styles of music were found. Shaw's trion model provided a theoretical back-ground for the much-publicized and controversial "Mozart effect" studies (Rauscher, Shaw, & Ky, 1993; Rauscher, Shaw, Ky, & Wright, 1994). This trion theory suggests that the musical and spatial processing areas of the brain are in some way shared, proximal, or overlapping. Thus, the relation-ship of music and spatial processing are linked by neurological connections in the cortex. Shaw and others write that a prewired neural connection is suggested because of the short-term effect of music instruction on spatial abilities (Graziano, Peterson, & Shaw, 1999).

Any theory including the trion theory is difficult to test with current brain imaging techniques. However, an EEG study and a study outlining a new method of analysis for EEG data have been used to empirically test the trion theory (Sarnthein et al., 1997; Bodner et al., 1999). In the EEG study a carry over of brain activity from listening to music to a spatial test was observed in 3 of 7 subjects. The lack of effect in the other 4 subjects was perhaps due to individual differences, problems in application of the theory, the lack of a general effect, or other unknown causes. Comparing and combining trion theory with other theories will be an interesting area for future research.

Neural Networks and Wiring

The concept of neural networks and wiring of the brain has appeared in our recent popular press, and there is a notion or theory that music (or other environmental experiences) "rewires" the neural networks of the brain. The idea is that babies are born with a basic "wiring" of neural networks. As the child interacts with the environment, the brain builds new connections between existing networks. The number of connections increase, and the way the data are transferred is also changed. As a child grows, connections are made and changed (see figure 1.2). One notion is that music and music instruction may affect the way, number, and quality of connections that are being made during development. The idea that the environment—and music can be part of the environment—interacts with heredity and influences the amount and quality of neural connections is not controversial. One research problem is that our knowledge does not include the extent to which music affects the connections.

Theories taken as a whole are not necessarily mutually exclusive and may in combination explain many of the effects of music on brain activity, musical development, and general development. One or two theories (e.g., modular and affective response) may prove to be useful in combination with another theory or prove the other theory to be incorrect.

General Findings

1. Human development hinges on the interplay between nature and nurture. Recent brain research challenges old assumptions about talent and innate ability—that the genes humans are born with determine how the brain develops. In general, neuroscience research has shown that nature or nurture alone do not determine brain development. The complex interaction among innate abilities, environment, and the variability inherent in individual differences influences brain development. Although there is much growth and activity during the young years, there is evidence that there is room for change in the brain during the later years.
2. Early care and nurture have a decisive, long-lasting impact on how people develop, their ability to learn, and their capacity to regulate their own emotions (Flohr, Miller, & Persellin, 1999). Children as young as 1 day old are able to make cognitive choices about their environment, including musical choices.
3. Experience changes the physiological structure and operation of our brains. Music and music instruction have an effect on brain activity.

Studies using various brain imaging techniques have documented some of these changes as well as differences between trained and untrained musicians.

4. There is fertile ground for research in the several theories of brain function and structure. These theories need to be tested, modified, and combined with research and new techniques of imaging the human brain. Students and scientists may use brain theories in their research by testing a theory in new situations or previously studied situations.

5. The human brain has a remarkable capacity to change, but timing is often important and at some points crucial. Windows of opportunity are either optimal windows or critical windows. Extant research has not yet determined critical windows of opportunity for music education (Flohr, 2004b).

6. Improved technology will permit further investigation of the influence of music on the brain. A clearer understanding of how music and music-related tasks are manifested in the activity of the brain is an initial step in developing better instructional strategies for music education.

7. For a period of time, beginning in the 1970s, much has been made of music being in the right side of the brain. This oversimplification has been modified. Music is *not* in the right side of the brain alone; both sides are involved. In fact, sophisticated musical processing most likely involves the front-back, top-bottom, and left and right sides of the brain in widely distributed but locally specialized neural networks.

8. It is important to keep results of recent brain research in perspective. Neuroscience findings can be overstated (Bruer, 1999). On the other hand, it is easy to discount neuroscience findings because of problems with the use of new technology, difficulties interpreting data, and unproven brain theory. The neuroscience technologies are complicated and in evolution. Researchers and consumers of research need familiarity with the limits of each technique to properly assess validity of research.

9. It is important not to overstate and emphasize the nonmusical outcomes of the influence of music on brain development. For example, if a small number of studies are used to emphasize a possible link between music study and mathematical skill, it becomes easy to interpret the goal of music study as the production of good mathematicians. There are clear and meaningful musical outcomes of music education (Leonhard & House, 1972). The expressive import of music does not need a nonmusical outcome to justify music education.

Future Directions

Future directions for neuroscience and music research probably will and should include the following:

1. Development and validation of theories of music learning and brain development supported by neuroscientific research; for example, one research problem is that our knowledge does not include the extent to which music affects the brain connections.

2. Increased infant research; studying fetal and infant responses to music

allows us to study the human brain with the least possible effect of prior environmental influence.

3. Music and neuroscience research may reveal activities that will help children develop musical skills more efficiently and effectively. Families and parents will be given information on specific enjoyable, interactive music strategies.

4. More projects dealing with the relation of music to emotion and temperament.

5. Continuing focus on music cognition. How does the human brain organize musical sounds into meaningful experiences? What are the developmental sequences in music cognition? Is music cognition completely autonomous, or are there relationships among various intelligences?

6. Increased use of more than one type of brain imaging to test theories through improvements in brain imaging technology and neurochemistry (Nakamura et al., 1999).

7. Increased collaboration between cognitive neuroscientists, neurobiologists, philosophers, and musicians; there is an increasing interest among neuroscientists in the study of music and the brain. Neuroscientists are interested in using music as a way in which other brain activity may be studied as well as examining music by itself. For example, music is different from language and can be used as a contrast in experiments designed to investigate brain activity and language (Besson, 2000).

8. Continued movement toward research with greater external validity; for example, focus on musical stimuli and musically valid tasks.

9. Better education of the general public and music education profession so that patience is developed for basic research and sophisticated findings are not reduced to promotional "sound bites."

10. Music educators and philosophers may bring to future neuroscience research the appreciation for the fluidity, creative constructs, and context-specificity of music. Music is more than sonorous stimuli; it is connected to cognitive, affective, kinesthetic, and social processes of each individual.

STUDY QUESTIONS

1. In what ways does neuroscience research influence your thoughts on the nature versus nurture debate?

2. Identify and discuss the differences between optimal and critical periods. In what ways are the two terms misused?

3. List and discuss three important summary statements from the chapter. Do you agree or disagree with those statements? Why?

4. Compare and contrast two theories or theoretical frameworks.

5. Describe two brain imaging techniques and discuss their strengths and weaknesses in imaging brain activity.

6. Compare and contrast animal and human research.

7. Briefly outline and describe brain development from infancy through adulthood, noting landmarks on the way. Where do most of these landmarks seem to occur?

8. In what ways might musical experiences change the brain?

9. How can studying cognitively impaired individuals lead to insights into musical behaviors of those who have not suffered cognitive impairment?

10. What evidence can be given to support the notion that all human beings are born (or not born) with a musical brain?

REFERENCES

Abeles, H., & Chung, J. (1996). Responses to music. In D. Hodges (Ed.), *Handbook of music psychology* (2nd ed., pp. 285–342). San Antonio, TX: IMR Press.

Abrams, R., & Gerhardt, K. (1997). Some aspects of the fetal sound environment. In I. Deliège & J. Sloboda (Eds.), *Perception and cognition of music* (pp. 83–101). East Sussex, England: Psychology Press.

Ackerman, S. (1992). *Discovering the brain.* Washington, DC: National Academy Press.

Altenmüller, E. (1993). Psychophysiology and EEG. In E. Niedermeyer & F. L. da Silva (Eds.), *Electroencephalography* (pp. 597–614). Baltimore: Williams and Wilkins.

Altenmüller, E., Gruhn, W., Parlitz, D., & Kahrs, J. (1996). Music learning produces changes in brain activation patterns: A longitudinal DC-EEG study. *International Journal of Applied Music, I,* 28–33.

Amunts, K., Schlaug, G., Jancke, L., Steinmetz, H., Schleicher, A., Dabringhaus, A., & Zilles, K. (1997). Motor cortex and hand motor skills: Structural compliance in the human brain. *Human Brain Mapping, 5,* 206–215.

Atkins, D., & Flohr, J. W. (2000, June). *Music style ratings in relation to emotional tone of the music and individual variation in emotionality.* Paper presented at the twelfth annual American Psychological Society Conference, Miami.

Avanzini, G., Faienza, C., Minciacchi, D., Lopez, L. & Majno, M. (Eds.). (2003). *The neurosciences and music. Annals of the New York Academy of Sciences,* vol. 999.

Avanzini, G., Lopez, L., Koelsch, S., & Majno, M. (Eds.). (2005). *The Neurosciences and Music II: From Perception to Performance, Annals of the New York Academy of Sciences,* Vol. 1060.

Barber, B. (1999). *An investigation of neural processes in music cognition using quantitative electroencephalography.* Unpublished doctoral dissertation, University of Melbourne.

Barber, B., McKenzie, S., & Helme, R. (1997). A study of brain electrical responses to music using quantitative electroencephalography (QEEG). *International Journal of Arts Medicine, 5*(2), 12–21.

Bartlett, D. (1996). Physiological responses to music and sound stimuli. In D. Hodges (Ed.), *Handbook of music psychology* (2nd ed., pp. 343–385). San Antonio, TX: IMR Press.

Bates, E., Thal, D., & Janowsky, J. S. (1992). Early language development and its neural correlates. In F. Boller, J. Grafman, S. J. Segalowitz, & I. Rapin (Eds.), *Handbook of neuropsychology* (pp. 69–110). Amsterdam: Elsevier.

Besson, M. (2000, June). *Comparisons between language and music.* Paper presented at Mapping Music in the Brain, a satellite symposium of the annual conference for Human Brain Mapping. San Antonio, Texas.

Blood, A. J., Zatorre, R. J., Bermudez, P., & Evans, A. C. (1999). Emotional responses to pleasant and unpleasant music correlate with activity in paralimbic brain regions. *Nature Neuroscience, 2*(4), 382–387.

Bodner, M., Shaw, G. L., Gabriel, R., Johnson, J., Murias, M., & Swanson, J. (1999). Detecting symmetric patterns in EEG data: A new method of analysis. *Clinical Electroencephalography, 30*(4), 143–148.

Brody, J. (1991, April 9). Not just music, bird song is a means of courtship and defense. *New York Times,* pp. C1, C9.

Brown, W., Marsh, J., & Ponsford, R. (1985). Hemispheric differences in event-related potentials. In D. Benson & E. Zaidel (Eds.), *The dual brain: Hemispheric specialization in humans* (pp. 163–180). New York: Guildford Press.

Bruer, J. T. (1999). *The myth of the first three years.* New York: Free Press.

Caine, R. N., & Caine, G. (1994). *Making connections: Teaching the human brain.* New York: Addison-Wesley.

Carpenter, P. A., Akira, M., & Just, M. A. (1995). Language comprehension: Sentence and discourse processing. *Annual Review of Psychology, 46,* 92.

Cheour, M., Ceponiene, R., Lehtokoski, A., Luuk, A., Allik, J., Alho, K., & Näätänen, R. (1998). Development of language-specific phoneme representations in the infant brain. *Nature Neuroscience, 12,* 351–353.

Chugani, H. T. (1998). A critical period of brain development: Studies of cerebral glucose utilization with PET. *Preventive Medicine, 27*(2), 184–188.

Chugani, H. T., Phelps, M. F., & Mazziotta, J. C. (1987). Positron emission tomography study of human brain functional development. *Annals of Neurology, 22*(4), 487–497.

Cohen, D., & Erez, A. (1991). Event-related potential measurements of cognitive components in response to pitch patterns. *Music Perception, 8*(4), 405–430.

Cossu, G., Faienza, C., & Capone, C. (1994). Infants' hemispheric computation of music and speech. In C. Faienza (Ed.), *Music, speech and the developing brain.* Italy: Edizioni Angelo Guerini.

Crystal, H., Grober, E., & Masur, D. (1989). Preservation of musical memory in Alzheimer's disease. *Journal of Neurology, Neurosurgery, and Psychiatry, 52,* 1415–1416.

D'Amato, M. (1988). A search for tonal pattern perception in cebus monkeys: Why monkeys can't hum a tune. *Music Perception, 5*(4), 453–480.

deBeus, R. (1999). The effects of music training on electroencephalographic coherence of preschool children. *Dissertation Abstracts International, 60*(09B), 4952.

Deliège, I., & Sloboda, J. (1996). *Musical beginnings: Origins and development of music competence.* Oxford: Oxford University Press.

Diamond, M., Scheibel, A., Murphy, G., & Harvey, T. (1985). On the brain of a scientist: Albert Einstein. *Experimental Neurology, 88,* 198–204.

Dissanayake, E. (2000). Antecedents of the temporal arts. In N. Wallin, B. Merker, & S. Brown (Eds.), *The origins of music* (pp. 387–410). Cambridge, MA: MIT Press.

Drayna, D., Manichaikul, A., de Lange, M., Snieder, H. Spector, T. (2001). *Science, 291,* 1969–1972.

Elbert, T., Pantev, C., Wienbruch, C., Rockstrub, B., & Taub, E. (1995). Increased cortical representation of the fingers of the left hand in string players. *Science, 270*(5234), 305–307.

Elliot, D. J. (1995). *Music matters: A new philosophy of music education.* New York: Oxford University Press.

Epstein, H. (1978). Growth spurts during brain development: Implications for educational policy and practice. In J. Chall & A. Mirsky (Eds.), *Education and the brain: seventy seventh National Society for the Study of Education.* Chicago: University of Chicago Press.

Epstein, H. (1986). Stages in human brain development. *Developmental brain research, 30,* 114–119.

Eriksson, P. S., Perfilieva, E., Björk-Eriksson, T., Alborn, A., Nordborg, C., Peterson, D. A., & Gage, F. H. (1998). Neurogenesis in the adult human hippocampus. *Nature Medicine, 4,* 1313–1317.

Faita, F., & Besson, M. (1994). Electrophysiological index of musical expectancy: Is there a repetition effect on the event-related potentials associated with musical incongruities? In I. Deliege (Ed.), *Proceedings of the third international conference for music perception and cognition* (pp. 433–435), University of Liège, Belgium.

Falk, D. (2000). Hominid brain evolution and the origins of music. In N. Wallin, B. Merker, & S. Brown (Eds.), *The origins of music* (pp. 197–216). Cambridge, MA: MIT Press.

Fein, G., Raz, F. F., & Merrin, E. L. (1988). Common reference coherence data are confounded by power and phase effects. *Electroencephalography and Clinical Neurophysiology, 69,* 581–584.

Flohr, J. W., Atkins, D., Bower, T. G. R., & Aldridge, M. A. (2000). *Infant music preferences: Implications for child development and music education* (Music Education Research Report). Austin, TX: Texas Music Educators Association.

Flohr, J. W. (2004a). *Musical Lives of Young Children.* Upper Saddle River, NJ: Prentice-Hall.

Flohr, J. W. (2004b). *Physiological music research with young children: Implications for public policy and parenting.* Proceedings of the 8th International Conference on Music Perception and Cognition, Evanston, IL.

Flohr, J. W., & Miller, D. C. (1993). Quantitative EEG differences between baseline and psychomotor response to music. *Texas Music Education Research,* 1–7.

Flohr, J. W., & Miller, D. C. (1995, February). *Developmental quantitative EEG differences during psychomotor response to music.* Paper presented at the Texas Music Educators Convention, San Antonio, Texas. (ERIC Document PS025653)

Flohr, J. W., Miller, D. C., & deBeus, R. (2000). EEG studies with young children. *Music Educators Journal 87*(2), 28–32, 54.

Flohr, J. W., Miller, D. C., & Persellin, D. C. (1999, June). *Recent brain research on young children: Teaching music.* Reston, VA: Music Educators National Conference, pp. 41–43, 54.

Flohr, J. W., Persellin, D. C., & Miller, D. C. (1996, July). *Children's electrophysical responses to music.* Paper presented at the twenty-second International Society for Music Education world conference, Amsterdam. (ERIC Document PS025654)

Fox, P., Sergent, J., Hodges, D., Martin, C., Jerabek, T., Glass, T., Downs, H., & Lancaster, J. (1995, June). *Piano performance from memory: A PET study.* Paper presented at the Human Brain Mapping Conference, Paris.

Freund, H., & Hefter, H. (1990). Timing mechanisms in skilled hand movements. In F. Wilson & F. Roehmann (Eds.), *Music and child development* (pp. 179–190). St. Louis, MO: MMB Music.

Frisina, R., Walton, J., & Crummer, C. (1988). Neural basis for music cognition: Neurophysiological foundations. *Psychomusicology, 7*(2), 99–107.

Gardner, H. (1985). *Frames of mind: The theory of multiple intelligences.* New York: Basic Books.

Gardner, H. (1999). *Intelligence reframed: Multiple intelligences for the twenty-first century.* New York: Basic Books.

Gaser, C. & Schlaug, G. (2003) Brain structures differ between musicians and non-musicians. *The Journal of Neuroscience, 23* (27), 9240–9245.

Geissmann, T. (2000). Gibbon songs and human music from an evolutionary perspective. In N. Wallin, B. Merker, & S. Brown (Eds.), *The origins of music* (pp. 103–124). Cambridge, MA: MIT Press.

Gibbs, W. W. (1998, November). Dogma overturned: Upending a long-held theory, a study finds that humans can grow new brain neurons throughout life—even into old age. *Scientific American,* 19–20.

Golden, D. (1994, July). Building a better brain. *Life,* 62–70.

Gopnik, A., Meltzoff, A., & Kuhl, P. (1999). *The scientist in the crib.* New York: Morrow.

Gordon, E. (1979). *Primary measures of music audiation.* Chicago: GIA.

Gordon, E. (1990). The nature and description of developmental and stabilized music aptitudes: Implications for music learning. In F. Wilson (Ed.), *Child development.* St. Louis, MO: MMB Music.

Graziano, A. B., Peterson, M., & Shaw, G. (1999). Enhanced learning of proportional math through music training and spatial-temporal training. *Neurological Research, 21,* 139–152.

Gur, R., & Gur, R. (1994). Methods for the study of brain-behavior relationships. In A. Frazer, P. Malinoff, & A. Winokur (Eds.), *Biological bases of brain function and disease* (pp. 261–280). New York: Raven Press.

Hantz, E., & Crummer, C. (1988). Neural basis for music cognition: Psychophysical foundations. *Psychomusicology, 7*(2), 109–115.

Hari, R. (1990). The neuromagnetic method in the study of the human auditory cortex. *Advances in Audiology, 6*(2), 222–282.

Hetland, L. (2000a). Learning to make music enhances spatial reasoning. *Journal of Aesthetic Education, 34*(3–4), 179–238.

Hetland, L. (2000b). Listening to music enhances spatial-temporal reasoning: Evidence for the "Mozart effect." *Journal of Aesthetic Education, 34*(3–4), 105–148.

Hodges, D. (1989). Why are we musical? Speculations on the evolutionary plausibility of musical behavior. *Bulletin of the Council for Research in Music Education, 99,* 7–22.

Hodges, D. (1996a). Human musicality. In D. Hodges (Ed.), *Handbook of music psychology* (2nd ed., pp. 29–68). University of Texas at San Antonio: IMR Press.

Hodges, D. (1996b). Neuromusical research: A review of the literature. In D. Hodges (Ed.), *Handbook of music psychology* (pp. 197–284). San Antonio, TX: Institute for Music Research.

Hodges, D. (2000). Why are we musical? Support for an evolutionary theory of human musicality. *Proceedings of the sixth International Conference on Music Perception and Cognition,* Keele University Staffordshire, U.K.

Hubel, D. H., & Wiesel, T. N. (1970). The period of susceptibility to the physiological effects of unilateral eye closure in kittens. *Journal of Physiology, 206,* 419–436.

Hutchinson, S., Lee, L., Gaab, N. & Schlaug, G. (2003) Cerebellar volume of musicians. *Cerebral Cortex, 13,* 943–949.

Ibatoullina, A. A., Vardaris, R. M., & Thompson, L. (1994). Genetic and environmental influences on the coherence of background and orienting response EEG in children. *Intelligence 19,* 65–78.

Imberty, M. (2000). The question of innate competencies in musical communication. In N. Wallin, B. Merker, & S. Brown (Eds.), *The origins of music* (pp. 449–462). Cambridge, MA: MIT Press.

Janowsky, J. S., & Carper, R. (1996). Is there a neural basis for cognitive transitions in school-age children? In A. J. Sameroff & M. M. Haith (Eds.), *The five to seven year shift: The age of reason and responsibility* (pp. 33–60). Chicago: University of Chicago Press.

Jensen, E. (1998). *Teaching with the brain in mind.* Alexandria, VA: Association for Supervision and Curriculum Development.

Johnson, J., & Ulatowska, H. (1995). The nature of the tune and text in the production of songs. In R. Pratt & R. Spintge (Eds.), *Music medicine: Vol. 2* (pp. 153–168). St. Louis, MO: MMB Music.

Juslin, P., & Sloboda, J. (Eds.). (2001). *Music and emotion: Theory and research.* New York: Oxford University Press.

Kaufmann, L., Curtis, S., Wang, J., & Williamson, S. (1991). Changes in cortical activity when subjects scan memory for tones. *Electroencephalography and Clinical Neurophysiology, 82,* 266–284.

Kimura, D. (1961). Cerebral dominance and the perception of verbal stimuli. *Canadian Journal of Psychology, 15,* 166–171.

Kimura, D. (1967). Functional asymmetry of the brain in dichotic listening. *Cortex, 3,* 163–178.

Krause, B. (1987). The niche hypothesis: How animals taught us to dance and sing [On-line]. Available: http://www.wildsanctuary.com.

Krumhansl, C. (2002). Music: A link between cognition and emotion. *Current Directions in Psychological Science, 11*(2), 45–49.

Languis, M. K., & Miller, D. C. (1992). Luria's theory of brain functioning: A model for research in cognitive psychophysiology. *Educational Psychologist, 27,* 493–511.

Lee, D., Chen, Y. & Schlaug, G. (2003). Corpus callosum: Musician and gender effects. *NeuroReport, 14,* 205–209.

Leng, X., & Shaw, G. L. (1991). Toward a neural theory of higher brain function using music as a window. *Concepts in Neuroscience, 2*(2), 229–258.

Leonhard, C., & House, R. (1972). *Foundations and principles of music education.* New York: McGraw-Hill.

Levitin, D., & Bellugi, U. (1998). Musical abilities in individuals with Williams syndrome. *Music Perception, 15*(4), 357–389.

McIntosh, G., Thaut, M., & Rice, R. (1996). Rhythmic auditory stimulation as an entrainment and therapy technique: Effects on gait of stroke and Parkinsonian's patients. In R. Pratt & R. Spintge, (Eds.), *Music medicine: Vol. 2* (pp. 145–152). St. Louis, MO: MMB Music.

Majkowski, J., Bochenek, Z., Bochenek, W., Knapik-Fijalkowska, D., & Kopec, J. (1971). Latency of averaged evoked potentials to contralateral and ipsilateral auditory stimulation in normal subjects. *Brain Research, 25,* 416–419.

Malyarenko, T. N., Kuraev, G. A., Malyarenko, Y. E., Khvatova, M. V., Romanova, N. G., & Gurina, V. I. (1996). The development of brain electric activity in 4-year-old children by long-term sensory stimulation with music. *Human Physiology, 22*(1) 76–81.

Marin, O., & Perry, D. (1999). Neurological aspects of music perception and performance. In D. Deutsch (Ed.), *The psychology of music* (2nd ed., pp. 653–724). New York: Academic Press.

Marler, P. (2000). Origins of music and speech: Insights from animals. In N. Wallin, B. Merker, & S. Brown (Eds.), *The origins of music* (pp. 31–48). Cambridge, MA: MIT Press.

Miller, D. C., & Flohr, J. W. (1995). Utilizing quantitative EEG techniques to evaluate processes elicited by music. In *Technological Directions in Music Education.* San Antonio: Institute for Music Research, University of Texas at San Antonio.

Miller, L. (1989). *Musical savants: Exceptional skill and mental retardation.* Hillsdale, NJ: Erlbaum.

Miller, R., Thaut, M., & Aunon, J. (1995). Event-related brain potentials in an auditory-motor synchronization task. In R. Pratt & R. Spintge (Eds.), *Music medicine: Vol. 2* (pp. 76–84). St. Louis, MO: MMB Music.

Moore, G. (1992). A computer-based portable keyboard monitor for studying timing performance in pianists. *Annals of the New York Academy of Sciences, 3,* 651–652.

Nakamura, S., Sadato, N., Oohashi, T., Hishina, E., Fuwamoto, Y., & Yonekura, Y. (1999). Analysis of music-brain interaction with simultaneous measurement of regional cerebral blood flow and electroencephalogram beta rhythm in human subjects. *Neuroscience Letters, 275,* 222–226.

Nelson, C. A., & Bloom, F. E. (1997). Child development and neuroscience. *Child Development, 68*(5), 970–987.

Paller, K., McCarthy, G., & Wood, C. (1992). Event-related potentials elicited by deviant endings to melodies. *Psychomusicology, 29*(2), 202–206.

Panksepp, J. (1998). *Affective neuroscience: The foundations of human and animal emotions.* New York: Oxford University Press.

Pantev, C., Oostenveld, R., Engelien, A., Ross, B., Roberts, L. E., & Hoek, M. (1998). Increased auditory cortical representation. *Nature, 392,* 811–813.

Parsons, L. (2000, June). *Functional anatomy of pitch, rhythm, melody, and harmony.* Paper presented at Mapping Music in the Brain, a satellite symposium of the annual conference for Human Brain Mapping, San Antonio, Texas.

Parsons, L. (2001). Exploring the functional neuroanatomy of music performance, perception, and comprehension. In R. Zatorre & I. Peretz (Eds.), *The biological foundations of music* (pp. 211–230). Annals of the New York Academy of Sciences, vol. 930.

Parsons, L., & Fox, P. (1997). Sensory and cognitive tasks: The cerebellum and cognition. In J. D. Schmahmann (Ed.), *International review of neurobiology, cerebellum and cognitio* (pp. 255–272). San Diego: Academic Press.

Parsons, L., Fox, P., & Hodges, D. (1998, November). *Neural basis of the comprehension of musical melody, harmony, and rhythm.* Paper presented at Society for Neuroscience, Los Angeles.

Pascual-Leone, A., Dand, N., Cohen, L., Braskil-Neto, J., Cammarota, A., & Hallett, M. (1995). Modulation of muscle responses evoked by transcranial magnetic stimulation during the acquisition of new fine motor skills. *Journal of Neurophysiology,* 74(3), 1037–1045.

Paulus, W. (1988). Effect of musical modelling on late auditory evoked potentials. *European Archives of Psychiatry and Neurological Sciences,* 237(5), 307–311.

Payne, K. (2000). The progressively changing songs of humpbackwhales: A window on the creative process in a wild animal. In N. Wallin, B. Merker, & S. Brown (Eds.), *The origins of music* (pp. 135–150). Cambridge, MA: MIT Press.

Peretz, I. (2001). Brain specialization for music: New evidence from congenital amusia. In Zatorre, R. & Peretz, I. (Eds.), *The biological foundations of music. Annals of the New York Academy of Sciences* (Vol. 930, pp. 153–165).

Petsche, H., Lindner, K., Rappelsberger, P., & Gruber, G. (1988). The EEG: An adequate method to concretize brain processes elicited by music. *Music Perception, 6,* 133–159.

Piaget, J. (1950). *The psychology of intelligence.* London: Routledge and Kegan Paul.

Platel, H., Price, C., Baron, J. C., Wise, R., Lambert, J., Frackowiak, R., Lechevalier, B., & Eustache, F. (1997). The structural components of music perception: A functional anatomical study. *Brain, 20(2),* 229–243.

Posner, M., & Raichle, M. (1994). *Images of mind.* New York: Scientific American Library.

Pratt, R., & Spintge, R. (1996). *Music medicine: Vol. 2.* St. Louis, MO: MMB Music.

Raichle, M. 1994. Visualizing the mind. *Scientific American, 270(4),* 58–64.

Rauscher, F. H., Shaw, G. L., & Ky, K. N. (1993). Music and spatial task performance. *Nature, 365,* 611.

Rauscher, F. H., Shaw, G. L., Ky, K. N., & Wright, E. L. (1994, August). *Music and spatial task performance: A causal relationship.* Paper presented at the American Psychological Association 102nd annual convention, Los Angeles.

Reilly, M. (1999). Music: A cognitive behavioral intervention for anxiety and acute pain control in the elderly cataract patient. *Dissertation Abstracts International,* 60(07B), 3195.

Reimer, B. (1999). Facing the risks of the "Mozart effect." *Music Educators Journal, 86,* 37–43.

Restak, R. (1994). *The Modular Brain.* New York: Scribners.

Robinson, G., & Solomon, D. (1974). Rhythm is processed by the speech hemisphere. *Journal of Experimental Psychology, 102(3),* 508–511.

Sarnthein, J., vonStein, A., Rappelsberger, P., Petsche, H., Rauscher, F., & Shaw, G. (1997). Persistent patterns of brain activity: An EEG coherence study of the positive effect of music on spatial-temporal reasoning. *Neurological Research, 19,* 107–116.

Schlaug, G., Jäncke, L., Huang, Y., & Steinmetz, H. (1994). In vivo morphometry of interhemispheric asymmetry and connectivity in musicians. In I. Deliege (Ed.), *Proceedings of the third international conference for music perception and cognition* (pp. 417–418), University of Liège, Belgium.

Schlaug, G., Jäncke, L., Huang, L., & Steinmetz, H. (1995). In vivo evidence of structural brain asymmetry in musicians. *Science, 267(5198),* 699–701.

Schlaug, G., Jänke, L., Huang, Y., Staiger, J. F., & Steinmetz, H. (1995). Increased corpus callosum size in musicians. *Neuropsychologia, 33,* 1047–1055.

Schlaug, G., Norton, A., Overy, K., Cronin, K., Lee, D.J. & Winner, E. (2004). *Effects of music training on children's brain and cognitive development.* Proceedings of the 8th International Conference on Music Perception and Cognition, Evanston, IL.

Schwent, V., Snyder, E., & Hillyard, S. (1976). Auditory evoked potentials during multichannel selective listening: Role of pitch and localization cues. *Journal of Experimental Psychology: Human Perception and Performance* 2(3), 313–325.

Sergent, J. (1993). Mapping the musician brain. *Human Brain Mapping, 1*(1), 20–38.

Shaw, G. L. (2000). *Keeping Mozart in mind.* San Diego: Academic Press.

Slater, P. (2000). Birdsong repertoires: Their origins and use. In N. Wallin, B. Merker, & S. Brown (Eds.), *The origins of music* (pp. 49–64). Cambridge, MA: MIT Press.

Sluming, V., Barrick, T., Howard, M., Cezayirli, E., Mayes, A. & Roberts, N. (2002) Voxel-based morphometry reveals increased gray matter density in Broca's Area in male symphony orchestra musicians. *Neuroimage, 17,* 1613–1622.

Snowdon, D. A. (1997). Aging and Alzheimer's disease: Lessons from the nun study. *Gerontologist, 37*(2), 150–156.

Snowdon, D. (2001). *Aging with grace: What the nun study teaches us about leading longer, healthier, and more meaningful lives.* New York: Bantam Books.

Spintge, R., & Droh, R. (1992). *Music medicine.* St. Louis, MO: MMB Music.

Standley, J. (1998). Pre and perinatal growth and development: Implications of music benefits for premature infants. *International Journal of Music Education, 31,* 2–13.

Sylwester, R. (1995). *A celebration of neurons: An educator's guide to the human brain.* Alexandria, VA: Association for Supervision and Curriculum Development.

Thatcher, R. (1998, September 11). *EEG database guided neurotherapy: Practical applications.* Presentation at the annual conference of the Society for the Study of Neuronal Regulation, Austin, Texas.

Thaut, M., Brown, S., Benjamin, J., & Cooke, J. (1995). Rhythmic facilitation of movement sequencing: Effects on spatio-temporal control and sensory modality dependence. In R. Pratt & R. Spintge (Eds.), *Music medicine: Vol. 2* (pp. 104–112). St. Louis, MO: MMB Music.

Thaut, M., McIntosh, G., Prassas, S., & Rice, R. (1993). Effect of rhythmic cuing on temporal stride parameters and EMG patterns in hemiparetic gait of stroke patients. *Journal of Neurologic Rehabilitation, 7,* 9–16.

Thulborn, K. R., Carpenter, P. A., & Just, M. A. (1999). Plasticity of language-related brain function during recovery from stroke. *Stroke, 30*(4), 749–754.

Trehub, S. (2004). Music Perception in Infancy. In J. Flohr, *Musical lives of young children* (pp. 24–29). Upper Saddle River, NJ: Prentice-Hall.

Trehub, S., Bull, D., & Thorpe, L. (1984). Infants' perception of melodies: The role of melodic contour. *Child Development, 55,* 821–830.

Trehub, S., Schellenberg, E., & Hill, D. (1997). The origins of music perception and cognition: A developmental perspective. In I. Deliège & J. Sloboda (Eds.), *Perception and cognition of music* (pp. 103–128). East Sussex, England: Psychology Press.

Trehub, S., & Trainor, L. (1993). Listening strategies in infancy: The roots of language and musical development. In S. McAdams & E. Bigand (Eds.), *Thinking in sound: Cognitive perspectives on human audition* (pp. 278–327). New York: Oxford University Press.

van Baal, G. C. M., de Geus, E. J. C., & Boomsma, D. I. (1998). Genetic influences on EEG coherence in 5-year-old twins. *Behavior Genetics, 28*(1), 9–19.

Wallin, N., Merker, B., & Brown, S. (Eds). (2000). *The origins of music.* Cambridge, MA: MIT Press.

Warren, R. (1993). Perception of acoustic sequences: Global integration versus temporal resolution. In S. McAdams & E. Bigand (Eds.), *Thinking in sound: Cognitive perspectives on human audition* (pp. 37–68). New York: Oxford University Press.

Whaling, C. (2000). What's behind a song? The neural basis of song learning in birds. In N. Wallin, B. Merker, & S. Brown (Eds.), *The origins of music* (pp. 65–76). Cambridge, MA: MIT Press.

Williamson, S., & Kaufman, L. (1988). Auditory evoked magnetic fields. In A. Jahn & J. Santos-Sacchi (Eds.), *Physiology of the ear* (pp. 497–505). New York: Raven Press.

Wilson, F. (1986). *Tone deaf and all thumbs?* New York: Viking Press.

Wilson, F. (1988). Brain mechanisms in highly skilled movements. In F. Roehmann (Ed.), *The biology of music making* (pp. 92–99). St. Louis, MO: MMB Music.

Wilson, F. (1991). Music and the neurology of time. *Music Educators Journal, 77*(5), 26–30.

Wilson, F. (1992). Digitizing digital dexterity: A novel application for MIDI recordings of keyboard performance. *Psychomusicology, 11,* 79–95.

Wilson, F. (1998). *The hand.* New York: Vintage Books.

Wilson, F., & Roehmann, F. (1992). The study of biomechanical and physiological processes in relation to musical performance. In R. Colwell (Ed.), *Handbook of research on music teaching and learning* (pp. 509–524). New York: Schirmer Books.

Woodward, S., Fresen, J., Harrison, V. C., & Coley, N. (1996). The birth of musical language. *Proceedings of the seventh International Seminar of the Early Childhood Commission,* Winchester, U.K.

Zatorre, R. (1994). Musical processing in the nonmusician's brain: Evidence for specialized neural networks. In I. Deliege (Ed.), *Proceedings of the third international conference for music perception and cognition* (pp. 39–40), University of Liège, Belgium.

Zatorre, R., Evans, A., & Meyer, E. (1994). Neural mechanisms underlying melodic perception and memory for pitch. *Journal of Neuroscience, 14*(4), 1908–1919.

Zatorre, R., & Peretz, I. (Eds.) (2001). *The biological foundations of music.* Annals of the New York Academy of Sciences, vol. 930.

Zimmerman, M. P. (1971). *Musical characteristics of children.* Washington, DC: Music Educators National Conference.

The Neurobiology of Music Cognition and Learning

2

WILFRIED GRUHN

FRANCES RAUSCHER

Music Learning and Cognition

The 20th century has provided a wealth of important data about cognition and learning. However, with the cognitive revolution in developmental psychology and the rise in Piagetian theory, the emphasis shifted from learning to thinking. Consequently, substantial knowledge about the development of children's thinking at different ages has been collected since then, but not as much knowledge has been provided about how children learn. This movement away from studying children's learning reflected more than a shift in interest; it rather reflected an assumption that cognitive development and learning are different processes. However, learning and cognition are two sides of the same coin. What one knows is largely based upon what one has learned, and learning, of course, generates knowledge. Therefore, any theory of cognitive development that has little to say about learning provides a limited perspective of development.

Over the past decades, the emergence of interdisciplinary studies in cognitive neuroscience produced evidence of neural correlates for cognition and learning. To the same degree neuroscientific research has extended our understanding of the basic structures of cognition and learning. This chapter reviews current research on the neural mechanisms of music learning and cognition. We will also refer the reader to relevant chapters elsewhere in this text for a greater degree of technical detail.

A brief survey of the literature on learning and cognition shall provide the framework for our particular neurobiological perspective. Four different approaches to investigating learning are reviewed: *behaviorism* (Watson

1913), *constructivsm* (Piaget 1947) *sociohistorical theory* (Vygotsky 1962), and *connectionism* (McClelland 1995).

Behaviorism

The behaviorists viewed developmental changes in behavior as relying on several basic principles of learning, particularly classical conditioning (Pavlov, 1927) and operant conditioning (Skinner, 1953), as initially demonstrated by animal experiments. For example, Ivan Pavlov's experiments with dogs revealed that a neutral stimulus (a bell) begins to elicit a response (salivation) after being repeatedly paired with another stimulus (food) that already elicits that response. A stimulus–response chain (S → R) can be strengthened by repetition and reinforcement, and the response will gradually generalize. Learning, according to the behaviorists, occurs when a behavioral change can be linked to a stimulus presumed to have caused that change and can thus be objectively measured. However, the behaviorists failed to do justice to the organization of human behavior and the complex inner processes that are responsible for generating it. For example, although the neuronal activity of learning in the human brain cannot be observed directly, it clearly plays a major role in behavior. From a behaviorist point of view, however, the mind remains a "black box" about which one can only speculate and which therefore cannot contribute very much to the scientific study of behavior. Any introspection into the processes of learning was seen by the behaviorists as neither reliable nor relevant to the understanding of behavioral processes. This limitation in the behaviorist view, along with the emergence of computer science, encouraged investigators to attempt to describe the cognitive processes that are necessary to generate and control complex human behavior. This event became known as the "cognitive revolution."

Cognitive Psychology

The cognitive revolution represented a qualitative shift from an emphasis on behavior toward an emphasis on understanding the inner processes involved in cognition and intellectual growth. The *constructivist* perspective emphasizes the active role of the child in constructing advanced forms of cognition that transcend less adequate earlier forms (Baldwin, 1894/1968). Constructivists believe that one should begin the study of children's cognitive development by exploring the foundational concepts with which children come equipped at birth and then go on to document any change that may take place in these concepts with age. Jean Piaget was perhaps the most influential developmental psychologist to carefully observe children's development. Based on his own observations of his three young children, Piaget built a cognitive theory of the awakening of intelligence in children. According to Piaget, children progress through a series of five universal stages of development, which are characterized by "sensori-motor intelligence," "preoperational and symbolic thinking," "intuitive thought," "concrete operations," and "formal operations" (1947, 1959). As they progress through these stages, children develop cognitive schemas through interaction with the environment and other persons. The forms of these schemas are different at different stages of their development, and it is this difference that gives the thought of young children its unique character. Piaget hypothesized that the progression of humans through the four developmental stages is biologically determined. In any given stage, new experiences are "assimilated" to the existing set of schemata. Transition from one form of thought to the next is driven by "accommodation," a process by which existing schemata are broken down and then reorganized into new and more adaptive patterns, in turn leading to a highly differentiated cognitive structure. This model was expanded, elaborated, and modified by others (Aebli, 1980/1981; Case, 1972; Pascual-Leone & Smith, 1969). Thus the term *mental representation* became a key signature of the cognitive revolution. Piaget's theory was applied to musical development by Pflederer Zimmerman (1984; Pflederer Zimmerman & Webster, 1983) and to music learning (slightly modified) by Bamberger (1991).

Piaget and successors to his theory have expanded our understanding of development by revealing substantial domain-specific cognitive capabilities that children possess from early in life. These theorists emphasize that learning at all ages involves an active interchange between structures in the mind and information from the environment. Mental structures are joined with processes, such as assimilation and accommodation, to actively contribute to cognitive development.

Sociohistorical Theory

Contextual models, sometimes called systems views, emphasize that the transformation from infant to adult takes place via a complex, multidirectional system of influences (Gottlieb, 1991). These theorists are concerned with understanding how the broad range of biological, physical, and sociocultural settings affect learning and development. For example, Lev S. Vygotsky's sociohistorical theory from the 1930s stresses the importance of cultural tools, symbols, and ways of thinking that the child acquires from more knowledgeable members of the community (1934/1962). Development is viewed as a dynamic, never-ending transaction that involves continuing, reciprocal exchanges: People and settings transform the child, who in turn affects the people and settings that surround him or her, which further reshape the child, in an endless progression. According to the sociohistorical view, knowledge does not originate in the environment alone (as the behaviorists claimed) or in the interaction between the individual and the environment (as the constructivists maintained). Rather, knowledge originates in the social, linguistic, and material history of the individual's culture and its tools, concepts, and symbol systems. Children's participation in cultural activities with the guidance of others allows them to "internalize" their community's tools for thinking. Thus efforts to understand individual cognitive development and learning must consider the social roots of both the tools for thinking that children are learning to use and the social interactions that guide children in use of these tools. Vygotsky's concept of the zone of proximal development posits that development proceeds through children's participation in activities slightly beyond their competence with the assistance of adults or more skilled children. These ideas were expanded by other Soviet researchers, most notably Luria (1961) and Leont'ev (1981). The translation of Vygotsky's work into English marked the beginning of widespread use of Vygotskian ideas in the United States and Western Europe.

Connectionism

Connectionism offers a fresh perspective to the understanding of learning by focusing research on the microstructure of cognition. Connectionist theory is extremely rich in terms of its implications for brain development. Highly sophisticated brain-imaging techniques, such as electro- and magneto-encephalography (EEG and EMG), event-related potential (ERP), magnetic resonance imaging (MRI), computer tomography (CT), and positron emission tomography (PET), permit a new view of the active brain. The topography of brain areas involved in aural perception and learning has been elaborated and transcribed into brain maps. The study of highly complex network structures and interconnections has laid the foundation for a connectionist model of "parallel distributed processing (PDP)" (Rumelhart & McClelland, 1986). The theory behind PDP is bound to the hypothesis of the modularity of mind (Fodor, 1983). Here the input systems refer to different brain areas that are highly specialized in processing particular properties of the incoming auditory stimulation, such as pitch, loudness, location of the sound source, melodic contour, and so forth. The possibility of exactly measuring the neural activation, the intensity and distribution of activation patterns, and the localization and lateralization of domain-specific processing tasks across the cortex have enabled new avenues for the investigation of the physiological foundations of music cognition and music learning (Hodges, 1996).

   Along with the development and implementation of the imaging techniques, computer models of artificial "neural" networks have been developed to investigate strategies in problem-solving and decision-making processes (Fiske, 1993; Griffith & Todd, 1999; Todd & Loy, 1991). The connectionist approach can be seen as a neurally inspired model of information processing, in which groupings of neurons are interconnected in input layers (by which signals enter the system), output layers (which represent the outcome of the network), and hidden layers (which compute the more complex nonlinear relationships within the network). (For a more detailed introduction to connectionist ideas, see Bechtel & Abrahamsen, 1991; Ellis & Humphreys, 1999.) Thus connectionist modeling can provide a functional understanding of the sequential structure of decision-making processes that are performed by an activation of units ("nodes") at an input layer, their gradual selection from a hidden layer, which corresponds to their semantic or syntactic weight, and finally their progression to an output layer. Cognition here is the result of a process of propagation and back-propagation within different layers of selection. Learning describes the tracing of paths and connections in that neural network.

In light of the neurobiological exploration of brain activities involved in music cognition and learning, mental representation has become a crucial component of learning. If neural networks function as the neural correlate for musical representations, then learning must be related to physiological conditions in the brain, that is, to the *activity* of neurons, to the *connectivity* among neurons, cell assemblies, and brain areas, and to the *neuronal plasticity* of the brain—especially the establishment, growth, and progressive differentiation of genuine musical representations with respect to their power, localization, and extension in both hemispheres (Zatorve & Peretz, 2001; Peretz & Zatorre, 2003; Avanzini et al., 2003).

Neurobiological Foundations of Cognition and Learning

Cognition can be seen as the result of a pattern-matching process by which mental representations are activated through perceived stimuli. The term *mental representation* covers a broad array of meanings and is often used synonymously with *mental models* (Johnson-Laird, 1983), *scripts* (Schank & Abelson, 1977), *frames* (Minsky, 1980), *schemas* (Aebli, 1980/1981; Piaget, 1959) or *neural networks* (Todd & Loy, 1991). In addition to the debate on the meaning of mental representations, there is also a debate on the nature of mental representations. In one view, representations are seen as veridical images that are stored in the mind and can be retrieved from it; that is, they are *depictive* in nature (Kosslyn, 1994), whereas another perspective holds that representations result from formal processes and accumulated experiences that are *propositional* in nature (Pylyshyn, 1973). In music, the depictive representation of a chord, for example, is reflected by the representation of the position of fingers on a keyboard or the picture of the notation, whereas propositional representation results from knowledge in terms of statements about that chord as a sum of many experiences.

In this section, we will only refer to the neuronal cortical substrates of musical representations which are defined as the neuronal networks that are involved in cortical activations caused by the processing of music (reading, writing, listening, performing, conducting, learning, memorizing etc.). Methodologically, four strategies are commonly employed to investigate the learning brain: (1) the observation of persons with brain lesions that cause par ticular deficits; (2) animal experiments that study neuronal brain reactions; (3) the measurement of infants' information processing, especially sensory and auditory temporal processing; and (4) the implementation of brain-imaging techniques for a clear and precise identification and localization of changes in brain activation.

Neurons are highly specialized to respond to particular qualities of stimuli, for example, to a section of a band of frequencies (pitch), to a movement of sounds up and down (direction), to the intensity of sound (loudness), and so forth. Neurons of a particular brain area represent different features. Unfortunately, little research exists on the auditory sensory mapping of the associative cortex. In cognition, distributed processing of sensory information must be coordinated for the creation of what is eventually perceived by the conscious mind. As M. E. Martinez (1999) has put it:

> The human mind is not a video camera. We do not process and store countless sensory bits; rather, we construct our inner and outer worlds according to the organizing principle of meaning. The fact that knowledge can be represented in different ways implies that knowledge is not a sensory transcription of the external world into the inner world of the mind. (p. 21)

Single cortical neurons with similar "interests" tend to be vertically arrayed in cortical columns like thin cylinders (Calvin, 1996). The best-known columns are the visual cortex's orientation columns, but little is known about aural orientation columns and representations. The data available, however, suggest the existence of complex musical structures that are processed in distributed areas and are connected in coherent networks or cell assemblies. What we perceive as music originates from distributed processing but combines into one conscious feature that forms a robust mental representation.

Experimental programs have demonstrated that formal training and informal experience in varied environmental situations cause measurable changes in the neurochemistry and even in the neuroanatomy of the brain (Black & Greenough, 1998). Even the cortical maps of adult primates can be radically altered through environmental input (Kempermann et al., 1997). This neuronal plasticity is crucial for the neurobiology of learning. As Ramon y Cajal stressed at the end of the 19th century, learning is deeply involved in, if not biologically based upon, the formation of new synaptic connections. Since Donald O. Hebb (1949) theorized that chemical changes in a cell's dendrites increase the likelihood that it will activate neighboring cells, remarkable empirical progress has been made in the investigation of synaptic connectivity and its impact on the electrochemical transmission between neurons. "This basic concept of a cooperative set of modifiable connections as the basis of learning and memory, along with the Hebb synapse, continues to have substantial influence on neural network theory" (Black & Greenough, 1998, p. 56).

If learning is associated with synaptic growth, the investigation of the formation of synaptic contacts in the human cerebral cortex becomes enormously important. It has been documented for animal and human brains that the synaptic density—the number of synapses per neuron or per unit volume of cortical tissue—changes over life spans and defines the limits of the processing capacity (Huttenlocher, 1979, 1984). In human beings, synaptogenesis takes place prenatally and in early infancy. By the age of 1 year it reaches a plateau stage, followed by a progressive synapse decline, which happens most rapidly during preschool years (Huttenlocher, 1984). However, there are regional differences in synaptogenesis in human brains. Huttenlocher (Huttenlocher & Dabholkar, 1997) compared the development in two cortical areas: the auditory and prefrontal cortex. He found that synaptic density increases more rapidly in the auditory cortex (maximum at age 3 months) than in middle frontal gyrus (peak after age 15 months). Here synaptic growth occurs concurrently with growth of dendrites and axons and with myelination of the subcortical white matter. The following phase of synapse elimination also starts earlier in the auditory cortex, where it reaches a mature level by age 12 years, than in the prefrontal cortex (Huttenlocher & Dabholkar, 1997). The exuberant overproduction of neuronal connections during infancy may be seen as an anatomical substrate for neural plasticity (Huttenlocher, 1990) that has a tremendous impact on the unique structure of early learning. The discovery of an inverted U-shaped structure in brain development is confirmed by the development of glucose metabolism. Cerebral glucose consumption rises from birth until about 4 years of age, maintains from 4 to about 9–10 years, and then gradually declines (Chugani, 1998). These findings have important implications for our understanding of brain plasticity and critical periods for learning.

Neuroscientists at Geneva University (Müller, Toni, & Buchs, 2000) have investigated the chemical changes that influence synaptic strength. The researchers stimulated rat brain slices to produce long-term potentiation (LTP). If a receiving neuron has been activated, the incoming neurotransmitter induces LTP by flooding calcium ions into the spine. An hour after treatment, 20% of the synapses had developed double spines, forming a second spine adjacent to the active one. Müller concludes that LTP triggers "a duplication of the active synapse" (Barinaga, 1999, p. 1661). Presumably this causes an increase in synaptic strength.

The neurobiological foundations for learning are derived from studies that suggest that experience or learning induces changes in the brain that relate to cortical thickness (Diamond et al., 1964), the size of cell bodies (Diamond, 1967), the size of synaptic contact areas (West & Greenough, 1972), an increase in dendritic spines (Globus et al., 1973), a parallel increase in the number of synapses per neuron (Turner & Greenough, 1985), the thickness of the corpus callosum (Schlaug, Jäncke, Huang, Stalger, & Steinmetz, 1995), an increase in hippocampal neurons (Kempermann et al., 1997), the size of the left planum temporale (Pantev et al., 1998), and the doubling of spines through LTP (Müller et al., 2000). These research findings relate either to the growth of number or size of new synaptic connections by formal training or enriched environmental experience or to the growth of stronger and bigger already-existing synapses. In any case, the evidence of neurochemical and neuroanatomical plasticity is basic for the neurobiology of learning, that is, for the formation and modification of mental representations. In particular for young children, it is evident—despite Bruer's reluctance (see "Discussions and Conclusions")—that early music training leads to an expansion of the representation of sound in the auditory cortex (Rauschecker, 1999).

For cognition and learning experiments, the localization of task-specific cortical areas has been empirically investigated (see "Brain Research on Music Cognition and Learning," p. 51). Even the specialization within the auditory cortex has been clarified by its subdivision into four distinct territories (Gaschler-Markefski, Baumgart, Tempelmann, Woldorff, & Scheich, 1998). The contribution of different cortical areas to music processing still remains a major focus of research in neuroscience. From patients with surgical lesions we know about different strategies of musical-information processing. They demonstrate, for example, that a right temporal cortectomy impairs the use of both contour and interval information, whereas a left temporal cortectomy interferes with interval information only (Liegeois-Chauvel, Peretz, Babai, Leguitton, & Chauvel, 1998). In general, the acquisition of implicit knowledge through neuronal self-organization that results from mere exposure to music (Peretz, Gaudreau, & Bonnel, 1998) should not be underestimated, as Tillmann, Bharucha, and Bigand have shown by experiments that dealt with tone, chord, and key relationships, including memory judgments, and expectancies (2000). Furthermore, the learning context plays an important role in memory retrieval, especially for infants who displayed a 7-day retention only when the music played during the retention test matched the training music (Fagen et al., 1997). However, all that knowledge about functional cortical areas cannot suffice as the only explanation for the neurobiological processes involved in music learning. In this section, learning is, therefore, exclusively defined as the process of incrementally developing and altering the structure of mental representations.

Following the experimental brain studies on learning primarily conducted with animals, researchers have recently conducted EEG studies on music learning of children (aged 12–14) and adults (aged 17–39) (Altenmüller & Gruhn, 1997; Altenmüller, Gruhn, Parlitz, & Liebert, 2000; Gruhn, 1997; Gruhn, Altenmüller, & Babler, 1997; Liebert, 2000). These studies reveal that significant changes in auditory activation patterns and neural networks are induced by different types of learning according to declarative and procedural leading strategies that correspond to formal instruction and informal musical exposure. Subjects who received informal instruction by singing and playing supported the efficiency of the phonological loop at the aural-oral level and, by this, developed procedural knowledge. This learning strategy evidenced increased activation patterns at the right frontal and bilateral parieto-occipital lobes, which may be ascribed to a global way of processing through the integration of visuo-spatial associations). However, music processing of subjects who received formal verbal instruction evidenced an in creased activation of left fronto-temporal brain regions, which might refer to a more local strategy (Altenmüller & Gruhn, 1997).

In another long-term learning experiment, subjects displayed different activation patterns depending upon how successfully they performed a task. Those who succeeded in the task, regardless of the type of learning (declarative versus procedural), demonstrated a shift to the *right* fronto-temporal lobes, whereas brain activation in those subjects who did not succeed focused in the *left* fronto-temporal regions. Therefore, it appears that a simple right-left dichotomy with music in the right hemisphere is an oversimplification. Any music processing involves both hemispheres equally but in an asymmetric specialization that depends upon many intra- and interpersonal factors. Perhaps different types of processing (global versus local processing; Peretz, 1990; see "Brain Research on Music Cognition and Learning," p. 51) produce a lateralization effect because different cognitive strategies are applied individually.

Brain activation patterns can also differentiate long-term from short-term learning. In a short-term ear-training experiment (Liebert et al., 1999), researchers found an overall increase of brain activation, whereas experiments with long-term learning demonstrated a general decrease of brain activation. Furthermore, the two methodical strategies caused different patterns of cortical networks. During the processing of the musical task, only procedural learners developed significant changes in their activation patterns (Liebert, 2001).

These findings suggest that learning causes a change in the reorganization of cortical networks and therefore affects the structure of the mental representation, which may be called *formal* (Bamberger, 1991; Gruhn, 1998). Formal representations produce a more distributed, widely spread neuronal network and may therefore need only a reduced cortical brain potential, presumably due to the involvement of subcortical regions in the representation of genuine musical qualities. (This must be shown by functional fMRI studies.) There is good reason to assume that, biologically, learning is accomplished by a move from one type of cortical representation (which might be called figural, according to Bamberger, 1991) to a different type of cortical representation that involves subcortical layers. The essence of this model is based upon different encodings of the processing and storing of musical information and knowledge. Learning, therefore, effects the transformation from cortical to integral cortical-subcortical representations.

In instrumental training, motor skills and auditory skills collaborate. The activation of representation in one area is linked to that of a corresponding area that is not directly stimulated. This process has been described as coactivation. Bangert, (Bangert & Altenmüller, 2003) demonstrated that subjects exhibit a slight coactivation of the sensorimotor cortex in a passive auditory task even 20 minutes after a keyboard-training session. Likewise, fronto-temporal regions were activated in pianists during a mute motor task. This clearly suggests that cortical activation patterns, even during a strictly limited task, display a widely distributed network far beyond a simple image of the involved activity. Learning, in a neurobiological sense, is due to the establishment of those networks.

Neurobiological Research on Music and Learning

Overview

A comprehensive review of brain development is beyond the scope of this chapter. However, M. H. Johnson (1998) has identified four factors that we believe are important to any understanding of the neurobiology of music learning and cognition.

First, there are neural structures in the brain that are common to both humans and other mammals, both primate and nonprimate. Differences between humans and other animals primarily concern the extent of the cerebral cortex. Subcortical structures, such as the hippocampus and cerebellum, are structurally similar across mammalian species.

Second, the cerebral cortex, hippocampus, and cerebellum continue to develop throughout childhood. Although the vast majority of neurons are present at birth (Rakic, 1995), synapses, dendrites, and fiber bundles continue to develop postnatally, perhaps as a function of experience. Myelin, the fatty sheath that surrounds neuronal pathways (and is thought to increase the efficiency of information transmission), also increases dramatically after birth. The immaturity of the human brain at birth may explain some of the limitations on learning and cognition present in infants and children. Similarly, the dynamic postnatal development of the cortex allows more intentional, purposeful behavior.

Third, different areas of the cerebral cortex develop at different rates. For example, Conel's (1939/1967) study of cortical development in the human infant led him to conclude that the cortex develops in an "inside-out" fashion, with outer brain layers developing in advance of inner layers. Differential development *between* cortical regions (i.e., visual cortex and frontal cortex) has also been documented (Huttenlocher, 1990). These patterns of development may influence information processing.

Finally, studies on cortical plasticity suggest that cortical specialization is heavily influenced by experience. Although primary cortices are genetically predetermined, there is a high degree of modulation with respect to the extension and connectivity of functional brain areas according to experience and learning. Therefore, brain plasticity can be seen as fundamental for the development of mental representations.

Empirical Methods

The recent explosion of knowledge of brain development makes the task of relating it to cognitive changes considerably more viable. Consequently, efforts to correlate neural changes to cognitive changes have increased dramatically over the past two decades. However, because a multitude of neuroanatomical variables change over the first decade of life, it is unwise to make causal inferences that regard the relationship between changes in specific brain areas to specific cognitive changes. Evidence of temporal correlation can, however, be supported by empirical methods. A variety of techniques are now available to developmentalists interested in the biological basis of cognitive development. Some of these methods, such as PET, require the injection of a radioactive dye and are therefore of limited use for studying the cognitive functioning of healthy children and adults. Others, such as EEG, ERP, and functional MRI (fMRI), are currently being employed. These imaging techniques are described by Hodges and Flohr in this volume (chap. 1).

While the new functional brain-imaging techniques promise to provide researchers with important information that regards the relationship of brain structure and function to learning and cognition, somewhat similar questions can be explored through the use of animals as subjects. Research on animals (mostly rodents) has contributed a great deal to our understanding of the relation between brain and behavior. The field of molecular genetics, for example, has opened up new possibilities for investigating this relationship. In particular, mice that undergo lesions in the alpha-calcium-calmodulin kinase II gene are unable to perform certain learning tasks in adulthood (Silva, Paylor, Wehner, & Tonegawa, 1992). These types of techniques, in which certain genes from the genome of an animal are either removed or lesioned, permit the investigator to answer questions that regard genetic contributions to learning and behavior and are particularly well suited when applied to established animal models of development.

Further insight into the relations between brain and behavior can be found in studies in which the brain is removed in order to examine it at the cellular level. For example, studies that used this technique suggest that rats reared in an "enriched" environment after weaning show a wealth of enduring neurobiological and behavioral changes. Rats raised with stimulus objects such as running wheels, rubber tubes, nibble bars, and such in their cages show morphological and biochemical alterations in cortical and hippocampal formation and perform better on learning and memory-dependent tasks than animals raised in normal laboratory conditions (see Renner & Rosenzweig, 1987, for review). Similar effects have been found for rats raised in socially enriched conditions, in which animals are housed with several siblings rather than in pairs or isolation (Pacteau, Einon, & Sindon, 1989). Furthermore, recent research has demonstrated that rats exposed to complex music learned a spatial maze faster and with fewer errors than rats exposed to minimalist music, white noise, or silence (Rauscher, Robinson, & Jens, 1998), results that appear to be a function of increased hippocampal dendritic density in the animals exposed to the complex music (Rauscher & Koch, 2000). A follow-up study explored the molecular mechanisms underlying these auditory enrichment effects (Li, Cai, Ying, Gomez-Pinila, Cooper,

& Rauscher, 2004). Rats exposed to complex music performed better in a spatial maze than rats exposed to silence. The music exposure also enhanced BDNF and its effectors on synaptic plasticity and learning, synapsin I and CREB, in the rat hippocampus. The results show that music exposure preferentially affected molecular systems related to synaptic plasticity. Music may therefore play an important role for improving cognitive abilities by modulating synaptic plasticity.

Marker tasks, behavioral tasks that have been linked to particular brain regions by neuroimaging studies, provide another useful approach to understanding brain development and learning. By testing individuals of varying ages with different versions of these tasks researchers can relate levels of task performance to the functional development of different brain regions. A number of marker tasks have recently been developed for the functioning of structures involved in oculomotor control and visual attention shifts (M. H. Johnson, 1998).

Brain Research on Music Cognition and Learning

There may be no other area of music psychology that has seen as much recent advancement as research on music-induced plasticity of the brain. For example, Gottfried Schlaug and his colleagues found that a small neural structure in the cerebral cortex that processes sound signals, the planum temporale, was larger in the left hemisphere and smaller in the right in the brains of musicians than of nonmusicians (Schlaug, Jäncke, Huang, & Steinmetz, 1994), an effect that was later found to be due to musicians who possessed perfect pitch and who began their musical training before the age of 7 (Schlaug et al., 1995). Schlaug and his colleagues also reported that musicians, particularly those who had begun their training before age 7, had thicker corpus callosi (the band of nerve tissue that connects the left and right hemispheres) than nonmusicians (Schlaug et al., 1994).

Other correlational studies also suggest that instrumental instruction affects brain development. Elbert, Pantev, Wienbruch, Rockstroh, and Taub (1995) asked string players and nonmusicians to move the fingers of their left hands while magnetoencephalography (MEG) measurements were taken. The researchers found that magnetic response from the right primary somatosensory cortex—a brain region that controls the left-hand fingers—was larger for the string players than it was for the nonmusicians. Furthermore, the magnitude of the response was related to the age at which the string players began instruction, with those who began lessons earlier evidencing the largest response. Finally, a recent paper by Pantev and his colleagues reported that auditory cortical representation was 25% larger in musicians than in nonmusicians, regardless of the instrument played and the presence of perfect pitch (Pantev et al., 1998). The younger the instrumental training began, the larger the cortical reorganization. Effects were found for subjects who began to practice before age 9. To help determine whether musical practice or heredity is responsible for brain attributes related to musical skill, researchers using MEG measured violinists' and trumpeters' cortical representations for violin and trumpet tones compared to sine wave tones (Pantev, Roberts, Schulz, Engelien, & Ross, 2001). The researchers found enhanced representations for timbres associated with the instrument of training, with trumpeters showing enhancement for trumpet tones and violinists showing enhancement for violin tones. These data suggest that cortical representations for musical timbre are use-dependent rather than coded genetically.

Many studies have compared cortical processing of aural imagery tasks with perception tasks (Reisberg, 1992; Zatorre & Halpern, 1993; Zatorre, Halpern, et al., 1996). Zatorre and Halpern (1993) hypothesized that similar neuronal mechanisms may underlie both imaginal and perceptual processing. A PET study demonstrated that although many of the same regions appear to be involved in imagined and perceived tonal-pattern processing, two inferior frontopolar regions showed significant increase of blood flow only for the imagery task (Zatorre et al., 1996). This may refer to different aspects of the generation of auditory information from memory. However, in an experiment on the effects of unilateral temporal-lobe excision on perception and imagery Zatorre and Halpern (1993) found that patients with right temporal-lobe excision showed a significant decrease in both perceptual and imagery tasks. The interaction of aural imagery and music perception plays an important role in music learning because aural imagery depends on already-established mental representations that are a prerequisite for any type of discrimination learning.

Correspondingly, different processing strategies influence lateralization effects and particular musical properties call for different activation areas. In a study with unilateral brain-damaged patients, Peretz (1990) found two types of musical-information processing that she called local and global processing. If, on the one hand, the processing is interval-based, focusing on local properties as single tones and distances, the left hemisphere is dominant; if, on the other hand, the processing is contour-based, focusing on the more global aspects of a tune, then the right hemisphere is dominant. Similar results support these findings. In an EEG study, Breitling, Guenther, and Rondot (1987) found different bilateral involvement for different stimulus conditions (single tone, scale, melody). Only in the melody condition (global processing) was the right hemisphere more activated.

In general, it can be stated that lateralization effects mirror the asymmetric specialization of brain functions, depending on acoustic aspects of stimuli as well as individual cognitive processing strategies.

Discussion and Conclusions

Until recently, the majority of the research on the neurobiology of learning in general and music learning in particular was descriptive and focused mainly on cerebral localization of function. (See Hodges and Flohr in this text, chapter 1 for a review of these studies.) However, neuropsychologists are now beginning to approach music learning from a more "cognitive" or "information-processing" position. Simply knowing that left unilateral neglect follows posterior right hemisphere lesions does not tell us anything about the specific mechanism(s) responsible, nor how these mechanisms operate to produce the symptom. Thus the goal today is to identify the particular *processes* that are enhanced, maintained, or disrupted after intervention or cerebral damage and determine how these processes relate to specific neural substrates or neural systems.

The purpose of the research cited earlier was to discover how developmental processes affect brain and cognition, particularly in the early years. These studies suggest that early instrumental instruction may actually physically shape and mold the young brain. However, Bruer (1999) cautions us against drawing excessive conclusions from these data. Although there may indeed exist a relationship between music cognition and brain development, our knowledge of this relationship is far from complete, and alternative explanations for the data should be considered. For example, Elbert et al.'s (1995) research with string players measured the brain's response to an overlearned skill—fingering a keyboard. It stands to reason that any overlearned motor activity, for example, typing, would produce similar brain reorganization. This study, therefore, was not directly about music. Furthermore, although Schlaug, Jäncke, Huang, and Steinmetz (1994, 1995) and Pantey, Oostenveld, Engellen, Ross, Roberts, and Hoke's (1998) findings suggest that early music engagement affects the brain's pitch/auditory processing regions, it is not clear that the age at which subjects began instruction, rather than how long they had been playing, produced the effects. In other words, the larger brain response may be the result of longer time on task, rather than age of task onset.

It is also not clear in these studies whether the morphological effects were caused by the music instruction. Studies that compare musicians to nonmusicians are correlational, not causal. They therefore do not address whether differences in brain structure between these two groups of subjects are a function of the music exposure or of inborn atypicalities in the brains of musicians that may attract them to music making in the first place. Clearly, longitudinal causal studies are needed to investigate the maturation of cognitive abilities and brain regions before and during early versus later onset music instruction. It is important to note that no scientific studies have directly investigated the effects of music instruction on the adult brain. We must be careful not to ignore the fact that brain development continues until death.

Transfer Effects

According to conventional opinion, music has an effect on cognitive achievement. Therefore, experimental findings that actually confirm transfer effects would have an important impact on educational policies with respect to school music curriculum. Consequently, there is an increasing interest in inquiries on whether music can really improve the mind (Overy, 1998). Thus several longitudinal observations of schoolchildren who received extra music lessons within their regular school curriculum were performed in Europe (Bastian, 2000; Spychiger, 1995). Here effects of music on social behavior and school achievement appeared.

In an experimental memory study, Chan, Ho, and Cheung (1998) found that music training improved verbal memory because verbal memory is mediated mainly by the left temporal lobe, which is larger in musicians than in nonmusicians. Although Chan used subjects from Hong Kong whose native language was tonal (a language in which verbal memory includes pitch memory), the greater effect on verbal than on visual memory tasks in musicians possibly indicates a general transfer effect.

Just recently, a meta-analysis of studies on the relationship between music and academic achievement (Winner & Hetland, 2000) has examined the outcome of studies on music and reading skills, music and mathematics, and music and spatial-temporal reasoning. Twenty-four correlational studies and six experimental studies on the impact of music on the development of reading skills were examined (Butzlaff, 2000). Whereas correlational studies showed that students who studied music scored significantly higher on standardized reading tests, there was no reliable effect supported by the experimental studies. With respect to an impact of music instruction on mathematics, a total of 25 correlational and experimental studies were examined. The analysis revealed a small but evident association between music and mathematics achievement: Individuals who voluntarily chose to study music privately and those who were exposed to a music curriculum in school produced higher mathematical scores than those who did not (Vaughn, 2000). However, a positive relationship is not sufficient to establish a causal link. Furthermore, listening to background music had no notable effect.

The explosion of studies that explore the transfer of musical processing to spatial processing compels us to examine these data from a neurophysiological perspective. Two lines of behavioral research have been pursued: the effects of *listening* to music on *adult* spatial abilities and the effects of *instrumental instruction* on *children's* spatial abilities. Two recent meta-analyses (Hetland, 2000a, 2000b) have examined the studies relevant to these inquiries. The first analysis explored the so-called Mozart effect, the finding that college students who listened to 10 minutes of Mozart's piano sonata K. 448 scored higher on spatial-temporal tasks than students who listened to taped relaxation instructions or silence (Rauscher, Shaw, & Ky, 1993). Hetland's (2000b) meta-analysis of 36 studies that involved approximately 2,500 subjects revealed a moderate, robust effect that "is limited, however, to a specific type of spatial task that requires mental rotation in the absence of a physical model" (p. 33). Despite Hetland's conclusion, it must be noted that attempts to reproduce Rauscher, Shaw, and Ky's (1993) findings have been inconsistent. For example, in a series of experiments designed to replicate the Mozart effect through use of the same musical composition as well as similar control conditions and dependent measures, Steele and his colleagues achieved negative results (e.g., Steele et al., 1999).

There is also a growing body of evidence implicating the role of arousal in the Mozart effect. Schellenberg and his colleagues found that changes in arousal, induced by listening to music, mediated performance on a spatial-temporal task (Nantais & Schellenberg, 1999: Thompson, Schellenberg, & Husain, 2001: Husain, Thompson, & Schellenberg, 2002). This research suggests that the Mozart effect may be due to differences in arousal, rather than to Mozart in particular or music in general.

McKelvie and Low (2002) were the first to investigate the Mozart effect in children. Twelve-year-old children listened to either a Mozart sonata or to popular music by the band Aqua. There were no differences in the children's spatial scores as a function of the music condition. A study with 10–11-year-old children, however, did find a Mozart effect (Ivanov & Geake, 2003). Children who listened to either Mozart or Bach scored significantly higher on a spatial-temporal task than children who sat in silence. The highest scores were achieved by the children who had studied a musical instrument.

A second meta-analytic review, also undertaken by Hetland (2000a), examined studies on the effects of instrumental instruction on children's spatial abilities (see, for example, Rauscher et al., 1997). Figure 2.1 portrays the effect for kindergarten children. The results of this analysis revealed an over-

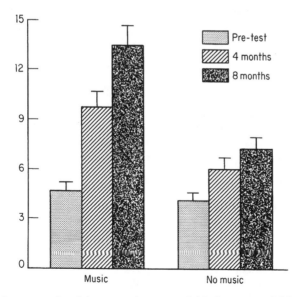

Figure 2.1. Spatial-temporal scores of kindergarten children (School District of Kettle Moraine) before and after music or no training: correct joins/minute.

all effect size of $r = .37$, an effect that was deemed "remarkably consistent" and could be "generalized to similar populations of preschool- and elementary-school-aged children, while they are engaged in similar kinds of active music programs, with or without keyboard instruments, taught in groups or individual lessons. The effect cannot be explained away by a Hawthorne effect, nonequivalence of experimental groups, experimenter bias, or study quality. It is a solid finding" (Hetland, 2000a, pp. 41–42).

We will not attempt to undertake a critical analysis of these studies, but instead, as per the focus of this chapter, we will comment on their possible neurophysiological implications. The motivation for research on the transfer of music listening or instruction to spatial task performance came from a neural connectionist model of the mammalian brain proposed by Xiaodan Leng and Gordon Shaw (Leng & Shaw, 1991). Based on Mountcastle's columnar principle of cortex, the model proposed that families of neural networks respond to and compare spatial features of objects. By mathematically deriving their firing probabilities the researchers determined that the networks evolved according to symmetries modified by Hebb learning rules. These neural network patterns (lasting tens of seconds over large cortical areas) corresponded to spatial-temporal task performance (requiring the transformation of mental images over time). Leng and Shaw therefore predicted that certain musical forms and instruction might stimulate these firing patterns, thereby enhancing spatial-temporal performance.

Although it is impossible to "prove" a neural model of brain function, Leng and Shaw's (1991) hypothesis is supported by data. For example, Alzheimer patients who listened to the Mozart sonata or silence demonstrated improved spatial-temporal performance following Mozart (J. K. Johnson, Cotman, Tasaki, & Shaw, 1998; J. K. Johnson, Shaw, Vuong, Vuong, & Cotman, 1999). Neuroscientists have investigated the effect through the use of EEG and fMRI. EEGs of subjects who performed a spatial-temporal task after listening to the Mozart sonata revealed a carryover effect in parietal and frontal cortex; no carryover was found when reading a story was substituted for the task (Sarnthein et al., 1997). EEGs of epilepsy patients, some comatose, showed decreased seizure activity during exposure to the sonata rather than silence or control music (Hughes, Daaboul, Fino, & Shaw, 1998; Hughes, Fino, & Melyn, 1999). The compositions differentially activated the prefrontal, occipital, and cerebellar regions—all regions associated with spatial-temporal reasoning. These findings, although specific to music listening, may also have neurophysiological implications for the effects of music instruction on certain spatial abilities.

An additional study utilized DC potential and ERP (Trimmel, Goger, & Geiss-Granadia, 2003). A measure of electrical activity, DC potential is considered to reflect ongoing cortical activation at the level of the neuron. ERP, on the other hand, measures electrical activity as a function of a stimulus event (such as performing a spatial-temporal task). It is considered to be a measure of cognitive activity. Subjects listened to either a composition by Mozart, Albinoni, Schubert, or brown noise. After each condition they per formed either a spatial-temporal task or a memory task. Behavioral dependent measures included preference for the musical selections as well as mood, alertness, and excitation. Results indicated that participants preferred all musical conditions more than brown noise. There were no differences between the musical compositions for mood, alertness, and excitation, which all registered higher than brown noise. However, the DC potentials for subjects listening to the Mozart condition were more positive than for those listening to the other musical compositions or brown noise, which did not differ from each other. This finding suggests enhanced cortical activation during listening to Mozart and not during listening to Albinoni, Schubert, or brown noise. The ERPs for the spatial-temporal task showed shorter latencies after listening to the Mozart sonata. There were no latency or amplitude differences for the memory task. The authors suggest that this finding indicates faster cognitive processing for spatial-temporal tasks following listening to Mozart.

Parsons, Hodges, and Fox (1998) have proposed an alternative theory. These researchers suggest that the rhythmic elements of music, processed in the cerebellum, are responsible for the enhancement of spatial tasks (such as mental rotation tasks) that also require cerebellar function. A recent experiment by Parsons and his colleagues (cited in Hetland, 2000a) supports this hypothesis. Subjects performed two spatial-temporal tasks following one of five conditions: auditory exposure to rhythm without melody (a popular song bass line), auditory exposure to melody without rhythm (a melody presented in a steady beat), visual exposure to rhythm (a pulsating square on a computer screen), auditory exposure to a continuous tone, or silence. Enhanced performance of the spatial-temporal tasks was found following only the auditory and visual rhythmic conditions. This suggests that the enhancement of spatial-temporal tasks is due to rhythm, regardless of the modality of presentation.

Other explanations for these transfer effects can be found in the cognitive literature. For example, Rauscher (1999) has proposed that several of the elements of music cognition described by Serafine (1988)—temporal succession and simultaneity, nontemporal closure, transformation, and abstraction—may be musically analogous to the cognitive processes required to solve certain visuo-spatial tasks. Perhaps some of the skills involved in learning music transfer to the performance of particular spatial skills.

The importance of studying the transfer of musical learning to spatial learning becomes evident when one considers the overall significance of spatial abilities to cognitive function. High levels of spatial ability have frequently been linked to creativity, not only in the arts but in science and mathematics as well (Shepard, 1978; West, 1991). Physicists (Albert Einstein, James Clerk Maxwell, Michael Faraday, and Hermann von Helmholtz), inventors (such as Nikola Tesla and James Watt), and other scientists displayed high levels of spatial abilities and reported that these abilities played an important role in their most creative accomplishments. In psychology, Shepard (1978) has given particularly lucid accounts of the role of spatial imagery in his own thinking. Involuntary dream images were the source of many of his most creative and influential contributions, including the idea for his research on mental rotation, the first method of nonmetric multidimensional scaling, and the computer algorithm that underlies additive nonhierarchical cluster analysis. Given the prominent role of spatial abilities both in models of human abilities and in models of cognition, studies that demonstrate that music instruction may influence spatial reasoning have important educational implications. However, due to the fact that there is as yet no commonly accepted theoretical approach that adequately accounts for these transfer effects, we recommend discretion in both the interpretation of research results and their application.

Music Learning by Individuals With Brain Disorders

Patients With Mental Disorders

The study of brain-damaged populations has always been a major area of research for investigating cognitive functioning of the human brain. Unfortunately, results of studies of brain-damaged patients are neither consistent nor easy to interpret, because the loss of a particular ability may not necessarily be attributed to a damaged brain area or specific module of information processing. Rather, loss of ability may instead be due to an interruption of important connections between collaborating cell assemblies. However, the effect on musical skills can be observed in musicians with brain injuries who suffer from music alexia and agraphia (Brust, 1980). Namely, developmental musical dyslexia in children who have difficulties reading music has been studied (N. Gordon, 2000; Overy, 2003), just as general dyslexia, which has significant effects on children's musical abilities to recognize musical tone sequences and differentiate tone colors and sound intensities (Kurth & Heinrichs, 1976). Therefore, investigations of the development of musical abilities in populations with brain disorders, as well as those with genetic abnormalities, offer valuable research. In particular, individuals with Williams syndrome, Down's syndrome, Alzheimer's and Huntington's disease, and musicogenic epilepsy are rather informative with respect to particular musical abilities.

There is an extended body of research that investigated Alzheimer's disease and its impact on musical abilities. It is well documented that previously acquired musical skills (e.g., singing and playing an instrument) remain accessible despite otherwise severe cognitive impairment. A case study of an 82-year-old musician reports relatively spared anterograde and retrograde procedural memory for music making (Crystal, Grober, & Masur, 1989). Similarly, J. Johnson and Ulatowska (1995) studied the progression of deterioration of Alzheimer's patients in music and language. They found that song texts in connection with the tunes persisted while speech was pro foundly disturbed. This supports Gardner's (1983/1985) theory of unique multiple intelligences, that is, that music as a manifestation of intelligence constitutes a faculty per se and is to a large degree uncorrelated with other cognitive abilities.

A notable affinity for music is documented for children with Down's and Williams syndromes. Quantitative studies of brain morphology demonstrate a distinctive dysmorphology unlike that of other forms of mental retardation (Lenhoff et al., 1997). A highly selective effect of brain development appears to accompany Williams syndrome, a neurodevelopmental disorder, which causes substantial deficits in cognitive domains but preserves skills in social domains, language and music (Levitin et al., 2003; Levitin et al., 2004). Patients demonstrate a reduced cerebral size and a significant increase of neocerebellar vermal lobules, whereas individuals with Down's syndrome evidence a reduction in both cerebellar components (Jernigan & Bellugi, 1990; Levitin & Bellugi, 1998). These individuals often possess relatively intact verbal working memory but are more impaired in spatial working memory (Levitin & Bellugi, 1995, p. 375). Therefore, they demonstrate deficient spatial coordination on the motoric level but perform general musical tasks sufficiently. Moreover, subjects with Williams syndrome have a striking independence of rhythmic abilities and show a propensity for creative rhythmic productions. The obvious evidence for this quality is called rhythmicity or rhythmic musicality by Levitin and Bellugi (1998). Although children with Williams syndrome fail in Piagetian conservation tasks, they demonstrate a clear conservation of musical time and rhythm. This may be linked with a general predominance of local over global processing strategies, especially in the processing of visual stimuli (Bellugi, Lai, & Wang, 1997). In a rhythm repetition task, children with Williams syndrome often do not repeat correctly the global structure but use local variations for creative completions (Levitin & Bellugi, 1998). A similar affinity for music and musical rhythm is reported for children with Down's syndrome. In a comparative study with other mentally challenged and normal children, children with Down's syndrome exhibited the same level of rhythm discrimination as normal children but did differ from other mentally challenged children (Stratford & Ching, 1983).

These findings with subjects with Down's and Williams syndrome suggest that musical abilities and other cognitive functioning may develop independently, perhaps due to neuroanatomical differences in the brain disorders of these patients. This suggests that music may not only serve a therapeutic goal, especially in Alzheimer's patients (Aldridge, 1994; Glynn, 1992; Lord & Garner, 1993), but it may also serve as a special tool for learning due to the evident interaction between *rhythmicity* and brain function (Thaut, Kenyon, et al., 1999) as well as movement and vocal sound production (Gruhn, 2001). This explanation also relates to the striking effect of music on the motor control of patients with Parkinson's disease. Also, researchers have shown that patients with Huntington's disease could significantly modulate their gait velocity during self-paced and rhythmic metronome cueing, but velocity adaptations did not fit with an exact synchronization of steps and metric impulses (Thaut, Miltner, et al., 1999). Effects are also reported from patients with epilepsy where brain-wave abnormalities occur during music-induced seizures (Critchley, 1977). Just recently, fewer clinical seizures and fewer generalized bilateral spike and wave complexes were reported from a patient with Lennox-Gastaut syndrome after regular exposure to Mozart's piano sonata K. 448 (Hughes et al., 1999).

Deaf Children With Cochlear Implants

During the last two decades, advanced technology has been applied to the treatment of deaf (or severely hearing-impaired) children who still have an active hearing nerve. An artificial cochlea can be implanted to stimulate the hair cells of the cochlea by electrodes that are activated through electric impulses from an outside microphone. Cochlear implant (CI) surgeries have become routine in Europe, Australia, and the United States since the 1980s, and younger and younger prelingually deaf children can be treated. The most appropriate time window for an efficient surgery is between age 2 and 4, that is, before the development of prosody has already been stabilized. Although there is only limited access to music transmitted by the available technology of today (Fujita & Ito, 1999), new generations of speech processors (such as Nucleus, Clarion, and Med-el) have expanded the range of formats by developing different strategies through use of either time resolution (CIS = continuous interleaved sampling strategy), spectral peak resolution (SPEAK strategy), or a combined strategy (ACE = advanced combined encoder).

In recent times, increasing research efforts have been directed towards the processing of nonspeech sounds, namely pitch, rhythm, melodies, and timbres in CI users (Gfeller et al. 1997; Pijl, 1997; Fujita & Ito, 1999; Abdi et al. 2001; Gfeller et al., 2002; Stordahl, 2002; Koelsch et al., 2004). The general findings are that rhythm is more easily and more successfully perceived than melodies, especially if they are presented without rhythm and verbal cues. Pitch perception, however, can be improved by training and the application of new processors that use spatial and temporal patterns of stimulation. In general, the appraisal of music tends to be much lower than in normal listeners (McDermott, 2004).

Up to now, little has been known about the cortical development of CI patients after they recover auditory cortex areas. These areas, like the visual cortices of children born blind, are underdeveloped and utilized by other sensory representations. Perception of different sounds evoked through electrical stimulation must be learned with respect to sound discrimination and the gradual attribution of meaning to discern ible sounds. A clear understanding of the neurobiological development of mental representation can facilitate this learning process, the goal of which relates to speech acquisition. As we know from neurolinguistics, even the semantics of a language are carried out through sequential structures in time. Therefore, music, especially rhythm patterns, may function as a cortex trainer for CI patients to gain or regain perceptive and expressive competence. Only EEG measurements (because MEG and MRI cannot be applied to the highly sensitive cochlear electrodes) can demonstrate whether sound stimulation actually arrives at the brain stem and how auditory and associative cortices develop during listening training and sound exposure. The aforementioned interaction of movement and brain function (Thaut, Kenyon, et al., 1999) plays an important role in the learning process here, because the motor system responds so sensitively to the auditory priming and, vice versa, rhythmic auditory stimulation corresponds with motor activation.

Applications to Music Education

Results from brain research and neurobiological findings alone can hardly lead to immediate applications and recommendations for music education. These data cannot be directly transferred to educational practice because scientific descriptions are essentially different from educational prescriptions. Empirical data are based upon objective facts and verifiable procedures; scientific research is committed to objectivity, reliability, and validity. Judgments in education, however, are value judgments to a large degree. Normative decisions on values can never be deduced objectively from empirical descriptions. As Gardner (1999) puts it: "We could know what every neuron does and we would not be one step closer to knowing how to educate our children," because "the chasm between 'is' and 'ought' is unbridgeable" (pp. 60, 79).

Mental representation has become the key notion of the cognitive revolution during the decade of the brain (Gardner, 1999). Therefore, one possible application to music education may involve the fostering of mental representations (see chap. 7 by Andreas C. Lehmann and Jane W. Davidson in this volume). As already mentioned, education is based on decisions that are grounded in value judgments that deal with the "what" and "why" of teaching, but findings in neurobiology may indicate new ways of "how" to teach. Teaching interacts with the disposition and potential of each individual. Although neurobiological findings cannot tell us why to teach music of a particular culture and what to select from the broad variety of musical traditions, empirical findings can advise us on how and when to teach so that mind, memory, perception, and cognition can be developed most effectively. This has established the new discipline of "neurodidactics" (Preisser, 1998) which provides a new foundation for viewing the learning processes in accordance with the state of brain development. If we know about electrochemical and hormonal processes that enhance synaptic strength and facilitate long-term representation that can be re-activated at any time, methods and teaching strategies (that is *didactics*) as well as the organization of environmental sets for teaching and learning, curriculum development and school policies can be related to the developmental state of the brain and its neurobiological conditions. From that perspective, the neurobiology of cognition and learning allows us to draw the following tentative conclusions:

1. Learning is the process by which one develops and incrementally differentiates mental representations. Therefore, music learning focuses on the development of genuine musical representations that are characterized by different forms of encoding.
2. Procedural knowledge (knowing how) is more appropriate in music cognition than formal declarative knowledge (knowing about). Immanent musical properties (pulse, meter, tonality, intervals, motifs, contours, etc.) are represented by neuronal connections that can only be recognized when activated through aural stimulation. Conversely, these musical entities can only be articulated in singing or playing if developed as mental representations. Conscious activation may be called audiation (Gordon, 1980/1997). It takes place when neuronal representations are activated in thinking, listening, or music making.
3. This calls for the idea of teaching music *musically* (Gruhn, 1997; Swanwick, 1999), that is, advancing those teaching strategies and learning modes that promote the development of genuine musical representations by priming an aural-oral loop.
4. There is some evidence that music learning may transfer to other areas of learning (e.g., spatial learning). The possible mechanisms of this transfer, either cognitive or neurophysiological, are still unknown. Much more work is needed before applications to educational practice can be derived from these studies.
5. The same caution should also be applied to studies on the lateralization effects in music. Music is processed in both hemispheres, but there exists an asymmetric predominance that depends on the applied cognitive strategy (global versus local; verbal versus procedural). Therefore, music teaching and learning should take into consideration that different strategies engage different brain areas. The more interconnected these areas are, the more stable the developed representations will become.
6. Research on individuals with mental disorders has clearly demonstrated that musical abilities develop independently of other domains of cognition. Therefore, these studies suggest that each person forms his or her individual intelligence profile. Music education should take advantage of the individual's potential within the musical domain rather than hoping for possible extramusical transfer effects. Music education must develop the individual's unique musical aptitude to its highest possible level.

Further research questions that regard the development of appropriate methods for teaching and learning remain, listed in the study questions at the end of this chapter.

The ongoing progress in brain research has spawned the investigation of many aspects of music learning in a more sophisticated way than was ever thought possible. In neurosciences music in particular has become a prominent example of neuroplasticity. This research may in the long run open new insights into the learning and understanding of music, with far-reaching applications for music education.

STUDY QUESTIONS

1. How do motor and aural activities interact in music learning processes?

2. What role does memory play in "formal" representation?

3. What are the neuronal correlates of different types of representation (*figural* versus *formal*)?

4. What are the effects of *declarative* and *procedural* strategies on the neuroplasticity evoked by long-term training?

5. What kind of subcortical activations are involved in music processing?

6. How do cortical and subcortical representations interact in music learning?

7. Do culture-specific types of brain processing exist and consequently are there different strategies for the development of mental representations? Then, what would be the best ways of teaching music within and between cultures?

8. What are the "near" effects of music making on cognitive development and achievement?

9. What are the effects of listening to music on children and adults' cognition? Do the data justify educational applications?

10. What are the effects of music instruction on cognition? What mechanisms might account for these transfer effects?

REFERENCES

Abdi, S., Khalessi, M. H., Khorsandi, M., & Gholami, B. (2001). Introducing music as a means of habilitation for children with cochlear implants. *International Journal of Pediatric Otorhinolaryngology* 59(2), 105–113.

Aebli, H. (1980/81). *Denken—das Ordnen des Tuns*, 2 vols. Stuttgart, Germany: Klett-Cotta.

Aldridge, D. (1994). Alzheimer's disease: Rhythm, timing and music as therapy. *Biomedicine and Pharmacotherapy,* 48(7), 275–281.

Altenmüller, E., & Gruhn, W. (1997). *Music, the brain, and music learning. Mental representation and changing activation patterns through learning* (GIML series vol. 2). Chicago: G.I.A.

Altenmüller, E., Gruhn, W., Parlitz, D., & Liebert, G. (2000). The impact of music education on brain networks. Evidence from EEG studies. *International Journal for Music Education, 35,* 47–53.

Avanzini, G., Faienza, C., Minciacchi, D., Lopez, L., & Majno, M. (Eds.) (2003). *The Neurosciences and Music.* Annals of The New York Academy of Sciences, vol. 999.

Baldwin, J. M. (1968). *The development of the child and of the race.* New York: Augustus M. Kelly. (Original work published 1894).

Bamberger, J. (1991). *The mind behind the musical ear: How children develop musical intelligence.* Cambridge, MA: Harvard University Press.

Bangert, M. & Altenmüller, E. (2003). Mapping perception to action in piano practice: A longitudinal DC-EEG study. *BMC Neuroscience 4*(1), S. 26.

Barinaga, M. (1999). Learning visualized, on the double. *Science 286,* 1661.

Bastian, H. G. (2000). *Musik(erziehung) und ihre Wirkung: Eine Langzeitstudie an Berliner Grundschulen* [Music education and its effects]. Mainz, Germany: Schott.

Bechtel, W., & Abrahamsen, A. (1991). *Connectionism and the mind: An introduction to parallel processing networks.* Cambridge, MA: Blackwell.

Bellugi, U., Lai, Z., & Wang, P. (1997). Language, communication and neural systems in Williams syndrome [Special issue: *Communication processes in children with developmental disabilities*]. *Mental Retardation and Developmental Disabilities Research Review, 3,* 334–342.

Black, J. E., & Greenough, W. T. (1998). Developmental approaches to the memory process. In J. Martinez & R. Kesner (Eds.), *Neurobiology of learning and memory* (pp. 55–88). San Diego, CA: Academic Press.

Breitling, D., Guenther, W., & Rondot, P. (1987). Auditory perception of music measured by brain electrical activity mapping. *Neurophysiologia, 25,* 765–774.

Bruer, J. T. (1999). *The myth of the first three years.* New York: Free Press.

Brust, J. C. (1980). Music and language: Musical alexia and agraphia. *Brain, 103*(2), 357–392.

Butzlaff, R. (2000). Can music be used to teach reading? *Journal of Aesthetic Education, 34*(3–4), 167–178.

Calvin, W. H. (1996). *How brains think.* New York: Basic Books.

Case, R. (1972). Learning and development: A neo-Piagetian interpretation. *Human Development, 15,* 339–358.

Chan, A. S., Ho, Y. C., & Cheung, M. C. (1998). Music training improves verbal memory. *Nature, 396,* 128.

Chugani, H. T. (1998). A critical period of brain development: Studies of cerebral glucose utilization with PET. *Preventive Medicine, 27*(2), 184–188.

Conel, J. L. (1967). *The postnatal development of the human cerebral cortex* (Vols. 1–8). Cambridge, MA: Harvard University Press. (Original work published 1939.)

Critchley, M. (1977). Musicogenic epilepsy. In M. Critchley & R. Hensen (Eds.), *Music and the brain* (pp. 344–353). Springfield, IL: Charles C. Thomas.

Crystal, H. A., Grober, E., & Masur, D. (1989). Preservation of musical memory in Alzheimer's disease. *Journal of Neurology, Neurosurgery, and Psychiatry, 52*(12), 1415–1416.

Deary, I. J. (2001). *Intelligence: A very short introduction.* Oxford: Oxford University Press.

Diamond, M. C. (1967). Extensive cortical depth measurements and neuron size increases in the cortex of environmentally enriched rats. *Journal of Comparative Neurology, 131,* 357–364.

Diamond, M. C., Krech, D., & Rosenzweig, M. R. (1964). The effects of an enriched environment on the histology of the rat cerebral cortex. *Journal of Comparative Neurology, 123,* 111–119.

Elbert, T., Pantev, C., Wienbruch, C., Rockstrub, B., & Taub, E. (1995). Increased cortical representation of the fingers of the left hand in string players. *Science, 270,* 305–307.

Ellis, R., & Humphreys, G. W. (1999). *Connectionist psychology: A text with readings.* Hove: Psychology Press.

Fagen, J., Prigot, J., Carroll, M., Pioli, M., Stein, A., & Franco, A. (1997). Auditory context and memory retrieval in young infants. *Child Development, 68*(6), 1057–1066.

Fiske, H. E. (1993). *Music cognition and aesthetic attitudes.* Lewiston: Edwin Mellen.

Fodor, J. A. (1983). *The modularity of mind.* Cambridge, MA: MIT Press.

Fujita, S., & Ito, J. (1999). Ability of nucleus cochlear implantees to recognize music. *Annals of Otology, Rhinology, and Laryngology, 108,* 634–640.

Gardner, H. (1985). *Frames of mind: The theory of multiple intelligences.* New York: Basic Books. (Original work published 1983)

Gardner, H. (1999a). *The disciplined mind.* New York: Simon & Schuster.

Gardner, H. (1999). *Intelligence reframed: Multiple intelligences for the 21st century.* New York: Basic Books.

Gaschler-Markefski, B., Baumgart, F., Tempelmann, C., Woldorff, M. G., & Scheich, H. (1998). Activation of human auditory cortex in retrieval experiments: An fMRI study. *Neural Plasticity, 6*(3), 69–75.

Gfeller, K., Woodworth, G., Rubin, D., Wih, S., & Knutson, J. (1997). Perception of rhythmic and sequential pitch patterns by normally hearing adults and adult cochlear implant users. *Ear and Hearing, 18*(3), 252–260.

Gfeller, K., Witt, S., Woodworth, G., Mehr, M. A., & Knutson, J. (2002). Effects of frequency, instrumental family, and cochlear implant type on timbre recognition and appraisal. *The Annals of Otology, Rhinology, and Laryngology 111*(4), 349–356.

Globus, A., Rosenzweig, M. R., Bennett, E. L., & Diamond, M. C. (1973). Effects of differential experience on dendritic spine counts in rat cerebral cortex. *Journal of Comparative and Physiological Psychology, 82,* 175–181.

Glynn, N. J. (1992). The music therapy assessment tool in Alzheimer's patients. *Journal of Gerontological Nursing, 18*(1), 3–9.

Gordon, E. E. (1997). *Learning sequences in music. A music learning theory* (5th ed.). Chicago: G.I.A. (Originally published 1980.)

Gordon, N. (2000). Developmental dysmusia (developmental musical dyslexia). *Developmental Medicine and Child Neurology, 42*(3), 214–215.

Gottlieb, G. (1991). Experimental canalization of behavioral development: Theory. *Developmental Psychology, 27,* 4–13.

Griffith, N., & Todd, P. M. (Eds.). (1999). *Musical networks: Parallel distributed perception and performance.* Cambridge, MA: MIT Press.

Gruhn, W. (1997). Music learning: Neurobiological foundations and educational implications. *Research Studies in Music Education, 9,* 36–47.

Gruhn, W., Altenmüller, E., & Babler, R. (1997). The influence of learning on cortical activation patterns. *Bulletin of the Council for Research in Music Education, 133,* 25–30.

Gruhn, W. (1998). *Der Musikverstand: Neurobiologische Grundlagen des musikalischen Denkens, Hörens und Lernens* [The music brain: neurobiological basis of musical thinking, listening, and learning]. Hildesheim, Germany: Olms.

Gruhn, W. (2001). Musikalische Lernstadien und Entwicklungsphasen beim Kleinkind. Eine Langzeituntersuchung zum Aufbau musikalischer Respräsentationen bei Kindern bis zum 4. Lebensjahr. *Diskussion Musikpädagogik, 9*, 4–33.

Hebb, D. O. (1949). *Organization of behavior.* New York: Wiley.

Hetland, L. (2000a). Learning to make music enhances spatial reasoning. *Journal of Aesthetic Education, 34*(3–4), 179–238.

Hetland, L. (2000b). Listening to music enhances spatial-temporal reasoning: Evidence for the "Mozart effect." *Journal of Aesthetic Education, 34*(3–4), 105–148.

Hodges, D. A. (Ed.). (1996). *Handbook of music psychology* (2nd ed.). San Antonio, TX: IMR Press.

Hughes, J. R., Daaboul, Y., Fino, J. J., & Shaw, G. L. (1998). The "Mozart effect" in epileptiform activity. *Clinical Electroencephalography, 29*, 109–119.

Hughes, J. R., Fino, J. J., & Melyn, M. A. (1999). Is there a chronic change of the "Mozart effect" on epileptiform activity? A case study. *Clinical Electroencephalography, 30*(2), 44–45.

Husain, G., Thompson, W. F., & Schellenberg, E. G. (2002). Effects of musical tempo and mode on arousal, mood, and spatial abilities. *Music Perception, 20*(2), 151–171.

Huttenlocher, P. R. (1979). Synaptic density in human frontal cortex— Developmental changes and effects of aging. *Brain Research, 163*(2), 195–205.

Huttenlocher, P. R. (1984). Synapse elimination and plasticity in developing human cerebral cortex. *American Journal of Mental Deficiency, 88*(5), 488–496.

Huttenlocher, P. R. (1990). Morphometric study of human cerebral cortex development. *Neuropsychologia, 28*, 517–527.

Huttenlocher, P. R., & Dabholkar, A. S. (1997). Regional differences in synaptogenesis in human cerebral cortex. *Journal of Comparative Neurology, 387*(2), 167–178.

Ivanov, V. K., & Geake, J. G. (2003). The Mozart effect and primary school children. *Psychology of Music 31*(4), 405–413.

Jernigan, T. L., & Bellugi, U. (1990). Anomalous brain morphology on magnetic resonance images in Williams syndrome and Down syndrome. *Archives of Neurology, 47*(5), 529–533.

Johnson, J. K., Cotman, C. W., Tasaki, C. S., & Shaw, G. L. (1998). Enhancement in spatial-temporal reasoning after a Mozart listening condition in Alzheimer's disease: A case study. *Neurological Research, 20*, 666–672.

Johnson, J. K., Shaw, G. L., Vuong, M., Vuong, S., & Cotman, C. W. (2002). Short-term improvement on a visual-spatial task after music listening in Alzheimer's disease: A group study. *Activities, Adaptation and Aging, 26*(3), 37–50.

Johnson, J., & Ulatowska, H. (1995). The nature of the tune and text in the production of songs. *Music Medicine 2.* St. Louis: MMB Music.

Johnson, M. H. (1998). The neural basis of cognitive development. In W. Damon (Ed.), *Handbook of child psychology: Vol. 2. Cognition, perception, and language* (5th ed.) (pp. 1–49). New York: Wiley.

Johnson-Laird, P. N. (1983). *Mental models: Toward a cognitive science of language, inference, and consciousness.* Cambridge, MA: Harvard University Press.

Kempermann, G., Kuhn, H., & Gage, F. (1997). More hippocampal neurons in adult mice living in an enriched environment. *Nature, 386,* 493–495.

Koelsch, S., Wittfoth, M., Wolf, A., Muller, J., & Hahne, A. (2004). Music perception in cochlear implant users: An event-related potential study. *Clinical Neurophysiology 115*(4), 966–972.

Kosslyn, S. M. (1994). *Image and brain: The resolution of the imagery debate.* Cambridge, MA: MIT Press.

Kurth, E., & Heinrichs, M. (1976). Musical-rhythmic discrimination ability and recall in children with reading and spelling disorders. *Psychiatrie, Neurologie und Medizinische Psychologie (Leipzig), 28,* 559–564.

Leng, X., & Shaw, G. L. (1991). Toward a neural theory of higher brain function using music as a window. *Concepts in Neuroscience, 2,* 229–258.

Lenhoff, H. M., Wang, P. P., & Greenberg, F. (1997). Williams syndrome and the brain. *Scientific American, 277*(6), 68–73.

Leont'ev, A. N. (1981). The problem of activity in psychology. In J. V. Wertsch (Ed.), *The concept of activity in Soviet psychology* (pp. 37–71). Armonk, NY: Sharpe.

Levitin, D., & Bellugi, U. (1998). Musical abilities in individuals with Williams syndrome. *Music Perception, 15*(4), 357–389.

Levitin, D. J., Cole, K., Chiles, M., Lai, Z., Lincoln, A., & Bellugi, U. (2004). Characterizing the musical phenotype in individuals with Williams syndrome. *Neuropsychology, Development, and Cognition. Section C, Child Neuropsychology 10*(4), 223–247.

Levitin, D. J., Menon, V., Schmitt, J. E., et al. (2003). Neural correlates of auditory perception in Williams syndrome: An fMRI study. *Neuroimage 18*(1), 74–82.

Li, H. H., Cai, Y., Ying, Z., Gomez-Pinila, F., Cooper, R., & Rauscher, F. H. (2004, April). *Music exposure improves maze learning and up-regulates genes related to synaptic plasticity.* Paper presented at the meeting of the Cognitive Neuroscience Society, San Francisco, CA.

Liebert, G. (2001). *Auswirkungen musikalischen Kurzzeitlernens auf kortikale Aktivierungsmuster.* Diss. med., Medical School, Hannover.

Liebert, G., Gruhn, W., Parlitz, D., Trappe, W., Bangert, M., & Altenmüller, E. (1999). Kurzzeit-Lerneffekte musikalischer Gehörbildung spiegeln sich in kortikalen Aktivierungsmustern wider. In *Proceedings of the 1999 Annual Meeting of the German Society for Music Psychology* (pp. 32–33). Karlsruhe, Germany.

Liegeois-Chauvel, C., Peretz, I., Babai, M., Laguitton, V., & Chauvel, P. (1998). Contribution of different cortical areas in the temporal lobes to music processing. *Brain, 121*(10), 1853–1867.

Lord, T. R., & Garner, J. E. (1993). Effects of music on Alzheimer patients. *Perception and Motor Skills, 76*(2), 451–455.

Luria, A. R. (1961). *The role of speech in the regulation of normal and abnormal behavior.* New York: Liveright.

Martinez, M. E. (1999). Cognitive representations: Distinctions, implications, and elaborations. In I. E. Sigel (Ed.), *Development of mental representation* (pp. 13–31). Mahwah, NJ.: Erlbaum.

McClelland, J. L. (1995). A connectionist perspective on knowledge and development. In T. J. Simon & G. S. Halford (Eds.), *Developing cognitive competence: New approaches to process modeling* (pp. 157–204). Hillsdale, NJ: Erlbaum.

McDermott, H. J. (2004). Music perception with cochlear implants: A review. *Trends in Amplification* 8(2), 49–82.

McKelvie, P., & Low, J. (2002). Listening to Mozart does not improve children's spatial ability: Final curtains for the Mozart effect. *British Journal of Developmental Psychology* 20, 241–258.

Minsky, M. (1980). K-lines: A theory of memory. *Cognitive Science, 4,* 117–133.

Muller, D., Toni, N., & Buchs, P. A. (2000). Spine changes associated with long-term potentiation. *Hippocampus, 10*(5), 595–604.

Nantais, K. M., & Schellenberg, E. G. (1999). The Mozart effect: An artifact of preference. *Psychological Science, 10,* 370–373.

Overy, K. (1998). Discussion note: Can music really "improve" the mind? *Psychology of Music* 26(1), 97–99. [See also responses to Overy's article, next issue, 26(2), 197–210.]

Overy, K. (2003). Dyslexia and music: From timing deficits to musical intervention. In *Neurosciences and Music* (pp. 497–505). Annals of The New York Academy of Sciences, vol. 999.

Pacteau, C., Einon, D., & Sinden, J. (1989). Early rearing environment and dorsal hippocampal ibotenic acid lesions: Long-term influences on spatial learning and alternation in the rat. *Behavioural Brain Research, 34,* 79–96.

Pantev, C., Oostenveld, R., Engellen, A., Ross, B., Roberts, L. E., & Hoke, M. (1998). Increased auditory cortical representation in musicians. *Nature, 392,* 811–814.

Pantev, C., Roberts, L. E., Schulz, M., Engelien, A., & Ross, B. (2001). Timbre-specific enhancement of auditory cortical representations in musicians. *NeuroReport, 12,* 169–174.

Parkinson, A. J., & Parkinson, W. S. (1998). Speech perception performance in experienced cochlear-implant patients receiving the SPEAK processing strategy in the Nucleus Spectra-22 cochlear implant. *Journal of Speech, Language, and Hearing Research, 41*(5), 1073–1087.

Parsons, L., Hodges, D., & Fox, P. T. (1998). Neural basis of the comprehension of musical harmony, melody, and rhythm. *Proceedings of the Cognitive Neuroscience Society Meeting,* San Francisco.

Pascual-Leone, J., & Smith, J. (1969). The encoding and decoding of symbols by children. A new experimental paradigm and a neo-Piagetian theory. *Journal of Experimental Child Psychology, 8,* 328–355.

Pavlov, I. P. (1927). *Conditioned reflexes* (G. V. Anrep, Trans.). New York: Oxford University Press.

Peretz, I. (1990). Processing of local and global musical information by unilateral brain damaged patients. *Brain, 113,* 1185–1205.

Peretz, I., Gaudreau, D., & Bonnel, A. M. (1998). Exposure effects on music preference and recognition. *Memory and Cognition, 26*(5), 884–902.

Peretz, I., & Zatorre, R. (Eds.). (2003). *The cognitive neuroscience of music.* Oxford: Oxford University Press.

Pflederer Zimmerman, M. (1984). The relevance of Piagetian theory for music education. *International Journal of Music Education, 3,* 31–34.

Pflederer Zimmerman, M., & Webster, P. (1983). Conservation of rhythmic and tonal patterns of second through six grade children. *Bulletin of the Council for Research in Music Education, 73,* 28–49.

Piaget, J. (1947). *La psychologie de l'intelligence.* Paris: Librairie Armand Colin.

Piaget, J. (1959). *La naissance de l'intelligence chez l'enfant.* Neuchâtel: Delachaux & Niestlé.

Pijl, S. (1997). Labeling of musical interval size by cochlear implant patients and normally hearing subjects. *Ear and Hearing, 18*(5), 364–372.

Preiss, G. (Ed.). (1998). *Neurodidaktik.* Herbolzheim: Centaurus.

Pylyshyn, Z. W. (1973). What the mind's eye tells the mind's brain: A critique of mental imagery. *Psychological Bulletin, 80,* 314–329.

Rakic, P. (1995). Corticogenesis in human and nonhuman primates. In M. S. Gazzaniga (Ed.), *The cognitive neurosciences* (pp. 127–145). Cambridge, MA: MIT Press.

Rauschecker, J. P. (1999). Auditory cortical plasticity: A comparison with other sensory systems. *Trends in Neurosciences, 22*(2), 74–80.

Rauscher, F. H. (1999). Music exposure and the development of spatial intelligence in children. *Bulletin of the Council for Research in Music Education, 142,* 35–47.

Rauscher, F. H., & Koch, J. E. (2000). *The effects of exposure to music on spatial processing sites.* Unpublished raw data.

Rauscher, F. H., Robinson, K. D., & Jens, J. J. (1998). Improved maze learning through early music exposure in rats. *Neurological Research, 20,* 427–432.

Rauscher, F. H., Shaw, G. L., & Ky, K. N. (1993). Music and spatial task performance. *Nature, 365,* 611.

Rauscher, F. H., Shaw, G. L., Levine, L. J., Wright, E. L., Dennis, W. R., & Newcomb, R. L. (1997). Music training causes long-term enhancement of preschool children's spatial-temporal reasoning. *Neurological Research, 19,* 1–8.

Reisberg, D. (Ed.). (1992). *Auditory imagery.* Hillsdale, NJ: Erlbaum.

Renner, M. J., & Rosenzweig, M. R. (1987). *Enrichment and impoverished environments: Effects on brain and behavior.* New York: Springer.

Rumelhart, D. E., & McClelland, J. L. (1986). *Parallel distributed processing: Explorations in the microstructure of cognition.* Cambridge, MA: MIT Press.

Sarnthein, J., von Stein, A., Rappelsberger, P., Petsche, H., Rauscher, F. H., & Shaw, G. L. (1997). Persistent patterns of brain activity: An EEG coherence study of the positive effect of music on spatial-temporal reasoning. *Neurological Research, 19,* 107–116.

Schank, R. C., & Abelson, R. P. (1977). *Scripts, plans, goals, and understanding: An inquiry into human knowledge structure.* New York: Wiley.

Schlaug, G., Jäncke, L., Huang, Y., & Steinmetz, H. (1994). In vivo morphometry of interhemispheric asymmetry and connectivity in musicians. In I. Deliège (Ed.), *Proceedings of the 3d International Conference for Music Perception and Cognition* (pp. 417–418). Liège, Belgium: ESOM (Centre de Recherches et de Formation Musicales de Walbnie).

Schlaug, G., Jäncke, L., Huang, Y., Staiger, J. F., & Steinmetz, H. (1995). Increased corpus callosum size in musicians. *Neuropsychologia, 33*(8), 1047–1055.

Serafine, M. L. (1988). *Music as cognition: The development of thought in sound.* New York: Columbia University Press.

Shepard, R. N. (1978). The mental image. *American Psychologist, 33,* 125–137.

Silva, A. J., Paylor, R., Wehner, J. M., & Tonegawa, S. (1992). Impaired spatial learning in a-calcium-calmodulin kinase II mutant mice. *Science, 257,* 206–211.

Skinner, B. F. (1953). *Science and human behavior.* New York: Macmillan.

Spychiger, M. (1995). *Mehr Musikunterricht an den öffentlichen Schulen?* Hamburg, Germany: Kovac.

Steele, K. M., Dalla Bella, S., Peretz, I., Dunlop, T., Dawe, L. A., Humphrey, G. K., Shannon, R. Z., Kirby, J. L., & Olmstead, C. G. (1999). Prelude or requiem for the Mozart effect? *Nature, 400,* 827.

Stordahl, J. (2002). Song recognition and appraisal: A comparison of children who use cochlear implants and normally hearing children. *Journal of Music Therapy, 39*(1), 2–19.

Stratford, B., & Ching, E. Y. (1983). Rhythm and time in the perception of Down's syndrome children. *Journal of Mental Deficiency Research, 27,* 23–38.

Swanwick, K. (1999). *Teaching music musically.* London: Routledge & Kegan Paul.

Thaut, M. H., Kenyon, G. P., Schauer, M., & McIntosh, G. (1999). The connection between rhythmicity and brain function. *IEEE Engineering in Medicine and Biology Magazine, 18*(2), 101–108.

Thaut, M. H., Miltner, R. Lange, H. W., Hurt, C., & Hoemberg, V. (1999). Velocity modulation and rhythmic synchronization of gait in Huntington's disease. *Movement Disorders, 14*(5), 808–819.

Thompson, W. F., Schellenberg, E. G., & Husain, G. (2001). Arousal, mood, and the Mozart effect. *Psychological Science, 12*(3), 248–251.

Tillmann, B., Bharucha, J. J., & Bigand, E. (2000). Implicit learning of tonality: A self-organizing approach. *Psychological Review, 107*(4), 885–913.

Todd, P. M., & Loy, D. G. (Eds.). (1991). *Music and connectionism.* Cambridge, MA: MIT Press.

Trimmel, M., Goger, C., & Geiss-Granadia, T. (2003). Brain DC potentials during listening to Mozart's sonata and ERPs of subsequent tasks. *Journal of Psychophysiology, 17* (Suppl.), 66.

Turner, A. M., & Greenough, W. T. (1985). Differential rearing effects on rats' visual cortex synapses. 1. Synaptic and neuronal density and synapses per neuron. *Brain Research, 329,* 195–203.

Vaughn, K. (2000). Music and mathematics: Modest support for the oft-claimed relationship. *Journal of Aesthetic Education, 34*(3/4), 149–166.

Vygotsky, L. S. (1962). *Thought and language* (E. Hanfmann & G. Vaker, Trans.). Cambridge, MA: MIT Press. (Original work published 1934.)

Watson, J. B. (1913). Psychology as the behaviorist views it. *Psychological Review, 20,* 158–177.

West, T. (1991). *In the mind's eye: Visual thinkers, gifted people with learning difficulties, computer images, and the ironies of creativity.* Amhurst, NY: Prometheus Books.

West, R. W., & Greenough, W. T. (1972). Effect of environmental complexity on cortical synapses of rats: Preliminary results. *Behavioral Biology, 7,* 278–284.

Winner, E., & Hetland, L. (2000). The arts in education: Evaluating the evidence for a causal link. *Journal of Aesthetic Education, 34*(3/4), 3–10.

Zatorre, R., & Halpern, A. (1993). Effect of unilateral temporal-lobe excision on perception and imagery of songs. *Neuropsychologia, 31*(3), 221–232.

Zatorre, R., Halpern, A., Perry, D., Meyer, E., & Evans, A. (1996). Hearing in the mind's ear: A PET investigation of musical imagery and perception. *Journal of Cognitive Neuroscience, 8,* 29–46.

Zatorre, R., & Peretz, I. (Eds.). (2001). *The biological foundations of music.* Annals of the New York Academy of Sciences, vol. 930.

Listening to Music

3

WILLIAM FORDE THOMPSON

E. GLENN SCHELLENBERG

Studies of music perception and cognition adopt a variety of theoretical viewpoints and use a diverse range of methods and analytic approaches. A survey of recent articles reveals a richly interdisciplinary field, comprising studies that range from psychophysical investigations of isolated tones to examinations of long musical segments in tonal, atonal, and non-Western styles. Although *cognition* is often distinguished from *perception,* the distinction is somewhat artificial and we will not delimit our discussion in this manner. Some perceptual phenomena, such as visual illusions, are relatively impervious to learning (e.g., knowledge of the illusion does not make it disappear), but most perceptual tasks elicit knowledge structures to some extent. The terms perception and cognition represent different points on a continuum of research on mental processing, ranging from studies of automatic processes that depend little on experience, to studies of processes that depend critically on learning and knowledge.

Research measures also vary widely. They include results of neuroimaging techniques, responses to music by special populations (e.g., brain-damaged patients, individuals with Williams syndrome), aesthetic judgments, measurements taken from music performances, infants' responses to musical stimuli, and subjective ratings of musical stimuli obtained from musically trained or untrained adults and children. Consequently, a vast and confusing body of data has been accumulated that has yet to be embedded within a widely accepted framework for understanding music cognition. The development of such a framework has been hampered by differences in opinion on at least three issues of substance: (1) the relative contributions of innate structures and exposure to music, (2) the most appropriate level at which to investigate and explain music cognition, and (3) the kinds of stimuli and methods that are most appropriate for studying relevant cognitive processes and mechanisms.

Perhaps the most contentious issue in the psychology of music concerns the relative role of innate structures and learning in musical experience. Some educators and researchers take a dim view of nativist constructs such as musical *talent* (Howe, Davidson, & Sloboda, 1998), and assume a prominent role of learning, education, and enculturation. To support their position, they point to patterns of within-group similarities and between-group dissimilarities across different musical cultures and historic periods (e.g., Walker, 1996). By contrast, others argue that although such instances of learning are conspicuous, they are nevertheless constrained by underlying cognitive principles. Three classes of evidence point to the importance of innate cognitive endowments. First, competence in many domains is achieved early and rapidly, despite large differences in experience. Second, competence is often domain specific, implicating specialized cognitive modules (Fodor, 1983). Third, there is often a marked disparity between models of environmental influences and the mental representations acquired by learners, which implies that information processing is constrained by cognitive biases and perceptual predispositions, and assimilated into pre-existing knowledge structures.

A second issue concerns the most appropriate level at which to investigate and explain psychological phenomena related to music. Are listening, performing, and composing music best understood in terms of neurons and networks, or in terms of mental schemata and prototypes? Studies directed at different analytic levels often pose different questions, use different methods, and promote different theories. Reductionism holds that explanations based on psychological constructs such as schemata and prototypes are reducible—with the help of yet-to-be-discovered bridging laws—to neurological events in the brain. In this view, theories of cognition should be reducible to neural models. The opposing position, argued by Fodor (1983), is that psychological explanations are not always reducible to neural states, or that they may be realized in multiple configurations. It would therefore be impossible to identify systematic bridging laws that connect psychological states (e.g., beliefs, desires) to specific brain states. Rather, psychology would need to construct its own autonomous generalizations using a specialized "language of thought." In this view, theories of music cognition can be developed somewhat independently of advances in neuroscience. One danger with this strategy is that when psychological principles are not linked to plausible physiological mechanisms, it can be difficult to evaluate their validity.

A third area of disagreement involves balancing concerns for experimental control with concerns for ecological validity. Recent collaborations between a well-known composer and a group of empirical psychologists illustrate the potential relevance of perceptual and cognitive data for composition (McAdams, 2004a, 2004b; Reynolds, 2004), but it is not obvious that all psychological studies involving musical materials are highly relevant to musical experiences. Can studies using stimuli comprised of a few pure tones tell us about the cognitive processes that are activated when one listens to a symphony played by an orchestra? Can the responses of Western listeners to Western music provide insight into cognitive mechanisms that operate independently of cultural knowledge?

In general, concerns about the use of artificial (non-musical) stimuli versus real pieces of music are empirical questions about whether a psychological process, mechanism, or neural resource generalizes to a wider range of stimuli than those used in a particular experiment. In cases where general auditory or cognitive mechanisms are at issue, concerns about ecological or cross-cultural validity may be unnecessary. For example, the neural resources involved in segregating multiple auditory sources (i.e., in *auditory stream segregation*) are almost certainly the same when listening to non-musical tone sequences, Western music, non-Western music, speech signals, and environmental sounds (Bregman, 1990).

It is also likely that the mechanisms engaged to process pitch contour (upward, downward, or lateral pitch movement) for short sequences of pure tones are the same as those engaged for long musical phrases. Such mechanisms are also likely to be involved in the processing of speech intonation. Dissanayake (2000) argues that music and speech intonation share a common ancestry as temporal-spatial patterns of emotional communication, which are particularly adaptive for promoting attachment between mothers and infants. If so, then the same neural resources may be responsible for processing contour in music and in speech (Patel, Peretz, Tramo, & Labreque, 1998; Patel, Foxton & Griffiths, in press; Thompson, Schellenberg, & Husain, 2004).

Some auditory processes are automatically invoked for all possible acoustic stimuli, including music, and therefore operate regardless of the style of the music or the cultural context in which music is heard. Many researchers, especially those with a strong background in cognition, are interested in precisely these basic processes. Because research on general auditory mechanisms and their connection to musical experience requires careful experimental control, the use of naturalized music-listening conditions is not always advantageous. Naturalized conditions introduce uncontrolled influences (and, consequently, variance in the data) related to personal, social, cultural, or historical knowledge, which can mask or distort the cognitive processes under investigation.

In other cases—when cognitive processes depend on musical context—it is necessary to use more naturalized conditions. For example, the expressive use of timing and loudness in music performance depends not only on local features (intervallic patterns, phrasing), but also on knowledge of harmony and key (Thompson & Cuddy, 1997), on composer-specific aspects of expression (Thompson, 1989), and on goals related to adjudication criteria (Thompson, Diamond, & Balkwill, 1998). Furthering our understanding of such issues *requires* an examination of actual music performances. Thus, despite thoughtful critiques of studies involving artificial stimuli and simple tone patterns (e.g., Serafine, 1988), a complete understanding of music cognition requires the convergence of data obtained using varying approaches and methods. Attempts to restrict the field to particular types of stimuli or experimental approaches will only delay progress in this regard.

In this chapter, we describe a sample of current discussions, debates, and empirical evidence in music cognition. Issues are not resolved quickly, and many that were raised by pioneers in the field continue to dominate. Certain shifts in focus have occurred over the past decade, however. First, there is a renewed interest in studies of brain function, following developments in neuroimaging techniques, advances in neural network modeling, and insights gained from studies of brain-damaged patients (see also chapter by Gruhn & Rauscher, this volume). A second shift has been to study listeners' perception of *emotions* expressed by music (see also chapter by Kopiez, this volume), mirroring attempts by researchers in cognition and neuroscience to understand the role of emotion in memory, reasoning, and problem solving. Third, there has been widespread effort to evaluate the psychological validity of influential theories that attempt to unify research on music and psychology within a single framework (e.g., Generative Theory of Tonal Music, Implication-Realization Model). Fourth, following a neo-Darwinian movement across a number of fields, there has been a renewed interest in evolutionary perspectives on music (e.g., Wallin, Merker & Brown, 2000). Examination of all of these issues would require considerably more than a single chapter, so we have limited our discussion to a sample of the issues that currently motivate the field.

Fundamentals of Pitch Perception and Cognition

Studies of pitch have dominated the field of music cognition over the past 20 years, paralleling a similar emphasis in music theory and education. Pitch studies have been a fruitful area of investigation because people are remarkably accurate at discriminating between pitches (Burns, 1999). Moreover, mental representations of pitch are richly structured. This structure partly reflects culture-specific conventions in music. Through passive or active exposure, listeners internalize regularities in the music of their own culture, forming long-term knowledge schemata into which novel music stimuli are assimilated. Nonetheless, processing limits and biases also constrain mental representations of pitch. For example, the limits of working memory constrain our ability to encode brief but unfamiliar melodies with accurate detail. Because of such limits, unfamiliar melodies are represented largely in terms of pitch contour (Dowling & Harwood, 1986).

Physical Acoustics: Sensory Consonance and Dissonance

Any naturally occurring sound, such as a cough or a piano tone, can be described as a complex of pure tones (i.e., sine waves) or *partials*, each with its own frequency, amplitude, and phase. *Fourier analysis* is the mathematical technique that allows us to analyse a complex sound into its pure-tone components. We do not normally perceive the individual partials of a complex sound because cognitive mechanisms operate to fuse them together, leading us to experience a unitary sound. According to *Ohm's acoustical law,* however, under certain listening conditions we have a limited ability to hear some of the individual partials of a complex sound.

Any sound with a discernable pitch has a *periodic waveform,* in that the waveform continuously repeats itself over time. The *period* is the time taken for one complete cycle of the waveform, and is the reciprocal of the repetition rate. The repetition rate usually determines the perceived pitch (exceptions include *circular tones,* discussed below), and is measured in cycles per second, or hertz (1 Hz = 1 cycle / sec). In general, when the repetition rate of a periodic sound is increased, the perceived pitch rises. The partials of any periodic waveform fall along the *harmonic series,* and are called *harmonics.* That is, if the lowest frequency component of the sound is "n" then the other harmonics—called *overtones*—are members of the set 2n, 3n, 4n, 5n, and so on. That is, each overtone has a frequency that is an integer multiple of the lowest or *fundamental* frequency of the complex. An important property of the harmonic series is that additional overtones do not alter the overall repetition rate of the waveform (which is determined by the fundamental frequency) and therefore do not change the perceived pitch of the complex.

Helmholtz (1863/1954) observed that several aspects of music, such as scale structure and harmony, have compelling parallels in physical acoustics. He noted that music from several cultures involves important scale notes that map onto the harmonics of complex tones. In the major scale, the fifth scale degree (*sol*) is equivalent (i.e., in note name, or tone *chroma*) to the third harmonic of a complex periodic tone built on the first note of the scale (*do*), and the third scale degree (*mi*) is equivalent to the fifth harmonic. The most important musical intervals used in Western music are also found in the harmonic series. The first and second harmonics are separated by an octave, the second and third harmonics are separated by a perfect fifth, the third and fourth harmonics are separated by a perfect fourth, the fourth and fifth harmonics are separated by a major third, and the fifth and six harmonics are separated by a minor third.

Harmonic overtones are not perceived as individual pitches. When presented with a periodic complex tone, only one pitch is usually perceived. Other mechanisms, however, are sensitive to harmonic spectra. For example, complex tones with different spectral contents are perceived as having different sound qualities, tone colors, or *timbres.* Harmonic overtones also affects the degree of *sensory consonance* and *dissonance* of tone combinations presented simultaneously. Tone combinations with fundamental frequencies that are related to each other by small-integer ratios, such as the octave (2:1) and the perfect fifth (3:2), have several harmonics in common and lead to sensory consonance. In contrast, tone combinations with fundamental frequencies that are not related to each other by small-integer ratios, such as the minor second (16:15), lead to sensory dissonance. Such combinations contain harmonic frequencies that are not identical but that fall within a *critical band* (a range of frequencies within which sensory interactions occur), resulting in rapid amplitude fluctuations that give rise to perceived *roughness and beating*. Sensitivity to sensory consonance and dissonance is thought to be independent of knowledge and enculturation. Long-term knowledge of music also affects judgments of consonance, and this aspect of music experience is referred to as *musical consonance*.

If sensitivity to sensory consonance and dissonance is independent of knowledge and enculturation, then young infants might be expected to exhibit a natural preference for consonance. Researchers have examined infants' preference for one type of music over another type by letting them "choose" which type of music they hear. Such experiments typically place an infant between two loudspeakers. When the infant looks toward the speaker on her left, she hears one type of music, but she hears a different type of music when she looks toward the speaker on her right. Hence, the infant is "controlling" what she hears by the direction of her gaze. Because infants tend to have a bias to look rightward, it is important to *counterbalance* the stimuli presentations. That is, half of the infants hear Piece A from the speaker on their left and Piece B from the speaker on their right, whereas the other half hear Piece B from the left and Piece A from the right.

Results based on this "infant preference" method reveal that infants look longer toward a speaker playing a consonant version of a musical piece than they do toward a speaker playing a dissonant version of the same piece. These findings suggest that listeners have an innate preference for sensory consonance and/or an innate dislike of sensory dissonance. As infants develop, these basic preferences are overlaid with effects of learning and enculturation, which contribute to the experience of *musical* consonance and dissonance. These effects of learning may run counter to initial predispositions: indeed, in so far as the aesthetic quality of chords can be judged outside of a musical context, the most beautiful may involve considerable dissonance.

Zentner and Kagan (1996) presented 4-month-old infants with a melody accompanied by a single "harmony" line. The melody and accompaniment were separated by minor seconds in the dissonant condition, but by major and minor thirds in the consonant condition. Infants preferred the consonant versions. Trainor and Heinmuller (1998) extended these findings by considering the influence of harmonics in pairs of complex tones, which can interact with each other and give rise to sensory dissonance. They found that 6-month old infants preferred to listen to perfect fifths and octaves compared to tritones and minor ninths (which give rise to greater sensory interference between harmonics). Trainor, Tsang, & Cheung (2002) tested the preferences of 2- and 4-month-old infants for consonant versus dissonant two-tone intervals. Using a looking-time preference procedure, they found that infants of both ages preferred to listen to consonant over dissonant intervals. The findings illustrate that infants are sensitive to sensory consonance and dissonance, and exhibit a preference for consonant over dissonant tone combinations.

Studies of discrimination provide further evidence that sensitivity to sensory consonance and dissonance is innate. Specifically, it comes naturally for listeners to discriminate combinations of tones on the basis of their consonance or dissonance. Schellenberg and Trainor (1996) presented 7-month-old infants and adults with a background pattern of simultaneous fifths (7 semitones) presented at varying pitch levels. Listeners were tested on their ability to discriminate the intervals in the background pattern from a new interval, which was either a tritone (6 semitones) or a fourth (5 semitones). Fifths and fourths are relatively consonant intervals, whereas tritones are relatively dissonant. Both age groups used the consonance and dissonance to discriminate these intervals. Although the fifth and fourth differ more from each other in terms of interval size, the fifth and tritone were better discriminated. Presumably, the dissonance of the tritone made it stand out from the perfect fifth, whereas the relative consonance of the perfect fourth made it sound similar to the fifth. In short, sensitivity to sensory consonance and dissonance is evident very early in development. Listeners can learn to appreciate dissonance, but they begin life with an initial preference for consonance.

If sensitivity to sensory consonance is a basic property of the auditory system, one might ask how this property affects scale structures and tuning systems. In most scales from around the world, consonant intervals (e.g., octaves, perfect fifths and fourth) are structurally important. For example, complex tones separated by octaves are considered to be similar in virtually all cultures. In North Indian scales, tones separated by a fifth (the *sa* and *pa*) are structurally important and are typically sounded continuously throughout a piece. The most common pentatonic scale (exemplified by the black notes on the piano), which is found in Chinese and Celtic music, can be formed by choosing any pitch as an arbitrary starting tone, adding a second tone a fifth higher, another tone a fifth higher than the second tone, and so on, until a collection of five pitches is obtained. The scale is formed by octave-transposing the collection of tones so that they fall within a single octave.

In Western music, a number of tuning systems have been used historically (for a review see Burns, 1999). One, called *Pythagorean tuning,* extends the pentatonic scale described above with additional tones that continue the "cycle of fifths." In another tuning system, called *just intonation,* the scale is formed by tuning notes so that their fundamental frequencies form small-integer ratios with the fundamental frequency of the first note of the scale (*do*). Both of these scales limit the possibility of transpositions between keys, because some instances of particular intervals (e.g., the perfect fifth between C and E) are tuned differently than other instances (e.g., C# and F).

Equal temperament represents a compromise solution. It guarantees that all intervals (i.e., all perfect fifths, or all major thirds) are tuned identically, and that important intervals do not deviate greatly from small-integer frequency ratios (fifths and fourths deviate from exact small-integer ratios by 2% of a semitone; major and minor thirds are slightly more mistuned). These minor deviations, although discriminable in some cases, are no greater than the typical tuning deviations observed in the performances of singers or stringed-instrument players. Moreover, such small departures from exact small-integer ratios have little effect on the perceived consonance of these intervals, which may explain why equal temperament has endured for many years.

Models of Pitch Perception

Pitch height is the most basic dimension along which pitches are perceived to vary; it refers to the continuum that extends from low to high pitches (which corresponds to a logarithmic function of frequency, or cycles per second). The psychological relevance of this continuum is evident in similarity judgments for pairs of pitches: tones closer in pitch are considered more similar than tones separated by greater pitch distance. The pitch-height continuum is also evident in neural activity in the cochlea. High frequencies stimulate the basal portions of the basilar membrane, low frequencies stimulate the apical portions, and intermediate frequencies affect intermediate portions.

In constructing a model of pitch perception, one may start with the basic dimension of pitch height, and then consider additional dimensions along which pitch seems to vary. In the most basic model, the perception of pitch height is determined by the logarithm of the fundamental frequency. Thus, the perceived size of a melodic interval spanning a given log frequency should not change under transposition or inversion. However, Stevens, Volkmann & Newman (1937) demonstrated that judgments of pitch height are not always consistent with a logarithmic relation between pitch and frequency. They derived a new scale, called the mel scale, using psychophysical scaling methods. A pure tone of 1000 Hz at 40 dB above threshold was first defined as 1000 mels, and the pitch in mels of other frequencies was determined by asking participants to adjust a comparison tone until it was perceived to be one half of the pitch height of a standard tone (method of fractionation). The mel scale and the logarithmic scale are roughly equivalent below 500 Hz, but the mel scale increases at a slower rate than the logarithmic scale above 500 Hz.

Most models of pitch perception consider the special status of the octave among intervals. As noted, complex tones with fundamental frequencies separated by an octave are perceived to be similar in virtually all musical cultures. *Pitch chroma* refers to the quality of pitch that is independent of the octave register in which it occurs. In Western music, tones separated by an octave are given the same name (e.g., A, B, C), implicating their equivalence in some sense. Further evidence for this view comes from listeners with musical training, who perceive similarities between tones that are separated by an octave (Allen, 1967; Kallman, 1982).

If pitch chroma and pitch height are basic dimensions of pitch perception, one should expect to find similar evidence among naïve listeners. When musically-untrained adults or children judge the similarity between *pure* tones, however, they tend to focus exclusively on the dimension of pitch height (Allen, 1967; Kallman, 1982; Sergeant, 1983). For example, C_4 and $C\#_4$ (notes separated by a semitone) are perceived to be highly similar, but C_4 and C_5 (notes separated by an octave) are perceived to be no more similar than C_4 and B_4 (notes separated by a major seventh). These findings do not rule out the possibility that sensitivity to the chroma dimension could be uncovered with tasks that measure *implicit* rather than *explicit* knowledge of musical associations. For example, Demany & Armand (1984) found that three-month-old infants are less surprised when one note of a melody is replaced by a note that is an octave apart than when it is replaced by a note that is a seventh or ninth apart. As another example, Humphreys (1939) showed that a conditioned galvanic skin response to one particular pitch generalises to pitches an octave apart. Nonetheless, the findings make it clear that music educators should not assume that octave equivalence is *explicitly* understood by naïve listeners.

An early psychological model of pitch perception incorporated the two dimensions of pitch height and pitch chroma. As shown in Figure 3.1, these two dimensions are depicted as orthogonal dimensions of a geometrically regular helix—a monotonic dimension of pitch height and a circular dimension of pitch chroma. Shepard (1964) reported evidence that these dimensions are psychologically relevant and orthogonal. He created tones with well-defined chroma but ambiguous height. Such *circular tones* were constructed by combining 10 pure-tone components spaced at octave intervals, and imposing a fixed amplitude envelope over the frequency range such that components at the low and high ends of the range approach hearing threshold.

Although the overall pitch height of any circular tone is somewhat indeterminate, listeners experience certain circular tones as "higher" or "lower" than others. In particular, listeners tend to perceive the relative height of these tones so as to maximize their pitch proximity. For example, when presented the circular tones C followed by D, one can perceive the second tone as either "higher" or "lower" than the first tone (C up to D, or C down to D). Both interpretations are possible because their individual pitch heights are ambiguous. Nonetheless, listeners typically perceive the second tone (D) as higher than the first tone (C), because this interpretation implicates a pitch distance of only two semitones. Listeners almost never perceive the second tone as lower than the first tone, because that interpretation would implicate a pitch distance of 10 semitones.

Shepard created fascinating patterns of circular tones in which chroma varied continuously around a "chroma circle" (see figure 3.1). For ascending patterns, he shifted all of the octave-spaced components up in frequency

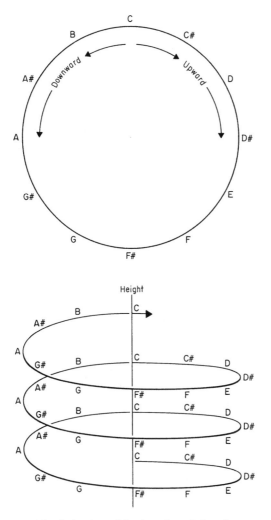

Figure 3.1. The *helical model of pitch* and the *chroma circle*.
The helical model combines two dimensions of pitch: height
and chroma.

(adding new components at the low end of the amplitude envelope) until
the complex returned to the initial configuration. When chroma was shifted
continuously in a clockwise direction around the chroma circle (C, C#, D,
D#, etc.), the pattern was perceived as ascending endlessly. When chroma
was shifted continuously in a counter-clockwise direction (C, B, A#, A, etc.),
the pattern was perceived as descended endlessly. That is, listeners perceived
changes in pitch chroma but not in overall pitch height. Most importantly,
these effects were perceived by musically trained and untrained listeners
alike. By making pitch height indeterminate, Shepard demonstrated that

pitch chroma has perceptual significance, even for untrained listeners. Thus, although untrained listeners may lack explicit knowledge of the similarity between tones with the same chroma, they nonetheless demonstrate sensitivity to chroma.

If pitch class and pitch height are orthogonal, then the relative height of circular tones that are directly opposite on the circle, such as C and F#, should be ambiguous or indeterminate. Deutsch addressed this prediction in a series of experiments (for a review, see Deutsch, 1999b). She reported that, for a given individual, certain circular tones (i.e., chromas) are reliably and consistently judged as being "higher" than the circular tone that is opposite on the circle, suggesting that the perceived height of a tone is systematically related to its pitch chroma. For example, some listeners reliably perceive a successive presentation of two particular circular tones separated by a tritone (e.g., C and F#) as upward pitch movement, whereas others perceive the same two tones as downward pitch movement. This so-called *tritone paradox,* and related findings, implies that pitch chroma and pitch height are not entirely independent.

Shepard (1982, 1999) and others have proposed more elaborate models of pitch perception with additional dimensions besides those based on height and chroma. These models account for affinities between tones separated by perfect fifths and fourths, which are said to be relevant for musically trained listeners tested with harmonically rich tones presented in musical contexts. Even more elaborate models have been proposed to account for affinities between tones separated by thirds. As described later, the establishment of a musical "key" also shapes pitch judgments (for a review, see Krumhansl, 1990). For example, in the context of the key of C major, C and G are perceived to be more strongly associated with each other than E and B, even though both tone pairs represent a perfect fifth interval (Krumhansl, 1979).

Absolute Pitch

It is often asserted that most listeners are sensitive to *relative* pitch but not to *absolute* pitch. Relative pitch refers to the ability to produce, recognize, or identify pitch relations, such as those that define a musical interval or a melody. To illustrate, *Twinkle Twinkle Little Star* can be sung in a high or a low voice, or performed on a tuba or a piccolo. As long as the pitch relations conform to those of the melody, it is usually recognizable. Absolute pitch refers to the ability to produce, recognize, or identify an individual pitch (e.g., middle C) without reference to any other pitch. Whereas relative pitch is the norm among trained and untrained listeners, absolute pitch is rare, occurring in about 1 in 10,000 people (Levitin & Rogers, 2005; Takeuchi & Hulse, 1993). Absolute pitch can be a valuable skill for musicians, but it can also interfere with the ability to perceive pitch relations (Miyazaki, 1993; 2004). Because melodies are defined by pitch and duration relations rather than with reference to any absolute pitch, relative pitch is arguably a more musical mode of pitch processing.

Nonetheless, some forms of long-term memory for pitch level may be quite common. Halpern (1989) asked participants to sing familiar tunes on different occasions (e.g., *Happy Birthday*), and Bergeson and Trehub (2002) asked mothers to sing the same song to their infant on two occasions. In both studies, singers varied minimally in pitch level across their different performances. In another study (Levitin, 1994), undergraduates were asked to sing the first few words of their favorite rock song. Their renditions were very close to the pitch level of the original recording (see also Terhardt & Seewann, 1983). Listeners also exhibit accurate memory for other surface (non-relational) features of recordings, such as tempo (Levitin & Cook, 1996) and overall sound quality (Schellenberg, Iverson, & McKinnon, 1999). These results confirm that memory for absolute aspects of musical recordings, which do not change from presentation to presentation, are more prevalent than previously assumed.

Finally, Schellenberg and Trehub (2003) devised a purely *perceptual* task in which they presented listeners with two versions of a 5-s excerpt from an instrumental TV theme song. One version was at the original pitch and the other version was shifted upward or downward by 1 or 2 semitones. Listeners were better than chance at identifying the original, even in the 1-semitone condition. A control experiment confirmed that successful performance was not due to electronic artifacts of the pitch–shifting process. Listeners also exhibit accurate memory for other surface (non-relational) features of recordings, such as tempo (Levitin & Cook, 1996) and overall sound quality (Schellenberg, Iverson, & McKinnon, 1999). These results confirm that memory for absolute aspects of musical recordings, which do not change from presentation to presentation, are more prevalent than previously assumed.

The discovery of good memory for pitch level in adults is pertinent to claims of a developmental shift in pitch processing. The traditional view (e.g., Takeuchi & Hulse, 1993) is that everyone is born with absolute pitch, although this ability typically disappears unless one receives musical training early in childhood (i.e., by age 6 or 7). Those without such early training are thought to shift to relative pitch processing, presumably as a consequence of hearing the same pitch relations (i.e., the same tunes, such as *Happy Birthday* or *Twinkle Twinkle*) at multiple different pitch levels (e.g., sung by a man or a woman). Findings indicating that young infants attend more to absolute than to relative pitch information are consistent with this perspective (Saffran, 2003; Saffran & Griepentrog, 2001). Nonetheless, in some instances, infants remember pitch relations rather than pitch level (Plantinga & Trainor, 2005). Moreover, an abundance of evidence confirms that infants are sensitive to relational pitch properties (contour and/or interval structure) of melodies (for review see Trehub et al., 1997). When considered as a whole, the available findings indicate that both absolute *and* relative pitch processing are evident across the lifespan. Although relative pitch is easily encoded and accessed from long-term memory, sensitivity to absolute pitch also plays a role in musical experience.

Melody

We now turn to a discussion of the perception and cognition of *melodies,* or tones presented sequentially. We begin with a focus on what listeners remember when they hear a melody. Which features of the melody are likely to be remembered, and which are likely to be forgotten? Melodies can be considered at different levels of analysis, including local structure (intervals, contours), higher-order structure (phrases, movements), and abstract structure (scales, keys).

Melodic Intervals

A melodic interval is created when two tones are sounded in sequence. They are experienced as large or small, consonant or dissonant, and for musically trained listeners, they are associated with category labels such as the major third, the minor sixth, and the octave. The ability to recognize and appreciate melodic intervals is one consequence of the more general skill known as *relative pitch*. Relative pitch allows us to perceive, appreciate, and remember melodies. Large melodic intervals or "leaps" form the basis for gap-fill melodies (Meyer, 1973) and are experienced as a point of accent (Boltz & Jones, 1986; Drake, Dowling & Palmer, 1991; Jones, 1987). Conversely, melodies sound more coherent or cohesive when they consist of a sequence of small intervals (Huron, 2001; Russo, 2002). Interval size may also influence melodic expectancy (Larson, 2004; Narmour, 1990) and grouping (Deliege, 1987; Lerdahl, 1989; Lerdahl & Jackendoff, 1983).

Interval size is normally defined according to the number of semitones that separate the lower and upper pitch of the interval, consistent with a logarithmic relation between frequency and pitch. Recent evidence by Russo & Thompson (in press; 2005), however, indicates that judgments of interval size are influenced by a large number of factors. Participants in these studies were presented with sequences of two pitches and judged the size of the melodic interval formed by them. Estimates were larger for intervals in the high pitch register than in the low pitch register, and for descending intervals than for ascending intervals. Ascending intervals were perceived as larger than descending intervals when presented in a high pitch register, but descending intervals were perceived as larger than ascending intervals when presented in a low pitch register (Russo & Thompson, in press). Moreover, if the upper pitch of an interval had a brighter timbre (i.e., higher spectral centroid) than the lower pitch, the interval was judged to be significantly larger than if the timbral properties of the two pitches were reversed (Russo & Thompson, in press b). The latter effect was so powerful that for some conditions participants judged a seven-tone pitch interval to be larger than a six-tone interval. Other evidence suggests that listeners even consider the facial expressions of performers when estimating the size of melodic intervals

(Thompson, Graham & Russo, 2005). Presumably, visual information related to the production of melodic intervals is integrated with auditory cues of interval size, leading to a perceptual representation that reflects the audio-visual experience.

Can infants remember melodic intervals? The answer is an unequivocal *yes,* but not all intervals are processed and remembered equally well. Rather, infants, as well as children and adults, have processing biases and preferences for consonant (pleasant sounding) intervals, which may account for the predominance of such intervals across musical cultures.

Experiments testing listeners' perception of intervals are similar to those testing their perception of contour. Listeners are typically asked to discriminate one interval from another. Because an interval change always involves a change in absolute pitch, the intervals are typically presented in transposition so that listeners must attend to interval size (i.e., pitch relations). Otherwise, they could perform the task merely by detecting shifts in absolute pitch. This type of "same/different" discrimination task allows researchers to determine which intervals are easy to process and remember, and which are difficult. If an interval is easily processed, then memory for it will be relatively stable and permanent, and listeners should find it easy to detect slight alterations to that interval. By contrast, if an interval is difficult to process, listeners will be unable to form a stable and lasting representation of the interval, making it less likely that a slight alteration would be detected.

In one series of experiments (Schellenberg & Trehub, 1996a), adults and 6-year-old children were required to detect 1-semitone changes in interval size. They were asked to discriminate two different intervals presented one after the other: fifths (7 semitones) from tritones (6 semitones); tritones from fourths (5 semitones); minor ninths (13 semitones) from octaves (12 semitones), and octaves from major sevenths (11 semitones). Each pair was presented in both orders, and all intervals were comprised of pure tones (sine waves). This discrimination task requires listeners to compare a memory representation for the standard interval (presented first) with a currently available comparison interval (presented second). Thus, if the standard interval is stable in memory, then it should be discriminated easily from the comparison interval. As predicted, performance was asymmetric in all instances. When the standard interval was relatively consonant and the comparison interval was dissonant, both children and adults could discriminate the intervals. When the standard was dissonant and the comparison was consonant, however, performance fell to chance levels. These findings suggest that listeners form relatively stable memory representations for octaves, fifths, and fourths.

Why do listeners form stable memories for these melodic intervals? One possibility is that they occur frequently in Western melodies, and are therefore well recognized. A related interpretation is that familiarity with octaves, fifths, and fourths within *simultaneous* combinations of tones (many chords contain these intervals) influences judgments of the same intervals presented melodically. Both "learning" hypotheses imply rather high-level abstraction and generalization of musical relations, however, and would not predict similar effects in young infants, who have very little exposure to music.

In a study with 6-month-old infants (Schellenberg & Trehub, 1996b), a similar processing advantage was identified for fifths and fourths over tritones. Infants heard a repeating pattern of alternating pure tones separated by one of three intervals, as shown in figure 3.2. After eight tones (four low-pitched and four high-pitched), the pattern was shifted upward or downward in pitch (figure 3.2a). On "no-change" trials, the shift was an exact transposition, such that the interval associated with the first eight tones was repeated at a new pitch register. On "change" trials, every other high-pitched tone was displaced downward by a semitone, creating intervals that were different from that associated with the first eight tones (figure 3.2b). Infants were capable of detecting these differences in interval size when the initial interval was a fifth or fourth, but not when it was a tritone. In other words, they demonstrated a clear processing advantage for consonant over dissonant intervals, even for pure tones presented sequentially in non-musical contexts. Similar findings have been obtained from infants tested with simultaneously presented pairs of tones (i.e., harmonic intervals; Schellenberg & Trehub, 1996b; Trainor, 1997). The results suggest that there is a basic

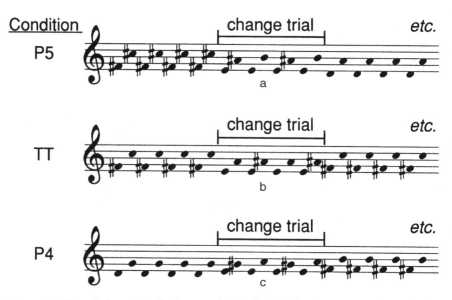

Figure 3.2. Stimuli from Schellenberg and Trehub (1996b). Sequences consisted of 2 alternating tones, transposed after the two tones were presented four times. The alternating tones were separated by a perfect fifth (P5, top panel), a tritone (TT, middle panel), or a perfect fourth (P4, lower panel). Infants 6 months of age were tested on their ability to detect displacements of the top tone during *change trials*

processing advantage for consonant intervals (see also Schellenberg & Trehub, 1994a, 1994b).

Melodic Contour

The *contour* of a melody refers to its pattern of upward and downward changes in pitch over time, irrespective of the absolute pitches involved, or the specific size of the intervals between pairs of adjacent tones. Figures 3.3a and 3.3b display melodies with a different contour, a different interval structure, and different absolute pitches. By contrast, figures 3.3a and 3.3c illustrate melodies with the same contour, but different intervals and absolute pitches. figures 3.3a and 3.3d display melodies with the same interval structure, yet different absolute pitches (one is an *exact transposition* of the other). Finally, figures 3.3a and 3.3e illustrate melodies that are identical in all respects: absolute pitch, intervallic structure, and contour.

How would these melodies be retained, or *mentally represented,* in memory? One possibility is that our mental representations are more-or-less veridical. As such, they would include absolute pitches, precise intervals between tones, and melodic contour. On this view, only the melodies displayed in figures 3.3a and 3.3e would be represented equivalently in memory. Although absolute pitches play a role in musical experience, as noted above, explicit memory for melodies is more often based on pitch relations.

A second possibility it that listeners' mental representations are determined by abstracting a sequence of intervals and discarding information about absolute pitch. If so, then the melodies shown in figures 3.3a, 3.3d, and 3.3e would be represented equivalently in memory, while the other two melodies would have different representations. For novel melodies, however, listeners often have difficulty retaining the exact pattern of intervals, which suggests that unfamiliar melodies are seldom represented with this degree of precision.

A third possibility is that listeners' mental representations are relatively crude, determined simply by the direction of the upward and downward shifts in pitch (i.e., melodic contour). In other words, fine-grained information about intervals and absolute pitch would typically not be perceived and encoded accurately during listening. The melody in figure 3.3a would be represented merely by its contour of up-down-up, and the mental representations of four of the five melodies would be equivalent (a, c, d, e).

Note that these melodic features (contour, intervals, and absolute pitch) are embedded hierarchically. If a listener remembers the absolute pitch of each of the tones in a melody, she can reconstruct the intervals between tones, and the melodic contour. If the listener remembers the sequence of intervals (but not the absolute pitches), then she can reconstruct the melodic contour. Conversely, melodies that differ in contour necessarily differ in interval size and absolute pitch. Melodies that differ in one or more intervals

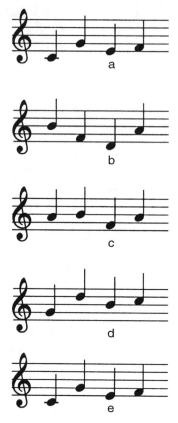

Figure 3.3. The "standard" melody in panel A has an up-down-up contour. The melody in panel B has a different contour, different intervals, and different pitches. The melody in panel C has the same contour as the standard but different intervals and pitches. The melody in panel D has the same contour and intervals as the standard, but different pitches; it is an exact transposition. Finally, the melody in panel E has the same contour, intervals, and pitches as those in the standard.

may or may not differ in contour, but at least one tone must differ in absolute pitch.

In general, research indicates that listeners' mental representations of novel melodies contain contour information but relatively little information about absolute pitch or exact interval size. Memory for the absolute pitches of novel melodies tends to be poor, and memory for the exact intervals between notes also tends to be poorer than memory for contour. Findings from studies of infants are particularly compelling in this regard (for a review, see Trehub, Schellenberg, & Hill, 1997). Moreover, the findings for adults' memories for novel melodies converge nicely with those from infants (for a review, see Dowling, 1994).

Studies with adults often adopt the same-different experimental method. On each experimental trial, listeners hear a "standard" (original) and "comparison" melody and judge whether they are the same or different. By systematically varying the ways in which the comparison differs from the standard (as in figure 3.3) and assessing the effects of such changes on judgment accuracy, one can determine which features are represented in memory. Listeners make errors about the interval and absolute-pitch information of novel melodies relatively soon after they are presented. By contrast, they retain contour information for longer periods of time.

The experimental method is necessarily altered for studies with infants. Infant listeners are trained to turn their head toward a loudspeaker when they hear a change in an auditory stimulus presented repeatedly (e.g., a melody), a process that occurs naturally anyway. By reinforcing this response with illuminated and activated toys, infants maintain their interest in the task. If they reliably turn their head toward the speaker for certain melodic changes but not for others, we can conclude that the former changes are relatively detectable for infants, whereas the latter changes are relatively undetectable. Several studies have confirmed that contour changes are very noticeable for infants, whereas changes that maintain contour but alter absolute pitch or interval size are far less noticeable (Trehub et al., 1997). In short, infants perceive and remember the contour of melodies.

Why is melodic contour so easy to remember? Many have speculated that our sensitivity to contour in music stems from the adaptive importance of contour in speech. Studies of speech perception in infancy reveal that infant-directed speech (i.e., *motherese*) differs from adult-directed speech in a number of systematic ways (Fernald, 1991), and that infants prefer to listen to infant-directed over adult-directed speech (Cooper & Aslin, 1990; Fernald, 1985). One of the distinctive aspects of infant-directed speech is its exaggerated use of pitch contour. Different pitch contours are used to express different messages to infants (e.g., approval, arousal, etc.), and the alterations that adults make in their speech to infants are remarkably similar across cultures (Fernald et al., 1989). Hence, sensitivity to contour patterns in speech could facilitate bonding between infants and their caregivers, and the language-acquisition process. Such sensitivity has obvious adaptive value, and could account for infants' sensitivity to contour in music. Researchers have identified a number of implications of this heightened sensitivity to melodic contour. First, melodies with fewer changes in contour are perceived as "simpler" than melodies with more contour changes (Boltz & Jones, 1986). Second, listeners attend more to notes at points of contour change than they do to notes that are embedded within an ongoing contour (Dyson & Watkins, 1984). For example, when presented with a 5-tone sequence with an up-up-down-down contour (see figure 3.4), listeners' attention is drawn more to the middle (third) tone—the point of contour change—than it is to the second or fourth tones. In other words, tones at *contour points* (at contour changes or at the beginning or end of melodies) are more likely to be represented in memory than are other tones. It follows, then, that melodies with a relative abundance of contour points contain a relative abundance of salient bits of information, and should be relatively challenging to process and remember.

A number of recent studies have examined the possible relation between contour sensitivity in melody and sensitivity to speech intonation. In particular, the ability to make sense of pitch changes in these two domains could be associated with shared neural resources. Patel, Foxton & Griffiths (in press) found, for example, that musically tone-deaf individuals have difficulty discriminating intonation contours extracted from speech. However, Peretz & Hyde (2003) showed that such individuals could sometimes discriminate intonation contours in speech at normal performance levels, as long as the discrimination required attention to coarse-grained aspects of pitch. Peretz & Hyde concluded that although sensitivity to pitch changes in music and speech may be associated with shared neural resources, music often involves fine grained changes in pitch such that correlated performance levels are not always expected.

The potential neural overlap between music and speech is not restricted to pitch contour. The ability to decode speech prosody might engage a range of processes that are involved in music listening, including sensitivity to contour, loudness, tempo, and rhythm (Ilie & Thompson, in press). In support of this idea, Thompson, Schellenberg & Husain (2004) reported that adults with extensive training in music were significantly better at decoding the emotional connotation of speech in an unfamiliar language. Because participants could not understand the verbal content of the speech, they relied on

Figure 3.4. The melody has an up-up-down-down contour. The first, middle, and last tones can be considered contour points.

prosodic features such as pitch contour, loudness, and temporal properties—properties that have musical significance. In the same study, the authors found that seven-year-old children assigned to one year of piano lessons were better at decoding speech prosody in their own language and in a foreign language than children who did not receive such training. The findings imply that training in music engages neural resources associated with both music and speech, such that the enhanced skill acquired from music lessons *transfers* to an enhanced ability to decode speech prosody.

Scale Structure and Enculturation

A survey of the scales of various musical cultures suggests rather strongly that music is constrained by basic psychological processes. For example, virtually all scales have 5 to 7 notes per octave. There is a consensus in the literature that the limited number of notes in these scales stems from limitations in the capacity of working memory. Several decades ago, Miller (1956) demonstrated that for any continuous dimension (e.g., brightness, loudness), adults can reliably categorize instances into a maximum of seven categories, give or take about two categories. Because this limitation of working-memory capacity extends across domains and modalities, one would expect that pitch categories would be similarly limited. Hence, music composed with scales that have more than seven tones is likely to exceed the cognitive capacities of many listeners. This constraint may explain why many people find it challenging to listen to 12-tone (serialized) music.

A second characteristic of scales that may stem from basic psychological constraints is the structural importance of intervals that closely approximate perfect consonances, such as octaves, perfect fifths, and perfect fourths. These structural features may reflect an innate preference for consonance, as well as an innate processing advantages for consonant over dissonant intervals (as noted above).

A third property of scales is that most have differently-sized steps between consecutive tones in the scale. For example, the major scale has intervals of 1 and 2 semitones in size between adjacent scale notes. The most common pentatonic scale has steps of 2 and 3 semitones. In fact, scales from around the world (except for the whole-tone and 12-tone scales) have this property of unequal-steps. One often-noted exception is a scale from Thailand, although there is doubt about its proposed equal-step structure in musical practice (Morton, 1976). Why would scales exhibit this "unequal-step" property?

One explanation is that unequal steps arise simply because consonant intervals (fifth, fourth, major third) are formed from a small number of scale notes. Balzano (1980) argued, however, that unequal steps also confer a psychological benefit, because they allow tones to have different functions within the scale. In the major scale, each note has a unique set of intervals that it forms with the other notes from the scale. In C major, for example,

F and B are related to each other by the interval of an augmented fourth, but C is not related to any scale note by that particular interval. This distinctive property allows listeners to differentiate scale tones from one another, and to isolate a focal or tonic tone (*do*). A focal or tonic tone functions as a mental referent to which other tones can be compared. The ability to determine a focal tone and differentiate scale tones may make unequal-step scales advantageous from a psychological standpoint.

In a test of whether the use of unequal steps confers a basic processing advantage to listeners, Trehub, Schellenberg, and Kamenetsky (1999) tested adults and 9-month-old infants on their ability to process and remember three scales (see figure 3.5). One was the unequal-step major scale, another was an unfamiliar scale formed by dividing the octave into seven equal steps (Shepard & Jordan, 1984), and a third was a completely unfamiliar unequal-step scale. This third scale was formed by dividing the octave into 11 equal steps, and then constructing a seven-tone scale that had four two-step intervals and three one-step intervals.

Both age groups were tested on their ability to detect when the sixth scale step was displaced upward slightly. Infants showed relatively good performance for the familiar (major) and the unfamiliar unequal-step scales, but poor performance for the unfamiliar equal-step scale. These results provide evidence that scales with unequal steps are inherently easier for infants to process and represent compared to equal-step scales. For infants, music composed with equal-step scales, such as whole-tone (e.g., music by Debussy) or 12-tone (e.g., music by Schönberg) scales, may be more difficult to perceive and remember than music composed with unequal-step scales.

Adults showed a different pattern of responding. For the familiar major scale, they could detect the upward displacement of the sixth scale step. By contrast, for both unfamiliar scales (equal- or unequal-step), adults had difficulty detecting when the sixth scale step was displaced upward. This finding suggests that with years of exposure to the scale (or scales) from one's musical culture, the initial processing advantage for unequal-step scales is eliminated. When the listener is fully enculturated, he is familiar and comfortable with conventional scales, whereas unconventional scales of all types (including unfamiliar unequal-step scales) sound foreign and are difficult to perceive and remember.

A related study reveals a similar pattern of findings, in which another basic predisposition is gradually overwhelmed by culture-specific knowledge. It is safe to assume that melodies with an abundance of repeated tones are "simple" and therefore easier to perceive and remember compared to less repetitive melodies. In other words, tone repetition is a basic feature of melodic simplicity. In support of this idea, Schellenberg and Trehub (1999) reported that infants 9 months of age found it easier to process and remember 5-tone sequences with two repeated tones than similar sequences with only one repeated tone. This finding held whether the sequences were conventional (based on a major triad) or relatively unconventional (based on a diminished triad).

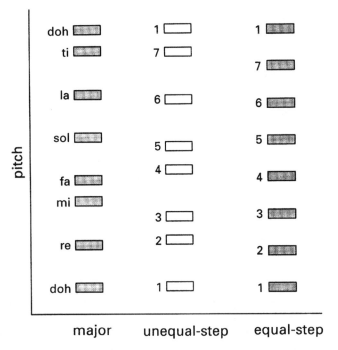

Figure 3.5. Schematic diagram of the scales used by Trehub, Schellenberg, and Kamenetsky (1999). Each scale had seven tones per octave. One was the familiar major scale (left). The other were completely artificial. The unequal-step scale (middle) was formed by dividing the octave into 11 equal steps and selecting a subset of 7 tones. The equal-step scale (right) was formed by dividing the octave into 7 equal steps.

Interestingly, this effect of tone repetition varied as a function of age and exposure to music. For 5-year-old children, processing advantages for tone repetition were also apparent, but the effect was greater for conventional than for unconventional melodies. For adults, however, such advantages were observed only for conventional melodies. Presumably, adult listeners had difficulty assimilating unconventional melodies into their existing schemata, and this difficulty overwhelmed any potential advantage of tone repetition. More generally, it appears that basic cognitive processes (such as processing advantages for tone repetition, or for unequal-step scales) can be strongly affected by age and experience.

Larger Melodic Structures

How do listeners know when one musical phrase ends and another begins? Do composers capitalize on perceptual predispositions? Are musical phrases structurally similar in any ways to linguistic utterances? Can infants use cues in the music to segment music properly?

Krumhansl and Jusczyk (1990) tested infants' preferences for Mozart pieces that were "correctly" or "incorrectly" segmented. Correctly segmented pieces had pauses inserted *between* phrases. Incorrectly segmented pieces had pauses inserted *within* phrases. To an adult listener, both versions sound somewhat strange, although the former version seems more musical because the pauses occur at "natural" breaks in the music. Looking times indicated that infants preferred the correctly segmented pieces, in which segments tended to end with relatively long notes and downward pitch contours. Interestingly, spoken utterances also tend to end with words of relatively long duration and downward pitch contour. This correspondence between spoken utterances and musical phrases leads to two related interpretations of the results: (1) infants might prefer the "correctly" segmented pieces because they bear structural similarities to spoken utterances, which infants have learned from being exposed to speech, or (2) downward contours and extended durations naturally mark the end of all auditory signals. Either way, the findings indicate that listeners implicitly understand at a very early age that melodic phrases tend to end with downward pitch motion and notes of relatively long duration. Such cues allow listeners to segment melodies into melodic groups such as phrases and motifs, and to identify boundaries between larger forms such as movements and sections.

In addition to phrase boundaries, the perception of melodic groups is influenced by other auditory cues such as pitch proximity and timbral similarity of notes (for a review, see Deutsch, 1999a). Such cues not only influence perceived connections between *adjacent* notes in a melody, they can also induce perceived connections between salient or significant notes across several melodic groups, leading to the perception of *higher-level* melodic structures. That is, melodic groups are perceived at multiple hierarchic levels, and excerpts with the same higher-level structure are perceived as similar despite differences in surface structure (Serafine, Glassman, & Overbeeke, 1989).

Lerdahl and Jackendoff (1983) proposed a comprehensive and influential theory of melody that emphasized its hierarchic structure. They first noted that Western tonal melodies can be analyzed into essential notes and ornamental notes. Ornamental notes are notes in the melody that can be removed without altering the essential character of the melody. After ornamental notes are removed, what is left is a simplified version of that melody. With this idea as a starting point, Lerdahl and Jackendoff (1983) used the term "reductional structure" to describe how large-scale melodic structures can be analyzed into simpler and simpler skeletons. They proposed two ways in which melodies can be simplified.

In time-span reduction, certain beats and groups in a melody are designated as ornaments on other groups and beats. This simplification process is continued in an interactive manner, resulting in a tree diagram that specifies the relative dominance of each event. In prolongation reduction, primary points of tension and relaxation are differentiated from subordinate points of tension and relaxation, again resulting in a tree diagram. Both types of tree diagrams illustrate how smaller melodic units combine to form large-scale melodic structure. Palmer and Krumhansl (1987a, 1987b) found that time-span reduction was able to predict listeners' judgments of phrase endings in music by Mozart and Bach. Other research supports the psychological validity of prolongation reduction (Bigand, 1990; Dibben, 1994).

Melodic Expectancies

As a listener hears a melody, she continuously forms expectancies about upcoming notes she will hear. Sometimes we expect a particular note, but usually our expectations are not so specific. Rather, some notes seem relatively likely, whereas other notes seem less likely. Learning and exposure to musical styles exert a large influence on such expectancies. Is there a role for basic cognitive processes in the formation of melodic expectancies?

According to Narmour (1990), the answer is *yes*. His theory of melodic expectancy, called the *Implication-Realization Model,* posits that listeners' expectancies are formed from a combination of bottom-up and top-down factors (see Thompson, 1996, for a reivew). In Narmour's use of these terms, "bottom-up" refers to innate or hardwired cognitive and perceptual tendencies; "top-down" refers to expectancies that result from experience, either with music in general, or with a particular musical piece. As examples, pitch proximity (expecting notes that are proximal in pitch) is considered to be an innate influence on melodic expectancy, whereas tonality (expecting notes in proportion to their importance in the scale) is thought to be based on long-term knowledge of Western music.

Two experimental methods have been used to test expectancies. In one method, listeners hear a fragment of a melody followed by a test tone. Their task is to rate how well the test tone continues the fragment. The assumption is that tones conforming to listeners' expectancies will be rated as relatively good continuations. The other method is a production task, in which participants play or sing a continuation to a stimulus provided by the experimenter. The main finding from all of the relevant studies is that *proximity* explains the lion's share of the variance in listeners' responses, regardless of experimental method, age, musical style, and participants' music training or cultural background (e.g., Cuddy & Lunney, 1995; Schellenberg, 1996, 1997; Schellenberg, Adachi, Purdy, & McKinnon, 2002; Thompson, Cuddy, & Plaus, 1997). In general, tones that are proximate in pitch to the last tone heard are the most expected (see von Hippel, 2000). This association is more-or-less linear, such that tones farther and farther away from the last tone heard receive lower and lower ratings, or are less likely to be sung or played.

Narmour (1990) proposed several bottom-up principles of melodic expectancy. In an examination of Narmour's theory, however, Schellenberg

(1997) observed that bottom-up expectancies can be explained by just two basic principles. The first principle is *pitch proximity,* described above. The second principle is *pitch reversal.* Pitch reversal describes expectancies for an upcoming tone to be proximate to the penultimate tone heard, as well as expectancies for a change in pitch contour after a large melodic leap (von Hippel & Huron, 2000). This simple model has proven to be equal or superior to Narmour's original model across listeners who vary in musical training, cultural background, or age, across stimulus contexts (real melodies or two-tone stimuli), with both production and perceptual-rating methods, and with melodies from Western tonal, atonal, and non-Western repertoires (Schellenberg, 1997; Schellenberg et al., 2002; see Thompson & Stainton, 1998, for another simplified model).

In short, there is strong evidence that proximity is an innate grouping principle that influences the formation of melodic expectancies. The role of proximity in melodic expectancy represents perhaps one of the clearest examples of a basic psychological process influencing music perception and cognition. Proximity is known to be a robust predictor of perceptual grouping in vision. Consider the illustration in figure 3.6. The average perceiver visually groups the elements on the basis of proximity: Items that are close together are perceived as a group. The same holds true for audition in general (see the section on auditory stream segregation) and for music in particular. Tones that are proximate in pitch tend to be grouped together. Hence, a melody that contains many large leaps in pitch is difficult to perceive as a unified whole, whereas a melody with mostly stepwise motion (rather than leaps) tends to be perceived as a unified group of tones.

Implicit Memory for Melody

The effects of learning that result from exposure to music are often subtle. Moreover, as the following section illustrates, they often occur without conscious awareness. It is widely acknowledged that experiences can affect our behavior in the absence of conscious awareness. Such effects are thought to reflect an *implicit* memory system that operates independently of conscious or *explicit* memory (Schacter, 1987). Recent advances in the understanding of implicit memory systems suggest an exciting direction for future studies of music cognition.

Implicit memory for music may explain how listeners develop an appreciation for the music of their culture. Indeed, most musical experiences are probably influenced by implicit memory. As Crowder (1993) argues, ". . . the re-entry of a fugue theme, the occurrence of a lietmotif, or the developmental section of a remembered sonata-movement subject may all be examples of implicit music memory" (p. 134). Empirical studies support Crowder's suggestion. Passive exposure to music leads to implicit knowledge of tonal relations (Tillman, Bharucha & Bigand, 2000), musical preferences (Peretz, Gaudreau, & Bonnel, 1998; Szpunar, Schellenberg, & Pliner, 2004),

Figure 3.6. The figure illustrates how *proximity* influences perceptual grouping in vision. The viewer sees four columns of letters. Note the similarity in shape between the second and third columns, and between the first and fourth columns. Nonetheless, the first and second columns form a group, as do the third and fourth columns, because of proximity.

and expectancies for melodic continuations (Thompson, Balkwill, & Vernescu, 2000).

Thompson, Balkwill & Vernescu (2000) presented listeners with atonal melodies (target melodies) as they performed a counting task or a visual task. The latter tasks reduced the *depth of processing* of the melodies, making it difficult for listeners to remember them explicitly. In a subsequent task, listeners heard the same melodies, as well as novel melodies that were constructed similarly. For each melody, listeners rated the extent to which they expected the final note, on a scale from 1 (unexpected) to 7 (expected). Ratings were higher for the melodies that were heard previously than for novel melodies, which illustrates that mere exposure to music affects melodic expectancy. Szpunar et al. (2004) presented the same melodies to listeners at a low volume while they were engaged in a demanding distractor task. Afterward, when the listeners were asked to rate how much they liked the previously heard melodies and novel melodies, they provided higher ratings for the exposed melodies. As in Thompson et al. (2000), they could not explicitly remember the melodies they had heard. In both studies, mere exposure led to *implicit* memory for melodies, either in the form of melodic expectancies or preferences. These results provide insight into how listeners internalize the music of their own culture, and how they learn to appreciate unconventional music. Repeated exposure to music composed in a consistent manner leads to the development of stable expectancies and preferences for typical melodic patterns. Over time, the music becomes somewhat predictable and "makes sense" to the listener.

Harmony and Tonality

Western Harmony

The term "harmony" refers to rules and conventions governing the simultaneous combination of tones into chords and chord progressions (sequences of chords). Although music from other cultures allows for more than one tone to be presented simultaneously, Western music is unique in its regular use of chords and rules governing chord progressions (i.e., monophonic music and solo singing are relatively rare). Because Western harmony is specific to Western music, its rules must be learned, either by regular music listening or by formal training in music. Accordingly, one might ask when listeners have acquired knowledge of the rules of Western harmony as a function of age and/or exposure to music.

In Western harmony, a sense of finality (i.e., *closure*) is expressed typically by having the tonic chord (the chord based on do) as the final event in a phrase or piece. Listeners with musical training are aware of this convention and they can identify the tonic chord when listening to a musical piece. By contrast, untrained listeners have no knowledge of tonic chords or harmonic rules, and they cannot articulate explicitly what they know about harmony. Nonetheless, they may have acquired extensive but *implicit* knowledge of harmony through years of exposure to Western music. In order to examine listeners' implicit knowledge of harmony, we can ask them to make an unrelated judgment about the final chord of a musical piece, such as whether it is sung with one of two vowels (e.g., /i/ or /u/), or played on one of two instruments (e.g., piano or trumpet). The listener is unaware that the harmonic function of the final chord is also being manipulated (i.e., either a tonic chord or a less stable chord in the key of the piece). If untrained listeners have implicit knowledge of harmony, they should expect a piece to end on the tonic. Accordingly, accuracy and response speed on the task they are asked to perform may improve when the final chord is consistent with their implicitly formed expectation.

Across a wide variety of implicit tasks, untrained listeners show a performance advantage when the final chord is the tonic—in accuracy, response speed, or both accuracy and speed (for a review see Bigand & Poulin-Charronnat, 2005). Musically trained and untrained participants show similar advantages for tonic chords, which indicates that the acquisition of implicit knowledge of Western harmony does not require formal training in music. In a developmental study of children who varied both in age and in amount of music lessons (Schellenberg, Bigand, Poulin, Garnier, & Stevens, 2005), 6-year-olds with no music lessons showed a performance advantage for tonic chords that was similar in magnitude to that of 11-year-olds who were studying music at a conservatory. These findings suggest that acquisition of implicit knowledge for Western harmony is rapid and effortless, such that some aspects of this knowledge are relatively mature by 6 years of age.

Implied Harmony

Because melodies are so often heard with a harmonic accompaniment, listeners gradually learn to associate isolated melodies with plausible harmonic accompaniments, even when none is present. Consider the melody illustrated in figure 3.7 (from Trainor & Trehub, 1992, 1994). The melody implies a shift from a tonic harmony in the first measure to a dominant harmony in the second measure. Musically trained listeners are highly sensitive to this implied harmony, and consistently identify the implied harmonic change. Are untrained listeners also sensitive to these shifts in implied harmony? If so, how does sensitivity to implied harmony change over development?

In one experiment (Trainor & Trehub, 1992), adults and 8-month-olds were tested on their ability to discriminate alterations to the melody shown in figure 3.7, which was presented repeatedly in varying transpositions. In each case, the alteration consisted of an upward displacement to the sixth tone in the melody. For some listeners, the displacement was a shift upward by 1 semitone (e.g., from G to G#), which is a small alteration in terms of interval size but inconsistent with the implied harmony. For other listeners, the displacement was a shift upward by 4 semitones (e.g., from G to B), which is a much larger change in interval size but consistent with the implied dominant harmony. Adult listeners found the former change—which violated the implied harmony—easier to detect than the latter change—which was consistent with the implied harmony. Infant listeners performed equally well in both conditions. Interestingly, infant listeners actually outperformed adults at detecting the larger but harmonically consistent shift in pitch. In

Figure 3.7. Stimulus melody used by Trainor and Trehub (1992, 1994). The melody implies a tonic-dominant shift in harmony from the first to the second measure. The melody was presented continuously in transposition. Listeners were tested on their ability to detect when the circled tone was displaced upward. Such displacements violated the key and the implied harmony (1 semitone up, to G#), the harmony but not the implied key (2 semitones up, to A), or neither (4 semitones up, to B).

other words, adult listeners appear to have a very well developed sense of implied harmony that they acquire through years of exposure to music, such that changes in a melody that are consistent with the implied harmony are relatively unnoticeable. By contrast, infants appear to be less sensitive to implied harmony.

When does sensitivity to implied harmony develop? A follow-up experiment (Trainor & Trehub, 1994) addressed this question by testing listeners 5 and 7 years of age. The children were asked to detect the 1-semitone harmony-violating change, the 4-semitone harmony-consistent change, and an intermediate 2-semitone shift (e.g., from G to A) which was consistent with the underlying key signature (C major) but violated the implied harmony. The 5-year-olds found the 1-semitone change easier to detect than the other changes. In other words, the shift that violated both the implied harmony and the underlying key signature was more noticeable than the other shifts. For the 7-year-olds, the 2-semitone shift that violated the implied harmony but not the key was easier to detect than the 4-semitone harmonically consistent shift. These data, considered in conjunction with those from the previous study, indicate a systematic developmental progression. Infant listeners have a relatively poor sense of key. By 5 years of age, children are sensitive to key membership but not to implied harmony. By 7 years of age, children are sensitive to implied harmony.

Tonality

Tonality is a basic organizing principle in Western tonal music. It refers to the organization of the twelve pitches in the chromatic pitch set around a reference pitch, called the tonic. The establishment of tonality, also called key, involves inducing a hierarchical organization of stability or importance on the chromatic pitch set. In this hierarchy, the tonic pitch (do) is most stable, followed by other pitches of the tonic triad (mi and sol), followed by other pitches in the scale (diatonic tones). Pitches that are not in the scale (nondiatonic tones) are perceived to be unstable.

A number of landmark studies have been conducted to investigate the effects of tonality on judgments of pitch (for a review, see Krumhansl, 1990). Krumhansl and her colleagues used the "probe-tone" technique to investigate the psychological implications of tonality (Krumhansl & Kessler, 1982; Krumhansl & Shepard, 1979). The method involves presentation of a musical stimulus that clearly defines a musical key (e.g., scale, cadence, chord sequence) followed by a "probe" tone. Listeners rate how well each probe tone in the chromatic scale fits with the established key. When musically trained listeners are tested with this method, probe-tone ratings are quite consistent across listeners and reflect a hierarchical organization that has become known as the tonal hierarchy.

The *tonal hierarchy* is more easily uncovered with musically trained than untrained participants, illustrating the influence of learning. School-age children's implicit knowledge of the hierarchy improves dramatically from 6 to 11 years of age (Krumhansl & Keil, 1982), although 6-year-olds know that different tones vary in goodness once a musical context is established (Cuddy & Badertscher, 1987). Thus, although sensory dissonance is perceived by infants and musically untrained adults, judgments of pitch relations are also influenced by musical training, suggesting that our perceptions of pitch and pitch relations result from a combination of innate and learned factors.

Evidence of sensitivity to the tonal hierarchy early in development can be explained—in part—by psychoacoustic influences (Leman, 2000; Schellenberg & Trehub, 1994): Probe tones with high stability values (*do, mi, sol, fa*) have the largest degree of sensory consonance with the established tonic. Alternatively, because the frequency of occurrence of tones in real pieces of music closely mirrors the tonal hierarchy, children may learn implicitly that tones heard more often in a musical piece are particularly stable (Krumhansl, 1990, chapter 3). Indeed, we know that listeners are highly sensitive to pitch distributional information in music. Oram and Cuddy (1995) presented listeners with atonal sequences in which one tone occurred eight times, another tone occurred four times, and four other tones occurred once each. Following each sequence, listeners rated the extent to which various probe tones fit with the sequence in a musical sense. Ratings reflected the frequency with which each pitch occurred in the context. Thus, when listening to unfamiliar music, listeners readily construct a hierarchy of pitch importance using frequency-of-occurrence information.

A number of researchers have proposed models of how listeners determine the tonality of a piece of music (e.g., Brown, 1988; Brown & Butler, 1981; Browne, 1981; Krumhansl & Schmuckler, 1986; Krumhansl, 1990, 2000; Leman, 2000). In Brown and Butler's (1988) *intervallic rivalry* model, tonality is determined through the identification of "rare" intervals that uniquely define a particular key. In Krumhansl & Schmuckler's *key-finding algorithm*, tonality is determined by comparing the frequency of occurrence or duration of the tones of a musical passage with "standard" profiles of stability values for various possible keys. The profile that best matches the tonal information in the musical passage is defined as the key. Smith & Schmuckler (2004) pointed out that two general processes—differentiation and organization—underly these two models and that both may be involved in tonality perception. That is, the perception of tonality requires differentiation among pitches, as well as hierarchical organization of these differentiated pitches. Other theories of tonality perception are reviewed by Vos (2000) and by Auhagen and Vos (2000).

With music that contains simultaneously sounded notes, listeners may derive a sense of key either from isolated voices or from the harmonies that are created by combining those voices (Thompson & Cuddy, 1992; Cuddy & Thompson, 1992). Interestingly, the tonal implications of a harmonic progression (i.e., a sequence of chords) are somewhat independent of the tonal implications carried by the individual voices, which, in turn, may be somewhat different from each other (Thompson, 1993). For example, attending to a sequence of chords might suggest an abrupt change from one key to a psychologically distant key. By contrast, attending to an individual voice (e.g., the melody line) in the same polyphonic texture might suggest a smoother transition between more related keys. The use of timing and loudness in expressive performance can further influence perceived movement from one key to another (Thompson & Cuddy, 1997). These findings suggest that melody, harmony, and key are not mentally represented in a strictly hierarchical manner. Rather, melodic features may implicate key and key movement somewhat independently of the harmony.

Perceiving Voices in Harmony

The interdependence of melody and harmony has been a focal point in theoretical discussions of Western music (e.g., Lerdahl & Jackendoff, 1983; Meyer, 1973; Narmour, 1990, 1992). Although mutually intertwined, these two aspects of music often work in different ways. For example, different levels of tension or dissonance in melodies and their harmonic accompaniments may be a source of aesthetic interest. This is often true in the music of Brahms, where intense dissonances outlined in the melodic line may be offset by warm supporting harmonies. Other evidence, described earlier, illustrates that melodies and their harmonic accompaniments may also differ in how they implicate key and key change. In short, melodies have psychological effects that are somewhat different from the harmonies in which they are embedded.

The composition of polyphonic music must therefore achieve a balance between melodic and harmonic goals. This balance is partially guided by established conventions of Western tonal composition, which are often formalized as "rules" of harmonic progression and voice-leading. Although these rules may be "broken" by composers for aesthetic purposes, a close examination of them reveals important insights into their cognitive origins. In particular, several rules of voice leading are related to more general principles of auditory scene analysis (Bregman, 1990; for a detailed discussion, see Huron, 2001). Auditory scene analysis refers to the set of general processes that allow perceivers to organize acoustic information arriving at the ear into distinct sound events or sources. These basic auditory processes allow listeners to hear an individual speaker in a crowded room or to track individual voices in polyphonic music.

Remarkably, music students are often taught skills of voice leading with no reference to principles of auditory scene analysis. Instead, educators explain voice-leading practices in terms of cultural and historical factors, or imply that voice-leading conventions cannot be understood outside of a particular cultural and historical context. This explanation provides an incomplete picture, and students would benefit from a basic understanding of au ditory scene analysis. Furthermore, advances in computer technology and sound synthesis now allow composers to explore timbres, melodies, and harmonies that are unconstrained by the acoustical properties of natural instruments. An understanding of the nature of auditory stream segregation is especially important for such compositions.

Huron (2001) identified several general principles of auditory scene analysis that play a critical role in voice-leading practices. These principles were established through over 20 years of research using both musical and nonmusical stimuli. This body of research is summarized by Bregman (1990) and will not be reviewed here. Rather, we will describe how the most well established of these principles are instantiated in our perceptions of individual tones and voices in polyphonic music, and culturally encoded as rules of voice leading.

Beginning with the perception of individual tones, the conditions that lead to a clear sense of pitch are linked to the pitch range conventionally used in harmonic writing. Pitch clarity varies with the fundamental frequency of tones. Pitch perception tends to be clearest in a region that corresponds roughly to the center of a piano keyboard (extending from F_2 and G_5 and centered at 300 Hz, which is approximately 2 semitones higher than middle C). By contrast, listeners' sense of pitch is much poorer for the lowest and highest notes on the piano. The distribution of pitches in both Western and non-Western music corresponds precisely with the region associated with high pitch clarity. This correspondence suggests that harmonic writing reflects a tacit goal of using tones with a clear sense of pitch.

Mechanisms of auditory scene analysis also operate to link acoustic events over time. Pitch proximity represents one of the most important cues for such temporal grouping. To reiterate an idea discussed earlier, a sequence of tones is most readily perceived as a group or "stream" when the pitch distance between temporally adjacent tones is small. Tones with pitches that are distant from each other tend to be perceptually segregated into separate streams. In music, this effect is exploited in pseudo-polyphony or compound melodies, where a single sequence of notes may be written so as to evoke the impression of two distinct melodic lines. As the pitch distance between successive tones is increased, creating alternating high and low pitched tones, listeners become more and more likely to perceive two streams (2 separate melodies). This effect of pitch separation is known to depend on tempo. As tempo is decreased, a larger pitch separation is needed to evoke an impression of two auditory streams (van Noorden, 1975).

Thus, the coherence of an individual voice is enhanced if temporally adjacent tones are proximate in pitch. When leaps in pitch are introduced in a voice, coherence can be maintained by reducing tempo. Consistent with these findings, rules of voice-leading restrict the use of large leaps in part writing. When wide leaps are unavoidable, composers tend to use long durations for the notes forming the leap (the first note, the second note, or both notes), a convention called *leap lengthening*. The convention of avoiding large leaps maps directly onto listeners' sensitivity to the effects of pitch proximity on auditory stream segregation. The convention of leap length-ening mirrors an additional sensitivity to the interactive effects of proximity and tempo.

Yet a third convention in voice leading is also relevant to pitch proximity. To ensure perceptual independence of voices, the pitches of temporally adjacent tones within each voice should be more proximate than the pitches of temporally adjacent tones in different voices; otherwise, confusions in voice attribution may occur. Such confusions are especially probable if voices "cross" in pitch register, in which case streaming mechanisms may group part of one voice with a continuation of the other voice. Not surprisingly, part-crossing is avoided in voice leading, especially for music with three or more voices (Huron, 1991a).

Independence of voices is also affected by "harmonicity." This principle describes the mechanism by which the partials of periodic sounds are grouped into unified auditory events. Specifically, frequencies that fall along the harmonic series tend to be fused (DeWitt & Crowder, 1987), giving rise to a single pitch sensation and a timbre associated with the spectral composition. In harmonic writing, the same mechanism may partially fuse tones from different voices, which works in opposition to the more general goal of creating independent voices. Such fusion among different tones helps to account for our perception of chords as higher-order musical units. In voice-leading practice, however, it is often desirable to avoid strong fusion effects in the interest of emphasizing the melodic component of individual voices.

The pitch intervals that most promote tonal fusion are the unison, octave, and perfect fifth (perfect consonances). For music that is composed to emphasize independence of voices, composers appear to avoid tonally fused intervals. Huron (1991b) showed that in the polyphonic writing of J. S. Bach, tonally fused intervals are avoided in direct proportion to the strength with which each interval promotes tonal fusion. Unisons occur less often than octaves, which occur less often than perfect fifths, which occur less often than other intervals. This observation implies a tacit understanding of how tonal fusion can undermine the musical goal of separation of voices.

Like harmonicity, pitch co-modulation (i.e., different voices or pure-tone components that vary similarly in contour and interval size) is used as a cue for unifying the harmonics of individual sound events. Here, tonal fusion is promoted between sounds that have positively correlated pitch motions. The mechanism described by this principle is especially important for unifying the components of sounds that involve inharmonic overtones, which would not be fused by mechanisms attuned merely to harmonicity. Tonal fusion is strongest if pitch motion is precise with respect to log-frequency (i.e., exactly the same shifts in interval size), although any positively correlated pitch motion contributes to tonal fusion.

Again, voice-leading conventions reflect this cognitive principle. Similar pitch motion between two voices is avoided, especially when voices are separated by an interval that promotes tonal fusion (unison, octave, fifth). Although identical or "parallel" pitch motion is particularly eschewed, all cases of similar motion are avoided as a general principle. This general psychological principle is formalized in rules that discourage parallel unisons, octaves, and fifths, and in rules that encourage contrary melodic motion among voices.

The spacing of tones within chords reflects another acoustic principle, namely the association between sensory dissonance and pitch register. Briefly, there is less potential for sensory dissonance between voices in the upper pitch register than between voices in the lower pitch register. Although we often think of certain intervals as consonant (e.g., the perfect fifth) and others as dissonant (e.g., the tritone), sensory dissonance is influenced by pitch register as well as interval size. A more direct measure of sensory dissonance considers the occurrence of interactions among partials, which is related to the concept of a critical band.

A critical band is defined as the range of frequencies within which *masking effects* (in which the presence of one tone affects the audibility of another tone), *loudness summation* (in which overall loudness corresponds to the sum of the amplitude of two tones), and other interactions among frequencies occur. Such interactions are the basis for sensory dissonance. Importantly, critical bandwidth decreases (as measured in log-frequency) as pitch register increases. The result is that a given musical interval (e.g., a major third) yields fewer interactive effects and is therefore associated with less sensory dissonance when that interval is played in a higher pitch register than when it is played in a lower pitch register. This effect is manifested in the spelling of chords; the pitch separation between lower voices is much larger on average than the pitch separation between upper voices (Plomp & Levelt, 1965). This aspect of polyphonic writing may function to maintain a balance of relative consonance and dissonance across pitch regions.

Interestingly, when dissonance between two voices occurs, it is possible to reduce its salience by emphasizing the melodic structure within which the dissonant tones occur. This may be accomplished by adhering more assiduously to the principles that enhance auditory stream segregation. When stream segregation is enhanced, tonal fusion and dissonance are inhibited (Wright & Bregman, 1987).

To summarize, the connection between voice-leading conventions and auditory scene analysis exemplifies multiple ways in which musical practice and basic cognitive mechanisms intersect. The connection also helps to explain how listeners perceive melodies within a harmonic context. Mechanisms of auditory stream segregation allow listeners to track individual melodies and voices, whereas tonal fusion emphasizes harmonic structure and the combining of individual voices into a unitary event (a chord). Other perceptual principles and their relation to rules of voice leading are outlined by Huron (2001). Cognitive principles other than those related to auditory scene analysis (e.g., short-term memory limitations) are also relevant to voice-leading practices, but are beyond the scope of this review.

Rhythm

Investigations of the perception and cognition of musical time include examinations of the limits of temporal discrimination, studies of temporal expectancies (e.g., *when* the next musical event will occur), and experiments that test listeners' experience of time in long musical passages. Most studies, however, focus on the perception of rhythm. Rhythm perception is strongly influenced by the inter-onset interval (IOI), which is the time between the onset of one tone and the onset of the next tone.

Experiences of rhythm, like experiences of pitch, are partly shaped by cognitive constraints. For example, listeners perceive temporal organization most readily when IOIs fall within a limited range. If IOIs are much less than 100 ms, listeners tend to hear the sequence as one continuous event; if they are greater than 1500 ms, listeners tend to hear a sequence of disconnected events. For temporal patterns involving IOIs between 100 and 1500 ms, listeners tend to perceive rhythmic patterns of up to 5 seconds in duration, which is the approximate limit of auditory sensory memory (Darwin, Turvey, & Crowder, 1972). Thus, cognitive constraints limit the range of IOIs within rhythmic patterns as well as the duration of rhythmic patterns.

Lerdahl and Jackendoff (1983) made a useful distinction between meter and grouping, which can be viewed as distinct aspects of rhythm. Meter refers to regular cycles of strong and weak accents. Listeners are highly sensitive to meter, and associate strong accents with phrase boundaries (Palmer & Krumhansl, 1987a, 1987b). Accent strength is determined by changes in intensity, note density, and musical structure (e.g., pitch contour, tonality). Listeners show a bias to hear metrical interpretations (alternations of strong and weak beats) as binary, even when sequences are ternary (Vos, 1978). More generally, small-integer ratios of durations (e.g., sequences that contain only quarter notes and eighth notes) are easier to process than more complex rhythms. Meter is hierarchically organized, with cycles at one level (e.g., groups of two beats) nested within cycles at higher levels (e.g., groups of four beats). Listeners tend to perceive one level of the metric hierarchy as more salient than others. Some models of meter identify this level as the *tactus*, or the level at which it is most natural to tap one's foot.

Metrical patterns are recognized and reproduced more accurately than nonmetrical patterns (e.g., Bharucha & Pryor, 1986; Essens, 1995). Moreover, perceptual asymmetries, similar to those noted above for pitch, are evident for rhythm. When listeners are asked to discriminate two patterns— one metrical and one nonmetrical—performance is better when the metrical pattern is presented first and the nonmetrical pattern second, compared to when the identical patterns are presented in the reverse order (Bharucha & Pryor, 1986). This response pattern implies that metrical frameworks facilitate the efficiency with which auditory temporal patterns are processed and represented. It is relatively easy to detect alterations to metrical patterns because they have relatively stable representations. Metrical patterns also place less demand on attentional resources compared to nonmetrical patterns, because they provide a frame of reference within which rhythmic structure can be processed and represented (Keller, 1999).

Grouping refers to perceived associations between events. As with metrical structure, temporal grouping structure is hierarchically organized, with small groups of two or three notes nested within larger groups, such as phrases. At the highest level of the hierarchy are groups corresponding to sections and movements of music. Empirical studies generally support the psychological reality of grouping structure in music (Deliege, 1987). The grouping mechanisms associated with music perception appear to be general cognitive mechanisms that are also implicated in the processing of speech and other auditory stimuli (Patel et al., 1998).

Although both meter and grouping are hierarchically structured, they need not coincide with each other. Rhythm is defined as the interaction between meter and grouping. Remarkably, there is little psychological work on this interaction; instead, researchers have examined these aspects of rhythm separately. Empirical studies have confirmed that listeners are sensitive to both metrical and grouping structure.

One issue examined in studies of rhythm is the concept of the musical pulse, which is related to meter and can be measured in cycles per minute. Fraisse (1982) noted that three distinct temporal phenomena (walking pace, heart rate, sucking rate in newborns) tend to have a rate of between 60 and 120 events per minute, a range that also includes the tempi of most pieces of music. The implication is that music may be linked to physiological motion. This link is manifested explicitly when listeners dance or tap to music. Early evidence for the link was provided by Gabrielsson (1973a, 1973b), who reported that judgments of the similarity between rhythmic patterns are strongly affected by a perceptual dimension related to movement. Other support for a link between music and physiological motion was provided by Kronman and Sundberg (1987), who showed that ritards in music have a close correspondence with deceleration when walking or running. Finally, research suggests that a listener's arousal level becomes higher after listening to fast-tempo music than after listening to slow-tempo music (Husain, Thompson & Schellenberg, 2002; Thompson, Schellenberg & Husain, 2001)

Several models of rhythm have been proposed, each designed to capture a particular aspect of rhythm perception. Some existing models consider only temporal cues to meter, such as onset times and durations, ignoring influences of pitch, phrasing, and harmony on the perception of rhythm. Parncutt's (1994) model assumes cognitive biases for certain metrical experiences. In particular, certain levels in the metrical hierarchy are assumed to be more salient than others, with a bias towards the metrical level that approximates the *tactus*.

Another question concerns the kinds of neural units that might be involved in tracking the meter of complex music. In Large and Jones' (1999) model, meter is tracked using a small set of oscillatory neural units that vary from each other in their natural resonance. Because the oscillators are able to adjust their phase and period to external periodicities, units with natural resonances closest to existing periodicities lock on and track the tempo (see also McAuley & Jones, 2003). Related to this issue is the question of how simple patterns (i.e., small-integer ratios of duration) are represented in memory when the durations and periodicities of actual performances are highly variable. In order to account for this *quantization problem*, Desain's (1992) connectionist model assumes that rhythmic experiences are biased towards temporal patterns defined by small integer ratios.

Some researchers have examined the extent to which pitch and rhythm interact in perception and memory. This question may be relevant to music educators because pitch and rhythmic skills are often assessed separately in traditional pedagogical exercises, implying distinct cognitive mechanisms for processing these dimensions. Music theory also suggests a separation between rhythm and pitch. For example, the Schenkerian reduction technique for analyzing tonal works assumes that surface temporal relations operate independently of pitch structure.

Results on this issue suggest that pitch and rhythm interact at some levels of processing, but operate independently at other levels. Jones, Boltz and Kidd (1982) reported that rhythmically accented tones in a melody are better recognized than unaccented tones. Similarly, if pitch and rhythm patterns imply different metrical groupings, memory for melodic sequences is generally poor (Boltz & Jones, 1986; Deutsch, 1980). Such findings suggest that pitch and rhythm are integrated in memory for music. Additional evidence for non-independence of pitch and rhythm processing comes from a study that required listeners to rate the emotionality (i.e., happiness, sadness, scariness) of melodies (Schellenberg, Krysciak, & Campbell, 2001). The melodies' pitch and rhythmic properties proved to be interactive in their influence on listeners' ratings.

Other researchers contend, however, that pitch and rhythm are processed independently. In some experiments, pitch and rhythm have made statistically independent contributions to judgments of melodic similarity (Monahan & Carterette, 1985), and to ratings of phrase completion (Palmer & Krumhansl, 1987a, 1987b). Moreover, memory for the pitch and rhythm patterns of a short melody is far better than memory for how those features are combined. Thompson (1994) presented listeners with two test melodies followed by two comparison melodies. The task was to indicate if the two comparison melodies were identical to the two test melodies, disregarding the order in which the melodies occurred. In one condition, participants performed a distractor task as the melodies were presented. In another condition, participants listened attentively to the melodies. When the comparison melodies involved a novel pitch pattern or a rhythm that was not present in the test melodies, performance was highly accurate for participants in both conditions. When the comparison melodies were constructed by combining the pitch pattern of one test melody with the rhythm of the other test melody (or vice versa), however, distracted participants performed poorly.

That is, distracted participants were relatively insensitive to the manner in which pitch and rhythm were combined.

Neuropsychological studies provide converging evidence that pitch and rhythm are processed separately. Whereas some brain-damaged patients exhibit normal pitch perception but impaired rhythm perception, other patients show the opposite pattern. One patient who sustained a lesion in the left temporal lobe was unable to discriminate between sequences differing in temporal structure, but he had no difficulty in discriminating between sequences differing in pitch structure. By contrast, another patient with damage to the right temporal lobe showed the opposite pattern of discrimination skills. Such impairments suggest that some areas of the brain are responsible for processing pitch, whereas other neuronally distinct areas are responsible for processing rhythm (Peretz, 1996; Peretz & Kolinsky, 1993; Peretz & Morais, 1989).

Recent evidence suggests that rhythmic qualities of speech, which are often dinstinguishing characteristics of different languages, exert a "gravitational pull" on rhythmic qualities of music (Patel & Daniele, 2003; Patel, Iversen, & Rosenberg, 2004). Analyzing melodic themes from the turn of the 20th century, Patel and his colleagues made two observations. First, adjacent notes in English melodies are characterized by a greater degree of durational contrast than adjacent notes in French melodies. Second, adjacent intervals in English melodies are characterized by a greater degree of intervallic difference than adjacent intervals in French melodies. The authors argued that these rhythmic qualities in melodies arise from composers' familiarity with the rhythmic qualities their language. As evidence for their claim, they showed that adjacent vowels in English sentences tend to differ more in duration than do adjacent vowels in French sentences, and consecutive pitch movements between syllables in English sentences tend to differ more from each other than do consecutive pitch movements between adjacent syllables in French sentences. (For more extensive discussions of rhythm, see Clarke, 1999 or Krumhansl, 2000a.)

Timbre

Timbre is notoriously difficult to define. It is often described as the attribute distinguishing sounds that are equivalent in pitch, duration, and loudness. Timbre is influenced by the pattern of partials that are present in complex waveforms, and how those partials change over time (i.e., *transient* or *dynamic* attributes). A sawtooth waveform, which contains all harmonics, has a timbre that is distinct from a square waveform, which contains only odd-numbered harmonics. The sound of a plucked instrument such as a harp has a relatively rapid amplitude onset, whereas the sound of a bowed instrument such as a violin has a more gradual onset. In naturally occurring sounds, inharmonic partials (i.e., partials with a frequency equal to a non-integer multiple of the fundamental) also affect timbre. When inharmonic partials are removed from a piano note, for example, the note sounds artificial and unfamiliar.

For many instruments, the fundamental frequency has the greatest intensity of all harmonics in the frequency spectrum. Intensity typically decreases for higher frequency components. An inverse relationship between harmonic number and intensity (called *spectral rolloff*) does not hold for all instruments, however. For some instruments, certain harmonics may be disproportionately intense, giving that instrument its unique timbral character. A "bright" sounding tone, such as that produced by a clarinet, typically contains high-frequency harmonics sounded at relatively high amplitudes.

When other aspects of a tone are held constant, differences in the frequency spectrum are associated with differences in timbre. We know, however, that the frequency spectrum is not entirely responsible for timbre, because tones with very different spectra can be perceived as having the same timbre. For example, examination of the frequency spectrum for a note played very softly on a trumpet reveals that most of the partials associated with trumpet sounds are absent. Nonetheless, the note is still perceived as emanating from a trumpet. More generally, the frequency spectrum associated with a given instrument may be quite different for soft and loud sounds despite their perceptual invariance.

Figure 3.8 provides an illustration of the dimensions of a musical instrument associated with its perceived timbre. The figure shows the partials that are present, their relative intensity, and how their intensity changes over time. For this particular instrument—a clarinet—the constituent frequency components vary in intensity at approximately the same rate. For other instruments, such as a piano, different partials change intensity at different rates. In many instances, onset or "attack" cues (i.e., transient cues during the initial portion of the spectrum) are important for perceiving timbre.

Formants are also thought to influence the perception of timbre. A formant is a range of frequencies with high amplitude relative to other frequencies, which is a consequence of the resonant properties of the sound source (e.g., the body of an acoustic guitar). Formants correspond to local peaks in a frequency spectrum. Fixed-frequency formants are particularly interesting because they remain relatively constant across the tessitura of an instrument. Whereas individual partials of a sound provide information about timbre by their relation to each other and to the fundamental frequency, fixed-frequency formants are resonant frequencies that do not change in proportion with changes in overall pitch. The harmonics that fall within the formant region resonate louder than other frequencies, giving the sound (e.g., a musical instrument) its particular timbral character.

Hajda, Kendall, Carterette, & Harshberger (1997) describe various methods that have been used to identify the acoustic properties that influence the perception of timbre. These include identification tasks (*name that timbre*),

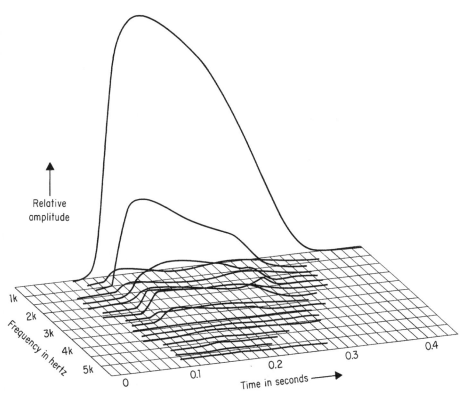

Figure 3.8. Transient attributes of sound. Frequency is displayed as a function of time and intensity.

grouping and classification tasks (*match similar sounding timbres*), semantic rating scales (*rate how bright or dull a timbre sounds*), discrimination tasks (*are two timbres the same or different?*), and various types of similar ratings (*rate how similar two timbres sound*). In a classic experiment, Grey (1977) asked musically trained listeners to provide similarity ratings for pairs of notes, which came from a set of nine different instrumental timbres. Notes were presented with the same fundamental frequency, intensity, and duration so that they varied only in timbre. His analysis revealed that three distinct dimensions could account for a good portion of the variance in similarity ratings.

Various follow-up studies have yielded different results regarding the underlying dimensions that influence the perception of timbre. In almost all cases, "brightness" appears to be a significant perceptual dimension. Instruments with a wide range of spectral energy (e.g., oboe) are perceived as having a brighter timbral character than instruments with a more restricted range of spectral energy (e.g., french horn). The influence of onsets (attacks) and other temporal properties—important in some studies but not in others—depends on the specific timbres used in the stimulus set and the duration of the stimuli (see Hajda et al., 1997).

Another way to identify acoustic attributes that are essential to instrument identification is to simplify the waveforms of instrumental notes without fundamentally changing the perceived timbre. Grey and Moorer (1977) showed that removing certain acoustic properties does not significantly affect judgments of instrument timbre. For example, removing amplitude and frequency modulations of individual partials resulted in subtle changes to timbre, but these manipulations did not alter the perceived instrument associated with the sound.

Yet another approach is to examine how readily tone sequences involving different timbres form separate auditory streams. Iverson (1995) presented listeners with sequences consisting of two different orchestral tones and asked them to rate the extent to which one or two sequences were being played. Auditory stream segregation was influenced by differences in both static spectra (the pattern of partials present) and dynamic attributes. Moreover, the results converged with similarity judgments obtained by Iverson and Krumhansl (1993) on the same tones. That is, similarity judgments predicted the extent to which timbres segregated into separate auditory streams, with similar timbres less likely than dissimilar timbres to split into separate streams.

How rapidly do listeners register timbre? Robinson and Patterson (1995) tested the limits of listeners' ability to identify the timbre and pitch of tones that varied in duration. Whereas identification of pitch proved to be a function of duration, identification of timbre was independent of duration. Listeners required several complete cycles of a periodic signal to identify pitch accurately, but only one or two cycles (i.e., milliseconds) to identify timbre. These results make intuitive sense when one considers that pitch is determined by frequency (number of cycles per second). Therefore, a listener needs to hear several cycles in order to determine how rapidly a cycle repeats. By contrast, one or two cycles of a tone contain information about the components present in the frequency spectrum, which allow for identification of timbre.

In a related investigation, researchers tested the limits of listeners' ability to identify recordings (Schellenberg, Iverson, & McKinnon, 1999). In an experimental version of *Name That Tune* (the song-identification game played on TV and radio), listeners matched extremely brief excerpts (100 or 200 ms) from recordings of popular songs with the song titles and artists. Listeners' performance was better than chance with excerpts of 1/5 of a second. Performance deteriorated with shorter excerpts (1/10 of a second) but was still better than chance. Other manipulations involved low-pass and high-pass filtering, and playing the excerpts backward. Performance fell to chance levels for the low-pass-filtered and backward excerpts, but was unaffected by high-pass filtering. In short, successful identification of the recordings required the presence of dynamic, high-frequency spectral information. Note that the excerpts were too brief to convey any relational information (re: pitch and duration), and that the absolute pitch of the excerpts would be identical whether they were played backward or forward. Thus, successful performance presumably stemmed from accurate and detailed memory of the recordings' timbres, which consisted of many complex tones from many different instruments.

By definition, timbre and pitch are different. Nonetheless, some studies suggest that timbre and pitch are not perceived independently. For example, it is easier to judge whether two tones (Crowder, 1989), two chords (Beal, 1985), or two melodies (Radvansky, Fleming, & Simmons, 1995) are the same when standard and comparison stimuli are played on identical rather than different musical instruments. This finding suggests that—despite our experience of pitch and timbre as distinct musical qualities—they interact with each other in music processing.

Krumhansl and Iverson (1993) used another approach to study interactions between pitch and timbre. Participants were asked to classify stimulus items into two groups as quickly as possible based on a specified "target" attribute (e.g., pitch). Not only did the target attribute vary; an irrelevant attribute (e.g., timbre) also varied from trial to trial. Performance on the categorization task was relatively good when variation in the irrelevant attribute was correlated with variation in the target attribute, but relatively poor when variation in the irrelevant attribute was uncorrelated with variation in the target attribute. That is, subjects were unable to attend to the pitch of a tone without being affected by its timbre, or vice versa. This finding provides converging evidence that pitch and timbre are not perceptually separable from each other.

Although pitch and timbre may be integrated successfully at some points in the information-processing system, listeners can also become confused about the ways in which pitches and timbres are combined. In one experiment, participants listened for particular combinations of pitch and timbre in arrays of tones that were presented simultaneously but emanated from different locations in the auditory field (Hall, Pastore, Acker, & Huang, 2000). An examination of errors indicated that participants often perceived an *illusory conjunction* of pitch and timbre. That is, participants often heard the timbre of one tone combined with the pitch of another tone. Estimates of illusory conjunction rate ranged from 23% to 40%. The findings provide evidence that after an initial stage in which individual features of musical tones are registered (e.g., pitch, timbre), there is a stage in which these separately registered features are integrated (feature integration). Illusory conjunctions arise when errors occur at the *feature-integration* stage of processing.

What is the relation between timbre and harmony? The principle of harmonicity, outlined by Bregman (1990), suggests that partials that fall along the harmonic series of a single note are fused together, such that listeners perceive the distinct timbral qualities of each note holistically. When two instruments play the same note, or two different notes with many harmonics in common, there may be some confusion in this process. Such fusion effects actually contribute to our perception of harmony. For example, if one plays two piano notes separated by a fifth, those two notes have several partials in common. Perceptual mechanisms will tend to fuse or "con-fuse" some of the components of the two different notes, giving rise to emergent timbral effects. Compositions by Debussy exemplify the varied timbral effects of combining tones.

Although pitch and rhythmic relations are usually considered to define musical structure, some contemporary composers and theorists (e.g., Lerdahl, 1987; Slawson, 1985) have considered the possibility that timbre might be used compositionally in a way that is analogous to the use of pitch. One challenge with this compositional approach is that timbre has a powerful influence on auditory stream segregation. Thus, any large shift in timbre is likely to signal a separate auditory stream, which would conflict with the goal of creating a coherent sequence analogous to a melody. Nonetheless, changes in timbre that correspond to reductions in sensory dissonance (i.e., fewer harmonics falling within a critical band)—and increases in fusion—may be perceived as a change from *tension* to *release,* which commonly occurs at points of musical closure (Pressnitzer, McAdams, Winsberg, & Fineberg, 2000). In other words, changes from relatively dissonant to relatively consonant timbres have some of the resolving properties of a perfect cadence. Moreover, it is clear that timbre has a profound influence on our appreciation of music. For example, imagine a piano piece composed by Chopin performed by a horn section, or a song by U2 played on an accordion. Such changes in instrumentation would undoubtedly affect our experience of the music.

Conclusion

At the outset, we identified the nature-nurture controversy as one of the most contentious issues in the psychology of music, as it is in the field of psychology as a whole. We argued that experiences of music are shaped by a combination of enculturation and cognitive constraints. We cited numerous sources of evidence for psychological constraints on music experience. Such constraints include working-memory limitations, sensitivity to sensory consonance and dissonance, the perceptual salience of pitch contours, perceptual grouping as a function of proximity, predispositions that favor simple meters and rhythms, processing biases for intervals with small-integer ratios, and reliable memories for the absolute pitch and timbre of frequently encountered auditory stimuli. Even rules of counterpoint and voice leading are strongly linked to cognitive constraints.

Influences of enculturation were also implicated throughout our review. A listener learns about her native musical system through formal training or from simple exposure. This knowledge then influences music cognition in several ways, acting in conjunction with unlearned factors. Examples of learning include the development of sensitivity to the hierarchy of various scale steps in music, and to the harmonies that are implied when listening to melodies. Even our expectations of what will happen next in a melody are shaped by implicit memory for music to which we have been passively exposed. In some cases, enculturation may actually overwhelm or reduce initial predispositions.

Distinguishing innate from learned factors in music perception and cognition is challenging because cognitive predispositions not only affect listeners' perceptions of music, they also affect music composition and hence musical structure. Exposure to musical structure, in turn, shapes listeners' perceptions, in that listeners internalize persistent regularities in music. What results is a bootstrapping process that entangles innate and learned influences on music perception. As an example, if pitch proximity is a basic principle of perceptual grouping, then most melodies should have a predominance of proximate tones (Dowling & Harwood, 1986). But if listeners are exposed repeatedly to melodies with an abundance of pitch proximity, a general expectancy for proximate tones could result from learning. Infant studies have provided a valuable technique for disentangling innate and learned influences on music perception.

Although extreme versions of cultural determinism have been proposed (Walker, 1996), the enormous body of evidence for cognitive constraints on music processing is far too compelling to dismiss. In this regard, it should be emphasized that the existence of innate processing abilities and biases need not limit our ability to appreciate or perceive music, because effects of learning and enculturation allow us to develop preferences and schemata that extend beyond our initial predispositions. Conversely, natural processing abilities allow our appreciation of music to extend beyond the limits of individual enculturation. For example, by attending to basic perceptual cues, Western listeners are able to appreciate emotional meaning in Hindustani ragas, even if they have never been exposed to such music and have no knowledge of the raga-rasa system (Balkwill & Thompson, 1999; 2004).

Although listeners are able to appreciate music from other cultures, existing evidence on innate processing abilities cannot account for the enormous diversity and complexity of musical styles both within and across cultures. No list of processing biases can readily account for the innovation and complexity of Bach fugues, serialized music, or Hindustani ragas. This complexity can only be explained in terms of a uniquely human mode of enculturation in which modifications of cultural traditions are accumulated over time (Tomasello, 1999). The music of Bach and Mozart was not invented in its entirety at a single point in time. Rather, other composers invented related versions of these styles, and these versions were then modified. This process of *cumulative cultural evolution* requires not only creative invention but also accurate transmission (i.e., learning) of existing innovations. Accurate transmission of a musical composition or style—whether through demonstration or recorded in notation—allows individuals to build upon existing levels of complexity. What results within each culture is an accumulation of modifications, leading to diverse range of musical styles within and between cultures. Underlying all of these unique styles, however, are the processing biases and predispositions that have fascinated scholars for over a hundred years.

STUDY QUESTIONS

1. Debates in music cognition tend to center on a small number of contentious issues. Discuss two of these issues.

2. Helmholtz observed that certain aspects of music have parallels in physical acoustics. Provide a critical review of his observations.

3. Summarize and evaluate an example of empirical evidence that sensitivity to sensory consonance and dissonance is innate.

4. Describe the research that led to the Mel scale, and discuss its significance.

5. Describe recent research suggesting that the skill of "absolute pitch" may be more prevalent than previously believed.

6. Why is melodic contour so easy to remember?

7. Describe similarities and differences between music and speech prosody, and discuss the implications of this comparison.

8. Describe the two ways that melodies are simplified according to Lerdahl and Jackendoff's theory of reductional structure.

9. When does sensitivity to implied harmony develop? What evidence was used to reach this conclusion?

10. Discuss how general principles of auditory scene analysis might play a critical role in voice-leading practices.

11. Discuss evidence for and against the view that pitch and rhythm are processed independently.

12. Outline the major acoustic properties that influence the perception of timbre.

REFERENCES

Allen, D. (1967). Octave discriminability of musical and non-musical subjects. *Psychonomic Science, 7,* 421–422.

Auhagen, W. & Vos, P. G. (2000). Experimental methods in tonality induction research: A review. *Music Perception, 17,* 417–436.

Balkwill, L. L. & Thompson, W. F. (1999). A cross-cultural investigation of the perception of emotion in music: Psychophysical and cultural cues. *Music Perception, 17*(1), 43–64.

Balkwill, L-L & Thompson, W. F. & Matsunaga, R. (2004). Recognition of emotion in Japanese, Western, and Hindustani music by Japanese listeners. *Japanese Psychological Research, 46*(4), 337–349.

Balzano, G. J. (1980). The group-theoretic description of 12-fold and microtonal pitch systems. *Computer Music Journal, 4,* 66–84.

Beal, A. L. (1985). The skill of recognizing musical structures. *Memory & Cognition, 13,* 405–412.

Bharucha, J. J., & Pryor, J. H. (1986). Disrupting the isochrony underlying rhythm: An asymmetry in discrimination. *Perception and Psychophysics, 40*(3), 137–141.

Boltz, M., & Jones, M. R. (1986). Does rule recursion make melodies easier to reproduce? If not, what does? *Cognitive Psychology, 18,* 389–431.

Bregman, A. S. (1990). *Auditory scene analysis: The perceptual organization of sound.* Cambridge, MA: MIT Press.

Brown, H. (1988). The interplay of set content and temporal context in a functional theory of tonality perception. *Music Perception, 5,* 219–250.

Brown, H., & Butler, D. (1981). Diatonic trichords as minimal tonal cue-cells. *In Theory Only, 5,* 37–55.

Browne, R. (1981). Tonal implications of the diatonic set. *In Theory Only, 5,* 3–21.

Burns, E. M. (1999). Intervals, scales, and tuning. In D. Deutsch (Ed.), *The psychology of music* (2nd ed., pp. 215–264). San Diego: Academic Press.

Butler, D. (1989). Describing the perception of tonality in music: A critique of the tonal hierarchy theory and a proposal for a theory of intervallic rivalry. *Music Perception, 6,* 219–242.

Cohen, A. J. (1991). Tonality and perception: Musical scales primed by excerpts from 'The Well Tempered Clavier' of J. S. Bach. *Psychological Research, 53,* 305–314.

Cooper, R. P., & Aslin, R. N. (1990). Preference for infant-directed speech in the first month after birth. *Child Development, 61,* 1584–1595.

Crowder, R. G. (1989). Imagery for musical timbre. *Journal of Experimental Psychology: Human Perception and Performance, 15,* 472–478.

Crowder, R. G. (1993). Auditory memory. In S. McAdams & E. Bigand (Eds.), *Thinking in Sound: The Cognitive Psychology of Human Audition* (pp. 113–145). Oxford: Oxford University Press, Clarendon Press.

Cuddy, L. L., & Badertscher, B. (1987). Recovery of the tonal hierarchy: Some comparisons across age and levels of musical experience. *Perception & Psychophysics, 41,* 609–620.

Cuddy, L. L., & Lunney, C. A. (1995). Expectancies generated by melodic intervals: Perceptual judgments of melodic continuity. *Perception & Psychophysics, 57,* 451–462.

Cuddy, L. L., & Thompson, W. F. (1992). Asymmetry of perceived key movement in chorale sequences: Converging evidence from a probe-tone investigation. *Psychological Research, 54,* 51–59.

Darwin, C. J., Turvey, M. T., & Crowder, R. G. (1972). An auditory analogue of the Sperling partial report procedure: Evidence for brief auditory storage. *Cognitive Psychology, 3,* 255–267.

Deliège, I. (1987). Grouping conditions in listening to music: An approach to Lerdahl & Jackendoff's grouping preference rules. *Music Perception, 4,* 325–360.

Demany, L. & Armand, F. (1984). The perceptual reality of tone chroma in early infancy. *Journal of the Acoustical Society of America, 76,* 57–66.

Desain, P. (1992). A (de)composable theory of rhythm perception. *Music Perception, 9,* 439–454.

Deutsch, D. (1999a). Grouping mechanisms in music. In Diana Deutsch (Ed.), *The Psychology of Music* (2nd ed.). New York: Academic Press.

Deutsch, D. (1999b). The processing of pitch combinations. In Diana Deutsch (Ed.), *The Psychology of Music* (2nd ed.). New York: Academic Press.

DeWitt, L. A., & Crowder, R. G. (1987). Tonal fusion of consonant musical intervals: The oomph in Stumpf. *Perception & Psychophysics, 41,* 73–84.

Dissanayake, E. (2000). Antecedents of the temporal arts in early mother-infant interactions. In N. L. Wallin, B. Merker, & S. Brown (Eds.). *The origins of music* (pp. 388–410). Cambridge, MA: MIT Press

Dowling, W. J. (1994). Melodic contour in hearing and remembering melodies. In R. Aiello & J. A. Sloboda (Eds.), *Musical perceptions* (pp. 173–190). New York: Oxford University Press.

Dowling, W. J., & Harwood, D. L. (1986). *Music cognition.* Orlando, FL: Academic Press.

Dyson, M. C., & Watkins, A. J. (1984). A figural approach to the role of meldic contour in melody recognition. *Perception & Psychophysics, 35,* 477–488.

Essens, P. J. (1995). Structuring temporal sequences: Comparison of models and factors of complexity. *Perception and Psychophysics, 57*(4), 519–532.

Fernald, A. (1985). Four-month-olds prefer to listen to motherese. *Infant Behavior and Development, 8,* 181–195.

Fernald, A. (1991). Prosody in speech to children: Prelinguistic and linguistic functions. *Annals of Child Development, 8,* 43–80.

Fernald, A., Taeschner, T., Dunn, J., Papousek, M., de Boysson-Bardies, B., & Fukui, I. (1989). A cross-language study of prosodic modifications in mothers' and fathers' speech to preverbal infants. *Journal of Child Language, 16,* 477–501.

Fodor, J. A. (1983). *The modularity of mind.* Cambridge, MA: MIT Press.

Garner, W. R. (1974). *The processing of information and structure.* Potomac, MD: Erlbaum.

Grey, J. M. (1977). Multidimensional perceptual scaling of musical timbres. *Journal of the Acoustical Society of America, 61,* 1270–1277.

Grey, J. M. & Moorer, J. A. (1977). Perceptual evaluations of synthesized musical instrument tones. *Journal of the Acoustical Society of America, 62,* 454–462.

Hajda, J. M., Kendall, R. A., Carterette, E. C., & Harshberger, M. L. (1997). Methodological issues in timbre research. In I. Deliège & J. Sloboda (Eds.), *Perception and cognition of music* (pp. 253–306). East Sussex, UK: Psychology Press.

Hall, M. D., Pastore, R. E., Acker, B. E., & Huang, W. (2000). Evidence for auditory feature integration with spatially distributed items. *Perception & Psychophysics, 62,* 1243–1257.

Halpern, A. R. (1989). Memory for the absolute pitch of familiar songs. *Memory & Cognition, 17,* 572–581.

Helmholtz, L. F. von (1954). *On the sensations of tone as a physiological basis for the theory of music* (A. J. Ellis, Ed. & Trans.). New York: Dover. (Original work published 1863).

Howe, M. J. A., Davidson, J. W., & Sloboda, J. A. (1998). Innate talents: Reality or myth? *Behavioral and Brain Sciences, 21,* 399–442.

Humphreys, L. F. (1939). Generalization as a function of method of reinforcement. *Journal of Experimental Psychology, 25,* 361–372.

Husain, G., Thompson, W. F. & Schellenberg, E. G. (2002). Effects of musical tempo and mode on arousal, mood, and spatial abilities: Re-examination of the "Mozart effect". *Music Perception, 20*(20), 151–171.

Huron, D. (2001). Tone and voice: A derivation of the rules of voice leading from perceptual principles. *Music Perception,* 19(1), 1–64.

Huron, D. (1991a). The avoidance of part-crossing in polyphonic music: Perceptual evidence and musical practice. *Music Perception, 9,* 93–104.

Huron, D. (1991b). Tonal consonance versus tonal fusion in polyphonic sonorities. *Music Perception, 9,* 135–154.

Ilie, G. & Thompson, W. F. (in press). A comparison of acoustic cues in music and speech for three dimensions of affect, *Music Perception.*

Iverson, P. (1995). Auditory stream segregation by musical timbre: Effects of static and dynamic acoustic attributes. *Journal of Experimental Psychology: Human Perception and Performance, 21,* 751–763.

Jones, M. R., & Boltz, M. (1989). Dynamic attention and responses to time. *Psychological Review, 96,* 459–491.

Kallman, H. J. (1982). Octave equivalence as measured by similarity ratings. *Perception & Psychophysics, 32,* 37–49.

Kronman, U., & Sundberg, J. (1987). Is the musical ritard an allusion to physical motion? In A. Gabrielsson (Ed.), *Action and Perception in Rhythm and Music* (pp. 57–68). Stockholm: Publications issued by the Royal Swedish Academy of Music, No. 55.

Krumhansl, C. L. (1995). Music psychology and music theory: Problems and prospects. *Music Theory Spectrum, 17,* 53–80.

Krumhansl, C. L. (1979). The psychological representation of musical pitch in a tonal context. *Cognitive Psychology, 11,* 346–374.

Krumhansl, C. L. (1990). *Cognitive foundations of musical pitch.* Oxford: Oxford University Press.

Krumhansl, C. L. (2000a). Rhythm and pitch in music cognition. *Psychological Bulletin, 126,* 159–179.

Krumhansl, C. L. (2000b). Tonality induction: A statistical approach applied cross-culturally. *Music Perception, 17,* 461–480.

Krumhansl, C. L., & Iverson, P. (1992). Perceptual interactions between musical pitch and timbre. *Journal of Experimental Psychology: Human Perception and Performance, 18,* 739–751.

Krumhansl, C. L., & Jusczyk, P. W. (1990). Infants' perception of phrase structure in music. *Psychological Science, 1,* 70–73.

Krumhansl, C. L., & Keil, F. C. (1982). Acquisition of the hierarchy of tonal functions in music. *Memory & Cognition, 10,* 243–251.

Krumhansl, C. L., & Kessler, E. (1982). Tracing the dynamic changes in perceived tonal organization in a spatial representation of musical keys. *Psychological Review, 89,* 334–368.

Krumhansl, C. L., & Shepard, R. N. (1979). Quantification of the hierarchy of tonal functions within a diatonic context. *Journal of Experimental Psychology: Human Perception and Performance, 5,* 579–594.

Large, E. W., & Jones, M. R. (1999). The dynamics of attending: How we track time-varying events. *Psychological Review, 106,* 119–159.

Leahey, T. H. (1997). *A history of psychology* (4th ed.). Upper Saddle River, NJ: Prentice Hall.

Leman, M. (2000). An auditory model of the role of short-term memory in probe-tone ratings. *Music Perception, 17,* 481–510.

Lerdahl, F. (1987). Timbral hierarchies. *Contemporary Music Review, 2,* 135–160.

Lerdahl, F., & Jackendoff, R. (1983). *A generative theory of tonal music.* Cambridge, MA: MIT Press.

Levitin, D. J. (1994). Absolute memory for musical pitch: Evidence from the production of learned melodies. *Perception & Psychophysics, 56,* 414–423.

Levitin, D. J. (1999). Memory for musical attributes. In P. R. Cook (Ed.) *Music, cognition, and computerized sound* (pp. 209–227). Cambridge, MA: MIT Press.

Levitin, D. J., & Cook, P. R. (1996). Memory for musical tempo: Additional evidence that auditory memory is absolute. *Perception & Psychophysics, 58,* 927–935.

Levitin, D. J. & Rogers, S. E. (2005). Absolute pitch: perception, coding, and controversies. *Trends in Cognitive Science, 9*(1), 26–33.

McAdams, S. (2004a). Problem-solving strategies in music composition: A case study. *Music Perception, 21,* 391–429.

McAdams, S. (2004b). Prolog. In D. J. Levitin (Ed.) The Angel of Death Project. *Music Perception, 22,* 171–172.

McAuley, J. D., & Jones, M. R. (2003). Modeling Effects of Rhythmic Context on Perceived Duration: A Comparison of Interval and Entrainment Approaches to Short-Interval Timing. *Journal of Experimental Psychology: Human Perception and Performance, 29,* 1102–1125.

Meyer, L. (1973). *Explaining music: Essays and explorations.* Chicago: University of Chicago Press.

Miller, G. A. (1956). The magical number seven, plus or minus two: Some limits on our capacity for processing information. *Psychological Review, 63,* 81–97.

Miyazaki, K. (1993). Absolute pitch as an inability: Identification of musical intervals in a tonal context. *Music Perception, 11,* 55–72.

Morton, D. (1976). *The traditional music of Thailand.* Los Angeles: University of California Press.

Narmour, E. (1990). *The analysis and cognition of basic melodic structures.* Chicago: University of Chicago Press.

Narmour, E. (1992). *The analysis and cognition of melodic complexity.* Chicago: University of Chicago Press.

Oram, N., & Cuddy, L. L. (1995). Responsiveness of Western adults to pitch-distributional information in melodic sequences. *Psychological Research, 57,* 103–118.

Palmer, C. & Krumhansl, C. L. (1987a). Independent temporal and pitch structures in determination of musical phrases. *Journal of Experimental Psychology: Human Perception & Performance, 13,* 116–126.

Palmer, C. & Krumhansl, C. L. (1987b). Pitch and temporal contributions to musical phrase perception. *Perception & Psychophysics, 41,* 116–126.

Parncutt, R. (1994). A perceptual model of pulse salience and metrical accent in musical rhythms. *Music Perception, 11,* 409–464.

Patel, A. D. & Daniele, J. R. (2003). An empirical comparison of rhythm in language and music. *Cognition, 87*:B35–B45.

Patel, A. D., Iversen, J. R., & Rosenberg, J. C. (2004). Comparing rhythm and melody in speech and music: The case of English and French. *Journal of the Acoustical Society of America, 116*:2645.

Patel, A. D., Foxton, J. M. & Griffith, T. D. (in press). Musically tone-deaf individuals have difficulty discriminating intonation contours extracted from speech. *Brain & Cognition.*

Patel, A. D., Peretz, I., Tramo, M., & Labreque, R. (1998). Processing prosodic and music patterns: A neuropsychological investigation. *Brain and Language, 61,* 123–144.

Peretz, I., Gaudreau, D., & Bonnel, A. (1998). Exposure effects on music preference and recognition. *Memory & Cognition, 26,* 884–902.

Plomp, R. & Levelt, W. J. M. (1965). Tonal consonance and critical bandwidth. *Journal of the Acoustical Society of America, 37,* 548–560.

Plomp, R., & Steeneken, J. M. (1969). Effect of phase on the timbre of complex tones. *Journal of the Acoustical Society of America, 46,* 409–421.

Pressnitzer, D., McAdams, S., Winsberg, S., & Fineberg, J. (2000). Perception of musical tension for nontonal orchestral timbres and its relation to psychoacoustic roughness. *Perception & Psychophysics, 62,* 66–80.

Radvansky, G. A., Fleming, K. J., & Simmons, J. A. (1995). Timbre reliance in nonmusicians' and musicians' memory for melodies. *Music Perception, 13,* 127–140.

Reynolds, R. (2004). Compositional Strategies in The Angel of Death for piano, chamber orchestra, and computer-processed sound. *Music Perception, 22*(2), 173–206.

Robinson, K., & Patterson, R. D. (1995). The duration required to identify an instrument, the octave, or the pitch chroma of a musical note. *Music Perception, 13,* 1–15.

Russo, F. & Thompson, W. F. (in press). The subjective size of melodic intervals over a two-octave range. *Psychonomic Bulletin and Review.*

Russo, F. & Thompson, W. F. (2005). An interval size illusion: Extra pitch influences on the perceived size of melodic intervals. *Perception & Psychophysics, 67*(4), 559–568.

Sergeant, D. (1983). The octave: percept or concept? *Psychology of Music, 11,* 3–18.

Schacter, D. L. (1987). Implicit memory: History and current status. *Journal of Experimental Psychology: Learning, Memory, & Cognition, 13,* 501–518.

Schellenberg, E. G. (1996). Expectancy in melody: Tests of the implication-realization model. *Cognition, 58,* 75–125.

Schellenberg, E. G. (1997). Simplifying the implication-realization model of melodic expectancy. *Music Perception, 14,* 295–318.

Schellenberg, E. G., Adachi, M., Purdy, K. T., & McKinnon, M. C. (2002). Expectancy in melody: Tests of children and adults. *Journal of Experimental Psychology: General, 131,* 511–537.

Schellenberg, E. G., & Trainor, L. J. (1996). Sensory consonance and the perceptual similarity of complex-tone harmonic intervals: Tests of adult and infant listeners. *Journal of the Acoustical Society of America, 100,* 3321–3328.

Schellenberg, E. G., & Trehub, S. E. (1996a). Children's discrimination of melodic intervals. *Developmental Psychology, 32,* 1039–1050.

Schellenberg, E. G., & Trehub, S. E. (1996b). Natural intervals in music: A perspective from infant listeners. *Psychological Science, 7,* 272–277.

Schellenberg, E. G., & Trehub, S. E. (1999). Culture-general and culture-specific factors in the discrimination of melodies. *Journal of Experimental Child Psychology, 74,* 107–127.

Serafine, M. L. (1988). *Music as cognition.* New York: Columbia University Press.

Serafine, M. L., Glassman, N., & Overbeeke, C. (1989). The cognitive reality of hierarchic structure in music. *Music Perception, 6,* 397–430.

Shepard, R. N. (1982). Structural representations of musical pitch. In D. Deutsch (Ed.), *The psychology of music* (pp. 343–390). New York: Academic Press.

Shepard, R. N. (1964). Circularity in judgments of relative pitch. *Journal of the Acoustical Society of America, 36,* 2345–2353.

Shepard, R. N. (1999). Pitch perception and measurement. In P. R. Cook (Ed.), *Music, cognition, and computerized sound* (pp. 149–165). Cambridge, MA: MIT Press.

Shepard, R. N., & Jordan, D. C. (1984). Auditory illusions demonstrating that tones are assimilated to an internalized scale. *Science, 226,* 1333–1334.

Slawson, W. (1985). *Sound color.* Berkeley, CA: University of California Press.

Smith, N. A., & Schmuckler, M. A. (2004). The perception of tonal structure through the differentiation and organization of pitches. *Journal of Experimental Psychology: Human Perception and Performance, 30* 268–282.

Takeuchi, A. H., & Hulse, S. H. (1993). Absolute pitch. *Psychological Bulletin, 113,* 345–361.

Terhardt, E., & Seewann, M. (1983). Aural key identification and its relationship to absolute pitch. *Music Perception, 1,* 63–83.

Thompson, W. F. (1996). A review and empirical assessment of Eugene Narmour's *The Analysis and Cognition of Basic Melodic Structures* (1990) and *The Analysis and Cognition of Melodic Complexity* (1992). *Journal of the American Musicological Society,* XLIX (1), 127–145.

Thompson, W. F. (1993). Modeling perceived relationships between melody, harmony, and key. *Perception and Psychophysics, 53,* 13–24.

Thompson, W. F. (1989). Composer-specific aspects of musical performance: An evaluation of Clynes' theory of "pulse" for performances of Mozart and Beethoven. *Music Perception, 7,* 15–42.

Thompson, W. F., Balkwill, L. L., & Vernescu, R. (2000). Expectancies generated by recent exposure to melodic sequences. *Memory & Cognition, 28*(4), 547–555.

Thompson, W. F., & Cuddy, L. L. (1997). Music performance and the perception of key. *Journal of Experimental Psychology: Human Perception and Performance, 23,* 116–135.

Thompson, W. F., & Cuddy, L. L. (1992). Perceived key movement in four-voice harmony and single voices. *Music Perception, 9,* 427–438.

Thompson, W. F., Cuddy, L. L. & Plaus, C. (1997). Expectancies generated by melodic intervals: Evaluation of principles of melodic implication in a melody completion task. *Perception & Psychophysics, 59,* 1069–1076.

Thompson, W. F., Diamond, C. T. P., & Balkwill, L. (1998). The adjudication of six performances of a Chopin Etude: A study of expert knowledge. *Psychology of Music, 26,* 154–174.

Thompson, W. F., Graham, P. & Russo, F. A. (2005). Seeing music performance:

Visual influences on perception and experience. *Semiotica, 156* (1/4), 203–227.

Thompson, W. F., Schellenberg, E. G., & Husain, G. (2004). Decoding speech prosody: Do music lessons help? *Emotion, 4,* 46–64.

Thompson, W. F., Schellenberg, E. G., & Husain, G. (2001). Arousal, mood, and the Mozart Effect. *Psychological Science, 12*(3), 248–251.

Thompson, W. F. & Stainton, M. (1998). Expectancy in Bohemian folksong melodies: Evaluation of implicative principles for implicative and closural intervals. *Music Perception.* 15(3), 231–252.

Tillman, B., Bharucha, J. J., & Bigand, E. (2000). Implicit Learning of Tonality: A Self-Organizing Approach. *Psychological Review, 107,* 885–913.

Trainor, L. J., & Heinmiller, B. M. (1998). The development of eveluative responses to music: infants prefer to listen to consonance over dissonance. *Infant Behavior and Development, 21,* 77–88.

Trehub, S. E., Schellenberg, E. G., & Hill, D. S. (1997). The origins of music perception and cognition: A developmental perspective. In I. Deliège & J. Sloboda (Eds.), *Perception and cognition of music* (pp. 103–128). East Sussex, UK: Psychology Press.

Trehub, S. E., Schellenberg, E. G., & Kamenetsky, S. B. (1999). Infants' and adults' perception of scale structure. *Journal of Experimental Psychology: Human Perception and Performance, 25,* 965–975.

Trainor, L. J., & Trehub, S. E. (1992). A comparison of infants' and adults' sensitivity to Western musical structure. *Journal of Experimental: Human Perception and Performance, 18,* 394–402.

Trainor, L. J., & Trehub, S. E. (1994). Key membership and implied harmony in Western tonal music: Developmental perspectives. *Perception & Psychophysics, 56,* 125–132.

Trainor, L. J., Tsang, C. D., & Cheung, H. W. (2002). Preference for sensory consonance in 2- and 4-month-old infants. *Music Perception, 20*(2), 187–194.

van Noorden, L. P. A. S. (1975). *Temporal coherence in the perception of tone sequences.* Doctoral dissertation. Technisch Hogeschool Eindoven; published Eindhoven: Druk vam Voorschoten.

von Hippel, P. (2000). Redefining pitch proximity: Tessitura and mobility as constraints on melodic intervals. *Music Perception, 17,* 315–327.

von Hippel, P. & Huron, D. (2000). Why do skips precede reversals? The effect of tessitura on melodic structure. *Music Perception, 18,* 59–85.

Vos, P.G. (2000). Tonality induction: Theoretical problems and dilemmas. *Music Perception, 17,* 403–416.

Vos, P. G. (1978). *Identification of meter in music* (Internal report 78 ON 06). Nijmegen, The Netherlands: University of Nijmegen.

Walker, R. (1996). Can we understand the music of another culture? *Psychology of Music, 24,* 103–114.

Wallin, N. L., Merker, B., & Brown, S. (Eds.) (2000). *The origins of music.* Cambridge, MA: MIT Press.

Wright, J. K. & Bregman, A. S. (1987). Auditory stream segregation and the control of dissonance in polyphonic music. *Contemporary Music Review, 2,* 63–92.

Zentner, M. R., & Kagan, J. (1996). Perception of music by infants. *Nature, 383,* 29.

The Development of Musical Abilities

4

HEINER GEMBRIS

A considerable amount of research on musical development has been published in recent years. This particular survey addresses the following questions: Which results of developmental psychology should parents and teachers be aware of? What should they know about the development of musical abilities? There are obviously no simple answers to these questions since they depend on individual interests of the reader. However, there are a lot of general aspects of musical development that can be of general interest to parents and educators.

A central aspect of this chapter will be the description of typical age-related characteristics and the different influencing factors of development. In addition, we will establish connections to developmental theories, to pedagogical considerations, and to the state of research in relevant areas. A detailed outline of developmental theories is not intended since it can be found in other chapters of this book. Since research in the area of development and cognition is often incomplete and controversial, our account will inevitably resemble a puzzle with some pieces missing rather than a painting with straight lines.

Areas of Research

The current developmental psychology of musical abilities may be in one of its most productive stages in history. We can distinguish at least five areas of research that have opened up new perspectives on musical abilities of humans in the last 10 to 15 years: the examination of fetal learning before and infant learning after birth, neurobiological research, expertise research, life span development of musical abilities, and the emergence of develop mental theories. Brief characterizations of these key aspects are presented in the following sections.

The Examination of Fetal Learning Before and Infant Learning After Birth

New research methods in infant studies (e.g., video and computer technology, habituation paradigm) have enabled reliable investigations of children's perceptual and cognitive abilities even at preverbal stages of development. The results show a surprising degree of competence not only in general development but also in the area of musical perception and communication. Moreover, research has clearly shown that the perceptions of sounds and music not only emerge after birth but already have started weeks and even months before birth (for reviews see Lecanuet, 1996; Trevarthen, 1999–2000).

This leads to the question of whether and, if so, how musical abilities should be fostered by educational activities with infants and perhaps even during prenatal stages of development. One consequence might be that music education in the future will start even earlier than today. In addition, research on infants has shown to be relevant beyond the developmental psychology of music, because it refers back to the anthropological and psychological basis of music, hence to the question of musical universals and basics of musical expression.

Neurobiological Research

In neurobiological research, the development of visual image-mapping procedures (e.g., magnetic resonance imaging [MRI], positron emission tomography [PET]) provided new evidence for neurobiological correlates of musical activities (see also chap. 2, by Gruhn and Rauscher, in this volume). Schlaug, Jäncke, Huang, Staiger, and Steinmetz (1995) showed that the planum temporale, a brain area in the left temple region, is anatomically more developed in musicians, especially those with absolute pitch, than in nonmusicians. It has also been shown that the corpus callosum, which connects the two hemispheres of the brain, is morphologically more highly developed in musicians than nonmusicians. Another study group found that the specific area of the motor cortex that coordinates the movements of the left hand is more anatomically extended in string players than in nonmusicians (Elbert, Pantev, Wienbruch, Rockstroh, & Taub, 1995). This enlargement, correlated with the age at which the persons started to play their instruments, suggests that the anatomical or neurological/neurobiological differences between musicians and nonmusicians are a result of musical training and development and that these differences may, in turn, be a factor in any variations in musical development (Schlaug, 2001; Pascual-Leone, 2001).

In a longitudinal study, Hassler (1991, 1992) found that biological parameters correlated with musical development. She observed female and male adolescents over a period of 8 years and examined the relationship between the level of the male sex hormone testosterone, which changes during puberty, and the development of spatial and musical abilities. Among other things, musical talent for composing was clearly related to a tendency toward androgyny (cf. Kemp, 1996, p. 109). Music education and research on musical development should direct more attention to the phase of puberty.

Expertise Research

Expertise research focuses on the crucial role of deliberate practice for the development of musical abilities (see chap. 7, by Andreas C. Lehmann and Jane W. Davidson, in this volume). From this point of view, expert performance can be seen as a result of the accumulated hours of training and deliberate practice over a lifetime. After the acquisition of expert performance in a number of areas like sports and chess was addressed, the expertise approach was successfully adapted to the domain of music (e.g., Ericsson, Krampe, & Tesch-Römer, 1993; Krampe, 1994; Jørgensen & Lehmann, 1997). Recently the expertise paradigm has also become a helpful approach to study other levels of instrumental performance (Sloboda & Davidson, 1996; Sloboda, Davidson, Moore, & Howe, 1994). On the other hand, there are clear limitations of the expertise approach. For instance, the motivation for practice or interindividual differences in the effects of practice remain open to question. Furthermore, the acquisition of expertise in composing and in musical creativity seems to differ from that in playing an instrument. While highly trained processes and automated routines are fundamental for high performance on piano, violin or other instruments, it is exactly these elements that are counterproductive to creativity (Simonton 2000). Expertise research, with its focus on environmental variables, and behavioral genetics and neurobiological research, with its emphasis on innate capacities, together have stimulated the old nature–nurture debate.

Life-Span Development of Musical Abilities

Investigating the development of musical abilities of adults was another force that led to new perspectives in developmental psychology. Until recently, music education and the psychology of music focused primarily on childhood and adolescence. However, the fact that the proportion of older people is increasing in our societies and more adults are looking for meaningful leisure activities resulted in a greater need for research on the development and influence of musical abilities in an aging population. The establishment of the life-span perspective for developmental psychology was an important premise for the awareness that the development of musical abilities was a lifelong process. Biographical studies on musicians were rediscovered and their relevance increased (e.g., Gembris, 1997; Manturzewska, 1990, 1995).

The Emergence of Developmental Theories

In the last 10 to 15 years, a remarkable change has also occurred in the area of theory development. For a long time, a number of general theories, for the most part not specific to music like the theory of Piaget or the earlier idea of the biogenetic and psychogenetic law, determined theories of musical development. In recent years, a number of theories specifically related to music or at least to particular areas of musical development were established, for example, for the usage of musical symbols (Davidson & Scripp, 1992), singing (e.g., Davidson, 1994 Stadler Elmer, 2002); the learning of newborns and infants (Gordon, 1990), composition (Swanwick, 1994), the development of musical and artistic competence (Hargreaves, 1996), or the professional careers of instrumentalists (Manturzewska, 1995) (see chapter 5 on theories, in this volume). These theories do not always agree whether or not the acquisition of musical abilities can be considered domain-specific processes of development. Hargreaves (1996, p. 153) concludes that domain-specific processes are likely to play a role especially in the acquisition of high levels of musical abilities. However, there are stages of development for cognitive abilities that appear at certain ages, and those can be observed in various domains. A future task for theory development will be to draw a clear distinction between domain-specific and general processes of development.

"Research findings often are not readily or obviously applicable to practices" (Haack, 1992, p. 461). What Haack says about research on the acquisition of music-listening skills is true of most developmental psychology of music. On the one hand, research should thus be more concerned with particular problems of music education. On the other hand, processes of musical development will also benefit from theory development and basic research, which cannot be easily adopted to practice but offer important explanations and orientations.

General Assumptions

Musical abilities have to be understood in inclusive fashion as an amalgamate of many factors, including instrumental and vocal abilities, music-specific cognitive processes, emotional experiences, musical experiences, motivation, musical preferences, attitudes, and interests.

The Universality of Musical Abilities

An important starting point for looking at the development of musical abilities is the assumption that every human being is musical and that it is possible and promising to develop this musicality. It is usually assumed that musical abilities are normally distributed, which means that most people are of average musicality in much the same way as most people are of average intelligence. Assuming that musicality is normally distributed means that 68% of people are of average musicality, while 14% are less musical and 14% are more musical than the average. Approximately 2% are highly gifted and a further 2% have a low musical talent. Therefore, there are no completely unmusical people, just as there are no totally unintelligent people. Since everybody possesses at least some degree of musical aptitude, everybody can also benefit from musical instruction despite individual difference in innate capacities (Gordon, 1987).

Musical Development as a Lifelong Process

It is another premise that musical development is a lifelong process. Musical development occurs as part of the general development of an individual over the life span. It does not end—as is often assumed—by the end of adolescence. Also, it is difficult to say exactly when musical development begins. Since children are able to perceive acoustic stimuli like voices and music in the last weeks before birth and recognize them in their first days of life, we may assume that musical experiences and musical learning start before birth. From a theoretical point of view, musical development does not end until the end of life. Unfortunately, for a lot of people the development seems to have ceased a long time before the end of their lives. Yet music therapy with older people is being undertaken and only makes sense if we assume that there is potential for development at this age.

Development as Changing Dynamics of Growth, Maintenance, and Loss

Development is understood here not just as positive changes like improvement and growth but as an interplay of benefits, maintenance, and loss of abilities (e.g., Baltes, Lindenberger, & Staudinger, 1998). This interaction changes over the life span, for example, due to specialization. Whereas benefits are prevalent during childhood and adolescence, the proportion of loss increases with age. If we consider musical development part of the general development that includes cognitive, emotional, sensorimotor, and social components, it is also affected by the interplay of benefit and loss. For instance, while sensorimotor abilities decrease throughout adulthood and can influence instrumental playing, musical experiences and musical knowledge can increase at the same time. Thus even though some loss of abilities may occur over the life span, teaching and learning music during adulthood may still be beneficial for musical development.

Individual Differences

It is well documented that large developmental differences in music abilities already exist at an early age and in adolescence. They are caused by differences in giftedness and talent and the sociocultural background as well as by lessons, motivation, and practice (e.g., Kelly & Sutton-Smith, 1987). During adulthood, these individual differences, for example, among professionals, amateurs, and people untrained in music, become even more pronounced due to commitment and practice in the case of professionals and lack of use in nonmusicians. Therefore, research on musical development, especially development in adulthood, requires a strong differential perspective. One approach distinguishes between "normative" and "specialist" development (Hargreaves, 1996, p. 150). Normative development is "that which naturally happens to children as they grow up in a given culture regardless of any specialized attention or guidance," while specialist development and specialist education "is consciously devoted to the development of high levels of musical skill or expertise" (Hargreaves, 1996, p. 150). Even though Hargreaves advises against the strict separation of these two aspects, further distinctions seem to be necessary. Different aspects also become obvious if the careers and the development of musicians in jazz, rock, and popular music are compared with those in classical music. In such nontraditional domains there is a lack of theoretical concepts to describe the musical development.

Cross-Generational Differences

Since musical development is culturally and historically embedded, it is affected by the changing historical and cultural surroundings, especially the changes in musical culture. Children's musical development depends much on the current musical culture, which can differ largely from their parents' culture. This becomes obvious when one compares the musical development of the generation that grew up with rock and popular music as a main influence to that of the generation before. Hence, contemporary history can affect musical development (Gembris, 1997). The rise of new media technology (e.g., computers and the internet) and the emergence of new musical styles contribute to an increasing variety of musical development in the fields of composition, performance, listening, and preferences. Therefore, parents and teachers should be aware that the children's and student's musical development may differ considerably from their own. Correspondingly, research on musical development should broaden its focus on traditional Western art music to include all styles (e.g., Hemming & Kleinen, 1999).

Musical Development: 0 to 10 Years

The basic musical abilities that are required for participation in one's own musical culture are developed in the first 10 years of life. This process of enculturation takes place automatically and subconsciously, without the need of formal instruction. Musical stimulations that arise from the individual social and cultural environment seem to be most important. A musically rich social environment can lead to certain musical abilities' being acquired earlier than in a social environment with less musical activity (Kelly & Sutton-Smith, 1987). But the development of basic musical abilities can also be positively influenced through teaching. Morrongiello (1992) observed that musical practice leads to more precise perception of melodies, better musical memory, and an earlier sensitivity for keys. Other studies confirm that the acquisition of certain musical abilities can be accelerated through teaching; however, students without lessons do catch up after a while (e.g., Behne, 1974). The possibility to accelerate the development of basic musical abilities through lessons may be constrained by their connection with general mental, emotional, and sensorimotor developmental processes (Gembris & Davidson, 2002). Note that since large individual differences can occur in both general and musical development, the age-related details that follow are points of reference, and divergent ages cannot easily be interpreted as indicating unusual talent or developmental retardation.

Prenatal Development

The onset of musical learning and musical memory occurs before birth. The nerve cells of the inner ear start to work in the fifth or sixth month of pregnancy and respond to midrange frequencies. Approximately in the seventh month of gestation, the fetus perceives extrauterine acoustic stimuli. When children are born, they have already had some acoustic experiences. An experiment by Feijoo (1981) showed that babies stopped crying when they listened to short melodies that had been presented to them over a period of 4 weeks during the sixth to eighth month of pregnancy. Satt (1984) provided evidence for the ability of 16 newborns to recognize a lullaby that they had heard every day during the last 2 months of pregnancy. Hepper (1991) demonstrated the ability of infants just a few days old to recognize the main tune of a television series that they already heard before birth. Another study showed that newborns seemed to remember single words from a story read out loud by their mothers during the last 6 weeks of pregnancy (DeCaspar & Spence, 1986). These results demonstrate that reactions to music must already occur during prenatal development. However, the methods used in these experiments still offer no reliable distinction between direct reactions of the child and indirect reactions influenced by the mother's reaction.

The fact that unborn children can react to music has been taken up by the music industry, which offers a number of CDs especially designed for pregnant women. These products supposedly have a positive influence on the health of the mother and the unborn child. Experiments with animals have demonstrated that prenatal auditory deprivation leads to a retarded development, while careful acoustic enrichment seemed to improve the structure and function of auditory tracts in the fetus (Lecanuet, 1996, p. 18).

Development of Musical Perception

Pitch.   Infants can show performance superior to adults in the ability to perceive small pitch differences. A study with American infants and adults demonstrated the ability of 6-month-old infants to recognize single tones that were played out of tune in Western (major/minor) and non-Western scales (Javanese *pelog* scale) (Lynch, Eilers, Oller, & Urbano, 1990). Adults who grew up in a Western music culture did recognize tones out of tune in major and minor scales but not those out of tune of the *pelog* scale. The authors concluded that children are born with a potential to perceive the scales of different cultures equally well. However, in the process of enculturation scale-related perception schemes develop regardless of formal musical instruction for scales in one's own culture, while other perceptual abilities for non-culture-specific scales decrease (Lynch & Eilers, 1991). Similar findings exist for speech perception.

A number of experiments with infants and adults investigate the possible existence of innate dispositions or perceptual capacities that would favor specific intervals or scales. The results are ambiguous and inconsistent; in general, there is some evidence for the special position of the octave and perfect fifth in interval perception. Demany and Armand (1984) found out that higher and lower octaves were perceived as equivalent by 3-month-old infants. Obviously, infants were already sensitive to pitch and timbre at that age, although there was only little influence of musical experience. Other experiments indicated that the perfect fifth could be an interval whose perception and brain processing were supported by some universal, prototypical-cognitive representation (Lynch, 1993).

Melody Perception.   Growing research over the last 20 years supports the idea that infants' sensations are not just vague and mellow; instead, their reactions can be interpreted as recognizing behavior (see Fassbender, 1996, for a review). By the age of 6 months, infants are capable of distinguishing several short melodies with the melodic contour as the most important distinguishing feature. At this age they cannot yet recognize absolute pitch or specific intervals (Dowling, 1988, 1999). Most of the present studies indicate that melodic perception in its early stages aligns itself with the melodic contour and moves on to more specific details with increasing age (Dowling, 1999). Lamont's (1998) experiments demonstrate that informal musical experience is more important for general musical enculturation than playing an instrument, at least for children aged 6 to 11. However, during adolescence (11 to 16 years) the accuracy of melodic perception only improves if someone is musically active (e.g., plays an instrument). She concludes: "Enculturation (and school music) alone is insufficient for continued development after the age of 11" (p. 23).

Schwarzer's (1997) results run contrary to those mentioned before. She observed a tendency toward analytic perception for children (ages 5 to 7), whereas adults perceived the presented melodies in a holistic fashion. The children's perception was based on melody-unspecific features like loudness and timbre and not on melodic contour, whereas adults were oriented toward melody-specific contour. These inconsistent results can possibly be explained by the different task settings.

Another important concept for the development of musical perception is the distinction between equal and different stimuli (Deliège, Mélen, & Bertrand, 1995; Gordon, 1981, p. 41). Structuring and processing of perception already take place at infant age according to the principles of Gestalt psychology: namely, grouping of stimuli according to similarity, closeness, and conciseness (Fassbender, 1996). These are also the basis for auditory grouping or auditory stream segregation and can be regarded as universal principles. They contribute to the transformation of temporal relationships of note sequences into a meaningful, rhythmical "Gestalt," just as pitch relations and pitch sequences are transformed into a melodic contour.

Cross-modal Perception.   Essential for the development of musical perception of infants is their ability to recognize connections among auditory stimuli, visual stimuli, and touch. This specific ability is called cross-modal perception and was demonstrated in different experiments (e.g., Meltzoff, Kuhl & Moore, 1991; Papoušek, 1996). The infant perceives the acoustical characteristics of the maternal voice (melody, contour, tempo, rhythmical structure, timbre) as synchronous with and analogous to his or her own sensory perception, to visual experiences, and to the movements of the mother. The development of such cross-modal perceptual schemata is likely to play an important role for the perception of musical expression.

Rhythmic Abilities.   There are different indicators and approaches to examine the development of rhythmic abilities, that is:

- the ability to distinguish between identical and different rhythms,
- the preference for simple or complex rhythms,
- the reproduction of rhythms through clapping,
- the ability to move to presented rhythms, and
- the investigation of rhythmical structure in children's songs.

Early studies in the 1960s already demonstrated that newborns are able to distinguish between regular and irregular heartbeat or click sounds (Spiegler,

1967). Other researchers found that 5-month-old infants could recognize changes of simple rhythms (long–short vs. short–long) (Shuter-Dyson & Gabriel, 1981, p. 107). Even though children already seem to have some rhythmic awareness and are able to distinguish between simple rhythms, a more precise perception of rhythms develops only gradually. Regular meter in singing first becomes noticeable during the 2nd year of life, first in very short then in increasingly longer segments (Dowling & Harwood, 1986, p., 194). These abilities are clearly age-related, and considerable individual differences exist.

The results from investigations about rhythm perception during preschool age are quite divergent. The children Rainbow (1980) observed over a period of 3 years took 2 years before a marked increase of rhythmic abilities was noted. Conversely, Ramsey (1983) identified a developmental jump in the perception and (sung) performance of rhythms in a melody between the third and fourth year of life. He also found corresponding progress in the perception of melodic intervals between the fourth and fifth year of life. The author concludes that the perception of rhythm precedes the perception of melody.

Between the third and fourth year of life, children start to distinguish roughly between slow and fast. Four-year-olds seem to be able to identify slow and fast tempi and use appropriate terms and can demonstrate their understanding with concomitant body movements. For children at this age, fast and slow seems to be the central aspect of music (Young, 1982). Yet most of them are not capable of making comparative judgments (e.g., slow and slower). Furthermore, these children start to prefer rhythms in which they can identify regular structures (Zenatti, 1993). To show this preference, 4-year-olds need simple rhythms without sixteenth and eighth notes or dotted eighths, while 5-year-olds seem to have no problem even with more complex rhythmic structures. This may be related to the fact that children age 5 and up have a more sophisticated notion of time in general (Pouthas, 1996, p. 136; also Dowling, 1999).

Synchronization of Rhythm with Movement.   The beginnings of synchronization between music and movements can be first observed with children aged 18 months to 2 years (Moog, 1976). Starting with the age of 2 ½ years, children seem to be able to match their movements to the music for a short period of time. Still, imitating someone's clapping, synchronized clapping, and marching to the beat of the music are tasks that 3- to 4-year-olds can hardly accomplish (Rainbow, 1980). However, it is possible that children at this age are able to perceive rhythms that they cannot reproduce themselves through movement. They can clap a given rhythm more easily if they speak it before clapping it. Also, it is easier for them to repeat a spoken rhythm than a regular meter (Rainbow & Owen, 1979). Generally, children have fewer difficulties representing or realizing rhythms through use of their voice. Therefore, the voice is the most appropriate educational medium to teach rhythms to 3- and 4-year-olds (Rainbow, 1980). At the age of 5, children seem to be able to synchronize their movements (taps) to rhythms with somewhat less than adult accuracy (Gerard & Auxiette, 1992).

While studies from the 1970s concluded that the concept of meter did not develop until the age of 7 and stabilized by the age of 9, more recent studies show that 5-year-old children can already maintain a given meter. An increase of rhythmic abilities could possibly be explained by a stronger and earlier influence of the mass media, which may accelerate the general musical enculturation. Alternatively, research methods and measurements may have simply become more sophisticated and sensitive.

Harmony and Tonality.   Even though findings about the development of tonal sensitivity are not consistent throughout, a clear tendency can be observed: More recent studies record younger ages than did previous studies for harmonic perception and the preference for consonance over dissonance. Based on experiments from 1913, Valentine (1962) found that children were able to distinguish between major and minor at the age of 9 and those with intensive musical training between the ages of 5 and 7. Imberty (1969) first noticed this ability in children at the age of 7, while it can be observed at the age of 5 and younger today. Again, the increased influence of the mass media could account for the fact that children become accustomed to the Western major-minor tonal system at an earlier age, which in turn may lead to an acceleration in the identification of harmonies (Zenatti, 1993, p. 192). With the use of refined research methods, these effects could possibly be observed at even younger ages.

In a number of experiments with 5- to 10-year-olds, Zenatti (1993) examined the musical preference for tonality versus atonality and consonance versus dissonance. The children listened to pairs of musical stimuli (e.g., a tonal and an atonal melody) presented from tape and were asked which melody, rhythm, or chords of the two versions they preferred. Children younger than 5 were still at chance level; that is, they had no clear preference. However, at the age of 6 the preference for consonant harmonization increased as rapidly as the dislike for atonal melodies and dissonance. By the age of 9 or 10 the preference for tonality and consonance was between 90 and 95% (cf. Zenatti, 1993, p. 182; also Minkenberg, 1991, for supporting results). This suggests that enculturation into the Western tonal system is virtually concluded at that age. As a result, the openness to contemporary music or music from non-Western cultures constantly decreases after the age of 5 or 6. An educational countermeasure could be presenting more nontonal music to preschool children and indicating to them that it can be enjoyed just the same as familiar music.

Timbre.   A question of interest to music educators is whether preschool and primary school children are able to recognize and distinguish different instruments by their sound. In a number of experiments with preschool children, Schellberg (1998) found an enormous increase in the ability to distinguish timbres by 4- to 6-year-olds. Most of the 5- and 6-year-olds were able to distinguish and recognize conventional musical instruments—which they knew from their music lessons—even in combination with other instruments from the orchestra.

Recognition of Emotional Expressions in Music.   The ability to perceive and distinguish basic acoustic-musical parameters is the premise for the understanding of musical expression and its emotional meaning. Recognizing emotional expressions in music requires a general emotional ability of perception and differentiation.

Even though infants are not able to distinguish between different face expressions in the first 6 weeks of their life, they are able to recognize familiar voices (cf. Rauh, 1995, p. 230). At an early age, they distinguish and express various emotions via the acoustic channel. With different types of crying they communicate their current feelings (Wolff, 1969). Based on their long-term efforts, M. and H. Papoušek demonstrated the infant's ability to understand the emotional-communicative meaning of different melodic-rhythmic contours in nonverbal vocalization in parent–child intereactions (e.g., H. Papoušek, 1996; M. Papoušek, 1996; Papoušek & Papoušek, 1986). Infants seem to attribute the same meanings to the same melody contours, independent of the culture they grow into.

Between the ages of 6 weeks and 4 months, infants begin to distinguish happy, sad, and neutral facial expressions, first in actual faces and later in schematic pictures. Another important aspect for the perception of expression can be identified between the fourth and the ninth month of life: By that age, infants are able to perceive cross-modal relationships between vocal and gestural qualities of facial expressions. Next infants start to recognize the reason for a person's happy or angry reaction; that is, they establish the connection between certain events and the corresponding facial expression of familiar adults (Rauh, 1995, p. 230).

There is currently very little work on the recognition of emotional expression in music for infants and children younger than 3, and we do not know to what extent infants or toddlers actually perceive expressions, say, in the music their parents play to them with the goal of improving the child's well-being.

Various studies focus on the understanding of musical expression at preschool age and at school age. For example, children had to match schematic pictures of face expressions to a number of musical excerpts. Some researchers also included verbal statements, and the children were asked to either indicate which emotions they identified or give free descriptions of what they felt (Cunningham & Sterling, 1988; Minkenberg, 1991; Trehub, 1993). Most of the studies are limited to fundamental emotions ("happy-sad," "angry-frightened," or "calm-excited"), although exceptions exist where more emotions are considered. One of the most important results is that children 3 to 4 years old matched a surprisingly large number of pictures correctly to the music (Cunningham & Sterling, 1988; Dolgin & Adelson, 1990; Kastner & Crowder, 1990).

The examples presented in these experiments usually consisted of short pieces or excerpts from classical instrumental music. It should be noticed that, despite its wide distribution and generally easier musical structure, none of the studies included rock or pop music as stimuli. Correctly matching the pictures to the music largely depended on the kinds of emotions expressed as well as on the kinds of musical stimuli; some emotions were recognized more easily than others. Children seemed to better recognize the emotions "happy" and "sad" than "angry-frightened" and "calm-excited" (Cunningham & Sterling, 1988; Dolgin & Adelson, 1990; Kratus, 1993; Terwogt & van Grinsven, 1988). In addition, emotions were not recognized equally well on different instruments. For example, Dolgin and Adelson (1990) found that 4-year-olds identified the intended musical expression of a melody more accurately in a sung presentation than in an instrumental presentation on the violin. Studies with adults showed a better understanding for "sadness" if the emotion was presented vocally or on a violin and a better understanding for "anger" when the emotion was presented on drums (Behrens & Green, 1993).

It appears that the ability to recognize musical expression is dependent both on the importance of music in the home and on the influence of music education. Some studies suggest that the ability to recognize musical expression improves through music education; however, the effect is rather weak (Behrens & Green, 1993; Kratus, 1993). There is hardly any evidence for gender-related effects, as boys and girls do not differ in the ability to recognize musical expression (Giomo, 1993).

Mechanisms for the Recognition of Expressions

Which musical characteristics contribute to the recognition of expressions of children? What role do the fundamental categories of major and minor play? Research results that concern the emotional perception of major and minor are ambivalent. Whereas adults clearly relate major to happy and minor to sad, 4- to 8-year-olds are quite inconsistent and uncertain in assigning expressions to certain modes (Trehub, 1993; see also chap. 3, by Thompson and Schellenberg, in this volume).

If 3- or 4-year old children are already capable of recognizing emotional expression in music although the feeling for tonality only stabilizes at primary school age, there must be other characteristics of expression than major and minor for the children's identification of emotional expression. Terwogt and van Grinsven (1991) found that adults as well as 5-year-olds seem to be oriented toward a rhythm and melody. In another experiment, Dolgin and Adelson (1990) copied the melodic gesture of melodies from emotional speech. Four-year-olds and adults correctly recognize the emotional expressions of most melodies. In an experiment with 4- to 8-year-olds, Trehub detected that fast notes and ascending melodies were perceived as happy. However, slow and low notes and descending melodies were perceived as sad. Similar effects can be found through use of prosody in language (Trehub, Trainor, & Unyk, 1993) or the nonverbal interactions between infants and their parents (see earlier). It can be concluded that there must exist some prototypical gestures or movements of acoustic expression that are independent from tonality and common to both language and music. Interestingly, the Italian composer Claudio Monteverdi (1567–1643) used the prosody of the language as a basis for his *stile concitato* compositions to increase the affective power of his music.

Perception of Further Nonmusical Meanings

Children are not only able to perceive emotional expressions in music, but they are also able to recognize metaphoric representations of extramusical content. Some informative experiments were carried out by Trainor and Trehub (1992) in which children between the ages of 3 and 6 were asked to match parts of Prokofiev's composition *Peter and the Wolf* to a number of pictures (wolf, bird, cat, duck, etc.). The results showed that 3-year-old children were already capable of identifying extramusical characters within music and this ability improved with age. Another study was carried out by Graml, Kraemer, and Gembris (1988) with children of primary and secondary schools. Starting with the first grade, children were already able to match—with relative accuracy—excerpts from Stravinsky's *Firebird* and other compositions with pictures of the characters described in the music. Starting with grade level 4, the children were capable of solving all items correctly.

Again we could ask ourselves which musical characteristics enable the children to assign the right pictures to the music. According to Trainor and Trehub (1992), imitative and metaphoric characteristics of the music give rise to the expression: For instance, musical tension and relaxation serves as an analogue to emotional tension and relaxation, and high and low pitches convey spatial aspects; musical movement is mapped onto nonmusical movement, musical onto nonmusical power and mass (e.g., the elephant in the *Carnival of the Animals* by Camille Saint-Saëns). Thus cross-modal perceptual schemata may play an important role (see earlier).

As soon as the children's linguistic development is sufficiently advanced, which commonly happens around the ages of 7 to 10, they can be interviewed about their musical experiences. In a longitudinal study, one author discovered three kinds of thoughts and feelings in children. The first kind included thoughts and moods directly related to the music, such as thoughts about the composer or the performer. The second kind included associations caused by the music, such as thoughts about the morning light or sad things. The third kind included thoughts about actual situations experienced by the children while listening to or performing music, such as listening to music at school or while going to bed (cf. Minkenberg, 1991, p. 267).

In summary, we can state that a basic understanding of musical expression already exists at the ages of 3 to 4 and becomes more differentiated as the children grow older. The current studies do not separate whether the emotions expressed by the music were just recognized or experienced concurrently. Other variables, such as musical home environment, music lessons, and gender had little or no effect on the children's recognition of musical expression.

Graphic Representation of Music

Research on musical development has recently been influenced by the symbol-system approach (Davidson & Scripp, 1992). This resulted in an increased interest in graphic and symbolic representations of melodies and rhythms, which allow interesting insights into the development of musical thinking (e.g., Gromko, 1994; Smith, Cuddy & Upitis, 1994). To study the ability to create graphic representations, children (or adults) are first asked to repeat a given rhythm, melody, or song by clapping or singing. Then they are instructed to generate a "notation" for the music that is supposed to enable a third person to reproduce the music without having heard it before. A number of researchers have offered typologies for the development of graphic representation of music and the underlying musical thinking. (e.g., Bamberger, 1991; Upitis, 1987).

The children's representations led the authors to postulate two different kinds of underlying processing strategies. A first strategy resulted in the production of a sequentially ordered series of symbols. For instance, children under the age of 5 tended to simply jot down the rhythmic impulses of the melody. Older children reproduced a single dimension of the melody, either its rhythmic structure or its melodic contour. All of this changes between the ages of 6 and 8: Then rhythmic impulses are grouped together and pitch representation becomes dominant. Hereafter, both aspects can be integrated from 7 years on.

Coordination of Different Aspects of Perception ("Conservation")

Although it is currently unclear if Piaget's theory of cognitive development can be adequately transferred to the domain of music (cf. Case, 1998; Haith & Benson, 1998; Gardner, 1991; Hargreaves, 1986), research based on this theory has undoubtedly produced central insights into musical development. According to Piaget's theory, children start to develop the ability to coordinate several different aspects of perception (*conservation*) around the age of 7 years during the *concrete-operational stage*. For the development of musical abilities this implies that, for instance, children have to reach at least 7 years before they can pay attention to and coordinate rhythm and melody simultaneously. Older work had already demonstrated that 8-year-old children identified different melodies as variations of the *same* melody when rhythmic, melodic, or tonal changes had been made (Pflederer, 1964; Pflederer & Sechrest, 1968). This ability to coordinate different aspects of music, that is, to *conserve*, increases with age, although, as Nelson (1987, p. 26) found, it does not necessarily develop at the same time in different domains. Other studies provided evidence for an intermediate stage, where children can perceive but not coordinate more than one dimension at a time (Flammer, 1996, p. 129). For example, children at this age are mostly able to identify transposed melodies, but they have difficulties describing pitch relations with the right words, like *high* and *low* (Flowers & Costa-Giomi, 1991; also Shuter-Dyson, 1982, p. 75). As a consequence, these abstract notions should not be used for pre-school-age music education and rather be replaced by metaphorical pictures.

The Development of Singing.   The common roots of singing and speaking are the nonverbal vocalizations of the infant, which are an immediate expression of its basic feelings. Parents intuitively tune in to the child's noises to establish communication with the infant. These child-directed vocalizations are called motherese and can be seen as a *prelinguistic alphabet* (M. Papoušek, 1996). It is likely that children during preverbal development experience and process musical impressions in the same way as the prosody of the language (Trehub et al., 1993). These nonverbal vocalizations represent at the same time prelinguistic and premusical means of expressions.

A number of authors agree on the fact that most of these melodic contours consist of descending glissando figures after the first 3 or 4 months of life (e.g., Fox, 1990). M. Papoušek (1994) describes four different types of melodic contours of vocalization in early childhood (descending, ascending-descending, ascending and complex, and repeated ascending and descending), the frequency of which depends on the age of the infant and the situational context. Descending contours prevail in the first months of life, but later the melodic contours become more varied and the proportion of other contours increases. The large range of observed interindividual variability could be caused by developmental differences as well as by problems of research methodology.

By the end of the first year of life, it becomes possible to separate singing and speaking in the preverbal vocalizations of most children. Children themselves experiment with the voice and seem to try out its range and possibilities in "vocal play" (Stadler Elmer, 2000). It is possible to understand vocal play in Piagetian terminology as a kind of sensorimotor play. This kind of behavior typically appears between the 12th and the 18th month of life. The two fundamental cognitive processes that underlie vocal play and imitation are assimilation and accommodation (cf. Stadler Elmer, 2000, p. 55). Accommodation takes place when children are trying to adapt their imagination and vocal expression to a given model such as the phrase of a song. Assimilation occurs when children receive new information (e.g., a new melody) and integrate it into an already-existing schema.

Another kind of singing was characterized by Dowling (1999) as an articulation of syllables with vowels that are slightly prolonged and appear on stable pitches. The author also observed a sequential organization of the *song,* referring to more or less stabilized tonal patterns. According to Dowling, the first actual singing can be observed between the 6th and the 18th month of life. At first, these glissando-like improvisations on single syllables occupy only a narrow pitch range. Later they turn into recognizable songs, often with a sequential organization of the sounds. Thus a typical song of an 18-month-old-child consists of an often-repeated phrase with a steady melodic contour at a continuously changing level of pitch. The song is quite often interrupted by breathing; however, the rhythmical contour remains within the phrase and sometimes even stretches over several phrases. These songs are often derived from the rhythm of language.

In their second year of life, children are able to sing single short phrases of a song, frequently turning them into spontaneous improvisations and repeating them quite often. Microtonal figures in spontaneous singing slowly make way for more accurate intervals, resulting in an overall impression that is clearly related to the diatonic system (cf. Moog, 1976). Between the ages of 3 and 4, children combine different songs and song fragments into something like a medley. They can repeat songs they hear and increase phrase contour of the presented song by trial and error. Other researchers observed that children could reproduce all of the lyrics, the main rhythms, and also the formal segments of a song starting at the age of 4 (cf. Shuter-Dyson & Gabriel, 1981, p. 117).

Children will have acquired the singing range of an octave with all its steps once they are 6 or 7 years old (Davidson, 1994; Minkenberg, 1991). Although they still might miss certain pitches, this does not mean they are unable to recognize the pitches (Goetze, Cooper, & Brown, 1990). The development of the ability to sing comes to an end around the age of 8 years. Generally, by this time children are able to sing a song correctly. This ability remains at this level unless music instruction and practice follow. As always, however, a broad range of interindividual differences are observable. The singing abilities of untrained adults are not much different from those of 8- to 10-year-old children (see Davidson, 1994; Davidson & Scripp, 1990, p. 66; Minkenberg, 1991; Stadler Elmer, 2000; 2002, for further details).

Theories on the Development of Singing.   According to Stadler (2000, for summary) the different concurrent theoretical approaches to the development of singing can be categorized into three groups. The first group comprises the speech-dominated *theories of sequence.* The principal argument here is that songs are learned in a certain order, namely, lyrics, rhythm, melody contour/phrases, precise intervals (e.g., Hargreaves, 1986; Moog, 1976; Welch & White, 1994). A second group consists of explanations that implicate the *order of intervals.* Here intervals or successions of notes appear developmentally in a specific and unreversible succession, namely, first the fifth, followed by the third and fourth and then the sixth. This theory assumes innate structures that are supposedly based on the acoustical prop erties of the harmonic series (e.g., Metzler, 1962; Werner, 1917). The third group could be labeled *contour theories*. Proponents of this approach advance the notion that the learning process begins with the melodic contour and that pitch and tonality follow. Learning to sing is thus assumed to proceed from global to more local features. According to Davidson's (1994) theory of contour schemata, the development of a contour schema starts with a falling third into which the other intervals are placed. The contour schema will then expand with the child's age: at first to a fourth and up to a sixth, which is mastered by the age of around 6 or 7. One author, however, raises a number of critical arguments against all of these theories and suggests the following course of development (Stadler Elmer, 2000):

1st step: Early beginnings; vocalizations as the expression of an infant's basic feelings

2nd step: Shifted imitations; development of rituals and extended vocal play

3rd step: Imitation without understanding of rules and inventing of arbitrary rules

4th step: Generalization of examples; ability to sing larger units

5th step: Implicit integration of conventional rules into actions; increasing control of one's own singing

6th step: Beginning reflecting on one's own actions, means, symbols and terms; use of notation for the production and reproduction of music (p. 144, see also Stadler Elmer, 2002, p. 208f).

Musical Development: 10 to 20 Years

Preferences, Aesthetic Values, and Cultural Identity

Whereas the first 8 to 10 years of life are characterized by musical enculturation with a concomitant adoption of the culture's principles and conventions, the ensuing 10 years are dominated by the search for and the establishment of one's own place within a musical culture. This own position is reached with the development of individual musical preferences and tastes. Generally, the term *preference* is used to describe the

affective reactions to a piece of music or a certain style of music that reflect the degree of liking or disliking for that music, and is not necessarily based on cognitive analysis or aesthetic reflection regarding the music in question. (Flinds, 1989, p. 2)

In contrast, *musical taste* refers to long-term preferences for certain musical styles.

The development of preferences is mainly influenced by one's socialization into a given sociocultural environment, including parents, school, social class, peers, and mass media (see Zillmann & Gan, 1997, for an overview). It is difficult to determine the degree of relevance of each of the factors, since their importance changes over the lifetime and may even vary depending on the context. In general, the influence of parents and school decreases during adolescence, at the same time when the importance of peers and media increases. Furthermore, the degree of certain influences is determined by a person's social class.

We should also realize that adolescents not only are passively influenced by their sociocultural environment in the development of their musical preferences but also are rather actively choosing and shaping their own environment. This view of self-socialization is a relatively recent one and has been adapted to music by Müller (1999). Musical self-socialization takes place in an unhampered fashion far away from the influences of formal education, preferably within the youth culture.

"Open-earedness" During Childhood

For children younger than 8, 9, or 10, musical preferences are less important and less stable than those of teenagers. Therefore, children are more open toward and tolerant of unfamiliar or unconventional types of music (LeBlanc, 1991, for an overview). This musical openness (open-earedness; Hargreaves, 1982) of children of preschool and primary school age stems from the less strong internalization of musical conventions and rules than that of adolescents and adults. In addition, the links between preferences on the one hand and cultural values, different ways of hearing, and functions of music on the other hand are less strong at that age. Open-earedness is an opportunity for music education to introduce children to all kinds of unfamiliar music, be it avant-garde or non-Western, against which adults or adolescents might already have established prejudices.

Current research provides evidence for a decrease of "open-earedness" with the beginning of adolescence (LeBlanc, 1991). Recent data show that the decrease of "open-earedness" begins as early as grade 2 or 3 in elementary school (Gembris & Schellberg 2002; Schellberg & Gembris 2003). At the same time, a preference for the music of one's peers starts to emerge. This process is closely related to the construction of a personal and social identity. Furthermore, LeBlanc (1991) observed a rebound effect at the end of adolescence, when listeners tended to return to the music that played a role in late childhood before the beginning of adolescence. This hypothesis awaits further investigation.

Significance of Music Listening for Teenagers

With the beginning of adolescence, sometimes even earlier, listening to music, the orientation toward music, and knowledge about musicians and stars become more and more important. On average, musical preferences and attitudes dramatically change between the 10th and 20th year of life. Around this time, musical preferences separate from the taste of parents and teachers. The close connections to the adult musical world that exist during childhood are replaced by the desire to establish one's own musical taste and world. In this context, the taste of peers plays an important role and also the music industry's current products and the identification with specific musical styles, groups, idols, and stars.

It is typical for teenagers to change their preferences quickly and to experience music with strong accompanying emotions (Behne, 1986). This becomes manifest in the strong enthusiasm for their currently preferred music and a correspondingly strong rejection of other musical styles. Because their preferences mirror the strong emotional impact of the music, adolescents are often quite adamant when it comes to defending *their* current preferences (Behne, 1997, p. 149). This close emotional relationship does not exist during childhood or adulthood to nearly the same degree.

As adolescence is relatively short compared to the entire life span, it is the time in which the greatest changes of musical preferences occur. This period is most important for the musical development not only because of the dramatic changes in preferences but also because the behavioral patterns of listening acquired by the end of adolescence will remain prevalent for adulthood (Behne, 1986, p. 56; Dollase, Rüsenberg, & Stollenwerk, 1986, p. 183; Holbrook & Schindler, 1989; Lehmann, 1994). A distinctive preference for the music of one's youth can be quite frequently observed at a much older age (e.g., Jonas, 1991). A study of Holbrook and Schindler (1989) demonstrated that preferences of adults from different generational cohorts were clearly related to the music that was popular when they were about 24 years old.

Emergence of Preferences for Popular Music

Musical preferences start to develop at primary school age but remain subject to change for a long time. Typically, the preference for popular music gradually increases while other music is getting less popular (e.g., Montgomery, 1996). Between the ages of 8 and 10, children begin to orient themselves toward popular music and lose interest in other, for example, classical, music.

A methodological remark is in order here. The fact that verbal and behavioral preferences do not match is quite well known (e.g., Behne, 1986, 1997; Finnäs, 1989; Lehmann, 1994). It is a peculiarity of preference research that evaluative statements about music that are based on verbal labels will be more negative than preferences reported after listening to an actual example. The reason is that verbal preferences seem to be influenced by social desirability to a greater extent than behavioral preferences. Verbal preferences therefore represent the publicly expressed musical taste of a peer group, while behavioral preferences represent a more *private* taste (compare

Behne, 1997, and Finnäs, 1989). Thus it is entirely possible for a student to generally dislike a genre like opera but, when confronted with a recording of, say, "Che gelida manina" from Puccini's *La Boheme,* be quite touched.

K.-E. Behne (1986) carried out an investigation into the verbal and listening (behavioral) preferences of over 1,000 students aged 10 to 22. He observed that different classical music styles, when presented verbally (word labels), were viewed as a homogenous complex by the majority of the adolescents. However, when actual examples of classical music styles were presented (listening preferences), classical music was not rejected as a whole.

Among the various youth subcultures there are those in which classical music is rated highest on preference scale (e.g., Bastian, 1989, p. 236). Naturally, this group represents a minority. Still, some music-listening studies have demonstrated a surprising tolerance for different classical music genres among younger and older people as well as openness to the "oldies but goldies" of popular music among older people (Gembris, 1995).

Increasing Consumption of Music and Use of Mass Media

The development of musical preferences is accompanied by an expanding music consumption, which can already be observed around the age of 10 and remains at a high level during adolescence. Different researchers found out that the amount of time watching television increases rapidly between childhood and early adolescence and decreases slowly thereafter (Huston & Wright, 1998, p. 1001). Current studies also provide evidence for an increase of the time spent listening to music from childhood to adolescence. For better or worse, the growing availability of music videos, compact discs, minidiscs, the internet, and mp3 players is likely to contribute to the ubiquity of music consumption. Children and adolescents who play an instrument seem to use the mass media less and in a more reflective manner than those who do not (e.g., Scheuer, 1988, p. 206). Taken together, the time allotted to music in formal settings (school) contributes only a small fraction to the overall amount of music to which young people listen. This does not necessarily mean that education has no influence at all upon the development of musical preferences.

Based on his own and other researchers' work, Dollase (1997) proposed a 3-stage model to explain the development of interest in music and of individual preferences: First, there is a rise, starting with the age of 10; interests plateau starting with the age of 13 during the second stage; finally, speed of development declines after the age of 25. As always, age details only serve as points of reference, while individual differences may be large.

Gender Differences

In general, there seem to exist hardly any differences between girls and boys regarding musical instruments or musical styles during childhood (Maidlow

& Bruce, 1999). However, the increase in preference for popular music during adolescence seems to be more pronounced for boys than for girls; that is, girls' dislikes of nonpopular music are less strong than those of the boys. Also, girls seem to like a broader range of classical music (Hargreaves, Comber, & Colley, 1996). The authors explain this with the fact that girls generally take more instrumental lessons and are thus ahead in music education, resulting in a wider acceptance of different musical styles. Some researchers do find gender differences. Martin, Clarke, and Pearce (1993), for instance, found that boys prefer rock and heavy metal music while girls had a preference for popular music. These differences are obviously related to the gender stereotyping of certain musical styles (see Green, 1997; and Maidlow & Bruce, 1999, for detail on gender differences with regard to preferences).

Functions of Music, Listening Styles, and Preferences

The functions that music can assume in an individual's life can be considered the essential influencing factors in the development of musical preferences (Behne, 1986; Dollase, 1997; Lehmann, 1994). Music already serves specific functions during infancy and childhood, yet this functionality is largely imposed on the child (e.g., lullabies, children's songs, etc.) rather than self-chosen. However, the wide distribution of tape recorders, compact disc players, and other technical media makes it possible even for small children to listen to music whenever they choose. The functional use of music expands in adolescence in parallel with the increase in amount of listening. Music is used consciously or unconsciously for various reasons in everyday life. For example, Baacke (1993) presents the following possible list of functions:

- Specific musical preferences act as a sign of identification for specific youth cultures which distinguishes them from one another
- Source of information on new lifestyles, fashion and habits
- Separation from adults who reject youth-specific music
- Stimulation for dreams and wishes
- Establishing of own physical identity by discovering movement through dancing
- Summons to be active and protest
- Escape from everyday life
- Possibility to identify with idols like rock music stars
- Expression of protest and opposition against everyday culture
- A means of stimulation and mood control (p. 232)

It is obvious from a number of further studies that musical preferences develop in response to functional aspects of music (e.g., Lehmann, 1994; Mende, 1991). The use of music as a coping strategy, for compensating for problems, or for mood management plays an important role. Depending on an actual situation, different styles of listening are used to invoke various functional aspects. Pronounced gender differences are found, and according to Behne (1997) boys gravitate toward a more stimulative listening style, whereas girls tend to adhere to a more sentimental listening style:

> Results show surprisingly clearly how strongly individual listening styles are connected with the experience of individual problems, depression appearing to be the most important experience in this context. In most cases, plausible explanations for the interrelations between problem experience and listening style are possible. (p. 157)

Musical Preferences and Music Education

Musical preferences must be reckoned with in music education. On the one hand, they may provide the impulse for music instruction; on the other hand, they may also be a result of teaching. Music education usually strives for a pluralistic and tolerant musical taste. However, there are diverging opinions about whether or not teachers should try to influence the musical tastes of their students (cf. Finnäs, 1989, p. 43). Current knowledge makes it appear unlikely that music education can have a lasting effect on young people's musical preferences, especially during the first stage in the development of preferences and during puberty. At this time, the open-earedness is limited and the emotions run high. A survey of research into the possibilities of influencing musical preferences (cf. Finnäs, 1989) finds that students will generally not prefer music that is slow or rhythmically, melodically, and harmonically complex or vocal music. However, the preference for music increases once it becomes more familiar. In light of this, it may be advisable to repeat the presentation of unknown music in more than one lesson. Also, information about composers or musicians as well as live concerts can positively influence an interest in unfamiliar music.

Puberty as a Critical Phase in Musical Development

Puberty is a time of significant change, not only with respect to the development of musical preferences. During this time, decisions are made about instrumental music education with far-reaching consequences. Even in the biographies of professional musicians, turning points and setbacks can be observed at the onset of puberty (Manturzewska, 1990). A study among violinists provided evidence for a critical stage between the ages of 12 and 16. The best musicians were able to increase their amount of practice more than the average during this period (e.g. Ericsson et al., 1993; Krampe, 1994; see chap. 7, by Andreas C. Lehmann and Jane W. Davidson, in this volume). Making music and practicing an instrument thus becomes an important part of one's personal identity. Many other students drop out of instrumental lessons during this time. The reason is that young people's longing for autonomy and their search for personal identity now require more freedom and less rigid guidance (see Grimmer, 1991). Unfortunately, many teachers' abilities to cope with these changed desires in instrumental music lessons are quite limited.

Parents and teachers know very well that puberty is a critical stage for musical development. It is surprising that research has not yet adequately addressed the influences of changes in personality, motivation, interests, and sociopsychological conditions typical for this developmental stage on music instruction.

Developmental Processes Throughout Adulthood

The development of basic musical abilities, musical preferences, and aesthetic values takes place in the first two decades of life even in the absence of music education. However, more refined musical development requires deliberate activities and instruction. The range of individual differences with regard to music in adulthood encompasses the results of impressive specialization of the professional musician as well as the stagnation and decrease of musical abilities due to a lack of interest and motivation. This section offers a survey of research on musical development in adulthood, which is still in its infancy. I will first present some general comments on biological and cultural aspects of general conditions of aging during adulthood (cf. Baltes et al., 1998).

General Conditions of Aging: Biological Aspects

A number of age-related cognitive, sensory, and physiological changes occur in adulthood that can impact musical activities. Although these changes also affect younger adults, their influence increase at older ages (see Birren & Schaie, 1996, for relevant chapters). Starting around the age of 30, human physiological functions lose about 1% of their efficiency every year. In addition, the speed of cognitive processing and the discrimination of stimuli already start to decrease in early adulthood (e.g. Baltes et al., 1998; Jennen & Gembris, 2000; Park, 1999; Swartz et al., 1994). Another generally accepted effect of aging is the continuous decline of hearing. However, the body's great capacity for compensation can hide this slow process of reduction for a long time. Only when a critical limit is reached do these changes in physiological processes start to become a problem (Maier, Ambühl-Caesar, & Schandry, 1994, p. 167). For example, at older ages the decrease of sensorimotor speed and dexterity along with a reduction of the sense of touch and other micromotor impasses can lead to difficulties in instrumental playing.

A severe problem for singers is the change of the voice with age. This change is not directly related to chronological but to biological age, and it can be accompanied by effects like the loss of the chest voice, the fast change of pitch and timbre of the voice, the loss of intensity and resonance, and the reduced ability to control the many parameters involved in singing. Fortunately, these characteristics do not emerge all at the same time (Habermann, 1986, p. 148; Moore, Staum, & Brotons, 1992; Sataloff, 1992; Seidner & Wendler, 1997, p. 180).

The beginning of age-induced decline of physiological functioning is subject to individual differences and cannot be linked to a specific age. In addition, the amount of age-related changes and their significance for musical activities differ widely and depend also on other factors such as the level of musical training. For example, due to their maintenance practice, professional piano players are less affected by the decline of manual abilities than untrained amateurs of similar ages (Krampe, 1994; Krampe & Ericsson, 1996).

General Conditions of Aging: Cultural Aspects

Whereas the influence of biological aspects in the changes of function increases with age, the opposite is true for cultural influences. Even though the direct influence of culture on development lessens as an individual matures, existing differences in musical development, which stem from the time of childhood and adolescence, give rise to continuously increasing differences in the course of adulthood. This becomes obvious when professional musicians are compared to amateurs and people who are untrained in music. Musicians broaden the gap between themselves and less trained individuals through constant work and further development, while nonmusicians suffer a continuous decline because of their different professions and other activities. This means that developmental courses of professional musicians and amateurs point in opposite directions.

Creative Productivity of Composers Over Their Lifetimes

One of the first studies on the life-span development of creative work was carried out by Charlotte Bühler (1933/1959). Depending on the domain, different trajectories and peaks of creativity were found. An early study by Lehman and Ingerham (1939) showed that the peak of creativity for composers of classical music was reached between the ages 35 and 45. However, the age with the highest productivity seemed to depend on the specific musical genre. For instance, the peak for instrumental music occurred between the ages of 25 and 29, while most of the operas were composed between the ages of 35 and 40. Similar differences were encountered that concerned other musical forms, like symphonic music, chamber music, and sacred music. Using a different methodology, Dennis (1966) obtained converging results. For example, composers of chamber music reached their creative peaks between the ages of 30 and 39, whereas composers of operas had their highest productivity between the ages of 40 and 49. A remaining methodological problem of these studies is how to define and measure musical cre ativity if one does not only want to consider the number of compositions but also quality and other aspects (cf. Gembris, 2002, p. 375f).

More recently, a barrage of studies by Simonton have investigated the possible influences of culture, society, history, and biographical situation on creative productivity (e.g., Simonton, 1997, for a review). Based on his work, the author put forth a mathematical model that suggests that the lifetime trajectory of musical productivity (composition) could be represented by a tilted J-shaped function. Hence, the creative process rises quickly up to a peak that falls around the age of 40 (give or take a few years depending on the musical genre), after which there is a steady decrease. Of course, these kinds of statistical and graphic representations of creative productivity over the life span are idealized and based on averages. Given that individual differences of adults increase with age (see earlier), actual composers can differ from one another to a large extent.

Developmental Trajectories of Professional Instrumentalists

The social and individual preconditions for musical careers have been addressed in a number of studies by Manturzewska (1990, 1995). She examined the careers of 165 successful Polish musicians of different generations. The data collected consisted mainly of biographical interviews supplemented by archival material and quantitative data. Sosniak's (1985) studies of the careers of pianists were also based on biographical interviews.

Manturzewska (1995) identified six stages in the careers of professional instrumentalists in Western art music and characterized those according to the activities undertaken by the instrumentalists during those phases. The final phase after skill acquisition and a life of concertizing was marked by the fact that professional musicians turned to teaching as their main activity (see also chap. 30 in this volume for a broader discussion of skill acquisition). In another study among retired members of a first-class American orchestra, D. W. E. Smith (1988) observed that most of the musicians stopped playing completely. Due to a lack of motivation, they gave up regular practice and their performance no longer met their expectations. Furthermore, health problems may have resulted from giving up musical activities (cf. Darrough & Boswell, 1992, for a review).

The developmental stages that Manturzewska (1995) observed for outstanding musicians and that Sosniak (1985) described for concert pianists cannot be generalized to all professional musicians. The data are based on exceptional and successful musicians. Nowadays musicians' careers change structurally because many instrumentalists or singers do not hold steady jobs anymore. Instead, they earn a living with multiple and frequently changing jobs that may include nonmusical ones. In addition, becoming a professional musician through a conservatory degree does not necessarily mean that one will be working as a musician throughout the whole professional life. Both tendencies are supported by empirical data (HEFCE, 1998; Gembris &

Langner, in prep. (2005a, b); Mills & Smith, in prep (2005), and the consequences for the musicians' personal and professional identity as well as for the development of musical abilities have yet to be explored.

Maintaining High Performance in Old Age Through Practicing

A study among younger (average age: 24) and older (average age: 60) amateur and professional pianists was carried out by Krampe (1994; see also Krampe & Ericsson, 1996), who provided evidence that continuous musical activity counteracted the decline of musical performance in old age. Famous piano players like Artur Rubinstein (1887–1982) and Vladimir Horowitz (1903–1989), who still played concerts and produced records when they were more than 80 years old, illustrate that even very old persons can produce outstanding instrumental achievements. However, the examples mentioned are rare exceptions, and normally age-related declines cannot be prevented. It is possible to ameliorate the situation through the use of deliberate strategies like optimization, selection, and compensation (cf. Baltes & Baltes, 1989). Baltes, Lindenberger, and Staudinger (1998) offer the following interpretation of a television interview given by the 80-year-old Rubinstein:

> First, Rubinstein said that he played fewer pieces (selection); second, he indicated that he now practices these pieces more often (optimization); and third, he said that to counteract his loss in mechanical speed he now used a kind of impression management such as introducing slower play before fast segments, so to make the latter appear faster (compensation). (p. 1055)

However, it is likely that only pianists and conductors can maintain these kinds of outstanding results at old age, while it might be impossible for woodwind, brass, or string players. Those will be affected earlier by the decrease of sensorimotor functions as a result of aging. Additional problems for violin players that would lead to weaknesses in intonation and bowing could be the decline of the sense of touch along with the reduction of the skin's sensibility and reduced agility and speed.

Even though biological changes of the voice are also unavoidable, singers can work against them to a certain degree. Sataloff (1992, p. 20) suggests that in order to maintain a good physical condition it is necessary to exercise. Also, regular technical practice eliminates undesirable tremolo and improves the smoothness, exactness, and stamina of the voice for old as well as for young singers. According to Sataloff, many functions of the voice could be maintained at higher levels much longer than it is generally believed. Thus a singing career could possibly be extended beyond the age of 60 and into the seventh decade of life.

Musical Learning of Adult Amateurs and Nonmusicians: Cognitive Aspects

Findings on the development of musical abilities and interests of adult amateurs and nonmusicians are still inconclusive. Some authors have examined musical learning in areas including instrumental playing, sight-reading or sight-singing, rhythmic-melodic imitation, and aural training (Gibbons, 1983). The hypothesis that performance generally decreases with age is not supported by these studies (e.g., Klüppelholz, 1993). Even though learning might be more difficult in middle-aged and old-age groups, the overall achievements remained the same. In general, musical learning seems to be possible at every age.

Low self-confidence with regard to one's own musical performance and learning capabilities due to age may be more detrimental to a positive musical development than the actual decline of learning abilities. A fresh evaluation of one's own expectations, along with the idea that making music is enjoyable and requires neither high-level performance skills nor great talent, may provide a suitable basis for successful learning. Optimistically speaking, most of the older people have a considerable potential quite comparable to that of younger people and this can be activated by learning, practice, and deliberate training (Baltes & Baltes, 1989, p. 90; Staudinger, Cornelius, & Baltes, 1989). At the same time, these capacities do have limitations that cannot be altered even by intensive training (Baltes & Kliegl, 1992). There is no reason to assume that these capacities do not exist for musical abilities. On the contrary, current studies with adult nonmusicians demonstrate the possibility of learning new musical abilities with appropriate training. According to Gordon (1987), only very few people make use of all their existing capacities for musical abilities.

A number of studies clearly point to the fact that limitations to musical achievement are likely to increase with age (as far as psychomotor skills go). Older people need more time and more repetitions than younger individuals to attain the same level of performance (Mack, 1982). Also, a poorer musical long-term memory was observed by Bartlett and Snelus (1980). Finally, D. S. Smith (1991) examined the short-term memory of older people. Depending on their health status and social living conditions, memory capacities turned out to vary greatly. On the whole, these and other studies demonstrate that the decline of short-term memory of old people also applies to music, while significant interindividual differences can occur.

Although adults do not seem to be at a larger disadvantage in the cognitive domain than children and adolescents, their learning potential for instrumental technique is clearly limited (Kluppelholz, 1993). It would be possible to detail the difference between children's and adults' instrumental achievements by applying a "testing-the-limits" paradigm, an approach already applied to cognitive abilities (Baltes et al., 1998, p. 1066). However, no such studies in music have yet been carried out.

Adults who want to learn music have different motivations, learning styles, and learning difficulties from those of children. They tend to address their learning tasks primarily cognitively. It is common for adults to start to learn an instrument because they want to play in an ensemble or because they want to create new social contacts. Indeed, making music increases well-being and contributes to a balanced personality (Klüppelholz, 1993). The actual level of achievement and the desire to perform as a soloist are less important. Taking into account what we know about adult cognition and motivation is important for designing appropriate educational goals and methods.

Preferences During Adulthood

Most studies on musical preferences focus on the time of adolescence. The few existing studies on old people's preferences have emerged from the context of music therapy. Their results have been used for developing music programs in retirement homes and musicotherapeutic interventions. It became obvious from these studies that musical preferences primarily depended on the age and also on the social class. The effect of the chronological age on a person's musical preferences is mixed as well with the effects of the present point of time and with the effects of belonging to a specific generation (cohort). Therefore, age effects on musical preferences of adults should be viewed as a result of a combination of these three factors.

Musical preferences primarily depend on the individual and social functions of music. Thus the developmental perspective has to take into account age-related functions of music and age-related changes of functions (cf. Dollase et al., 1986; Mende, 1991). Lehmann (1994) showed convincingly that not only preferences changed with age but also the reasons for listening to music and the approaches to music. For example, with increasing age physiological and motor aspects relinquished their importance to the need for relaxation and empathy (Lehmann, 1994, p. 176).

A number of studies have demonstrated that older people, depending on their educational level and social environment, disliked current popular music and instead preferred other musical styles like country music, classical music, or traditional jazz. Quite often, older people's favorite music was the popular music of their youth (e.g. Gibbons, 1977; Holbrook & Schindler, 1989; Jonas, 1991; Moore et al., 1992). They also tended to prefer lower sound volumes and slower musical tempi (Moore et al., 1992).

Affective processes also undergo a lifelong development, as does the ability to recognize emotional expression in music. Current findings based on psychological data suggest that older persons experience fundamental emotions at a generally lower level of intensity than younger persons and that, in the case of geriatric patients, they show a decline in recognition of facial expression (Brosgole et al., 1983; Brosgole, Kurucz, Plahovinsak, Sprotte, & Haveliwala, 1983; Filipp, 1996). Complex emotions like those that arise from a musical experience have not yet been examined.

Even though experimental studies on the recognition of musical expression and on the ability to experience music in adulthood and old age are lacking, we can still derive some hypotheses for future research. The recognition of musical expression and the ability to experience music ought to depend on general factors (e.g. health status, social environment, etc.). Also, the development of recognition of musical expression is likely to be influenced by how much time a person devotes to music, if he or she is listening to music or actively making music, and if music in general holds a special status in that person's life. Just as existing abilities in other areas disappear as a result of lack of use and training, it is likely that musical abilities will decrease (disengagement or disuse hypothesis). This explanation could serve as a good reason for a lifelong active contact with music, especially since research on emotion has shown that even the most brilliant intelligence is hampered by the lack of emotional abilities (e.g., Damasio, 1997). Thus music seems to be an agreeable way to create and to maintain rich emotional experiences over the lifetime.

Conclusion

Considering the large individual differences in the musical development, the future psychology of life-span development of musical abilities will have to be a differential psychology. There is no such thing as a "normal" or average musical biography. For adult age in particular, it would appear to be more promising to focus on the existing diversity instead of trying to establish an "average."

Developmental psychology of music should not focus only on those cognitive or instrumental abilities that are readily measured. Instead, the ability to experience music, musical skills, and attitudes are also part of the musical development. Furthermore, changes of musical desires, interests, and motivations take place throughout life. Thus what we mean by *musical development* may be entirely different at different stages of life. While the first 10 years of life consist of the acquisition of basic musical abilities, musical development during adulthood possibly includes an expansion of musical preferences and the growth of musical understanding. Therefore, the notion of musical development as a continuum will in itself have to be reconsidered and subsequently expanded.

The idea of optimization through selection and compensation (see Baltes et al., 1998) and the concept of plasticity should provide new starting points for research on musical development. During adulthood or old age, musical activities are not merely leisure activities but rather play an important role in an individual's life as they help form identities, establish and maintain social contacts, and activate cognitive and emotional functions. Thereby musical activities contribute to a person's quality of life and well-being. Studies in the context of music therapy showed that the use of music in nursing homes and in geriatrics had a positive effect on cognitive functioning such as memory, mobilization, and social behavior (for an overview see Brotons, Koger & Pickett-Cooper, 1999). Although more research is badly needed, these facts illustrate the great importance of musical activities, especially during late adulthood and old age. As the number of older people in our society increases, the research results mentioned earlier will gain political importance, because if musical activities increase the quality of life and have positive effects on health, then they are extremely useful to society.

Encouraging musical learning in childhood and adolescence is an investment sure to produce long-term benefits at more mature ages. Even if no explicit support of the musical development has taken place during the early part of life, musical learning, musical activities, and some musical development are still possible during adulthood. Thus we can agree with the composer Robert Schumann who, in his musical rules for home and life ("Musikalische Haus-und Lebensregeln"), stated that "there is no end to learning."

STUDY QUESTIONS

1. Describe some generally important assumptions concerning musical development.

2. Name some fields of research on musical development which have generated significant new results in the research on musical development.

3. What do we know about prenatal hearing experiences?

4. Describe the development of pitch perception in the first ten years of life.

5. Describe the development of melody perception.

6. Describe the development of rhythmic abilities.

7. Describe the development of the sense for harmony and tonality.

8. Describe the development of the recognition of musical emotions.

9. Describe the development of singing abilities.

10. How do musical preferences develop in the course of childhood?

11. What functions do musical preferences have?

12. Are there gender differences in musical preferences?

13. Which general developmental processes in adulthood are important with respect to musical development?

14. Which decades are evidently the most productive years in the lives of composers of classical music?

15. Describe three principles which have proven to be effective in counteracting the age-related decline in musical performance.

16. Which aspects are important with respect to the musical learning of adult amateurs?

17. Explain how musical activities in adulthood can contribute to life quality and well-being.

NOTE

I am grateful to Mirjam Schlemmer and Jan Hemming for their indefatigable help with the English manuscript and the reviewers for their insightful comments.

REFERENCES

Baacke, D. (1993). Jugendkulturen und Musik. In H. Bruhn, R. Oerter, & H. Rösing (Eds.), *Musikpsychologie: Ein Handbuch* (pp. 228–237). Reinbek, Germany: Rororo.

Baltes, P. B., & Baltes, M. M. (1989). Optimierung durch Selektion und Kompensation: Ein psychologisches Modell erfolgreichen Alterns. *Zeitschrift für Pädagogik, 35,* 85–105.

Baltes, P. B., & Kliegl, R. (1992). Further testing of limits of cognitive plasticity: Negative age differences in a mnemonic skill are robust. *Developmental Psychology, 28,* 121–125.

Baltes, P. B., Lindenberger, U., & Staudinger, U. M. (1998). Life-span theory in developmental psychology. In W. Damon & R. M. Lerner (Eds.), *Handbook of child psychology: Vol. 1. Theoretical models of human development* (5th ed.) (pp. 1029–1143). New York: Wiley.

Bamberger, J. (1991). *The mind behind the musical ear: How children develop musical intelligence.* Cambridge, MA: Harvard University Press.

Bartlett, J. C., & Snelus, P. (1980). Lifespan memory for popular songs. *American Journal of Psychology, 93,* 551–560.

Bastian, H. G. (1989). *Leben für Musik. Eine Biographie-Studie über musikalische (Hoch-) Begabungen.* [A life for music: A biographical study on high ability in music]. Mainz, Genmany: Schott.

Behne, K.-E. (1974). Psychologische Aspekte der Musikalität. In *Forschung in der Musikerziehung* (pp. 74–94) Mainz, Germany: Schott.

Behne, K.-E. (1986). *Hörertypologien: Zur Psychologie des jugendlichen Musikgeschmacks.* Regensburg, Germany: Bosse.

Behne, K.-E. (1997). The development of "Musikerleben" in adolescence: How and why young people listen to music. In I. Deliège & J. Sloboda (Eds.), *Perception and cognition of music* (pp. 143–159). Hove, UK: Psychology Press.

Behrens, G. A., & Green, S. B. (1993). The ability to identify emotional content of solo improvisations performed vocally and on three different instruments. *Psychology of Music, 21,* 20–33.

Birren, J. E., & Schaie, K. W. (Eds.). (1996). *Handbook of the psychology of aging* (4th ed.). San Diego, CA: Academic Press.

Brosgole, L., Kurucz, J., Plahovinsak, T. J., Boettcher, P., Sprotte, C., & Haveliwala, Y. A. (1983). Facial-affect recognition in normal pre-school children and in elderly persons. *International Journal of Neuroscience, 20*(1–2), 91–102.

Brosgole, L., Kurucz, J., Plahovinsak, T. J., Sprotte, C., & Haveliwala, Y. A.

(1983). Facial and postural-affect recognition in senile elderly persons. *International Journal of Neuroscience, 22*(1–2), 37–46.

Brotons, M., Koger, S. M., & Pickett-Cooper, P. (1999). Music and dementias: A review of literature. *Journal of Music Therapy, 34*(4), 204–245.

Bühler, C. (1959). *Der menschliche Lebenslauf als psychologisches Problem* (2nd. ed.). Göttingen, Germany: Hogrefe. (Original work published 1933.)

Case, R. (1998). The development of conceptual structures. In W. Damon, D. Kuhn, & R. Siegler (Eds.), *Handbook of child psychology: Vol. 2. Cognition, perception and language* (5th ed., pp. 745–800). New York: Wiley.

Cunningham, J. G., & Sterling, R. S. (1988). Developmental change in the understanding of affective meaning in music. *Motivation and Emotion, 12*(4), 399–413.

Damasio, A. R. (1997). *Denken, Fühlen und das menschliche Gehirn.* Munich, Germany: dtv.

Darrough, G. P., & Boswell, J. (1992). Older adult participants in music: A review of related literature. *Council for Research in Music Education, Bull. no. 111,* 1–24.

Davidson, L. (1994). Songsinging by young and old: A developmental approach to music. In R. Aiello (Ed.), *Musical perceptions* (pp. 99–130). New York: Oxford University Press.

Davidson, L., & Scripp, L. (1990). Education and development in music from a cognitive perspective. In D. J. Hargreaves (Ed.), *Children and the arts* (pp. 59–86). Philadelphia: Open University Press.

Davidson, L., & Scripp, L. (1992). Surveying the coordinates of cognitive skills in music. In R. J. Colwell (Ed.), *Handbook of research on music teaching and learning: A project of the Music Educators National Conference* (pp. 392–413). New York: Schirmer Books.

Davidson, L., & Welsh, P. (1988). From collection to structure. The developmental path of tonal thinking. In J. A. Sloboda (Ed.), *Generative processes in music: The psychology of performance, improvisation, and composition* (pp. 260–285). Oxford: Clarendon Press.

DeCasper, A. J., & Spence, M. J. (1986). Prematernal speech influences newborn's perception of speech sounds. *Infant Behavior and Development, 9,* 133–150.

Deliège, I., Mélen, M., & Bertrand, D. (1995). *Development of music perception: An integrative view.* Paper presented at the Seventh European Conference on Developmental Psychology (pp. 23–27). Kraków, Poland.

Demany, L., & Armand, F. (1984). The perceptual reality of tone chroma in early infancy. *Journal of the Acoustical Society of America, 76* (1), 57–66.

Dennis, W. (1966). Creative productivity between the ages of 20 and 80 years. *Journal of Gerontology, 21,* 1–8.

Dolgin, K., & Adelson, E. (1990). Age changes in the ability to interpret affect in sung and instrumentally-presented melodies. *Psychology of Music, 18,* 87–98.

Dollase, R. (1997). Musikpräferenzen und Musikgeschmack Jugendlicher. In D. Baacke, (Ed.), *Handbuch Jugend und Musik* (pp. 341–368). Opladen, Germany: Leske + Burich.

Dollase, R., Rüsenberg, M., & Stollenwerk, H. J. (1986). *Demoskopie im Konzertsaal.* Mainz, Germany: Schott.

Dowling, W. J., & Harwood, D. L. (1986). *Musical cognition*. Orlando, FL: Academic Press.

Dowling, W. J. (1988). Tonal structure and children's early learning of music. In J. A. Sloboda (Ed.), *Generative processes in music: The psychology of performance, improvisation, and composition* (pp. 113–128). Oxford: Clarendon Press.

Dowling, W. J. (1999). The development of music perception and cognition. In D. Deutsch (Ed.), *The psychology of music* (2nd ed., pp. 603–627). San Diego, CA: Academic Press.

Elbert, T., Pantev, C., Wienbruch, C., Rockstroh, B., & Taub, E. (1995). Increased cortical representation of the fingers of the left hand in string players. *Science, 270*, 305–307.

Ericsson, K. A., Krampe, R. T, & Tesch-Römer, C. (1993). The role of deliberate practice in the acquisition of expert performance. *Psychological Review, 100*(3), 363–406.

Fassbender, C. (1996). Infants' auditory sensitivity towards acoustic parameters of speech and music. In I. Deliège & J. A. Sloboda, (Eds.), *Musical beginnings: Origins and development of musical competence* (pp. 56–87). Oxford: Oxford University Press.

Feijoo, J. (1981). Le foetus Pierre et le loup: Ou une approche originale de l'audition prenatale humaine. In E. Herbinet & M. C. Busnel (Eds.), *L'aube des Sens* (pp. 192–209). Paris: Stock.

Filipp, S. H. (1996). Motivation and emotion. In J.-E. Birren & K. W. Schaie (Eds.), *Handbook of the psychology of aging* (4th ed., pp. 218–235) San Diego, CA: Academic Press.

Finnäs, L. (1989, Fall). How can musical preferences be modified? *Council for Research in Music Education, Bull. no. 102*, 1–58.

Flammer, A. (1996) *Entwicklungstheorien: Psychologische Theorien der menschlichen Entwicklung* (2nd ed.). Bern, Switzerland: Huber.

Flowers, P. J., & Costa-Giomi, E. (1991). Verbal and nonverbal identification of pitch changes in a familiar song by English- and Spanish-speaking preschool children. *Council for Research in Music Education, Bull. no. 107*, 1–12.

Fox, D. B. (1990). An analysis of the pitch characteristics of infant vocalizations. *Psychomusicology, 9*, 21–30.

Gardner, H. (1991). *The unschooled mind*. New York: Basic Books.

Gembris, H. (1995). Musikpräferenzen, Generationswandel und Medienalltag. [Music preferences, change of generation and everyday life with media]. In G. Maas (Ed.), *Musiklernen und Neue (Unterrichts-) Technologien*, Musikpädagogische Forschung, Vol. 16 (pp. 124–145). Essen, Germany: Die blaue Eule.

Gembris, H. (1997). Time specific and cohort specific influences on musical development. *Polish Quarterly of Developmental Psychology, 3*(1), 77–89.

Gembris, H. (2002). Grundlagen musikalischer Begabung und Entwicklung. [Foundations of musical talent and development]. Second edition: Augsburg, Germany, Wissner.

Gembris, H. (2004) A new approach to pursuing the professional development of recent graduates from German music academies: The alumni project. In J. W. Davidson (Ed.), *The music practitioner. Research for the music performer, teacher and listener*. London: Ashgate, 309–317.

Gembris, H., & Davidson, J. (2002). Environmental influences. In R. Parncutt & G. E. McPherson (Eds.), *The science and psychology of musical performance*. New York: Oxford University Press, 17–30.

Gembris, H., & Langner, D. (2005a). What are instrumentalists doing after graduating from the music academy? Some results of the alumni project. In H. Gembris (Ed.), *Musical development in a life-span perspective*. Frankfurt: Lang.

Gembris, H., & Langner, D. (2005b). What are singers doing after having left the music academy? In H. Gembris (Ed.), *Musical development in a life-span perspective*. Frankfurt: Lang.

Gembris, H., & Schellberg, G. (2003). Musical preferences of elementary school children. Paper presented at the 5th ESCOM Conference, Hanover. In R. Kopiez, A. C. Lehmann, I. Wolther, & C. Wolf, *Abstracts of the 5th triennial conference of the European Society for the Cognitive Sciences of Music (ESCOM)*. Hanover University of Music and Drama, September 8–13, 2003, Hanover University of Music and Drama: Hanover, 324.

Gerard, C., & Auxiette, C. (1992). The processing of musical prosody by musical and non-musical children. *Music Perception, 10*, 93–126.

Gibbons, A. C. (1977). Popular music preferences of elderly people. *Journal of Music Therapy, 14*(4), 180–189.

Gibbons, A. C. (1983). Primary measures of music audiation scores in an institutionalized elderly population. *Journal of Music Therapy, 20*(1), 21–29.

Giomo, C. J. (1993). An experimental study of children's sensitivity to mood in music. *Psychology of Music, 21*, 141–162.

Goetze, M., Cooper, N., & Brown, C. J. (1990). Recent research on singing in the general music classroom. *Council for Research in Music Education, Bull. no. 104*, 16–37.

Gordon, E. E. (1981). Wie Kinder Klänge als Musik wahrnehmen. Eine Längsschnittuntersuchung zur musikalischen Begabung. In K.-E. Behne (Ed.), *Musikalische Sozialisation: Musikpädagogische Forschung* (Vol. 2, pp. 30–63). Laaber, Germany: Laaber Verlag.

Gordon, E. E. (1987). *The nature, description, measurement, and evaluation of music aptitudes*. Chicago: GIA.

Gordon, E. E. (1990). *A music learning theory for newborn and young children*. Chicago: GIA.

Graml, K., Kraemer, R. D., & Gembris, H. (1988). Filmdokumentation Musikpädagogische Forschung "Der Feuervogeltest": Studien zum musikalischen Gedächtnis. In C. Nauck-Börner (Ed., Arbeitskreis Musikpädagogische Forschung), *Musikpädagogische Forschung* (Vol. 9, pp. 163–178). Laaber, Germany: Laaber Verlag.

Green, L. (1997). *Music, gender, education*. Cambridge, UK: Cambridge University Press.

Grimmer, F. (1991). *Wege und Umwege zur Musik: Klavierausbildung und Lebensgeschichte*. Kassel, Germany: Bärenreiter.

Gromko, J. E. (1994). Children's invented notations as measures of musical understanding. *Psychology of Music, 22*, 136–147.

Haack, P. (1992). The aquisition of listening skills. In R. J. Colwell (Ed.), *Handbook of research on music teaching and learning: A project of the Music Educators National Conference* (pp. 451–465). New York: Schirmer Books.

Habermann, G. (1986). *Stimme und Sprache: Eine Einführung in ihre Physiologie und Hygiene* (2nd ed.). Stuttgart, Germany: Thieme.

Haith, M. M., & Benson, J. B. (1998). Infant cognition. In D. Kuhn & R. S. Siegler (Eds.), *Handbook of child psychology: Vol. 2. Cognition, perception, and language* (5th ed., pp. 199–254). New York: Wiley.

Hargreaves, D. J. (1982). The development of aesthetic reaction to music [Special issue], *Psychology of Music, 51–54.*

Hargreaves, D. J. (1986). *The developmental psychology of music.* Cambridge: Cambridge University Press.

Hargreaves, D. J. (1996). The development of artistic and musical development. In I. Deliège & J. A. Sloboda, (Eds.), *Musical beginnings: Origins and development of musical competence* (pp. 145–170). Oxford: Oxford University Press.

Hargreaves, D. J., Comber, C., & Colley, A. (1996). Effects of age, gender, and training on musical preferences of British secondary school students. *Journal of Research in Music Education, 44*(3), 242–250.

Hassler, M. (1991). Maturation rate and spatial, verbal, and musical abilities: A seven-year longitudinal study. *International Journal of Neuroscience, 58,* 183–198.

Hassler, M. (1992). The critical teens: Musical capacities change in adolescence. *European Journal of High Ability, 3,* 89–98.

Hemming, J., & Kleinen, G. (1999). The beginning of musical careers in jazz, rock & pop: A practice diary study among school bands. In N. Jeanneret & K. Marsch (Eds.), *Opening the umbrella: An encompassing view of music education: Proceedings of the 12th National Conference of the Australian Society for Music Education (ASME)* (pp. 69–75). Baulkham Hills, Australia: Margret McMurtry.

Hepper, P. G. (1991). An examination of foetal learning before and after birth. *Irish Journal of Psychology, 12,* 95–107.

HEFCE [Higher Education Funding Council for England]. (1998). Report 98/11. Retrieved January 15, 2001, from http://www.hefce.ac.uk/pubs/hefce/1998/98=_11.htm

Holbrook, M. B., & Schindler, R. M. (1989, June). Some exploratory findings on the development of musical tastes. *Journal of Consumer Research, 16,* 119–124.

Huston, A. C., & Wright, J. C. (1998). Contributions of television toward meeting the informational and educational needs of children. *The Annals of the American Academy of Political and Social Science, 557,* 9–23.

Imberty, M. (1969). *L'acquisition des structures tonales chez l'enfant.* Paris: Klincksieck.

Jennen, M., & Gembris, H. (2000). Veränderungen des musikalischen Tempos bei Dirigenten: Eine empirische Untersuchung anhand von Schallplattenaufnahmen von Mozarts "Don Giovanni" und "Die Zauberflöte." In K.-F. Behne, G. Kleinen, & H. de la Motte-Haber (Eds.), *Musikpsychologie: Bd. 15. Die Musikerpersönlichkeit* (pp. 29–46). Göttingen, Germany: Hogrefe.

Jonas, J. L. (1991). Preferences of elderly music listeners residing in nursing homes for art music, traditional jazz, popular music of today, and country music. *Journal of Music Therapy, 28*(3), 149–160.

Jørgensen, H., & Lehmann, A. C. (Eds.). (1997). *Does practice make perfect?*

Current theory and research on instrumental music practice. Oslo: Norwegian State Academy of Music.

Kastner, M., & Crowder, R. G. (1990). Perception of the major/minor distinction. IV. Emotional connotation in young children. *Music Perception, 8*(2), 189–202.

Kelley, L., & Sutton-Smith, B. (1987). A study of infant musical productivity. In J. C. Peery, I. Weiss Peery, & T. W. Draper (Eds.), *Music and child development* (pp. 35–53). New York: Springer.

Kemp, A. (1996). *The musical temperament: Psychology and personality of musicians.* Oxford: Oxford University Press.

Klüppelholz, W. (1993). *Projekt Musikalische Erwachsenenbildung an Musikschulen, 1990–1992: Abschlussbericht der wissenschaftlichen Begleitung.* Bonn, Germany: Verband Deutscher Musikschulen.

Krampe, R. T. (1994). *Studien und Berichte des Max-Planck-Instituts für Bildungsforschung: Vol. 58. Maintaining excellence: Cognitive-motor performance in pianists differing in age and skill level.* Berlin, Germany: Vertries edition sigma.

Krampe, R. T., & Ericsson, K. A. (1996). Maintaining excellence: Deliberate practice and elite performance in young and older pianists. *Journal of Experimental Psychology: General 125,* 331–359.

Kratus, J. (1993). A developmental study of children's interpretation of emotion in music. *Psychology of Music, 21,* 3–19.

Lamont, A. (1998). Music, education, and the development of pitch perception: The role of context, age and musical experience. *Psychology of Music, 26,* 7–25.

LeBlanc, A. (1991). *Effect of maturation/age on music listening preference: A review of literature.* Paper presented at the Ninth National Symposium on Research in Music Behavior, Cannon Beach, OR.

Lecanuet, J.-P. (1996). Prenatal auditory experience. In I. Deliège & J. A. Sloboda (Eds.), *Musical beginnings: Origins and development of musical competence* (pp. 3–34). Oxford: Oxford University Press.

Lehmann, A. C. (1994). *Habituelle und situative Rezeptionsweisen beim Musikhören: Eine einstellungstheoretische Untersuchung* [Habitual and situational music listening patterns]. Frankfurt, Germany: Peter Lang.

Lehman, H. C., & Ingerham, D. W. (1939). Man's creative years in music. *Scientific Monthly, 48,* 431–443.

Lynch, M. P. (1993). Prototypical representations of musical structure in infancy: Theoretical exploration and a pilot study. *Psychomusicology, 12,* 31–40.

Lynch, M. P., & Eilers, R. E. (1991). Children's perception of native and non-native musical scales. *Music Perception, 9*(1), 121–132.

Lynch, M. P., Eilers, R. E., Oller, D. K., & Urbano, R. C. (1990). Innateness, experience, and music perception. *Psychological Science, 1*(4), 272–276.

Mack, L. S. (1982). *Self-concept and musical achievement in the adult learner.* Unpublished dissertation, University of Illinois at Urbana-Champaign.

Maidlow, S., & Bruce, R. (1999). The role of psychology research in understanding the sex-gender paradox in music—Plus ça change. *Psychology of music 27*(2), 147–158.

Maier, K., Ambühl-Caesar, G., & Schandry R. (1994). *Entwicklungspsychophysiologie: Körperliche Indikatoren psychischer Entwicklung.* Munich, Germany: Beltz Psychologie Verlags Union.

Manturzewska, M. (1990). A biographical study of the life-span development of professional musicians. *Psychology of Music, 18,* 112–138.

Manturzewska, M. (1995). A biographical study of the life-span development of professional musicians. In M. Manturzewska, K. Miklaszewski, & A. Bialkowski (Eds.), *Psychology of music today (Proceedings of the International Seminar of Researchers and Lecturers in the Psychology of Music)* (pp. 311–337). Radziejowice, Poland: Warsaw Fryderyk Chopin Academy of Music.

Martin, G., Clarke, M., & Pearse, C. (1993). Adolescent suicide: Music preference as an indicator of vulnerability. *Journal of the Academy of Child and Adolescent Psychiatry, 32*(2), 530–535.

Meltzoff, A. N., Kuhl, P., & Moore, M. K. (1991). Perception, representation, and the control of action in newborn and young infants towards a new synthesis. In M.J.S. Weiss & P. R. Zelazo (Eds.), *Newborn attention: Biological constraints and the influence of experience* (pp. 377–411). Norwood, NJ: Ablex.

Mende, A. (1991). Musik und Alter: Ergebnisse zum Stellenwert von Musik im biographischen Lebensverlauf. *Rundfunk und Fernsehen, 39*(3), 381–392.

Metzler, F. (1962). Strukturen kindlicher Melodik. *Psychologische Beiträge, 7,* 218–284.

Mills, J., & Smith, J. (2005) Working in music: Becoming successful. In H. Gembris (Ed.), *Musical development in a life-span perspective.* Frankfurt: Lang.

Minkenberg, H. (1991). *Das Musikerleben von Kindern im Alter von fünf bis zehn Jahren.* Frankfurt, Germany: Peter Lang.

Montgomery, A. P. (1996). Effect of tempo on music preferences of children in elementary and middle school. *Journal of Research in Music Education, 44*(2), 134–146.

Moog, H. (1976). *The musical experience of the pre-school child* (C. Clarke, Trans.). London: Schott.

Moore, R. S., Staum, M. J., & Brotons, M. (1992). Music preferences of the elderly: Repertoire, vocal ranges, tempos, and accompaniments for singing. *Journal of Music Therapy, 29*(4), 236–252.

Morrongiello, B. A. (1992). Effects of training on children's perception of music: A review. *Psychology of Music, 20,* 29–41.

Müler, R. (1999). Musikalische Selbstsozialisation. In J. Fromme, S. Kommer, J. Mansel, & K.-P. Treumann (Ed.), *Selbstsozialisation, Kinderkultur und Mediennutzung* (pp. 113–125). Opladen, Germany: Leske + Budrich.

Nelson, D. (1987). An interpretation of the Piagetian model in light of the theories of Case. *Council for Research in Music Education, Bull. no. 92,* 23–34.

Papoušek, H. (1996). Musicality in infancy research: Biological and cultural origins of early musicality. In I. Deliège & J. A. Sloboda (Eds.), *Musical beginnings: Origins and development of musical competence* (pp. 37–55). Oxford: Oxford University Press.

Papoušek, M. (1994). *Vom ersten Schrei zum ersten Wort. Anfange der Sprachentwicklung in der vorsprachlichen Kommunikation* [From the first cry to the first word. Beginnings of language development in the pre-verbal communication]. Bern, Switzerland: Huber.

Papoušek, M. (1996). Intuitive parenting: A hidden source of musical stimulation in infancy. In I. Deliège & J. A. Sloboda (Eds.), *Musical beginnings:*

Origins and development of musical competence (pp. 88–112). Oxford: Oxford University Press.

Papoušek, M., & Papoušek, H. (1986). *Structure and dynamics of human communication at the beginning of life.* European Archives of Psychiatry and Neurological Science, vol. 236, no. 1, 21–25.

Park, D., & Schwarz, N. (Eds.). (1999). *Cognitive aging. A primer.* London: Psychology Press.

Pascual-Leone, A. (2001). The brain that plays music and is changed by it. In R. J. Zatorre & I. Peretz (Eds.), *The biological foundations of music* (pp. 315–329). Annals of the New York Academy of Sciences, vol. 930. New York: The New York Academy of Sciences.

Pflederer, M. (1964). The responses of children to musical tasks embodying Piaget's principle of conservation. *Journal of Research in Music Education, 12,* 251–268.

Pflederer, M., & Sechrest, L. (1968). Conservation-type responses of children to musical stimuli. *Council for Research in Music Education, Bull. no. 13,* 19–36.

Pouthas, V. (1996). The development of perception of time and temporal regulation of action in infants and children. In I. Deliége & J. Sloboda (Eds.), *Musical beginnings: Origins and development of musical competence* (pp. 115–141). Oxford: Oxford University Press.

Rainbow, E. (1980). A final report on a three-year investigation of the rhythmic abilities of preschool aged children. *Council for Research in Music Education, Bull. no. 62,* 69–73.

Rainbow, E., & Owen, D. (1979). A progress report on a three-year investigation of the rhythmic ability of preschool aged children. *Council for Research in Music Education, Bull. no. 59,* 84–86.

Ramsey, J. H. (1983). The effects of age, singing ability, and instrumental experiences on preschool children's melodic perception. *Journal of Research in Music Education, 31,* 133–145.

Rauh, H. (1995). Frühe Kindheit. In R. Oerter & L. Montada (Eds.), *Entwicklungspsychologie* (3rd ed.), (pp. 167–309). Weinheim, Germany: Psychologie Verlags Union.

Sataloff, R. T. (1992). Vocal aging medical considerations in professional voice users. *Medical Problems of Performing Artists, 7*(1), 17–21.

Satt, B. J. (1984). *An investigation into the acoustical induction of intrauterine learning.* Unpublished dissertation, University of California at Los Angeles.

Schellberg, G. (1998). *Zur Entwicklung der Klangfarbenwahrnehmung von Vorschulkindern.* Münster, Germany: Lit Verlag.

Schellberg, G., & Gembris, H. (2003). Was Grundschulkinder (nicht) hören wollen. Eine Studie über Musikpräferenzen von Kindern in der 1. bis 4. Klasse. In Musik in der Grundschule, Heft 4/2003, S. 48–52.

Scheuer, W. (1988). *Zwischen Tradition und Trend: Die Einstellung Jugendlicher zum Instrumentalspiel* [Between tradition and trend: Adolescents' attitudes toward playing a musical instrument]. Mainz, Germany: Schott.

Schlaug, G. (2001). The brain of musicians. A model for functional and structural adaptation. In R. J. Zatorre & I. Peretz (Eds.), *The biological foundations of music* (pp. 281–299). Annals of the New York Academy of Sciences, vol. 930. New York: The New York Academy of Sciences.

Schlaug, G., Jäncke, L., Huang, Y., Staiger, J. F., & Steinmetz, H. (1995). Increased corpus callosum size in musicians. *Neuropsychologia, 33*(8), 1047–1055.

Schwarzer, G. (1997). Analytic and holistic modes in the development of melody perception. *Psychology of Music, 25,* 35–56.

Seidner, W., & Wendler, J. (1997). *Die Sängerstimme: Phoniatrische Grundlagen der Gesangsausbildung* (3rd ed.). Berlin: Henschel.

Shuter-Dyson, R. (1982). Musical ability. In D. Deutsch (Ed.), *The psychology of music* (pp. 391–412). New York: Academic Press.

Shuter-Dyson, R., & Gabriel, C. (1981). *The psychology of musical ability.* London: Methuen.

Simonton, D. K. (1997). Products, persons, and periods: Historiometric analyses of compositional creativity. In D. Hargreaves & A. North (Eds.), *The social psychology of music* (pp. 107–122). Oxford: Oxford University Press.

Simonton, D. K. (2000). Creative development as acquired expertise: Theoretical issues and an empirical test. *Developmental Review, 20* (2), 283–318.

Sloboda, J., & Davidson, J. (1996). The young performing musician. In I. Deliége & J. Sloboda (Eds.), *Musical beginnings: Origins and development of musical competence* (pp. 171–190). Oxford: Oxford University Press.

Sloboda, J. A., Davidson, F. W., Moore, D., & Howe, M. (1994). Formal practice as a predictor of success and failure in instrumental learning. In I. Deliège (Ed.), *Proceedings of the 3rd International Conference for Music Perception and Cognition* (pp. 124–128). Liège, Belgium: ESCOM (European Society for the Cognitive Sciences of Music).

Smith, D. S. (1991). A comparison of group performance and song familiarity on cued recall tasks with older adults. *Journal of Music Therapy, 28* (1), 2–13.

Smith, D.W.E. (1988). The great symphony orchestra—A relatively good place to grow old. *International Journal of Aging and Human Development, 27*(4), 233–247.

Smith, K. C., Cuddy, L. L., & Upitis, R. (1994). Figural and metric understanding of rhythm. *Psychology of Music, 22,* 117–135.

Sosniak, L. A. (1985). Learning to be a concert pianist. In B. S. Bloom (Ed.), *Developing talent in young people* (pp. 19–67). New York: Ballantine Books.

Spiegler, D. M. (1967). *Factors involved in the development of prenatal rhythmic sensivity.* Unpublished dissertation, West Virginia University.

Stadler, S. (2000). *Spiel und Nachahmung: Über die Entwicklung der elementaren musikalischen Aktivitäten* [Play and imitation: About the development of basic musical activities]. Aarau, Switzerland: Nepomuk.

Stadler Elmer, S. (2002). *Kinder singen Lieder: Über den Prozess der Kultivierung des vokalen Ausdrucks.* Münster: Waxmann.

Staudinger, U. M., Cornelius, S. W., & Baltes, P. B. (1989). The aging of intelligence: Potential and limits. *Annals AAPSS, 503,* 44–58.

Swanwick, K. (1994). *Musical knowledge: Intuition, analysis and music education.* London: Routledge & Kegan Paul.

Swartz, K. P., Walton, J. P., Hantz, E. C., & Goldhammer E. (1994). P3 event related potentials and performance of young and old subjects for music perception tasks. *International Journal of Neuroscience, 78,* 223–239.

Terwogt, M. M., & van Grinsven, F. (1988). Recognition of emotions in music by children and adults. *Perceptual and Motor Skills, 67*(3), 697–698.

Terwogt, M. M., & van Grinsven, F. (1991). Musical expression of moodstates. *Psychology of Music, 19,* 99–109.

Trainor, L. J., & Trehub, S. E. (1992). The development of referential meaning in music. *Music Perception, 9*(4), 455–470.

Trehub, S. E. (1993). The music listening skills of infants and young children. In T. J. Tighe & W. J. Dowling (Eds.), *Psychology and music: The understanding of melody and rhythm* (pp. 161–176). Hillsdale, NJ: Erlbaum.

Trehub, S. E., Bull, D., & Thorpe, L. A. (1984). Infant's perception of melodies: The role of melodic contour. *Child Development, 55,* 821–830.

Trehub, S., Trainor, L., & Unyk, A. (1993). Music and speech processing in the first year of life. In H. W. Reese (Ed.), *Advances in child development and behavior* (Vol. 24, pp. 1–35). New York: Academic Press.

Trevarthen, C. (1999–2000). Musicality and the intrinsic motive pulse evidence from human psychobiology and infant communication [Special issue], *Musicae Scientiae,* 155–199.

Upitis, R. (1987). Children's understanding of rhythm: The relationship between musical development and music training. *Psychomusicology, 7*(1), 41–60.

Valentine, C. W. (1962). *The experimental psychology of the beauty.* London: Methuen.

Welch, G. F., & White, P. (1994). The developing voice Education and vocal efficiency—A physical perspective. *Council for Research in Music Education, Bull. no. 119,* 146–156.

Werner, H. (1917). Die melodische Erfindung im frühen Kindesalter: Eine entwicklungspsychologische Untersuchung. In *Sitzungsberichte der Kaiserlichen Akademie der Wissenschaften in Wien, Philosophisch-historische Klasse* (Vol. 182, pp. 1–100). Vienna: Tempsky.

Wolff, P. H. (1969). The natural history of crying and other vocalizations in early infancy. In B. Foss (Ed.), *Determinants of infant behavior* (Vol. 4) (pp. 81–109). London: Methuen.

Young, L. P. (1982). *An investigation of young children's music concept development using nonverbal and manipulative techniques.* Unpublished dissertation, Ohio State University.

Zenatti, A. (1993). Children's musical cognition and taste. In T. J. Tighe & W. J. Dowling (Eds.), *Psychology and music: The understanding of melody and rhythm* (pp. 177–196). Hillsdale, NJ: Erlbaum.

Zillman, D., & Gan, S.-L. (1997). Musical taste in adolescence. In D. Hargreaves & A. North (Eds.), *The social psychology of music* (pp. 161–187). Oxford: Oxford University Press.

A Comparative Review of Human Ability Theory

5

Context, Structure, and Development

BRUCE TORFF

A quick look around the world yields abundant examples of impressive human accomplishments. People are able to set new records in athletics, publish groundbreaking scientific works, and produce beautiful and challenging new music and art. Examples such as these raise old and vexing questions about the human abilities involved in complex performances like those in athletics, science, music, and art. To what extent do complex performances require abilities unique to particular domains and disciplines (e.g., language, mathematics)? To what extent are complex performances dependent upon general abilities that cut across domains and disciplines? How and why did abilities take this form, over the aeons? How do abilities change with age and experience? How can they be fostered?

These questions have been tackled over the centuries by a diverse group of psychologists, philosophers, sociologists, anthropologists, educators, and others focused on cognition, learning, development, and education. Historically, complex performances have posed a daunting challenge for these researchers. Accordingly, psychological work in the last century has made more headway with simpler performances that are easily measured, especially ones in laboratory settings that allow researchers to control the context in which tasks and instruments are implemented. Complex performances are far harder to study, and the psychological literature reflects this fact. As a result, practitioners and educators in many disciplines find the psychological literature too remote to be of much value (Egan, 1992).

But in recent decades, new theory and research have offered fresh perspectives on the development and nurturance of human abilities. Since the "cognitive revolution" that began in the late 1950s, attention has focused on the intellectual aspects of performances previously thought to be outside the realm of the cognitive. Traditionally, abilities in disciplines such as athletics, music, and art have been cast as "talents" that are conceptually distinct from "cognitive" abilities such as language and mathematics. The new perspective encompasses the cognitive underpinnings of all human abilities, even in matters athletic and aesthetic. Across the vast range of domains and disciplines, cognitive aspects of performance are coming under scrutiny, with human abilities cast increasingly as developing intellectual competences rather than fixed and innately specified aptitudes. It should be noted that this new body of cognitive work accompanies related investigations by researchers interested in other aspects of human experience, including philosophical, social, affective, moral, and practical ones.

The wealth of new ideas makes it a propitious time for a review of the literature in recent decades, with the goal of addressing anew some old questions about human abilities, especially as they are used in complex performances. It turns out that new theory and research dispute some widely held assumptions about human abilities and their development. In this chapter I review recent trends in theoretical conceptions of human abilities and explore their educational implications.

It may seem strange for this chapter to appear in a handbook on music education, since I make no effort here to examine musical ability specifically. This chapter takes a more general perspective on the abilities that underlie complex performances, for two reasons: to provide a review of theory in the psychological literature that may prove of interest to musical practitioners and educators and to stimulate discussion about the larger framework of which musical abilities are part, especially concerning the extent to which musical ability is unique to the domain of music or linked to other, extramusical abilities.

Psychology of Abilities: Past and Present

No discipline has a longer and more contentious history than studies of the human mind. Beginning perhaps with Plato's *Meno,* two millennia of scholarly attention have focused on the mind's structure, development, and nurturance. For most of this history, the workings of the mind have been viewed as issues of interest largely in the discipline of philosophy. But the industrial revolution brought forth a great flurry of activity in the sciences, and scholars interested in the mind sought "scientific" methods for studying their quarry. Psychology diverged from philosophy in the late 19th century, armed with newly crafted research methods modeled on the hard sciences. The new science of the mind put forward three theoretical models of human abilities.

First, the new focus on instrumentation and research methods led to a particular theoretical/methodological perspective of the mind, one that focused exclusively on observable behavior. This perspective is known variously as *behaviorism* and *learning theory* (e.g., Skinner, 1954; Thorndike, 1932; Watson, 1924). Eschewing constructs that can only be inferred to exist and cannot be observed directly (e.g., cognitive structure, knowledge), behaviorists explain human behavior in terms of the rewards and punishments associated with it. As such, behavior is under the control of externally imposed contingencies of reinforcement, and studying how these contingencies affect behavior is the goal of psychology. From the behaviorist perspective, abilities are patterns in behavior forged by a reinforcement history.

A second theory of human intellect became prominent in the 20th century—the "genetic epistemology" of Piaget, Inhelder, and associates (Piaget, 1983; see Gruber & Voneche, 1977). What is commonly known as *Piagetian theory* posits the mind as a general computational device that develops in predictable stages of development given the right kind of environmental interaction. Terms such as *equillibration, assimilation,* and *accommodation* were coined to describe the psychological processes involved in interaction and stage change. According to Piaget, abilities are outward manifestations of underlying cognitive structures that are innately specified but triggered through action on the environment.

The third theory of the psychology of human abilities is the notion of *general intelligence* (e.g., Eysenck, 1986; Thurstone, 1938). From this viewpoint, the human mind is structured with a single overarching cognitive ability called general intelligence, or *g.* The theory of general intelligence aims to predict individual differences in performance on intelligence tests and tests of other abilities. The high correlations among these various tests, the argument goes, support the claim that a general processing capacity constrains all intelligent action.

For decades, proponents of behaviorism, Piagetian theory, and general intelligence showed little regard for one another's perspective, underscoring the preparadigmatic character of psychological research. No widely accepted paradigm organizes modern psychology, as in physics, for example.

But disparate as these historically important models may be, they have in common a set of three related assumptions about human abilities. First, the three theories focus on the action of individual people. Each assumes that environmental elements such as language and culture have little impact on underlying cognitive structures and processes. Since abilities are viewed as fundamentally context-independent, it follows that the individual mind is the unproblematic unit of analysis for psychological research. Second, the three theories focus on domain-general universals of human development— structures and processes that are common to all individuals and that function similarly in different domains and disciplines. The three theories seek the basic laws of psychology, akin to the basic laws of physics. Third, the three theories assume that cognitive growth and learning occur along a smooth and unimpeded developmental path, given the right care and experiences. This trio of assumptions has done much to frame the debate about the structure and development of human abilities, outline the methods by which abilities have been studied, and establish the pedagogies by which abilities have been nurtured at home and in school.

These assumptions have come under fire in the decades since the cognitive revolution, as the traditional models have waned in influence. In what follows I examine each assumption in turn in light of recent theory and research in human abilities.

Contexualization of Psychological Theory and Research

Surrounding the individual learner is an environment filled with social, physical, and symbolic elements (e.g., languages, tools, notations). These environmental elements form the *context* in which abilities are developed and used. At issue in this section is the role of contextual factors in the structure and development of abilities—and the related methodological point that concerns the appropriate unit of analysis in psychological research.

Behaviorists, Piagetians, and *g* researchers have in common the pursuit of universals of learning and development that operate in all unimpaired individuals in a similar manner across domains and disciplines. Environmental elements are thought to provide the content used by human abilities but not to influence underlying patterns of thought, which are presumed to stem from domain-general structures or processes. It follows from this view that the individual person is the appropriate unit of analysis in psychological research.

Role of Context and Culture in Cognition.   Recent theory and research do not dispute the biological basis of abilities but make a persuasive case for sociocultural factors. There is now a substantial literature that demonstrates striking cultural differences in patterns of thought (see Bakhtin, 1981; Cole, 1996; Hutchins, 1990; Kaiping & Nisbett, 1999; Rogoff, 1990; Torff, 1999a). For example, Asians and Westerners give consistently dissimilar interpretations of a visual display, interpreting the figure-ground relationship in fundamentally different ways (Kaiping & Nisbett, 1999).

A host of similar findings have yielded the broad consensus that abilities are far more context-dependent than previously thought. Environmental elements such as languages and notations influence underlying patterns of thought. Thus the range of factors relevant to studies of human abilities must be expanded to include contextual ones, and the pursuit of universals ought to be viewed in new and less expansive light. After a century of largely ignored calls for a "second psychology" based on culture and context (Cahan & White, 1992), a new view emerged: In the course of development in a culture, the individual is exposed to (and becomes dependent upon) a variety of contextual elements that guide the way the individual mind develops. These contextual elements are products of culture. For a comprehensive understanding of abilities to be crafted, theory and research must take into account the culture in which abilities are created and given meaning.

The emergence of contextualism has coincided with a surge of interest in a sociocultural theory of cognitive development put forth by Vygotsky and independently by Mead in the 1930s (Mead, 1934/1956; Vygotsky, 1978; see also Cole, 1996; Wertsch, 1985). The essence of sociocultural theory is the claim that the mind is socially formed—that is, the structure and function of cognitive abilities are *constituted* by culture as the individual interacts with the sociocultural environment. The individual's performance is supported by a variety of culturally created *mediators,* which include physical tools, social conventions, and symbolic media. Learning (*internalization*) occurs as individuals construct mental representations and habituate actions as guided by mediational elements. According to sociocultural theory, cultural concepts form the foundation of the way individuals make sense of the world, and the individual's thought processes are thus imprinted through interaction with the cultural environment. In recent decades, four new lines of sociocultural theory and research have appeared, under the headings "Everyday Cognition," "Socially Shared Cognition," "Distributed Cognition," and "Situated Cognition."

Everyday cognition: With the rise of sociocultural theory came a spate of studies of thinking and learning in nonacademic contexts, much of it under the banner of *everyday cognition* (Lave, 1988; Lave & Wenger, 1993; Rogoff & Lave, 1984). Researchers who looked outside the classroom at instances of everyday activity—on the job and at home—found examples of ingenious strategies that people devised to exploit environmental affordances and overcome situational constraints. For example, truck drivers were found to stack milk crates through use of a context-embedded method of counting that is remarkably effective, if remote from the school-oriented approach of making a formal count (Scribner, 1984). Studies of everyday cognition reveal how seldom the strategies people use in life and on the job resemble the formal knowledge taught in schools. Sociocultural theory points up the learning inherent in everyday settings—visiting a restaurant, completing a tax form, programming a VCR. Focusing on the ubiquity of mediators in the world around us, sociocultural theory underscores that learning occurs everywhere, all the time—even when there is no intent to teach or learn. From this perspective, the terms *education, socialization,* and *enculturation* are closely related notions, if not outright synonyms.

Socially shared cognition: Sociocultural theory pays particular attention to one form of cultural mediation—the efforts made and encouragement given by other people. The growing interest in *socially shared cognition* refers to the study of how people come to engage in shared belief (Resnick, Levine, & Teasley, 1991). Apart from knowledge people hold through direct observation, all knowledge is the result of entering into a shared belief with a group of like-minded others called a *community of practice.* According to researchers focused on socially shared cognition, learning occurs when the learner comes to agreement with other people with whom the learner interacts in a community of practice. People in the United States share the belief that John Wilkes Booth assassinated Lincoln because we participate in a community of practice—the one that concerns the historical beliefs of American culture as taught in secondary schools. Of course, such beliefs may later be rethought and changed; as with any other cultural product, beliefs about history are dynamic and evolve as the culture does.

Bruner (1990, 1996) uses the term *intersubjectivity* to describe interactional processes through which individuals come to share beliefs with others. Through intersubjective exchange, Bruner suggests, people fail to arrive at the exact same construal of events but come to enough of a shared understanding to make sense of what's going on and continue the interaction. Intersubjectivity is at the heart of sociocultural theory, because it is shared belief in communities of practice that orients the individual and gives the world meaning.

Distributed cognition: If cognitive activities are shared between person and context, it follows that part of the resources (the "intelligence") required to get something done is handled by the environment, like a sort of prosthetic (Perkins, 1995). In communities of practice, people are assisted by the *intelligences of the cultural environment*—the physical, social, and symbolic elements that do part of the job. Abilities are thus said to be *distributed*—spread between person and environmental elements. For example, lawyers have at their disposal thick books that detail laws and precedents; we expect a lawyer not to memorize everything but to also know how to look things up. From the perspective of distributed-cognition researchers, the abilities needed in law are in part in the practitioners' heads but in part distributed among the various intelligences of the cultural environment.

Situated cognition: A strong form of sociocultural theory has come forward under the headings "situated" and "situative" cognition (Greeno, 1998; Lave & Wenger, 1993; Seely Brown, Collins, & Duguid, 1989). From this perspective, individuals and situations cocreate activity and thus cannot be studied separately. Abilities are seen as outgrowths of particular situational affordances and constraints, and only in context do they make sense. People develop strategies for doing things that depend on a certain context, and only in this context are they able to work without difficulty.

Dependence on situational affordances and constraints means that it is very difficult for individuals to transfer knowledge across contexts, even isomorphic ones. (Every teacher has had the experience of teaching something only to find that the lesson did not transfer as needed to a nearby context.) According to situated-cognition researchers, transfer occurs through generalization of knowledge, but this process can be fraught with difficulty. As a result, people often find it hard to work unless the environmental support is just right. Consider, for example, that there are places to which you are able to drive but to which you are unable to give another person adequate directions. You know the route, but only well enough to get yourself there, as if by "feel." Embedded in the environment are memory cues—environmental objects that, when presented to your senses and intermingled with your memories of the terrain, help you to make all the necessary turns. Memory and learning, it turns out, are not simply mental achievements—they are collaborations between the individual and a particular set of environmental circumstances.

The situative perspective underscores that all learning is a product not only of the person's intellectual efforts but also of whatever situational elements are present when the learning occurs. All learning is thus linked to its situation of origin, and it is of utmost importance for educators and researchers to explore how situational affordances and constraints influence learning.

Abilities as Situated Knowledge and Skill.   Abilities, according to sociocultural theory, are culturally established but individually internalized patterns of knowledge and skill crafted to fit situational affordances and constraints. Some of these constraints and affordances cohere into specific disciplines, (e.g., bowling, psychology), while others are everyday shared ways of doing things (e.g., restaurant scripts). From this perspective, abilities are patterns in socially shared and physically distributed knowledge in a community of practice. As a result, to see all the elements of the working psychological system that supports complex performances, one must look at the larger system, the person and cultural context.

Methodological Implications.   Sociocultural theory also raises new issues, ones that challenge key methodological assumptions in psychology. Years ago it was observed that animals in zoos behave differently from their counterparts in the wild; it follows that human behavior might well be as artificial in typical laboratory experiments in psychology. A concern for "ecological validity" prompts sociocultural psychologists to question the extent to which the bulk of laboratory work in psychology provides an accurate indication of the way people act in the real world (Cole, 1971, 1996). The experimental laboratory is by no means a context-neutral environment; rather, it has a set of procedures, expectations, and scripts all its own. From this perspective, a truer measure of human behavior comes from studies in real-world settings, despite the methodological difficulties involved.

Hence, the unit of analysis in research changes from individual person to *person-in-cultural context.* As a result, many research initiatives have shifted from laboratory settings, where variables can be controlled, to the larger world, where the full range of factors can be addressed. Sociocultural theory has as its burden the need to study processes that are supremely difficult (and often impossible) to operationalize and control. As difficult as it is to do good psychology and sociocultural theory at the same time, this has the benefit of reflecting the full range of influences on human cognition and learning (Olson & Bruner, 1996).

Taking Stock: Contexualization of Theory and Research.   Sociocultural theory yields some novel views of how cognition is structured, how it develops, what learning is, and how psychological research ought to proceed. This work rebuts the assumption that abilities are context-independent "talents" undergirded by mental structures that can be teased out for isolated analysis. Sociocultural theory emphasizes that abilities are stitched together by situational elements—products of culture. The view of abilities as situated actions calls into question the assertion that psychological work ought to focus on the functioning of the individual person. Analysis of the person–in–social context is a significant methodological complication but one that promises to provide psychological studies that seem more meaningful to practitioners interested in the abilities used in complex performances.

Human Abilities: Multiple and Interconnected

The second set of recently questioned assumptions about human abilities concerns the *range* of cognitive processes involved in abilities. The three traditional theories have in common a pursuit of overarching domain-general processes, structures, or principles that apply to all areas of human cognition (e.g., spatial cognition, language). Behaviorists posit a single law of learning in which abilities are shaped by contingencies of reinforcement. Piaget's theory views abilities as evidence of domain-general thought processes linked to predictable stagelike developmental changes in underlying cognitive structure. Finally, general-intelligence theorists posit a general cognitive capacity (g) that underlies all abilities. The question is, in a nutshell: To what extent are abilities domain-general or domain-specific?

In contrast to the traditional theories, recent theories offer a profusion of "pluralistic" (domain-specific) views. As the following review indicates, this literature is remarkably diverse but with a common thread. Widespread is the view that abilities are supported by a range of cognitive skills, some typically hidden, and these multiple abilities include ones that are particular to a domain (e.g., pitch and rhythm are essential elements of music) as well as cross-domain capacities (e.g., language figures in countless domains). In what follows I describe four bodies of such work: evolutionary psychology, cognitive-developmental psychology, pluralistic models of intelligence, and expertise.

Evolutionary Psychology.   Applying Darwin's work to the evolution of the human mind, evolutionary psychologists examine the adaptive pressures that have caused the mind to develop the way it has over time (see Barkow, Cosmides, & Tooby, 1992). This line of theory and research has included an explicit claim that the human mind is configured with a variety of *modules*—separate, task-specific cognitive abilities that evolved in response to the environmental challenges faced by the human species (Cosmides & Tooby, 1987; Tooby & Cosmides, 1990). Here the mind is considered to be something like a Swiss Army knife, designed with mechanisms specialized to meet the challenges that have arisen in particular environments. According to evolutionary psychologists, these modules are numerous and include innately specified capacities for facial recognition, spatial relations, rigid objects mechanics, tool use, social exchange, motion perception, and a great many others. These modules are thought to be content-rich; that is, modules provide not only sets of procedures for solving problems but also much of the information needed to do so.

According to evolutionary psychologists, culture is involved in phylogenetic change but not ontogenetic change (as posited in sociocultural theory). Modules are seen as forms of innate hardwiring that are largely unaffected by environmental influences such as social norms or educational practices and thus are not thought to undergo significant developmental changes as the individual ages. As a result of this adevelopmental view, cultural contexts are not thought to initiate change of any kind in the cognitive activities of individuals.

It is through culture, however, that people have responded to most, if not all, of the adaptive pressures that face them; for example, the need to communicate has given rise to language, a cultural product that serves the needs of individuals and guides the evolution of the species through natural selection. Evolutionary psychologists find it useful to study cultures to see how they respond to different environmental challenges. Hence, evolutionists, like sociocultural theorists, take the person-in-context as the relevant unit of analysis in psychological research. According to evolutionary psychologists, cultures do not change individual minds, but culturally manifested responses to adaptive pressures direct the evolution of the human species.

From the perspective of evolutionary psychology, abilities comprise patterns in behavior that draw upon combinations of multiple but independent cognitive capacities that have evolved over time. Abilities are the product of a long history of evolution, and therefore the close scrutiny of complex performances offers a glimpse of how cultures exploit such abilities, effectively guiding the development of the species. (Although Darwin pondered why music is so prevalent across cultures despite an apparent lack of adaptive advantages, it remains unclear a century later how natural selection has resulted in musical ability.)

Cognitive-Developmental Psychology.   With the three traditional models of human abilities in decline in recent decades, researchers have been emboldened to investigate entities that these influential theories explicitly proscribed—innately specified cognitive mechanisms that emerge early in life without interaction with the environment. Recent cognitive-developmental theory and research are rooted in the work of Chomsky (1968), whose nativist account of language acquisition dealt a devastating blow to its behaviorist and Piagetian rivals, and Fodor (1983), whose theory that posited a modular set of hardwired input systems ushered in a new era of skepticism about domain-general constructs and a new focus on domain-specific processes. Cognitive-developmentalists have presented a variety of nativist constructs under such monikers as first principals, p-prims, constraints, and early-developing modules (S. Carey & Gelman, 1991; Gelman & Au, 1996). These innately specified structures are seen as guiding frameworks for specific types of cognitive activity, and they need not be called into conscious awareness in order to work (Torff & Sternberg, 2001b).

From this perspective, human cognition is to a significant extent domain-specific rather than domain-general (Gelman & Au, 1996; Hirschfeld & Gelman, 1994). Domains are thought to be modular components of an innately specified cognitive system and are thus not equivalent to culturally specified "disciplines" described by socioculturists and evolutionists, among others. Detailed studies of human performances rooted in innately specified structures have been reported in several domains, including language (Pinker, 1994, 1998); psychology or "theory of mind" (Astington, 1993; Wellman, 1990); quantitative reasoning (Gelman & Brenneman, 1994); spatial cognition (Kellman, 1996; Spelke, 1994; Spelke & Hermer, 1996); and biology (Atran, 1994; C. Carey, 1985; S. Carey & Smith, 1993; Keil, 1989, 1994).

The extent to which these intuitive constructs "develop" in any meaningful sense of the word is a contentious issue among psychologists. Some see these innately specified constructs as guiding all subsequent cognition, throughout the life span, without evincing significant developmental changes (Spelke, 1994; Spelke & Hermer, 1996). This is Mother Nature's programming for thought, and it grows but does not significantly change, much as infants have 10 fingers that grow larger and more dexterous but not fundamentally different in structure.

Other psychologists argue that profound developmental changes are evident in innately specified structures. Perhaps the leading proponent of the development of cognitive abilities is Susan Carey, whose "conceptual change" model has proven influential (S. Carey, 1985; S. Carey & Smith, 1993). Conceptual judgments change significantly as the child develops, the argument goes, as a new set of beliefs replaces an old set with which the new one is qualitatively different and inconsistent (in Carey's term, incommensurable). Educational interventions, Carey argues, have the power to usher along developmental changes that individuals need to make if they are to develop accurate representations of the physical, mathematical, psychological, and biological worlds, and perhaps others as well.

The adevelopmental view also has been criticized by Karmiloff-Smith (1993), who puts forth a general theory of developmental changes in psychological structure and function called representational redescription. Karmiloff-Smith describes cognitive development in terms of three phases of representational character of knowledge in a domain: (1) implicit (unavailable to conscious awareness; (2) explicit level 1 (conscious but unavailable to verbal report), and (3) explicit level 2 (available to verbal report). Moreover, as this developmental progression occurs, knowledge from one domain becomes increasingly available to other modules, and thus knowledge that begins as domain-specific becomes increasingly generalized. Developmental change therefore involves a process of increasing connections ("mapping") across domains, as knowledge becomes increasingly available to conscious awareness.

From the perspective of cognitive-developmental theory and research, human abilities are deployments of domain-specific cognitive structures and processes. Moreover, complex performances require the interconnection of multiple sets of modules. This view is similar to that of the evolutionary psychologists. Where the majority of cognitive-developmentalists depart from the evolutionists is in the extent of ontogenetic development of the cognitive structures that underlie human abilities. According to cognitive-developmentalists, as individuals gain experience in the world, developmental changes occur in the structure and function of abilities.

Pluralistic Models of Intelligence.   Psychologists interested in human intelligence also have a long and disputatious history about the generality or specificity of abilities (Anderson, 1992). General-intelligence theories have been offset by pluralistic models in the antiquity from Plato and more recently with Guilford's multifactorial model (1967). This debate has changed considerably of late as a new set of pluralistic views has appeared (Torff & Warburton, 2003). As noted, these views tend to blur the line between talent and intelligence, gathering them together in a unified but multifaceted model of human abilities.

The most influential among these new pluralistic models is the theory of multiple intelligences, or MI (Gardner, 1983/1993, 1999; Torff & Gardner, 1999). MI theory holds that human abilities can be understood as combinations of eight underlying sets of neurobiological potentials or intelligences: logical-mathematical, linguistic, spatial, bodily-kinesthetic, musical, naturalistic, interpersonal, and intrapersonal. According to MI theorists, these intelligences are combined as needed in real-world disciplines. For example, cello performance requires, at a minimum, logical-mathematical (dealing with mathematical aspects of notation), linguistic (working with terms such as *legato*), musical (information processing of pitch, rhythm, and timbre, among other things), interpersonal (working collaboratively with conductor, orchestra, and audience), and intrapersonal (expression, self-regulation). In accordance with the cognitive developmentalists, MI theory calls for ontogenetic change, making the suggestion that abilities change as combinations of intelligences are elaborated. According to Gardner and colleagues, the individual's abilities are shaped by the way a domain uses and blends the various intelligences.

Sternberg's "triarchic" theory parses human intelligence differently from MI but continues the latter's emphasis on ontogenetic development (Sternberg, 1988). Sternberg's theory holds that human abilities comprise three related cognitive processes—analytic (capacity to render critical judgments), creative (capacity to generate novel responses), and practical (capacity to adapt to the situation at hand). Like MI theorists, Sternberg suggests that individuals pull together these three sets of abilities as needed to accomplish

objectives in real-world disciplines and domains. Hence, successful performances result from using these three abilities as disciplines require them. At
the same time, there is a tendency in educational settings to overemphasize
analytical ability and underplay creative and practical abilities. Educational
benefits follow from an educational regimen that restores balance to the
three sets of abilities (Sternberg, Torff, & Grigorenko, 1998).

Expertise.   The final set of pluralistic views of human abilities is put forth
by researchers interested in expertise (see Bereiter & Scardamalia, 1993).
Here the emphasis is on the development of discipline-specific expertise—
the capacity to engage successfully in the tasks required in a real-world
discipline (e.g., chess, auto mechanics). In this view, what is important about
abilities is structured not by underlying modules of cognitive functioning (a
domain-specific view) but by the external world of disciplines and canons
of knowledge and skill they contain (a discipline-specific view). Researchers
have investigated the discipline-specific abilities in disciplines as diverse as
chess (Chase & Simon, 1973), physics (Chi, Glaser, & Farr, 1988), and
teaching (Shulman, 1990). The functionalist tack taken by expertise researchers concentrates on the disciplinary organization of thought; placing
less emphasis on underlying structural changes such participation might
cause. From this perspective, abilities are a direct response to the requirements of the task, discipline, and culture at hand. Expertise researchers see
abilities as forms of developing expertise, and this development is structured
by the way the discipline does things. The literature on expertise is akin to
the sociocultural theory in that it examines culturally crafted knowledge;
however, only the socioculturalists focus on changes in cognitive structure
that result from real-world activities.

Taking Stock: Multiple and Interconnected Human Abilities.   A brief review
of several theoretical models that posit multiple forms of human abilities
has revealed diverse ways of parsing these abilities. It may seem a chaotic
picture, but these models converge to support a new view of the structure
of human abilities with a pair of important insights. First, these models
predicate themselves on the idea that abilities are multiple, not singular. No
domain-general or discipline-general laws, structures, or principles underlie
abilities, according to the new views. Second, complex performances are
supported by vital combinations of skills. Some of these skills operate primarily within a particular domain or discipline, but many abilities are used
across domains. With complex performances supported by multiple abilities,
it is unsurprising but significant that important abilities are sometimes hidden from view.

Developmental Challenges in Integration of Abilities

The third broad shift in the psychology of abilities involves a new view of
the extent of (and character of) developmental changes in abilities as indi-

viduals gain age and expertise. The traditional models of human abilities—behaviorism, Piaget, and general intelligence—share an optimistic view of the trajectory of human development. Behaviorists assume that abilities gradually accrue as reinforcement is administered. Piagetians assume that stage changes in cognitive functioning occur as the individual is afforded appropriate opportunities to act on the environment. General-intelligence researchers assume that people gain knowledge and skill given individual differences in general processing capacity.

These optimistic stances are called into question by a burgeoning body of theory and research in the psychology of human abilities. The assumption that "natural" human development is a smooth and unfettered process has been undermined by evidence that development can be hindered when the abilities needed in a domain or discipline are not integrated.

Most teachers have had the experience of teaching something to a group of students, only to find that the students' previously existing ideas have interfered with the lesson. These experiences have been corroborated by some troubling research. For example, studies in the domain of physics show that students hold fast to misconceived notions about force and agency (notions derivative of "Aristotelian" dynamics), even after successfully passing a course that features the prevailing "scientific" view of the physical world ("Newtonian" dynamics) (diSessa, 1993; Larkin, 1983; McCloskey, Camarazza, & Green, 1980). Even students who perform in an exemplary manner in the course revert to intuitive but inaccurate ideas about physics when tested outside the classroom.

In this example, educational outcomes are influenced by *intuitive conceptions*—knowledge or knowledge structures that need not be available to conscious reflection but act to facilitate or constrain task performance (see Torff & Sternberg, 2001a, 2001b). The domain of physics has provided the "smoking gun" that shows that learning can be impeded, sometimes severely, by intuitive conceptions. Similar phenomena have been noted in a variety of other domains, which include biology (e.g., Keil, 1989, 1994), numerical reasoning (e.g., Gelman, 1991; Gelman & Brenneman, 1994), and psychology (or "theory of mind") (e.g., Astington, 1993; Leslie, 1987; Wellman, 1990).

A set of three themes emerges from these bodies of work. First, as illustrated in the physics example, individuals employ a variety of intuitive conceptions that exert a powerful force on the kind of thinking they do in all sorts of situations, inside and outside the classroom. Seldom brought to conscious awareness, intuitive conceptions are typically hidden from view and often take the form of assumptions on which patterns of thought and action are predicated. One need not, for example, have conscious awareness of one's thinking to successfully recognize faces or add small quantities. Abilities, in this view, are constituted in part by knowledge and skill of which people have conscious access and also by intuitive forms of knowledge and skill.

Second, powerful as intuitive conceptions are for making commonsense judgments, at times they are oversimplified, misleading, or inaccurate. In some instances, intuitive conceptions may be consistently and unambiguously helpful; for example, innately specified facial recognition capacities that operate nonconsciously have little in the way of a downside. However, intuitive conceptions have the power to assist or detract from learning, depending on the context at hand. For example, intuitive conceptions about number and quantity make it seem sensible to people that larger numbers correspond to greater quantities. This intuitive conception makes decimals a breeze and fractions a nightmare, since the latter counterintuitively decrease in quantity as the denominator grows larger. Gardner (1991) classifies these difficulties into three categories: simplifications (e.g., analysis of political debates as bifurcated between the good guy and bad guy), misconceptions (e.g., naive beliefs about the physical world), and rigidly applied algorithms (e.g., inflexibility in quantitative reasoning that underlies difficulties with fractions).

The third theme emergent in the intuitive-conceptions literature is the most vexing for educators. Substantial evidence supports the claim that intuitive conceptions often persist despite efforts to improve or replace them. For example, S. Carey and Smith (1993) report little success that results from efforts to initiate conceptual change from misconceived intuitive notions to accurate scientific ones (in the domain of epistemological beliefs). Gardner (1991) and Gardner, Torff, and Hatch (1996) review research that yields similar results. Intuitive conceptions are often difficult to dislodge, even by the best of teachers.

Taken together, the three themes point to a complex trajectory for the development of abilities. Complex performances require the intermingling of various forms of ability, intuitive and otherwise, and these multiple abilities may fail to integrate as needed. Or they may conflict outright. The abilities required in complex performances are not only numerous; they also are in danger of discordance, resulting in difficulties in gaining needed knowledge and skill.

Theoretical Models of Disjunctures Between Abilities.   The question arises why such a situation should emerge. What conditions or characteristics produce such disjunctures? Answers to this question come from both sides of the nature–nurture aisle.

Evolutionary psychologists put forth an explanation that centers on the suggestion that not all of our genetic inheritance (of evolved, innately specified modules) serves the modern human well. Evolutionary pressures work slowly, but in the last two millennia human cultures have moved at a breakneck pace. In that time, the genetic makeup of the human mind has not evolved significantly, but cultures have changed human life in countless ways. So, while modern humans are adapted to the life of the Pleistocene-era hunter-gatherer, most people live in a different and more complex sort of world—society in the information age. The modern human is, in this view, fundamentally maladapted to the current environment. It follows, then, that modern humans should evince ways in which their behavior seems ill suited to contemporary challenges, intellectual and otherwise. Evolutionary psychologists suggest that not always does the adaptive legacy we have from our forebears support our performance in the modern world.

A similar view can be seen among cognitive-developmental psychologists. Part of Piaget's legacy was his demonstration that young children often exhibit distinctive conceptions of the world. More recent theory attributes these conceptions to a combination of innate constraints on learning and early experience (S. Carey & Gelman, 1991). Together with the evolutionists, cognitive-developmentalists press the case that the human genetic endowment is a root cause of the challenges of integration of abilities. But cognitive-developmentalists place additional emphasis on ontogenetic changes in the development of abilities. At the heart of these disjunctures lie the problems inherent in the developmental interplay of endogenous factors (nature) and exogenous ones (nurture).

Sociocultural theorists have little quarrel with evolutionist and cognitive-developmental theory, but they locate the primary causes for disjunctures elsewhere, at least in part: in interactions between the individuals and the ambient culture. Consider, for example, the concept of *folk psychology*—a set of socially shared ideas about how the mind works and what learning and knowledge are (Bruner, 1990, 1996; Olson & Bruner, 1996). A culture's folk psychology is a shared conception of how people think, how they should act, and how they learn, among other things. But not always do the precepts of a culture's folk psychology prove to be a boon to educators. Rather, folk beliefs can come into conflict with the formal concepts created and taught by experts in a discipline, leading to the disjunctures between abilities noted earlier.

Beliefs about teaching and learning called *folk pedagogy* help to make the point. In Western culture, especially in the United States, a popular folk belief holds that learning occurs when students absorb information from the environment and thus the best teaching occurs when the environment is made rich with information transmitted to students from teachers, books, and other sources. Studies of teachers' beliefs show that prospective teachers often hold fast to a "transmission model" of teaching, despite the "constructivist" view (taught in most teacher-education programs) that knowledge is constructed individually by each learner, based on environmental input and individual reflection (e.g., Brookhart & Freeman, 1992; Bruner, 1996; Doyle & Carter, 1996; Hollingsworth, 1989; Kagan, 1992; McLaughlin, 1991; Morine-Dershimer, 1993; Shulman, 1990; Strauss, 1993; 1996; Strauss & Shilony, 1994; Torff, 1999b; Torff & Sternberg, 2001a, 2001b); Woolfolk Hoy, 1996; Zeichner & Gore, 1990). Of course, the constructivist pedagogy might ultimately be found wanting. But it seems clear that people who are trained in education hold powerful intuitive conceptions about teaching and learning and these intuitive conceptions exert a great deal of influence on the way people think and act in classroom settings.

Folk pedagogy predisposes individuals to think and teach in particular ways, some of which are inconsistent with the concepts and practices characteristic of expert teaching. As with intuitive conceptions in other domains, folk pedagogy may tend to persist despite successful participation in preservice training programs. Becoming an expert teacher, then, is not simply a matter of gaining new knowledge or of replacing inadequate preconceptions in a straightforward manner. Rather, explicit efforts by teachers of educational psychology are needed to counter these uncritically held beliefs, principally by encouraging prospective teachers to engage in activities that facilitate relevant forms of cognitive change.

This example makes clear that intuitive conceptions held by teachers—as well as those held by students—influence educational outcomes, and not always for the better. The example also illustrates how sociocultural theory, as well as the cognitive-developmental and evolutionary theory, accounts for disjunctures between abilities. The shared beliefs in a community of practice may ill fit the time-honored procedures and practices created by disciplinary experts, resulting in disjunctures between abilities.

Taking Stock: Developmental Challenges in Integration of Abilities.   The traditional models portray development as a smooth process of acquisition of knowledge and skill in a discipline, but the psychological literature tells a more disquieting tale. Disjunctures between abilities exert a hidden and problematic force on the development of abilities. The literature on intuitive conceptions supports the view that the development of complex performances entails the intermingling of various forms of ability, intuitive and otherwise, and these multiple abilities may fail to integrate as needed, or they may come into conflict. The abilities required in complex performances are not only numerous; they also are in danger of discordance, resulting in difficulties in gaining the knowledge and skill needed in complex performances.

Educational Implications

Complex performances, it turns out, are supported by multiple context-dependent abilities that integrate with development but sometimes require specific educational interventions to integrate adequately. The next sections explore the educational implications of this viewpoint. Following the three shifts discussed earlier, the call here is for pedagogy that is contextualized, pluralistic, and integrative.

Education in Context

If knowledge and skill are shaped through context and only in context do tasks make sense, then any pedagogy begins with a detailed analysis of the abilities the domain or discipline requires, with the goal of crafting educational practices to foster the needed abilities. Chess masters, for example, ought to analyze their craft to determine its constituent abilities. Such an analysis focuses on a set of reflective questions. What abilities are needed in the discipline, and in what contexts are they used? To what extent does schooling help people to develop the full range of culturally situated skills needed for success in a career? To what extent does schooling give people the skills needed to be knowledgeable participants in lay discourse outside one's career area? These questions probe the ecological validity (in education the notion is typically called authenticity) of educational interventions. At issue is *contextualization*—the extent to which vehicles for curriculum and assessment appropriately reflect (and prepare students for) the challenges of adult life in the real world (Gardner, 1999). Contextualization prompts educators to ground their work more soundly in the disciplines, for example by making science teaching less like school (typically emphasizing memorizing of scientific facts) and more like professional science (e.g., designing and executing studies) and avocational science activities (e.g., reading and discussing a science article in a newsweekly).

But to say that contextualization of curriculum and assessment is a laudable aim is not to say that each and every lesson should consist of real-world activities. After all, scales are not played at musical recitals, but they have a rich purpose in the practice room. Decontextualized activities can be a means to an end; the key, however, is the connection ultimately made with the authentic activity in the discipline.

Contextualization of assessment has long been a vexing concern in education. High-stakes testing remains a key component in educational decision making in many countries, including the United States. At the same time, the strands of theory and research reviewed earlier support *assessment in context*: assessment procedures that are performance-based (allowing students to participate in assessment as they have in the classroom) and ongoing (as opposed to single-administration testing).

The Full Range and Interconnection of Abilities

A key component of contextualized educational practices concerns teaching for the full range of abilities needed in a domain or discipline. Detailed analysis of a domain inevitably yields a broad range of intradomain and interdomain abilities. As noted, no general laws explain all in a domain, so a domain-specific view is vital to understanding human abilities. At the same time, domain-specific work can lead to fragmented, insular pockets of theory and research. This in turn obfuscates vital interdomain connections of abilities, narrowing the scope of theory and research. Clearly, a key objective is to teach for abilities that are unique or specific to a domain or discipline (e.g., timbre in music). But the second, more overlooked abilities are the interdomain (interdiscipline) ones.

Contextualized learning of the diversity of skills needed in a domain or discipline has led many investigators to analysis and expansion of *appren-*

ticeship models of learning and teaching. Viewing teaching as multiple forms of assisted performance, not just instruction, apprenticeships feature three qualities in accord with the modern psychology of abilities. First, apprenticeships allow students access to useful forms of expert models. Models range from distal (watching golf on television) to proximal (watching your golf teacher) (Torff, 1997). Instructor modeling provides proximal encounters with expert performance, as well as opportunities for coparticipation and successive approximation. Rudimentary as this point is, many a golf and music lesson includes little performance by the mentor. Second, apprenticeship-type learning can be extended in fruitful ways, leading to the term *cognitive apprenticeship* (Collins, Brown, & Newman, 1989). The idea here is to make often-hidden expert thinking available to students. The goal is to make expert thinking visible and audible, encompassing not just how the expert works but also how he or she thinks when working—how the expert identifies, defines, operationalizes, and solves problems. *Cognitive apprenticeship* refers to the practice of engaging students in all the aspects of expert performance, not just the public ones. Third, apprenticeships have the virtue of stressing distributed knowledge. The sociocultural theory discussed earlier makes persuasive the claim that only a portion of the wherewithal of a performance resides in the head; the remainder is distributed in symbolic media, physical tools, and social conventions. Apprenticeships focus on combinations of person and context, a distributed approach to learning and teaching.

Integration of Abilities

The research reviewed earlier supports the conclusion that not always is the path to expertise in a domain or discipline a smooth one. The specter of conflicts between abilities calls for diagnostics that identify the difficulties that obtain in a particular domain or discipline. This is seldom done, as in the physics example discussed earlier. The finding about intuitive physics came as a surprise to many in the world of science teaching. Similar surprises may await educators in other disciplines.

Psychologists and educators are working to counter these difficulties, and the emerging consensus among them is that learners must confront naive views, to think about them and question them, not work around them. Learning about Newton did not dislodge the flawed intuitive physics. What's needed is pedagogy that requires students to critically analyze their intuitive responses and to consider ways in which they might be improved. In what is in essence a constructivist response to the problem, the focus falls on teaching for integration between abilities, with the aim of strengthening the relationships among abilities required in a discipline.

Promising initiatives that aim to enhance this integration fall under the various headings *reflective thinking* (Gardner, 1991; Paris & Ayres, 1994), *reflective teaching* (Liston & Zeichner, 1996), and *teaching for understand-*

ing (Wiske, 1993). These programs in reflective thinking engage learners in their own assessment by requiring them to answer questions about their work, the way it was made, and ways in which it could be improved. Reflective thinking takes place formally in critique sheets attached to student work but also less formally in conversations between and among students and teachers. Teachers have much to gain by asking questions that encourage students' involvement in their own assessment. These practices help students to build their own understandings of the discipline but also to examine the extent to which their naive views require revision. Telling students how their intuitions are inadequate holds little hope; a better approach is to encourage students to engage in the kind of reflective thinking that critically analyzes intuitive views.

The foregoing educational suggestions are hardly new, and they are not presented as such. Traditional educational methods have much to offer educators interested in fostering human abilities. But they also are lacking in some respects, namely, in terms of contextualization of learning and assessment, range of abilities covered, and integration of the abilities required in a domain or discipline. The bottom line for educators interested in abilities: Look closely at the domain and contextualize your practices in it, pay attention to the numerous and diverse abilities the domain requires, and take care that students can integrate these abilities as needed in complex performances.

Conclusion

In the psychology of abilities since the cognitive revolution, no paradigm has been secured, but it has been a fertile period. A set of hoary assumptions has come under fire as new theory and research have appeared. The emerging view highlights that abilities are context-dependent and thus culturally situated, multiple with important interconnections between different abilities, and sometimes difficult to draw together as needed even by the best of teachers.

The science of human abilities is still not a coherent picture, so practitioners and educators interested in complex performances still have much to wonder about in terms of the psychology and nurturance of the abilities that underlie tasks in their disciplines. But the new view portends well for future theory, research, and practice in the psychology of abilities, as the emerging views are explored across a broad range of domains and disciplines.

STUDY QUESTIONS

1. The psychology of human abilities is said to be preparadigmatic, with three historically important theoretical frameworks vying to explain the vast

array of human capacities and talents. What are these theoretical frameworks, how do they compare and contrast, and what are their shortcomings (according to contemporary psychologists)?

2. In the last two decades, the "contextualization" of theory and research in the psychology of human abilities has been emphasized. How does this "contextual" psychology differ from earlier theoretical frameworks, what theoretical notions have grown out of this approach, and what are its implications for methodology in psychological research?

3. Historically, psychologists have sought a single mechanism or process to explain the full range of human abilities, but in recent years psychologists have suggested that individuals benefit from multiple, theoretically-distinct abilities (i.e., "modules") that combine as individuals perform tasks. What are these pluralistic models of human abilities, what sets of mental modules have been posited, and how do these pluralistic approaches differ in ontogeny and phylogeny of abilities?

4. Human development has traditionally been seen as smooth process of acquiring knowledge and skill, but recent theories suggest that various human abilities may fail to integrate as needed, or come into outright conflict. What causes such difficulties, according to these theorists?

5. As diverse as contemporary theoretical perspectives on human abilities are, they suggest a set of educational implications. What are these implications?

REFERENCES

Anderson, M. (1992). *Intelligence and development: A cognitive theory.* Oxford: Blackwell.

Astington, J. (1993). *The child's discovery of the mind.* Cambridge, MA: Harvard University Press.

Atran, S. (1994). Core domains versus scientific theories. In L. Hirschfeld & S. Gelman, (Eds.), *Mapping the mind: Domain-specificity in cognition and culture* (pp. 316–340). Cambridge: Cambridge University Press.

Bakhtin, M. (1981). *The dialogic imagination.* Austin: University of Texas.

Barkow, J., Cosmides, L., & Tooby, J. (Eds.). (1992). *The adaptive mind: Evolutionary psychology and generation of culture.* New York: Oxford University Press.

Bereiter, C., & Scardamalia, M. (1993). *Surpassing ourselves: An inquiry into the nature and implications of expertise.* New York: Open Court.

Brookhart, S., & Freeman, D. (1992). Characteristics of entering teacher candidates. *Review of Educational Research, 62,* 37–60.

Bruner, J. S. (1990). *Acts of meaning.* Cambridge, MA: Harvard University Press.

Bruner, J. (1996). *The culture of education.* Cambridge, MA: Harvard University Press.

Cahan, E., & White, S. (1992). Proposals for a second psychology. *American Psychologist, 47*(2), 224–235.

Carey, C. (1985) *Conceptual change in childhood.* Cambridge: Bradford/MIT.

Carey, S., & Gelman, R. (Eds.). (1991). *The epigenesis of mind.* Hillsdale, NJ: Erlbaum.

Carey, S., & Smith, C. (1993). On understanding the nature of scientific knowledge. *Educational Psychologist, 28*(3), 235–251.

Chase, W., & Simon, H. (1973). Perception in chess. *Cognitive Psychology, 4,* 55–81.

Chi, M., Glaser, R., & Farr, M. (Eds.). (1988). *The nature of expertise.* Hillsdale, NJ: Erlbaum.

Chomsky, N. (1968). *Language and mind.* New York: Harcourt Brace Jovanovich.

Cole, M. (1971). *The cultural context of learning and thinking.* New York: Basic Books.

Cole, M. (1996). *Cultural psychology: A once and future discipline.* Cambridge, MA: Harvard University Press.

Collins, A., Brown, J., & Newman, S. (1989). Cognitive apprenticeship: Teaching the crafts of reading, writing, and mathematics. In C. Resnick (Ed.), *Knowing, learning, and instruction: Essays in honor of Robert Glaser* (pp. 453–494). Hillsdale, NJ: Erlbaum.

Cosmides, L., & Tooby, J. (1987). From evolution to behavior: Evolutionary psychology as the missing link. In J. Dupre (Ed.), *The latest and the best: Essays on evolution and optimality* (pp. 227–306). Cambridge, MA: MIT Press.

diSessa, A. (1993). Toward an epistemology of physics. *Cognition and Instruction, 10,* 105–225.

Doyle, W., & Carter, K. (1996). Educational psychology and the education of teachers: A reaction. *Educational Psychologist, 31*(1) 51–62.

Egan, K. (1992). Review of "The Unschooled Mind" (by Howard Gardner). *Teachers College Record, 94,* 2, 397–406.

Eysenk, H. (1986). The theory of intelligence and the psychopsysiology of cognition. In R. J. Sternberg & D. R. Detterman (Eds.), *What is intelligence: Contemporary viewpoints on its nature and definition* (pp. 1–34). Norwood, NJ: Ablex.

Fodor, J. A. (1983). *The modularity of mind.* Cambridge, MA: MIT Press.

Gardner, H. (1991). *The unschooled mind.* New York: Basic Books.

Gardner, H. (1993). *Frames of mind:* The theory of multiple intelligences. New York: Basic Books. (Original work published 1983).

Gardner, H. (1999). *Intelligence reframed.* New York: Basic Books.

Gardner, H., Torff, B., & Hatch, T. (1996). The age of innocence reconsidered: Preserving the best of the progressive tradition in psychology and education. In D. Olson & N. Torrance (Eds.), *Handbook of psychology in education* (pp. 28–55). Cambridge, MA: Blackwell.

Gelman, R. (1991). First principles organize attention to and learning about relevant data: Number and animate–inanimate distinction as examples. *Cognitive Science, 14,* 79–106.

Gelman, R., & Au, T. (Eds.). (1996). *Perceptual and cognitive development.* New York: Academic Press.

Gelman, R., & Brenneman, K. (1994). First principles can support both universal and culture-specific learning about number and music. In E. Hirschfeld & S. Gelman (Eds.), *Mapping the mind: Domain-specificity in cognition and culture* (pp. 369–390). New York: Cambridge University Press.

Greeno, J. (1998). The situativity of knowing, learning, and research. *American Psychologist, 53*(1), 5–26.

Gruber, H., & Voneche, P. (1977). *The essential Piaget.* New York: Basic Books.

Guilford, J. (1967). *The nature of human intelligence.* New York: McGraw-Hill.

Hirschfeld, L., & Gelman, S. (Eds.). (1994). *Mapping the mind: Domain-specificity in cognition and culture.* Cambridge: Cambridge University Press.

Hollingsworth, S. (1989). Prior beliefs and cognitive change in learning to teach. *American Educational Research Journal, 26,* 160–189.

Hutchins, E. (1990). *Culture and inference.* Cambridge, MA: Harvard University Press.

Kagan, D. (1992). Implications of research on teacher belief. *Educational Psychologist, 27,* 65–90.

Kaiping, P., & Nisbett, R. (1999). Culture, dialectics, and reasoning about contradiction. *American Psychologist, 54*(9), 741–754.

Karmiloff-Smith, A. (1993). *Beyond modularity.* Cambridge, MA: MIT Press.

Keil, F. (1989). *Concepts, kinds, and cognitive development.* Cambridge: MIT Press.

Keil, F. (1994). The birth and nurturance of concepts by domains: The origins of living things. In E. Hirschfeld & S. Gelman (Eds.), *Mapping the mind: Domain-specificity in cognition and culture* (pp. 234–254). New York: Cambridge University Press.

Kellman, P. (1996). The origins of object perception. In R. Gelman & T. Au (Eds.), *Perceptual and cognitive development* (pp. 3–48). New York: Academic Press.

Kuhn, D. (1989). Children and adults as intuitive scientists. *Psychological Review, 96*(4), 674–689.

Lave, J. (1988). *Cognition in practice.* Cambridge, MA: Cambridge University Press.

Lave, J., & Wenger, E. (1993). *Situated learning.* Cambridge, MA: Cambridge University Press.

Leslie, A. (1987). Pretense and representation: The origins of "theory of mind." *Psychological Review, 94,* 412–426.

Liston, P., & Zeichner, K. (1996). *Reflective teaching.* Mahwah, NJ: Erlbaum.

McCloskey, M., Camarazza, A., & Green, B. (1980). Curvilinear motion in absence of external forces: Folk beliefs about the motion of objects. *Science, 210,* 1141–49.

McLaughlin, J. (1991). Reconciling care and control: Authority in classroom relationships. *Journal of Teacher Education, 40*(3), 182–195.

Mead, G. (1956). *The social psychology of George Herbert Mead.* A. Strauss (Ed.). Chicago: University of Chicago Press. (Original work published 1934)

Morine Dershimer, G. (1993). Tracing conceptual change in preservice teachers. *Teaching and Teacher Education, 9,* 15–26.

Olson, D., & Bruner, J. (1996). Folk psychology and folk pedagogy. In D. Olson & N. Torrance (Eds.), *Handbook of education in human development* (pp. 9–27). Oxford: Blackwell.

Paris, S., & Ayres, L. (1994). Promoting students' reflections through classroom activities. In *Becoming reflective students and teachers with portfolios and authentic assessments.* Washington, DC: American Psychological Association Books.

Perkins, D. (1995). *Outsmarting I.Q.: The emerging science of learnable intelligence*. New York: Free Press.

Piaget, J. (1983). Piaget's theory. In P. Mussen (Ed.), *Handbook of child psychology* (Vol. 1, pp. 103–128). New York: Wiley.

Pinker, S. (1994). *The language instinct*. New York: Morrow.

Pinker, S. (1998). *How the mind works*. New York: Morrow.

Resnick, L., Levine, J., & Teasley, S. (Eds.). (1991). *Perspectives on socially shared cognition*. Washington, DC: American Psychological Association Books.

Rogoff, B. (1990). *Apprenticeship in thinking*. Cambridge, MA: Harvard University Press.

Rogoff, B., & Lave, J. (Eds.). (1984). *Everyday cognition*. Cambridge, MA: Harvard University Press.

Scribner, S. (1984). Studying working intelligence. In B. Rogoff & J. Lave (Eds.). (1984), *Everyday cognition* (pp. 9–40). Cambridge, MA: Harvard University Press.

Seely Brown, J., Collins, A., & Duguid, P. (1989). Situated cognition and the culture of learning. *Educational Researcher, 18*(1), 32–42.

Shulman, L. (1990). Reconnecting foundations to the substance of teacher education. *Teachers College Record, 91*(3), 300–310.

Skinner, B. (1954). The science of learning and the art of teaching. *Harvard Educational Review, 24*, 86–97.

Spelke, E. (1994). Initial knowledge: Six suggestions. *The Cognition, 50*, 431–445.

Spelke, E., & Hermer, L. (1996). Early cognitive development: Objects and space. In R. Gelman, & T. Au (Eds.), *Perceptual and cognitive development* (pp. 72–107). New York: Academic Press.

Sternberg, R. (1988). *The triarchic mind: A new theory of human intelligence*. New York: Viking.

Sternberg, R. (1998). Abilties are forms of developing expertise. *Educational Researcher, 27*, 11–20.

Sternberg, R., Torff, B., & Grigorenko, E. (1998, September). Teaching triarchically improves school achievement. *Journal of Educational Psychology, 90*(3), 374–384.

Strauss, S. (1993). Teachers' pedagogical content knowledge about children's minds and learning: Implications for teacher education. *Educational Psychologist, 28*(3), 279–290.

Strauss, S. (1996). Confessions of a born-again constructivist. *Educational Psychologist, 31*(1), 15–22.

Strauss, S., & Shilony, T. (1994). Teachers' models of children's minds and learning. In L. Hirschfeld & S. Gelman (Eds.), *Mapping the mind: Domain-specificity in cognition and culture* (pp. 455–473). Cambridge: Cambridge University Press.

Thorndike, E. (1932). *The fundamentals of learning*. Englewood Cliffs, NJ: Merrill/Prentice Hall.

Thurstone, L. L. (1938). *Primary mental abilities*. Chicago: University of Chicago Press.

Tooby, J., & Cosmides, L. (1990). On the universality of human nature and the uniqueness of the individual: The role of genetics and adaptation. *Journal of Personality, 58*, 375–424.

Torff, B. (1997). Into the wordless world: Implicit learning and instructor modeling in music. In V. Brummet (Ed.), *Music as intelligence* (pp. 77–92). Ithaca, NY: Ithaca College Press.

Torff, B. (1999a). Beyond information processing: Cultural influences on cognition and learning. In S. Ulibarri (Ed.), *Maria Montessori explicit and implicit in the 20th century* (pp. 8–39). Mexico City: Association Montessori Internationale.

Torff, B. (1999b). Tacit knowledge in teaching: Folk pedagogy and teacher education. In R. Sternberg & J. Horvath (Eds.), *Tacit knowledge in professional practice* (pp. 195–214). Mahwah, NJ: Erlbaum.

Torff, B., & Gardner, H. (1999). The vertical mind: The case for multiple intelligences. In M. Anderson (Ed.), *The development of intelligence* (pp. 139–160). London: University College Press.

Torff, B., & Sternberg, R. (2001a). Intuitive conceptions among learners and teachers. In B. Torff & R. Sternberg (Eds.), *Understanding and teaching the intuitive mind: Student and teacher learning* (pp. 3–26). Mahwah, NJ: Erlbaum.

Torff, B., & Sternberg, R. (Eds.). (2001b). *Understanding and teaching the intuitive mind: Student and teacher learning.* Mahwah, NJ: Erlbaum.

Torff, B., & Warburton, E. (2003). Old and new models of intelligence: The assessment conundrum. In M. Pearn (Ed.), *Individual deveopment in organisations.* London: Wiley.

Vygotsky, L. (1978). *Mind in society.* Cambridge, MA: Harvard University Press.

Watson, J. (1924). *Behaviorism.* New York: Norton.

Wellman, H. (1990). *The child's theory of mind.* Cambridge, MA: Bradford/MIT.

Wertsch, J. (1985). *Vygotsky and the social formation of mind.* Cambridge, MA: Harvard University Press.

Wiske, M. (Ed.). (1993). *Teaching for understanding.* San Francisco: Jossey-Bass.

Woolfolk Hoy, A. (1996). Teaching educational psychology: Texts in context. *Educational Psychologist, 31*(1), 35–40.

Zeichner, K., & Gore, J. (1990). Teacher socialization. In W. Houston (Ed.), *Handbook of research on teacher education* (pp. 329–349). New York: Macmillian.

Making Music and Making Sense Through Music

6

Expressive Performance and Communication

REINHARD KOPIEZ

Music and Meaning

Music itself seems to be an ideal medium to communicate meaning, perhaps much more effective than language. This may apply even if the meaning is not directly related to the musical structure itself but rather to associations evoked from listening to it. As Cook (1998, p. 3f.) demonstrates in his functional analysis of television commercials, "advertisers use music to communicate meanings that would take too long to put into words, or that would carry no conviction in them . . . Rock stands for youth, freedom, being true to yourself. . . ." Seen from this point of view, we participate daily in a continual experiment in which meaning is attributed to music by watching commercials. This is true regardless of the situation in which we encounter music. Generalizing more broadly: whatever stimuli human beings encounter or whichever activities they take part in, there is a constant wish to seek meaning.

Already by 1894 Bolton and Meumann had published two remarkable studies. Meumann's review investigated the impressions formed by 17 subjects upon listening to an isochronous sequence of clicks, that is, a series of events with equal temporal distance. Similarly, the 28 subjects in Bolton's study listened to isochronous clicks and were then "invited to say anything that suggested itself to them, whatever the character" (p. 184). When asked to count the clicks, the subjects—even those with no musical appreciation at all—used counting systems that grouped the clicks into units of 2 or 4. Both authors termed the effect tic-toc effect, which has today become known as subjective rhythmization. (Some subjects in Bolton's study reported a rhythmic grouping but also in larger groups that depended on the rate of the isochronous sequence; see p. 215.) Although these findings were concerned with little more than fundamental levels of perception, it would seem that the input of isochronous clicks is enough to stimulate our tendency to attribute meaning to rhythmic events. The same phenomenon can be experienced when listening to the metronomically exact version of a composition from a MIDI file, where all notes have been set to the same intensity and nominal duration—a so-called deadpan rendition. If you do not listen to this artificial product for too long, this extreme realization sounds surprisingly better than one would suppose, and although it may not be aesthetically pleasing, it is not completely "dead" in the sense of being meaningless (see also Thompson & Robitaille, 1992).

This simple experiment sheds light on the importance of the composed structure for the perception of meaning in music: Despite the absence of expressive shaping, the musical structure itself conveys meaning and can communicate sense—at least to some degree. Even in an unexpressive realization it is possible to perceive sections, modulations, and so on. At the same time, it would seem that musical communication consists of at least two layers: First, there is a structural layer (given by the composer's score); and second, there is an expressive layer (added by the performer's realization of the score). Bear in mind that musical communication is not complete until these two layers are related, implemented, and communicated to the listener. It is important to note that as of this day, music psychologists have not yet fully understood the complex processes of musical communication.

The Meaning of Music

In the history of music aesthetics and music psychology, three possible answers have been proposed to the question of what meaning music might possess:

Answer 1. Music does not have any meaning at all. Although there are no authors of musical aesthetics who assume that music has no meaning at all and is little more than "a tickle in the ear," there are indications in the writings of Kant (1790/1987, sect. 16, p. 2) that assume that music without text does not express a specific statement and can be described as "amusement of the senses" (*Spiel der Empfindungen*). This does not mean, however, that purely instrumental music (e.g., a free fantasy) can be described within the category of pleasant only and not of beautiful. As far as I can see, Burke (1852, part 3, sect. 25) comes closest to a sensually "objective" aesthetic. In his treatise, he argues that the initial impact of a musical performance causes a spontaneous emotional impression, which is subsequently followed by a rational aesthetic judgment (cf. Allesch, 1987, p. 148).

Meaning, of course, does not exist in the sense that it does in spoken language, but from the "no meaning at all" point of view it would be hard to explain why, even in the case of purely instrumental compositions, listeners attribute emotions such as happiness and sadness to a piece of music. Behne (1982, p. 128) offers a different theoretical explanation that suggests it would be naive to assume that a composer's intention was to communicate in a one-way fashion what he himself felt while composing a specific piece. On the contrary, the fascination of music is caused by the listener's impression of a two-way "quasi communication." Music not only offers perceived expression but also requires the listener to tune into a "simulation of communication." This point of view is also shared by Kraut (1992, p. 21) in his reflections on musical indeterminacy and how it relates to the understanding of music. In his view, the fact that music is not a spoken language does not represent any deficit. Rather, he indicates that the ambiguous characteristics of all music can be considered a strength of this communication medium.

Answer 2. The meaning of music is its musical form. There are two sources that support the idea that the meaning of music can be found in cognitive acts only, such as the perception of musical form. The first of these is the 19th-century position adopted by music aesthetics and succinctly summarized by the music critic Eduard Hanslick (1891/1986, p. 29). His opinion that music comprises only "tonally moving forms" (*tönend bewegte Formen*) is confirmed in the title of the second chapter of his book, which states that "the representation of feeling is not the content of music" (p. 8). Despite the fact that Hanslick's ideas and assertions are often considered to be extremely formalist, they may still contain a fair amount of accuracy. Suggesting that music is not free of feelings, although not necessarily represented directly but instead dynamically, he asks:

> What, then, from the feelings, can music present if not their content? Only that same dynamic mentioned above. It can reproduce the motion of a physical process according to the prevailing momentum: fast, slow, strong, weak, rising, falling. Motion is just one attribute, however, one moment of feeling, not feeling itself. (p. 11)

A secondary source dates from the late 1950s, a time when psychology was largely dominated by cognitive psychology, which had deliberately excluded emotions and feelings from their discussions (see, e.g., Gardner, 1985). The influence of this tendency upon music psychology can be seen in the second edition of Deutsch's *Psychology of Music* (1999), with its surprising lack of a chapter on music and emotion. Fortunately, this trend is changing and emotion is now viewed as a very important topic in both psychology and music psychology.

Answer 3. The meaning of music is the expression of emotion. The extreme opposite of purely formal aesthetics is Hausegger's (1885) aesthetics of expression (*Ausdrucksästhetik*). In his evolutionary approach, influenced by Darwin's 1872 treatise *The Expression of the Emotions in Animal and Man* (Darwin, 1872/1965), Hausegger developed a theory of "listening to and understanding music" based on an intuitive and universal understanding of emotional expression (*Mitempfindung*). In his view, musical expression is a strong force that guarantees emotional understanding without prerequisites. Today Hausegger's position is supported by the fact that for most people, namely, those without professional involvement, music does not satisfy a cognitive function, such as the understanding of musical form, but an emotional function. A supporting position is maintained by Cooke (1959, p. 12), who writes: "And those who have found music expressive of anything at all (the majority of mankind) have found it expressive of emotions."

While the educational importance of this last point offers potential for discussing not only musical knowledge but also emotional musical experiences in the classroom, there is still a long way to go before a unifying theory of musical meaning or a theory of emotion in music can be posited. The three possible answers to our opening question provided in this section are only representative of the wide range of possibilities of meaning in music. Important related topics such as programmatic music, metaphysical phenomena, and music as an expression of motion are outside the scope of this chapter.

Focus of This Chapter

As outlined earlier, musical communication is a complex, multifaceted subject and still lacks a comprehensive definition. Therefore, in this chapter I will focus primarily on the following questions:

1. Is a performance the result of an intentional process that tries to communicate the performer's view of a piece with a minimum amount of ambiguity, or is it the result of ad hoc decisions, generated in the course of performance?
2. Does a composition have only one meaning, thus limiting the various interpretations of a piece, or is there unlimited freedom of individuality in performance?
3. Are there any rules for the expressive shaping of performance that would facilitate the communication of meaning?
4. How reliable are the performer's so-called expressive acoustical cues decoded by the listener, and how do they serve as a basis of emotional communication?
5. Finally, is music a "universal language" understood by everybody without prerequisites?

In this chapter I will discuss musical communication from three points of view: the performer's and the listener's standpoints and the side of the music itself (i.e., what is communicated by the structural elements of the music?). Without an understanding of these three perspectives it may not be possible to fully understand the concept of musical communication.

Excluded from this chapter, however, are basic cognitive processes such as stream segregation and models of tonal relations and developmental as pects that could be relevant to the understanding of music by children. In addition, only limited space has been afforded to the area of skill acquisition (see chap. 7, by Lehmann and Davidson, this volume). Furthermore, this chapter does not intend to be a review of literature on performance research (this means research on a musician's performing activities and acoustical results). The interested reader can obtain such an overview in the three existing extensive publications by Gabrielsson (1999), Kopiez (1996), and Palmer (1997).

The Development of Performance Plans

If we suppose that all performing musicians have a "message" for their audience and use the expressive and technical means to communicate their personal view of a composition, the question still remains: How does this message develop within the preparatory phase of a performance? Two different answers can be considered that are located at opposite ends of a continuum: First, we could assume that the complete concept of the performance of a composition is present from the initial contact with the music and stays invariant throughout the entire preparation; second, it could be that the development of a performance plan is characterized by an interactive process that affects the whole preparation phase. In the latter case, aspects such as expressive performance plans, fingering, coping with difficult passages, analytical insight into the structure of the piece, and listening to recordings of other musicians would all interact. Thus the performance plan would emerge over the entire preparation phase, making the performer's message increasingly clear, strong, and coherent. For a scientific explanation of these performance plans, we need analytical tools to describe the sounding results. We will refer to the tempo variations of a performance in the form of a curve as "timing profile" and to the time span within which expressive shaping occurs as the "time frame." Timing has been chosen as the dominant parameter since it is the most widely investigated one in performance research. This does not, however, imply that other parameters such as dynamics are less important for the understanding of expressive intentions.

Results of Performance Research

Performance as Imaginary Narration.   A performance plan does not simply consist of the formal representation of music only but also includes noncognitive components that encompass, among other things, images, moods, and imaginative musical characters (Gabrielsson, 1999, p. 502). In this respect, the reduction of meaning to musical structure would be an oversimplification of the complex situation of musical communication. Yet as Shaffer (1992) points out, musical meaning also includes so-called narrative elements such as "imaginary protagonists." Seen in this light, "the performer's interpretation can be viewed as helping to define the character of the protagonist" (p. 265). The theoretical foundations of this narrative performance theory can be found in E. Tarasti's (1994) *Theory of Musical Semiotics,* the strength of which is demonstrated through a comparative and phenomenological analysis of 22 recordings of the *Mélodie française* "Après un rêve" and a sample analysis (by writing a so-called modal grammar) of Chopin's G-Minor Ballad. Tarasti's theory can be applied easily to the analysis of performance or can be used by music critics. Such a perspective of performance planning suggests that a performer uses a top-down strategy in developing an overall performance plan as well as a bottom-up strategy with more relevance to local events. In addition, expression marks in the score play an important role in the development of these local and global strategies. Experimental support for this view was obtained by Shaffer (1992) by removing expression marks from the edited score and comparing the resulting performances to renditions performed from the original score (1995). He also found that playing from an unedited score induced less consistent timing across repeated renditions. This observation encourages the idea that expression markings clarify the musical character and thereby contribute to the communication of musical meaning. Similarly, these findings are supported by a listening study carried out by Watt and Ash (1998), which used unfamiliar pieces of music to investigate the attribution of personal traits such as "gender" (male/female) and "age" (young/old). Due to the high consistency between evaluators involved in this experiment, the authors concluded that "music is perceived as if it were a person making a disclosure" (p. 47) and went on to suggest that because of the similarity between psychological reactions to both real people and music, "music creates a virtual person" (p. 49). One consequence for further investigations in musical communication is that it would be more effective to ask subjects to refer to elements relevant to the narrative structure of music as indices for successful communication, instead of free associations or nonmusical entities.

Strategies for the Development of Performance Plans.   To obtain greater insight into the strategies employed during the creation of an interpretation, Hallam (1995) interviewed 22 pianists about their study techniques for learning an unknown composition. Only a minority of the subjects (9%) were purely holistic learners who would initially play through the piece and attempt to acquire an idea of the overall conception of the work before starting their detailed practice. Thirty-two percent of the players employed an intuitive/serialistic strategy (playing of small sections) and developed their interpretation as the music was learned (p. 120). The majority of the players were so-called versatile learners (45%), who used a holistic as well as a serial strategy—a learning style that can be classified as a combined top-down and bottom-up strategy. It follows, then, that a balanced relationship between integration (global perspective) and differentiation (local perspective) is a feature of every outstanding work of art and a fundamental issue in musical aesthetics. As an educational consequence Hallam argues for the use of either holistic or versatile strategies after analyzing the piece or listening to different recordings, yet it is also possible that learning styles may depend on the musical style of a composition. As Childs (1992) demonstrated in a self-report study with professional musicians, the practice of contemporary music was characterized by a certain sequence of phases: The rhythmic structure, which is often highly complex, is practiced in the first phase; the "correct notes" are practiced in the second; and details of expression become part of the performance plan in the third phase.

A methodological flaw in many studies is the unwanted effects of "rationalization" that result from retrospective interviews. Consequently, researchers are sometimes better advised to directly observe musicians' practice. Such a method of direct observation with tape recording was used by Gruson (1988) for her analyses of piano practice behavior among advanced and novice pianists and by Miklaszewski (1989) who video-recorded a single case study of a pianist.

Representation of Performance Plans.   We now know that musicians use elaborate strategies to develop a performance plan that guarantees a high degree of reproducibility, but how are these performance plans represented in memory and controlled during execution? Already Skinner (1932; also Seashore, 1936) has shown in her groundbreaking studies on timing that musical interpretation is not accidental, but that note durations can be repeated consistently across several renditions. This observation is supported by the findings of Repp (1992a), who demonstrated that the correlation between the repetition of the first section in 28 recordings of Schumann's *"Träumerei"* varied, in most cases, between $r = .80$ and $r = .90$. Likewise, Skinner made the interesting observation that even if a player tries to play inexpressively and metronomically (in a so-called deadpan version), he or she will produce measurable tempo deviations, for example, with ritardandi corresponding to phrase endings. From this it is possible to conclude that, on the one hand, musical knowledge seems to be organized in phrases and that, on the other hand, a player is unable to ignore the perceived phrase units.

As Palmer (1989) explains in her "parameter theory" of performance, an interpretation is stored in memory as a basic performance pattern, the timing profile of which is modified when the player intends to give a different interpretation of a piece (instead of generating a completely new profile or program). We have to keep in mind that Palmer's timing analyses as well as those of most other authors are based on note-to-note interonset durations where the term *interonset interval* refers to the time span between the onset of two consecutive events. As long as we use analytical methods that concern timing within only a specific time frame (represented by means of a timing curve), we cannot conclude that only this time layer is affected by parameter changes. Therefore, we ought to compare the simultaneous shaping of time in time frames of various sizes (for a new theoretical approach see Langner,

2000, 2002; Langner, Kopiez, & Feiten, 1998). In a recent approach, Chaffin et al. (2002) revealed that the existence of a global musical concept (the so-called "big picture") at the beginning of the practice of a new piece is a characteristic feature of professional musicians.

The Coding/Decoding Process of Musical Expression

The Relation Between Structure and Expression

Musical expression can be investigated from two perspectives. On the one hand, there is the "emotional expression" of music (such as the communication of different moods), and on the other hand there is "structural expression," which is strongly related to the structural features of music. These structural features, such as cadences that indicate segment boundaries to the listener, help the listener to separate the stream of music into sections such as motifs or phrases. Although both perspectives are relevant for the explanation of the communicative processes in music, the structural expression is relevant for the communication on different hierarchical levels.

The Assumption of "Isomorphism."   The dominant structure-expression theory of expressive communication of meaning assumes that there is a strong relationship between compositional structure and musical expression. The theoretical foundation for this concept was provided by S. Langer (1953) with the assumption of isomorphism, that is, a close relationship between the structural features of a composition—such as hierarchical organization—and the expression intended by the composer. This assumption has been influential in this field of study (e.g., Palmer, 1997, who assumes that structure constrains expression). As early as 1936, Henderson was able to show that performers obviously use a hierarchical categorization of the compositional structure to modify with different weightings the nominal values in the score; for example, more important events on higher levels such as phrase boundaries would be emphasized through use of a dynamic accent, lengthening of the duration, or asynchronization. Following this theory, it would seem to be the performer's priority to uncover the musical structure encoded in the score and to communicate these insights to the audience—a view that has received wide support in empirical research.

Presenting melodies in different metrical contexts, Sloboda (1985) observed that pianists changed certain note parameters, namely, articulation and note length, in accordance with the different metrical positions on which a note fell. In a subsequent listening experiment, listeners could clearly identify the performer's intention. The importance of structural expression was also shown in a study by Repp (1997b) where the timing curves of a Debussy prelude played by 10 famous pianists were compared to the timing profiles of 10 graduate students, recorded nearly unrehearsed. Despite large inter individual differences in preparation and experience, timing curves were found to be extremely similar. A further experiment, based on the theoretical predictions of Lerdahl and Jackendoff's (1983) *Generative Theory of Tonal Music,* was carried out by Todd (1985). He discovered that the extent of a ritardando was proportional to the importance of the affected phrase boundary: More important phrase boundaries received more slowing than less important ones.

Clarke (1987, 1988, 1993) also showed that this close relationship between expression and musical structure is a necessary (but not wholly sufficient) prerequisite for adequate understanding of the performer's interpretive intention. In a series of experiments, he found that listeners gave a more qualified evaluation of a performance when the expressive modifications were congruent with the musical structure. Thus it would seem that expressive phrasing is determined by structural features, descriptions, and "mental representations of musical structure" (Palmer, 1992, p. 249). While the performer may use expressive cues to communicate his intention and understanding to the listener, we have to keep in mind that the listener not only perceives the musical structure but also evaluates whether or not the performer has understood the music.

Beyond Structural Constraints: Irrational Components of Expressive Performance.   The question remains open as to whether a performance is simply the result of structural constraints and can be described by the process of "rational composition of performance," meaning that the performer synthesizes a performance by analytically weighting structural features (see Mazzola & Beran, 1998). While there has been very little research aimed at investigating the extent to which performances are influenced by factors that include structure, gesture, and mood, Clarke (1993; also Clarke & Baker-Short, 1987) has indicated a need to modify the strict rationalistic model of performance generation.

Clarke set up manipulated performances that required players to imitate a rubato passage, the timing profile of which had been inverted or shifted by one eighth note or one measure. Such a transformation resulted in a contradiction between musical structure and expressive intention. When the subjects (skilled pianists) tried to imitate these versions, it could be seen that timing was more accurate and stable in the original than in the manipulated version. Consequently, it appears that the relationship between structural and expressive features is a necessary but not sufficient condition for the explanation of expressive performance. As of now, little is known about the impact of the performer's emotions or sense of movement on the shaping of a performance. It may therefore come as no surprise that completely synthesized performances of complete pieces based on complex mathematical transformations of pitch, harmony, and time parameters (e.g., Mazzola & Beran, 1998) sound musically plausible, albeit artistically unspectacular.

The recordings of Glenn Gould, whose performances have been evaluated by music critics as intentionally unconventional, bear witness to the claim that there has to be artistic individuality in addition to some rule-governed performance. Although experience of musical performance suggests strong evidence for the importance of an additional "human factor," current research cannot provide any explanations as to the nature of such an irrational component (see Shaffer, 1989). Consequently, more analysis of unconventional performances is necessary in order to gain a deeper insight into the scope of artistic individuality beyond the limits of the accepted "rules."

Rule-Based Performance Grammar

The Analysis-by-Synthesis Approach.   In everyday life, rules facilitate communication and help to avoid ambiguity. If this is the case, could it not then be possible that a similar mechanism also operates in the communication of musical expression? The observation that alike musical structures cause parallel expressive features has already been pointed out by Lussy (1873/1882). In his treatise on the application of musical expression to performance, Lussy analyzed expression marks in the scores of several different composers and identified 17 rules for the application of accelerando (e.g., through the course of repeated notes, at harmonic changes, or at rising melodic lines) and 32 rules for the application of ritardando (e.g., at falling melodic lines, at phrase endings, or at groups of lower notes that follow a series of high notes). Each of these rules, he argued, was illustrated by a vast number of notated examples for pupils to practice. It is this work that provides the backdrop to the scientific investigation of rule-based systems of musical expression developed by Scandinavian researchers (e.g., Friberg, 1995; Gabrielsson, 1999; Sundberg, Frydén, & Askenfelt, 1983; for a review). In the early studies, Sundberg, Frydén, and Askenfelt used an analysis-by-synthesis approach to test the adequacy of the output of their generative system. The approach outlined earlier has been labeled generative in view of the fact that performances are generated by the application of expressive grammars and rule-based systems. In simple terms, the procedure is the following: First rules of expression are formulated by listening to recordings of outstanding artists. (It is interesting to note that most of the rules were suggested by an experienced violinist, Lars Frydén!). Then these rules are implemented in a computer program that generates artificial interpretations. Finally, the synthesized and original versions are compared and the rule system subsequently improved. Recent progress of the performance synthesis project is documented in Friberg (1999), and models are implemented in software such as *Melodia* by Roberto Bresin and *Director Musices* by Anders Friberg. Thompson, Sundberg, Friberg, and Frydén (1989, p. 63) assert that "the musical quality of performances is improved by applying rules." However, the same authors remark that the simple addition of rules generated only "unmusical" results, due to the overemphasis on detail. In most cases, the application of no more than five rules was sufficient to produce an acceptable result.

Critical Assessment of the Rule-Based Approach.   Oosten (1993) seriously criticizes the generative approach, arguing that rules are a necessary but not entirely sufficient condition for the generation and communication of musically accepted performance synthesis. This is due in part to the primarily local effect of a rule (instead of being concerned with elements of greater structural importance; see experiment by Todd [1985] described earlier) and to the intuitive nature of the generative approach. Moreover, the simple application of a rule set seems to be a "hit the wall" strategy for the most part, which considers neither the style-specific application of an expression rule nor the fact that rules are not always applied consistently by a performer within a composition. Current performance research still has no theoretical framework for the shaping of expressive parameters within larger time frames. The experience of outstanding live performances, however, confirms that there must be an expressive layer responsible for the communication of, for instance, tension and resolution, which cannot be analyzed by any of the existing scientific methods. Langner and Kopiez (1995) showed that large-scale oscillations, triggered by the timing profile of a performance with a time frame of 60 seconds or more, can be important features of professional performances. In the same way, existing analyses support the assumption that the depth of a performer's musical thought influences the communication of expressive tension and perhaps of a performance's overall musical quality, yet such a hypothesis still awaits confirmation. In summary, it can be argued that the rule-based approach only partially explains the phenomenon of expressive interpretation and cannot account entirely for its complexity. In other words, the rule-based approach can *simulate* but not *imitate* a real performance.

Are Interpretations Uniform or Individual?

Music cannot be performed using just any method, and performance variability seems to be limited by a criterion of "correctness." The national anthem, for example, can be jazzed up only so much before it ceases to be the national anthem. Similarly, with regard to the parameter tempo, it is impossible to double or triple the tempo of music and have it remain the same piece of music or communicate the same message. Being too fast or too slow makes some music unmusical and changes its character completely. What does this mean for the performance of pieces from the classical repertoire?

Historical Background of Performance Individuality   The limited standard repertoire of our musical culture relies on individuality to distinguish one performer from another. Although it is usual for listeners to prefer specific artists, it remains unclear how this individuality can be identified in the acoustical data of a particular interpretation. In order to produce the unmistakable characteristics that identify a particular performer, the performer has to reproduce his or her personal rendition of a composition with great consistency, thereby practically minimizing the intraindividual variability. The historical situation of performance expectations has not always been that of the present day. On the contrary, Czerny's (1839/1991) treatise on musical performance (Czerny was Beethoven's piano teacher and one of the foremost piano teachers of his time) advocated the idea that performances should be variable from one time to another instead of being uniform. He demanded from competent performers an "always different" performance ("jedesmal eine andere Vortragsweise anzuwenden," p. 25), especially when repeating a passage several times within a composition. From this we can assume that, at least in the 19th century, performers gave a wider variety of performances than today and different artistic aspects of a composition could be communicated—as long as the character of the work was not compromised.

Performance Individuality in Schumann's "Träumerei."   The current state of performance research points to a different situation in recent times. Repp (1992a) analyzed the timing of 28 recordings of Schumann's "Träumerei," played by 24 different pianists. Analysis of interonset intervals in the first eight measures showed that players could be grouped, by means of a principal component analysis, into four categories: Group 1 was dominated by the recordings of Horowitz, Group 2 by those of Cortot, Group 3 represented the mainstream, and Group 4 contained the remaining performers. The author concluded that a tendency toward uniformity could be observed due to timing constraints at phrase boundaries that allowed only a small degree of freedom. In a subsequent study, Repp (1992b) concentrated on the principle melodic gesture of "Träumerei" (which consists of six notes) and found instances of additional constraints that could limit artistic individuality. Subsequent experiments revealed that when the timing profile of this motif was shifted only those timing profiles whose shapes were parabolic were judged positively by the listeners. This result was explained by "classes of optimal temporal shapes for melodic gestures . . . that musically acculturated listeners know and expect . . . within which artistic freedom and individual preference can manifest themselves" (p. 221). Similar experiments that concern the variability of performance still continue to the present day, as shown in a recent study by Repp (1998) in which the author analyzes 115 recordings of Chopin's Etude in E major, op. 10, no. 3, by 108 artists. Using a principal component analysis, the first five bars of the Etude could be described by four factors, accounting for most of the timing variance (76%).

Do Timing Curves Represent Individuality in Performance?   At this point, some criticism should be made concerning the validity of Repp's (1992a) results: By including the timing data of the whole piece, he obtained only one general factor with no differentiation among the 28 recordings and found also that a reduction in the number of included notes increased the

number of factors. In addition, the timing clusters for the first melodic gesture did not correspond to the three main factors found in the principal
component analysis of the first eight measures. Also, the perceptual experience when listening to the recordings does not correspond to such an un-
differentiated statistical grouping. Where does this mismatch arise? We could
assume that such a method of analyzing timing (or other variables) on a
note-to-note level offers only a very limited insight into the nature of musical
interpretation and the ideas communicated by the player. Consequently, we
suggest that future methods of timing analysis include the possibility of *simultaneous* timing analysis of layers with different time-frame sizes (on a
bar-to-bar level or a phrase-to-phrase level) of the same performance. Only
such an approach would be commensurate with the complexity of musical
thought observed in outstanding performers.

The considerations outlined earlier raise a further question: Is the performer's ability to shape time and intensity limited by the listeners' expectancies? Inspired by research into the attractiveness of human faces, Repp
(1997a) carried out a so-called average performance experiment, in which
listeners were asked to rate 11 performances of "Träumerei" in terms of
quality and originality. One of the listening examples had been generated
from the average timing and intensity data of the 10 other MIDI recordings.
The pedaling sequence remained constant throughout all 11 versions. Repp
found that the "average version" was ranked second-highest in terms of
performance quality but second-lowest in terms of individuality. A plausible
interpretation of the results offered by the author assumes that listeners develop a performance prototype that guides their expectancies; the average
version could fulfill this expectancy and provide an ideal interpretation due
to the compensation of extremes through the averaging. Despite the absence
of a convincing theoretical explanation for this effect, the same preferential
tendency for "averaged versions" can be observed in the evaluation of rhythmic performances. In a cross-cultural study on the perception of rhythm,
Kopiez, Langner, and Steinhagen (1999) found a consistently high evaluation
of the average performance of rhythm samples.

Different Perspectives of Analysis: Local and Global Expressive Shaping.   One
of the priorities for performance analysis in the future should be to develop
methods and theories that allow for the analysis to take place within time
frames of varying levels. Only the consideration of local as well as global
levels of expressive shaping in the same performance will enable adequate
analysis of the complex phenomenon of musical interpretation and communication. One example of how such a theoretical framework could function is given by Mazzola (1995, 2002) in his "inverse performance theory,"
which uses analytical data (so-called analytical weights) from a score analysis by a special software (Rubato[1]). These weights are used as predictor
variables for the individual timing curves in multiple regression analysis. As
demonstrated in Beran and Mazzola (2000), this decomposition of a complete performance (the authors call it analytical semantics) into analytical

weights for the melodic, metric, and harmonic structure explained between 65 and 85% of the microstructure timing of a performance. This finding strongly supports the assumption that a close relationship exists between expressive intentions and compositional features, where the first can be explained with reference to the second. Such an approach goes far beyond the surface analysis of a small section by Repp (1992a) and gives detailed insight into the complexity of musical thought. Although Beran and Mazzola (2000) were able to confirm the fundamental structure of Repp's principal component analysis, large individual differences were shown to exist in relation to the relative importance of single structural parameters (harmony, melody, metric). In the case of Horowitz's three performances of "Träumerei," the performer's view of the piece obviously changed over time: After his first recording of the piece, in 1947—which was dominated by a very localized melodic and metrical thinking (a kind of "performance near-sight")—Horowitz's interpretation became more coherent in his 1963 and 1965 recordings. The different time perspectives in the studies by Repp (1992a) and Beran and Mazzola (2000) also go some way toward explaining the seemingly contradictory results achieved. As a result, it could be argued that although the timing of the first eight bars and the single melodic gestures remain unchanged over decades, more global timing concepts reveal changes when the piece is analyzed as a whole.

In light of these considerations, it is evident that inverse performance theory is also of great practical importance since it offers the transformation of the metaphorical language of musical criticism into an exactly defined parametric space. At the same time, however, it must be pointed out that research that concerns the relationship between performance features and the structural properties of the score is still new and expanding.

Decoding Expression: The Role of Acoustical Cues

In his famous treatise on flute playing from the 18th century, Quantz (1752/1966, p. 164) writes: "Hence in playing you must regulate yourself in accordance with the prevailing sentiment, so that you do not play a very melancholy Adagio too quickly or a cantabile Adagio too slowly." Clearly, in terms of the Adagio mentioned here by Quantz, tempo is a global cue that supports the dominant character and affect of a piece, yet nowadays there are other factors, such as original instrumentation and tuning, that should be kept in mind. In addition, Quantz's statement sheds light on the relationship between the structural features of a composition and the expressive intentions of a performer. As Meyer (1956, p. 199) notes, the score gives more or less specific indications as to the composer's intention, but it depends on the performer to intensify or integrate these structural cues into a form that can be communicated to the listener. Thus a useful contribution for music theory is elaboration of the basic principles of emotive importance, such as expectancy or gestalt continuation. As the famous "Tristan chord" from the prelude to Wagner's *Tristan and Isolde* paradigmatically shows, emotional meaning will always be contextually dependent on structural features, which prevents the simple categorization of structural elements into a "catalog of emotions."

We assume that musical performance contains numerous so-called acoustical cues, such as timbre, tempo, and articulation, which help to facilitate the communication of the performer's intentions. A necessary condition for the communicative function, however, is the reliable decoding of such cues from the auditory stream. Research of the last decades into music performance as well as research into cross-modal perception of expressive qualities of object (see Beldoch, 1961, for less recent research) has given us some insight into the basic mechanisms of this cue extraction process: When measuring the degree of identification of 10 feelings, including anger, joy, and love, in different media (vocal, visual arts, and music), Beldoch found expressive qualities to be relatively consistent, yet the total congruence did not exceed 40% of correct identifications.

The Interdependence of Expressive Cues.   Our next question concerns the parameters of musical expression, their hierarchy, and their interrelation. Concerning the hierarchy of expressive parameters, Kamenetzky, Hill, and Trehub (1997) presented short, 30-second-long musical examples played in four versions: one with no variations in tempo and dynamics, another with variations in tempo and dynamics, another with variations in tempo only, and another with variations in dynamics only. The results showed that variation in tempo only caused a significantly lower evaluation on the "expressive" scale than variations in dynamics only or in tempo and dynamics. Although caution must be exercised regarding generalizations because of the very limited duration of the examples, a possible hierarchy of expressive parameters seems to exist.

In the same manner, two further studies produced more evidence of the interactive nature of expressive parameters. Dudek (1992), for example, carried out a recognition experiment of piano performances with interchanged velocity and timing data, holding one parameter constant in each version. In total, timing and intensity were used equally frequently for the identification of performances, but substantial individual differences were noted within the sample of 16 compositions played in different styles. Rather than provide a simple hierarchy of expressive factors, these findings emphasize the importance of the interaction between structural features of the composition and the listener's preferences for expressive parameters.

The second study, carried out by Dougherty in 1993, used the method of cross synthesis of four emotions (i.e., the transfer of spectral features from one item to the other) from spoken language (anger, fear, joy, and sadness) to a short sequence of notes played on the violin with three specific expressive parameters (timbre, pitch contour, and speech tempo). The fact that the emotional state of "non-cross-synthesized" violin tones was identified as accurately as that of unmanipulated speech led the author to conclude that there was no single-feature mechanism for cue detection. Since the reliability of identification improved with the increasing number of expressive parameters involved in cross-synthesis, it is possible to conclude that the interaction between expressive parameters plays a decisive role in the correct identification of emotional intentions in performance.

Communicating Expressive Intentions to the Audience.   An early study that concerned the communication of the more complex aspects of a player's ideas to the audience was undertaken by Senju and Ohgushi (1987). Subjects who rated 10 performances of the opening of Mendelssohn's Violin Concerto through use of a semantic differential most commonly identified the intention of a "powerful" performance. Having subjects verbalize performance impressions, however, did not result in effective identification of the relevant aspects of expressive performance. Concerning the communication of dynamics, Patterson (1974) found that most woodwind players had a dynamic range too small to cover the six different degrees of intensity (from *pianissimo* to *fortissimo*) that require a range of roughly 30 decibels. Oboists, for example, often produced a span of only two dynamic levels. Since greater dynamic contrasts make music more exciting, the author suggests the use of exercises to enlarge the dynamic range. However, we have to remember that the perception of dynamics is also influenced by instrument-specific expectations of the listener. Perception can differ from reality.

Nakamura's 1987 study focuses on the fundamental role of dynamics (and not timing!) in the communication of expressive intentions. In his experiment, subjects heard musical excerpts and identified instances of crescendo much more reliably than instances of decrescendo in the corresponding score. It is possible, however, that such an effect is both instrument- and context-specific. Here the perceptual basis could form a template for the recognition of increases in intensity. This last assumption is supported by the results of Huron (1991), who, in his analysis of the frequency of crescendo and decrescendo markings in 435 piano works by 14 composers, found a significantly greater number of crescendos than decrescendos. This bias in dynamic markings is termed ramp archetype and is based on a neural mechanism that facilitates detection of increasing rather than decreasing intensities.

A categorization of three levels of expression (no expression, appropriate, exaggerated) across different instruments was observed in a study by Kendall and Carterette (1990), which revealed that both musicians and nonmusicians were able to distinguish, to a certain and not totally reliable degree, between performances of a short melody on different instruments with different levels of expression. Besides the fact that the subjects appeared to use timing as an expressive cue, the authors stress that there was no support for the idea of an all-encompassing grammar that mediates the communication between performer and listener (p. 160). Of course, the perceived expression of a performance is influenced not only by acoustical cues but also by visual ones.

Conditions of Successful Recognition of Expressed Emotions.   Is formal music education a necessary condition for the successful recognition of expressive cues, or can an expressive intention be communicated by a performer even to "uneducated" listeners or children? In a perception experiment with 4- to 9-year-old children, Rodriguez (1998) conducted a "same-or-different" discrimination test that used mechanical and expressive versions of a tune. He found that subjects answered with 66% overall accuracy, but that the degree of correct answers increased with age, starting from 46% among kindergarten children and ending with 70% accuracy among fourth graders. Giomo (1992) investigated whether mood in music, as a holistic impression, was correctly recognized by 5- to 9-year-old children. Using a pictorial, non-verbal response paradigm, she was able to show that age played no role in the effective categorization of classical music examples into three mood dimensions (softness, pleasantness, solemnity). While no positive influence could be attributed to taking instrumental lessons, the author discovered an effect of sociocultural background that pointed to the influence of both the subjects' home music environment and musical experience.

These findings provide evidence for the idea that the perception of expressive features in music is perhaps an ability that must be nurtured and developed through education and listening experience. On the background of other studies that relate to age-dependent recognition of emotional expression in music, a more complex picture emerges. In a labeling task devised by Cunningham and Sterling (1989), for example, it was noted that preschoolers were already astonishingly consistent in associating certain attributes (happiness, sadness, anger, and fear) with musical excerpts presented to them. Dolgin and Adelson (1990) also found age differences in the recognition of emotional expression between 4- and 9-year-olds. Similarly, Terwogt and Grinsven (1991) noted that the agreement in recognition of happiness, anger, and sadness in music excerpts increased between the ages 5 and 7 years; conversely, Kratus (1993) found no developmentally based effect in the recognition of emotional states in 30 musical excerpts among 6- to 22-year-old subjects. Bear in mind that there is, as yet, no standardized mood-recognition task in music that uses a fixed repertoire of music examples from clearly defined selection criteria. As long as each study uses different stimuli, the varying results can be attributed not only to this incomparability but also to other relevant factors such as age and gender. Unfortunately, this is a serious methodological difficulty for all studies in the field.

Physical Correlates of Emotional Characters.   A Swedish research group led by Alf Gabrielsson has recently started to focus on the coding/decoding process of acoustical cues in the communication of expressive intentions. They are interested in knowing "what . . . performer[s] do to generate the intended emotional character of the music" (Gabrielsson, 1995, p. 35). In their opinion, musical expression includes both, structure and performance.

The principal method employed is experimental in the sense that a performer is instructed to play a given passage with different emotional characters (happy, sad, solemn, angry, soft, and indifferent). Upon completion of this task, the acoustical parameters of the performance are analyzed. An important result that arose out of the analysis of the recordings was that performers used a wide variety of durational modifications, especially concerning the proportional relationships between different note lengths. However, dynamics, articulation, and timbre also played an instrument-dependent role and were modified in correspondence with the intended expression. For example, "angry" and "happy" versions were played faster than those excerpts meant to illustrate other characters, and in happy versions the durational proportions were softened.

There are obvious reasons to investigate the connection between motion and musical expression. For example, Clynes's "theory of sentics" (1977) assumes that for each basic emotion there exists a specific dynamic form. Although Clynes's theory is not uncontroversial (see Edgewater, 1999, p. 167; Repp, 1989, 1990 for critiques), Gabrielsson used Clynes's Sentograph device to assess the correspondence between the expressive parameters and the expressive finger movements of an imagined performance for the same musical excerpt. The results indicated a close relationship between emotion and motion, which supports the central hypothesis that "we may consider emotion, motion, and music as being isomorphic" (Gabrielsson, 1995, p. 37).

An early experimental investigation into communicative processes was undertaken by Gabrielsson and Juslin (1996). In this study, musicians were asked to perform melodies from different styles of music (folk songs, classical tunes) on different instruments (violin, electric guitar, voice) with different emotional characters (happy, sad, angry, fearful, tender, solemn). Listeners then rated the performances regarding how clearly they perceived the intended character, a task that represents a basic paradigm for all research in expressive communication. Results showed that listeners were in general agreement and that a wide range of expression among instruments, styles, and players was observed. Analysis of the acoustical data showed an astonishingly flexible handling of the musical structure: One of the melodies was played on a flute with a "sad" character at 50 beats per minute and another by a violinist with a "happy" character at 250 beats per minute. Although the authors compiled a provisional "feature-catalogue" of musical characters, the results raise an important issue, namely, that of the constraints of musical material. If the same melody can be played five times faster, achieving a different expressive character, the question of the existence of a "natural character" determined by the compositional structure remains open to discussion! Therefore, we suggest that the term *character* should be used to denote a unique "fingerprint" of a piece that gives it its unifying impression. Beethoven's *Pastoral* Symphony (Kirby, 1970) and the powerful atmospheric spell of the "Wolfsschluchtszene" (Wolf's glen scene) in Weber's *Freischütz* (Ruiter, 1989) might serve as famous examples of such characters. In this sense, the term *character* has two connotations: It is connected first to the specific expressive individuality of a piece and second to the unmistakable emotions presented in a performance.

The Cue-Utilization Paradigm.   The most recent research in the analysis of acoustical cues generated by the performer and their relevance for musical communication is best represented by Juslin (1997, 2000, 2001; Juslin & Madison, 1999). This approach can be characterized as a cue-utilization paradigm where performers are instructed to play a short popular tune with different fundamental emotions, such as happiness, sadness, anger, and fear. The players may use all expressive parameters in free variation. In a subsequent "labeling task," listeners decode and rate the intensity of the communicated emotions. In principle, Juslin adopted the research paradigm that Scherer and Oshinsky (1977) used in their research on the perception of expression in synthesized 8-tone sequences. They also produced a catalog of expressive code. Juslin's theoretical framework was taken from functionalistic emotional psychology and Brunswik's functionalistic and probabilistic approach to perception: It assumes that "basic" emotions are perceived much more clearly than "other" emotions due to their importance for the phylogenetic development—a basic mechanism that could also be important in musical communication. Such an assumption is supported by Juslin, who showed that the decoding of expressive intentions reaches an overall stability of nearly 80%. For further information on the project "Feedback-learning of musical expressivity" see http://www.psyk.uu.se/hemsidor/musicpsy.

At this point, some critical points that concern research on the communication of emotion and the validity of results should be made:

- *Impact of structural features.* At present, the cue-utilization paradigm offers no predictions that regard the impact of the composition's structural features, such as tone system, scale, or orchestration. In order to develop a clearer understanding of such features, research would have to consider the interaction between a "happy" tune played with "sad" intentions in a very slow tempo and vice versa. As long as little is known about structural constraints, the validity of any results should be considered preliminary. A more complex picture emerges in the most recent reports on "inherent expression" (see Lindström, 2000; Madison, 2000): Emotional expression is determined by the musical structure itself, an adequate performance, and the interaction between performance variability and structure. While the intensity of emotional expression can be both reinforced as well as reduced by performance variability, some emotional characters are not influenced at all when performance variability is experimentally removed.
- *Relationship between global and local cues.* There is currently no theory to explain the relationship between local and global expressive elements. Listening experience produces strong evidence for the complex and hierarchical nature of the influence of single emotional features; we do not simply extract emotional cues locally. The 200-year-long debate in musical aesthetics about the term *musical character* underscores the importance of a

unifying mechanism called character, which "rules" a whole composition (see Ruiter, 1989). Nevertheless, as long as samples with durations of only a few seconds are used (such as in the study by Gabrielsson and Juslin, 1996), we cannot reach an adequate understanding of this emotional hierarchy. At the same time, we should not forget the results of other researchers (e.g., Karno & Konecni, 1992; Tillman & Bigand, 1996) that showed that listeners are "embarrassingly" insensitive to global structural properties when judging the emotional expression of manipulated (so-called scrambled) versions of a piece of music.

• *"Subjective" induction of emotions versus "objective" labeling.* Listeners in Juslin's study were given a labeling task, but there was no control over whether they could objectively label the perceived expressive code and keep this decision uninfluenced by the emotions induced by the music. Quite simply, it is uncertain exactly what was judged—expression or impression. This problem of separating impression from expression is a fundamental problem in all "music and emotion" research. A further problem is the immediate induction of emotions. As Nyklicek and Doornen (1997) were able to show, heartbeat as well as breathing patterns were strongly influenced by selected structural parameters of the music such as tempo. Despite the fact that the authors chose only very extreme and basic emotions for their examples, this effect was intensified when subjects were initially introduced to the expected emotions. From an evolutionary perspective, it follows that there is a basic mechanism for the immediate detection of certain emotional states; Juslin is right with regard to this point. And his view is supported by the findings of Peretz, Gagnon, and Bouchard (1998) in a judgment study with brain-injured listeners. The subjects' emotional judgment was quite consistent, immediate, and seemingly uninfluenced by their condition regardless of whether presented musical excerpts were "happy" or "sad": The judgment was mostly influenced by musical structure (mode and tempo). In addition, we do not know how an individual's "emotional quotient" influences the perceived emotional intensity. At the same time, it should be remembered that most musical states are not based on clear, fundamental emotions. For example, music may well result in "boredom"— a feeling/emotion that can surely not be classified as a fundamental emotion.

• *Model of emotion and consciousness.* The theoretical model used in the explanation is an "umbrella" model in which all emotions are assembled under one "hat." Criticizing the use of this model, LeDoux (1996) argues that each emotion should be considered as a complex and autonomous system that works along with psychophysiological reactions. As long as our understanding of just one of those systems is incomplete, it is impossible to reach any conclusion as to the nature of the whole emotional system. If we believe that listening to music can activate memorable musical experiences, it follows that the only way to investigate the complex phenomenon of musical communication is to adopt a systemic approach. This approach would cover the ongoing (conscious or unconscious) process of evaluation and interpretation while listening to music.

• *Ambiguity.* If musical communication aspires to being unambiguous, would a functionalistic approach be adequate for the explanation of emotional communication? Aesthetic experience appears to be characterized only by the paradoxical mechanism of ambiguous input (musical message) that results in unambiguous output (listening experience). If certainty in identification of expression were a genuine priority of music, we could be sure that human evolution would have created a form of music less ambiguous (maybe with fewer possible emotions)—in a communicative sense—than that already observed. We may conclude that in spite of its importance, cue utilization is only a secondary phenomenon of the listening process and that the functionalistic perspective remains limited to a few basic emotions.

Can We Understand Music Without Prerequisites?
The Myth of Music as a "Universal Language"

The idea that music might be a universal language that can be understood without prerequisites and independently from the individual's cultural background is a widely held conviction. Although this belief is asserted with great persistence in both politics and everyday life, this issue is not simple, judged from the standpoint of music psychology. It is already clear that the study of musical universals and the biological foundations of music have contributed a new perspective characterized by comparative research methodologies (see Carterette & Kendall, 1999). While this has resulted in the creation of new research disciplines such as biomusicology (Wallin, Merker, & Brown, 2000), aimed at providing us with a fascinating insight into the auditory perception among animals (see Fay, 1988, for an extensive data collection), it is still very difficult to draw conclusions from the literature relevant to the human music perception. Very often, the studies of comparative music psychology, based on studies of animal behavior, are obtained with simple stimuli that have little resemblance to real music. Although interesting in themselves, the results that concern "virtual pitch in cats" (Hefner & Whitfield, 1976), "octave stretching" (Carterette & Kendall, 1999, p. 739), or "octave identity" (surely not a universal; see Hulse & Page, 1988; Hulse, Takeuchi, & Braaten, 1992) have little immediate bearing on the human listening experience.

Having said this, it is important to recognize the contribution of researchers who investigate auditory perception in animals and newborn infants, which allow great insight into the importance of the basic processes in music listening and have shown that such processes appear on a "hardware" basis in all vertebrates regardless of cultural influences. For instance, studies by Porter and Neuringer (1984) revealed that pigeons can first learn to distinguish between musical styles (e.g., Bach and Stravinsky) and then successfully transfer their acquired stylistic knowledge to unfamiliar examples in a discrimination test. Hulse and Cynx (1986) found that auditory stream segregation already works in starlings, while Fassbender's (1996) study of auditory capacity in early infancy concluded that most musically relevant perceptual mechanisms, such as contour perception, are probably developed at a very early age. It is essential here to realize that music is not considered a spoken language and, as Sloboda (1985, p. 12) points out, it would indeed "be foolish to claim that music is simply another natural language." It should, however, be kept in mind that music shares certain structural similarities with spoken language, such as its hierarchical organization. Temporal proximity alone does not rule the perception of music; in fact, we as listeners construct hierarchical relationships while listening to music in real time.

The Cultural Dependency of Expressive Decoding.   A review I have written (Kopiez, 2004) argues that unfortunately most of the research concerned with so-called perceptual invariants is a long way away from explaining relevant aspects of musical experience. This can be seen in a study by Hulse, Takeuchi, and Braaten (1992), who demonstrated that the ability to recognize the transposition of a melody—a musically relevant universal—was lacking in young children (3-year-olds and younger) and animals. Similarly, investigations into the communication of meaning and emotion in music show disappointing results. In their study of the cross-cultural understanding of Indian raga modes in excerpts of Hindustani music, Balkwill and Thompson (1999) asked Western listeners to rate the degree of joy, sadness, anger, and peace displayed in 12 excerpts. Their results showed that listeners were sensitive to the intended emotions of "joy" and "anger" in the music, but that the impressions of "peace" and "sadness" could not often be so clearly distinguished. (Incidentally, impressions of peace and sadness are not always easily distinguished in Western music, either.) In addition, the researchers noticed that an association between emotional and structural features could be observed: impressions of "joy" were associated with fast tempi and low melodic complexity while "sadness" was linked to slow tempi and high melodic complexity. Despite the importance of the findings outlined earlier, it would seem that assigning emotional labels to music still does not reach far beyond the surface of the complex interaction between humans and music. As a result, we are encouraged to further question whether or not the emotional responses reported may in fact be influenced by musical features as well as by cultural factors.

In a series of studies designed to investigate the cross-cultural understanding of emotional content in music, examples were chosen from Western classical music, new age genres, and traditional Asian Indian music (Gregory & Varney, 1996). These were then rated for their emotional content by both Western listeners and listeners with also an Indian background (bicultural). The fact that these were unable to demonstrate clear consistency in their identification of, for example, the various seasons in Antonio Vivaldi's *Four Seasons* led the authors to conclude that "the affective response to music is determined more by cultural tradition than by the inherent qualities of the music" (p. 47). The most recent and extensive of these cross-cultural studies on emotional response (Bhatti & Gregory, 2000) used samples of religious music from both Asian Indian and Western cultures with durations of between 2 and 15 minutes. These excerpts were then rated by Western and Pakistani listeners in order to establish similarities and differences in the affective ratings. Western listeners gave lower ratings than Pakistanis to the spiritual content of religious Qawwali music, while Christian rock music was only considered to be "arousing" and "uplifting" by those Western listeners familiar with Christian practices. From this short review of cross-cultural research in music, it is clear that the search for universals in musical experience results in an inconsistent and contradictory pattern of results.

The most obvious conclusion to be drawn from the aforementioned findings is that music experience is heavily constrained by the listener's individual background and that it would require *tremendous* efforts to adapt to an unfamiliar cultural system. Those cultural experiences come into play especially in the affective response to unknown music. Despite a current lack of sound factual evidence, the issues of musical universals and music as a universal language are touted persistently. This suggests a need for explanation and research, and if we do not want to reject this appealing claim, we will have to seek alternative answers.

Proposal for Culturally Independent Universals in Music

It could be that an alternative approach is needed. Guided by the hypothesis that there are at least three factors that could be commonly associated with musical perception in all cultures, we would suggest that the potential over-simplification that results from the focus on premusical variables be avoided by focusing on the variables of synchronization, expectancy, and musical tension and movement.

Synchronization.   When people listen to music, reactions in the form of synchronized tapping or clapping can often be observed—a form of behavior that, according to Merker (2000a, 2000b), is not limited to humans but has also been observed in the glowing of fireflies and the chirping of crickets. This entrainment of living beings into an existing rhythmic pulse raises the issue of the possible existence of an evolutionary fundamental for this specific behavior. In attempting to provide a rationale for this idea, Merker (2000a) refers to a primarily sociobiological function, reminding us that synchronized chorusing increases the signal range, thereby increasing the probability of attracting potential mates. Furthermore, as observed in chimpanzees, synchronized calling at the site of a recently discovered food source indicates cooperation with external individuals, also attractive for possible mating partners. This capacity to synchronize to an external trigger pulse is indeed an astonishing phenomenon, and, as Fraisse (1982) indicates, it is a form of behavior that is strongest in humans at an interonset interval of 500 to 600 milliseconds. Nevertheless, there is a substantial difference between the synchronous calling of monkeys and the performance of music by humans in the sense that chimpanzees cannot keep time independently (e.g., continue a given pulse). This leads us to conclude that the ability to synchronize seems to be an indispensable condition for most kinds of human musical activities. Neither drumming ensembles, groups of dancers, nor a string quartet would be able to perform together without this fundamental capacity. Although synchronization can also be observed for visual stimuli (yet it is superior for auditory stimuli), this capacity would appear to be a musically relevant universal that can be found in the cross-cultural ubiquity of metric music that exists in present-day cultures. Furthermore, it is clear that the capability to desynchronize is equally important since only the variation between exact synchronization and intentional desynchronization produced the "human touch" in musical performance.

Expectancy.   Expectancy is a general cognitive mechanism that makes assumptions that concern the further processing of an event. While it can be applied to whatever phenomena we meet, it is also relevant to the concept of music perception. In the case of musical rhythm, for example, we can observe that all listeners create hypotheses as to how a given pattern will be continued or what the metrical position of the next beat will be (e.g., Desain, 1992). Yet expectancy also influences the perception of harmony and other musical parameters, and even when one is listening to unfamiliar (e.g., non-Western) music there is still a tendency to build expectancies. Using a probe tone paradigm, Castellano, Bharucha, and Krumhansl (1984) demonstrated that when Western listeners were able to perceive tonic (first) and dominant (fifth) degrees in an Indian raga, they did not assimilate the modal system to the Western diatonic system. The importance of culturally specific knowledge was also identified in a study by Krumhansl and Keil (1982), in which Western listeners were asked to complete a melody based on the Indonesian equidistant 5-tone *sléndro* scale. The findings suggest that although the cross-cultural familiarity of perception was limited to processing strategies, further culturally specific knowledge was needed to achieve a deeper understanding of the genre.

In relation to melodic perception, the theory of musical expectancy has been developed to a more advanced degree in the writings of Meyer (1956) and Narmour (1990). According to Meyer, listening to music can best be described using a "smoker" metaphor:

> If, for example, a habitual smoker wants a cigarette and, reaching into his pocket, finds one, there will be no affective response. . . . If, however, the man finds no cigarette . . . and then remembers that the stores are closed . . . he will very likely begin to respond in an emotional way. (p. 13)

Meyer (p. 5) regards the idea of universalism as one error of music psychology, besides hedonism and atomism, and claims that "music in a style with which we are totally unfamiliar is meaningless" (p. 35). However, I propose that the general tendency to build up expectancies while listening to music (regardless of the specific cultural experience) is worthy of consideration as a potential musical universal. In Narmour's theory of expectancy, his "implication-realization model" (which is similar to Meyer's ideas yet more formalized), we find a universally applicable perceptual model for melody. Broadly speaking, the first component, namely, implication, derives from the similarity/dissimilarity of melodic elements and causes us to hypothesize about a likely continuation of the melody. Subsequently, the "realization" part confirms or rejects any hypotheses and leads to aesthetic interest. The two characteristics of this model are: that top-down processes (such as acquired style-specific knowledge) work together with bottom-up processes (mainly innate Gestalt laws) and that small intervals imply the continuation of a melody with similar intervals and in the same direction, while large intervals imply following smaller intervals, a change in direction, and closure. Although verification is still needed for Narmour's model and some criticisms have been voiced (e.g., the model's bias for tonal Western music; see Krumhansl et al., 2000), we can assume that expectancy may play an important role in the debate that surrounds musical universals.

In their recent cross-cultural study on melodic expectancy among North Sami *yoiks*, Krumhansl, Toivanen, Eerola, Toiviainen, and Louhivuori (2000) found evidence to support the claim that "listeners are sensitive to statistical information in novel styles which gives important information about basic underlying structures" (p. 14). Moreover, despite general similarities among the responses given by Western, Finnish, and Sami subjects in the probe tone experiment, the authors concluded that style knowledge strongly influenced melodic expectancy and that the judgments of the Sami subjects familiar with the *yoik* style were least influenced by schematic Western tonal knowledge.

Musical Tension and Movement.   Another fundamental experience in musical perception that may be relevant to other factors besides rhythm is that of movement. When talking about movement, we are not so much concerned with the tapping of one's foot to a piece of music, but we are referring to the sensation of psychoenergetic forces—an inner phenomenon that manifests itself physically through observable body movements. Although Gabrielsson (1995, p. 37) has claimed that "we may consider emotion, motion, and music as being isomorphic," there is to the present day no theoretical framework that can explain these processes. The fact is that the degrees of belief in psychoenergetic effects varies among authors.

A strong belief in the psychoenergetic effects of music is apparent in the writings of Jaques-Dalcroze (1921, chap. 12). He posits that the main function of rhythmic education is to enable the student to play or symbolize the rhythms he or she experiences. Interestingly, the author does not refer to any explanation of the inner processes but chooses to concentrate exclusively on the expression of inner sensations through bodily movement, culminating in the exclamation that "rhythm is movement" (Moore, 1992). Due to a lack of research into the relationship between expressed and perceived movement, we cannot speak to the relation between strength of musical feelings and strength of physical sensation. The very sophisticated theoretical framework of the Swiss musicologist Kurth (1931) seems to come closest to the musical experience. In his view, analysis of the sensation of psychic movement is the key to the understanding of musical communication. Although terms such as *power, space,* and *matter* seem to refer to a physicalist approach, Kurth identifies more differences than similarities between physical and psychic processes. His writings contain a complete research program for future music psychology—centered around the term of *movement*—which has not yet been widely recognized.[2] However, difficulties with the implementation of this program may result because modern experimental methods may not necessarily be compatible with the type of predictions that Kurth made.

Researchers have also presented evidence for the importance of perceived movement. Repp (1992b), for example, found that the optimal temporal shaping for the principal melodic gesture of "Träumerei" could best be described by a parabolic timing function, referring to a motion metaphor. As Sloboda (1998, p. 24) points out, musical experience involves sensations such as tension and resolution: "The structural description does not in itself *incorporate* . . . [these] feeling[s]." This implies that the feeling of being moved must have an internal, psychoenergetic basis and that therefore any kinematic model (models that try to explain an experience of motion that is caused by music, e.g., an ascending scale), such as those reviewed in Palmer (1997), can only account very superficially for this phenomenon. It is also difficult to describe the relationship between perceived tension or movement and aesthetic experience. Fredrickson (1995) found that the resulting curve for the "perceived tension" when listening to a Haydn symphony (measured in real time with a Continuous Response Digital Interface [CRDI]) showed more variability and local changes than continuous ratings of the "aesthetic experience" (see Krumhansl, 1997, for a review of tension research). The variable "aesthetic experience" could be interpreted as the result of an integration of several other psychoenergetic aspects. As long as we do not have a theoretical framework or a definition of what musical tension is and how it is perceived, we cannot be certain what exactly the CRDI measures. Gjerdingen (1988) attempted to map the changes in pitch and intensity of the human singing voice onto a two-dimensional so-called Gjerdingen melogram in the form of a moving line. This way the author hoped to communicate the microstructure of vocal lines in Indian music, in which the microstructure of a single note is at the same time relevant to the impression of a lively character of singing but also hard to transcribe into our staff notation. Gjerdingen (1994) also investigated the related phenomenon of "apparent motion" induced by music. To summarize, support has been found for the assumption that musical movement and tension are, together, a further culturally independent fundamental.

Implications for Music Education

This chapter set out to show that the process of musical communication was dependent on the existence of relevant knowledge and experience on the part of the listener. As I have argued elsewhere (Kopiez, 2002), there is some convincing evidence that suggests that listeners always listen to music with "their own ears" and that music appreciation is based on culturally specific knowledge and education. The multicultural makeup of today's classroom, with its accompanying disparity of cultural knowledge and experience, does not allow for a simple, unified way to nurture communication skills. One suggestion seems tenable, however: The listening (and music-making) experience should take precedence over normative rules; this means that teachers should avoid oversimplified "labeling" of musical expression to explain the contents of music. Rodriguez (1998, p. 57) claims that "learning experiences in the music classroom should be designed to nurture sensitivity to musical expression," but how can this be realized under such difficult conditions? We would like to propose a few simple methods as starting points for the teacher who is trying to impart to his or her students the peculiarities of musical communication:

- *Spoken language.* It is relatively easy to read and record a short poem with and without different states of expression. Listeners' attention can be focused on parameters such as accents, accelerations, and dynamic shaping. With more technically advanced means, it would be interesting to extract parameters such as speech melody as cues for specific emotional states in language by using appropriate software (e.g., Boersma, 2004). Students can also be confronted with the impact of different speech melodies that correspond to different intended expressions.
- *Mechanical versus expressive performance in music.* As Burnsed (1998) has shown, a significant preference for folk songs played with expressive dynamics over those played without expression already exists in elementary school students from Grades 1 to 5, and even in musically less educated students expressive shaping increases aesthetic attractiveness. The basic experience of expression in music can be imparted on any instrument and by using any simple melody with the following setting. The required technical equipment amounts only to a simple MIDI sequencer for the generation of the unexpressive version and editing of the expressive deviations in the editor window. In order to demonstrate the difficulty of consistent expressive shaping, nominal note values can also be manipulated by the use of a graphic MIDI editor.
- *Synthesis of emotions.* Another approach, which would allow pupils to gain more insight into the communication of musical meaning, involves the use of software such as Director Musices (see Friberg, 1999) or the simple program referred to by Rodriguez (1998) for the synthesis of emotions in a given piece of music. These files or other synthesized versions of MIDI files can be evaluated by means of a semantic differential (scale with polar adjectives) regarding the intended emotion. Moreover, to demonstrate the importance of different expressive parameters in music, the expressive deviations in melodies can be "deconstructed" by setting the timing and intensity deviations to their nominal value.
- *Improving expressive communication.* As a result of the insight that expressive performance is based on a rule system that has to be learned by

player and listener, Woody (1999) showed that successful imitation of expressive dynamics in a short piano composition by a student correlated with the correct verbal identification of the expressive features used in the aural model before attempting an imitative performance. To improve communication between teacher and student on the one hand and performer and listener on the other, the author suggests that verbal instructions about the intended aural model are given to the student before trying an imitative performance. Finally, only a conscious and clear performance plan can guarantee easy perception of expressive intentions by the listener. Such an imitative exercise (accompanied by verbal reports of the perceived expressive intentions) could easily be realized through the use of simple melodies played with different expressive features. In a recent investigation by Juslin and Laukka (2000), performers were instructed to communicate different emotions to the subjects. After cognitive feedback about intended and perceived acoustical cues was given, accuracy of expressive communication increased by about 50%. These findings suggest that cognitive feedback is a useful tool in improving communication between player and audience. Actually, both of these approaches might be adapted to group situations.

Although some myths and illusions in the field of musical communication may have been shaken in this chapter, I would like to close with an optimistic perspective: Music psychology is still far from fully explaining the mechanisms of musical communication. It is certain, however, that this form of communication functions reliably in everyday life, in spite of its vague character. Much research remains to be undertaken if we are to gain deeper insight into the nature of musical communication. Although spoken language offers a much greater degree of communicative clarity, some commonalities between language and music exist. The famous physicist Niels Bohr used a metaphor to explain the general problem of communication in language; his words can easily be applied to the situation of musical communication:

> Washing dishes is just like language. Both the water and the tea towels are dirty, but we can still succeed in cleaning the plates and glasses. Similarly, language involves unclear concepts and a logic that is limited—in ways that we do not directly understand—to specific areas of application. In spite of this, we can develop a clear understanding of the natural world. (cited in Heisenberg, 1986, p. 190)

STUDY QUESTIONS

1. If you think of a piece of music you are currently practicing, what is the "musical message" you would like to communicate to the audience?

2. Listen to two recordings of the same composition (e.g. Schumann's piano piece "Träumerei" from op. 15) by different performers. What are the expressive means the performers use to communicate their version of the piece and how do they differ?

3. Where in everyday life can you find evidence that supports the idea of music as a 'universal language' that can be understood without prerequisites?

4. Covering is a means of interpretation in popular music. Listen to famous cover versions (e.g. "My way" originally performed by Frank Sinatra and covered by Sid Vicious from the 'Sex Pistols' or "With a little help from my friends" originally performed by the 'Beatles' and covered by Joe Cocker). Try to identify the intended 'musical message' and the musical means used (e.g. instrumentation, tempo). How does the 'message' change in the covered version?

NOTES

I would like to thank the following people for stimulating discussions and invaluable comments on earlier drafts of this chapter: Alf Gabrielsson, Patrik Juslin, Gunter Kreutz, Jörg Langner, Guerino Mazzola, Richard Parncutt, Ulrich Pothast, and four anonymous reviewers.

1. For the software *Rubato* see Mazzola (2002), for *Melodia* and *Director Musices* see *http://www.speech.kth.se/music/performance/download*

2. Although there are certain similarities between the ideas of Kurth and those of the German pianist Truslit (1938; partially translated by Repp [1993]), there is no evidence of any personal contact. The writings of Kurth have partially been translated into English (see Rothfarb, 1988, 1989; and Rehding, 1995).

REFERENCES

Allesch, C. G. (1987). *Geschichte der psychologischen Ästhetik* [History of psychological aesthetics]. Göttingen, Germany: Hogrefe.

Balkwill, L.-L., & Thompson, W. F. (1999). A cross-cultural investigation of the perception of emotion in music: Psychophysical and cultural cues. *Music Perception, 17*(1), 43–64.

Behne, K.-E. (1982). Musik—Kommunikation oder Geste? [Music—Communication or gesture?] *Musikpädagogische Forschung, 3,* 125–143.

Beldoch, M. (1961). *The ability to identify expressions of feelings in vocal, graphic, and musical communication.* Unpublished doctoral dissertation, Columbia University, New York.

Beran, J., & Mazzola, G. (2000). Timing microstructure in Schumann's "Träumerei" as an expression of harmony, rhythm, and motivic structure. *Computers and Mathematics with Applications, 39,* 99–130.

Bhatti, S., & Gregory, A. (2000). Cross-cultural study of affective responses to Qawwali. In C. Woods, G. Luck, R. Brochard, F. Seddon, & J. A. Sloboda (Eds.), *Proceedings of the 6th International Conference on Music Perception and Cognition,* (pp. 1321–1328). Keele, UK: Keele University.

Boersma, P. (2004). Praat [Computer software] Retrieved October 22, from http://www.praat.org.

Bolton, T. L. (1894). Rhythm. *American Journal of Psychology, 6,* 145–238.

Burke, E. (1852). *The works and correspondences: Vol. 8. A philosophical inquiry into the origin of our ideas of the sublime and beautiful.* London: Rivington. (Original work published 1756/57.)

Burnsed, V. (1998). The effect of expressive variation in dynamics on the musical preference of elementary school students. *Journal of Research in Music Education, 46,* 396–404.

Carterette, E. C., & Kendall, R. A. (1999). Comparative music perception and cognition. In D. Deutsch (Ed.), *The psychology of music* (2nd ed., pp. 725–791). San Diego, CA: Academic Press.

Castellano, M. A., Bharucha, J. J., & Krumhansl, C. L. (1984). Tonal hierarchies in the music of North India. *Journal of Experimental Psychology: General, 113,* 394–412.

Chaffin, R., Imreh, G., & Crawford, M. (2002). *Practicing perfection: Memory and piano performance.* Mahwah, NY: Lawrence Erlbaum.

Childs, C. (1992, February). The identification of style-specific performance practices in contemporary music. *Abstracts of the 2nd International Conference on Music Perception and Cognition, 95–96,* Los Angeles.

Clarke, E. F. (1987). Levels of structure in the organization of musical time. *Contemporary Music Review, 2,* 211–238.

Clarke, E. F. (1988). Generative principles in music performance. In J. A. Sloboda (Ed.), *Generative processes in music: The psychology of performance, improvisation, and composition* (pp. 1–26). Oxford: Clarendon Press.

Clarke, E. F. (1993). Imitating and evaluating real and transformed musical performances. *Music Perception, 10*(3), 317–341.

Clarke, E. F., & Baker-Short, C. (1987). The imitation of perceived rubato: A preliminary study. *Psychology of Music, 15*(1), 58–75.

Clynes, M. (1977). *Sentics: The touch of emotions.* New York: Anchor Press.

Cook, N. (1998). *Music: A very short introduction.* Oxford: Oxford University Press.

Cooke, D. (1959). *The language of music.* London: Oxford University Press.

Cunningham, J. G., & Sterling, R. S. (1988). Developmental change in the understanding of affective meaning in music. *Motivation and Emotion, 12,* 399–413.

Czerny, C. (1991). *Von dem Vortrage* [On performance] (Third part of the piano textbook, Op. 500) (U. Mahlert, Ed.). Wiesbaden, Germany: Breitkopf. (Original work published 1839)

Darwin, C. (1965). *The expression of the emotions in animal and man.* Chicago: University of Chicago Press, 1965. (Original work published 1872.)

Desain, P. (1992). A (de)composable theory of rhythm perception. *Music Perception, 9*(4), 439–454.

Deutsch, D. (Ed.). (1999). *The psychology of music* (2nd ed.). San Diego, CA.: Academic Press.

Dolgin, K. G., & Adelson, E. H. (1990). Age changes in the ability to interpret affect in sung and instrumentally-presented melodies. *Psychology of Music, 18*(1), 87–98.

Dougherty, T. J. (1993). *The perception of emotional content in non-speech audio.* (Doctoral dissertation, Claremont Graduate School, California, 1993). *Dissertation Abstracts International 54*(1), 524–525B.

Dudek, J. A. (1992). Listener's choice of timing or intensity information as prominent in piano performance style recognition (Doctoral dissertation, Ohio State University, 1992). *Dissertation Abstracts International, 53*(5), 1315A.

Edgewater, I. D. (1999). Music hath charms . . . : Fragments toward constructionist biocultural theory, with attention to the relationship of "music" and "emotion." In A. L. Hinton (Ed.), *Biocultural approaches to the emotions* (pp. 153–181). Cambridge: Cambridge University Press.

Fassbender, C. (1996). Infants' auditory sensitivity towards acoustic parameters of speech and music. In I. Deliège & J. Sloboda (Eds.), *Musical beginnings: Origins and development of musical competence* (pp. 56–87). Oxford: Oxford University Press.

Fay, R. R. (1988). *Hearing in vertebrates: A psychophysics databook.* Winnetka, IL: Hill-Fay.

Fraisse, P. (1982). Rhythm and tempo. In D. Deutsch (Ed.), *The psychology of music* (pp. 149–180). San Diego, CA: Academic Press.

Fredrickson, W. (1995). A comparison of perceived musical tension and aesthetic response. *Psychology of Music, 23*(1), 81–87.

Friberg, A. (1995). *A quantitative rule system for musical performance.* Unpublished dissertation, Royal Institution of Technology, Stockholm.

Friberg, A. (1999). Director Musices [Computer software] retrieved May 1999 from http://www.speech.kth.se/music/performance.

Gabrielsson, A. (1995). Expressive intention and performance. In R. Steinberg (Ed.), *Music and the mind machine* (pp. 35–47). Berlin, Germany: Springer.

Gabrielsson, A. (1999). Music performance. In D. Deutsch (Ed.), *The psychology of music* (2nd ed., pp. 501–602). San Diego, CA: Academic Press.

Gabrielsson, A., & Juslin, P. N. (1996). Emotional expression in music performance: Between the performer's intention and the listener's experience. *Psychology of Music, 24*(1), 68–91.

Gardner, H. (1985). *The mind's new science: A history of the cognitive revolution.* New York: Basic Books.

Giomo, C. J. (1992). The development of children's esthetic sensitivity to mood in music: An experimental study comparing five- and nine-year-olds using a non-verbal mode of response. (Doctoral dissertation, University of Colorado, Boulder, 1992). *Dissertations Abstracts International 53*(6), 1715-A.

Gjerdingen, R. O. (1988). Shape and motion in the microstructure of song. *Music Perception, 6*(1), 35–64.

Gjerdingen, R. O. (1994). Apparent motion in music? *Music Perception, 11*(1), 335–370.

Gregory, A. H., & Varney, N. (1996). Cross-cultural comparisons in the affective response to music. *Psychology of Music, 24*(1), 47–52.

Gruson, L. M. (1988). Rehearsal skill and musical competence: Does practice make perfect? In J. A. Sloboda (Ed.), *Generative processes in music: The psychology of performance, improvisation, and composition* (pp. 91–112). Oxford: Clarendon Press.

Hallam, S. (1995). Professional musicians' approaches to the learning and interpretation of music. *Psychology of Music, 23*(2), 111–128.

Hanslick, E. (1986). *On the musically beautiful: A contribution towards the revision of the aesthetics of music* (G. Payzant, Trans. and Ed.). Indianapolis: Hackett. (Original work published 1891 as *Vom musikalisch Schönen: Ein Beitrag zur Revision der Ästhetik der Tonkunst.*)

Hausegger, F. von (1885). *Die Musik als Ausdruck* [Music as expression]. Vienna: Konegen.

Hefner, H., & Whitfield, I. C. (1976). Perception of the missing fundamental in cats. *Journal of the Acoustical Society of America, 59,* 915–919.

Heisenberg, W. (1986). *Der Teil und das Ganze: Gespräche im Umkreis der Atomphysik* [Physics and beyond: Encounters and conversations] (6th ed.). Munich, Germany: Piper.

Henderson, M. T. (1936). Rhythmic organization in artistic piano performance. In C. E. Seashore, (Ed.), *Studies in the psychology of music: Vol. 4. Objective analysis of musical performance* (pp. 281–305). Iowa City, IA: University of Iowa Press.

Hulse, S. H., & Cynx, J. (1986). Interval and contour in serial pitch perception by a passerine bird, the European starling (*Sturnus vulgaris*). *Journal of Comparative Psychology, 100,* 215–228.

Hulse, S. H., & Page, S. C. (1988). Toward a comparative psychology of music perception. *Music Perception, 5*(4), 427–452.

Hulse, S. H., Takeuchi, A. H., & Braaten, R. F. (1992). Perceptual invariances in the comparative psychology of music. *Music Perception, 10*(2), 151–184.

Huron, D. (1991). The ramp archetype: A score-based study of musical dynamics in 14 piano composers. *Psychology of Music, 19*(1), 33–45.

Jaques-Dalcroze, E. (1921). *Rhythm, music, and education* (H. Rubinstein, Trans.). New York: Putnam.

Juslin, P. N. (1997). Perceived emotional expression in synthesized performances of a short melody: Capturing the listener's judgment policy. *Musicae Scientiae, 2*(1), 225–256.

Juslin, P. N. (2000). Cue utilization in communication of emotion in music performance: Relating performance to perception. *Journal of Experimental Psychology: Human Perception and Performance, 26,* 1797–1813.

Juslin, P. N. (2001). Communicating emotion in music performance: A review and a theoretical framework. In P. N. Juslin & J. A. Sloboda (Eds.), *Music and emotion: Theory and research* (pp. 309–337). New York: Oxford University Press.

Juslin, P. N., & Laukka, P. (2000). Improving emotional communication in music performance through cognitive feedback. *Musicae Scientiae, 4*(4), 151–183.

Juslin, P. N., & Madison, G. (1999). The role of timing patterns in recognition of emotional expression from musical performance. *Music Perception, 17*(2), 197–221.

Kamenetzky, S. B., Hill, D. S., & Trehub, S. E. (1997). Effect of tempo and dynamics on the perception of emotion in music. *Psychology of Music, 25*(2), 149–160.

Kant, I. (1987). *Critique of judgment* (W. S. Pluhar, Trans. and Ed.). Indianapolis: Hackett. (Original work published 1790 as *Kritik der Urteilskraft*)

Karno, M., & Konecni, V. J. (1992). The effects of structural interventions in the first movement of Mozart's symphony in G-Minor, K. 550, on aesthetic preference. *Music Perception, 10*(1), 63–72.

Kendall, R. A., & Carterette, E. C. (1990). The communication of musical expression. *Music Perception, 8*(2), 129–164.

Kirby, F. E. (1970). Beethoven's Pastoral Symphony as a "sinfonia caracteristica." *Musical Quarterly, 56,* 605–623.

Kopiez, R. (1996). Aspekte der Performanceforschung [Aspects of performance research]. In H. de la Motte-Haber, *Handbuch der Musikpsychologie* [Handbook of music psychology], (2nd ed., pp. 505–587). Laaber, Germany: Laaber Verlag.

Kopiez, R. (2004). Der Mythos der Musik als universell verständliche Sprache [The myth of music as a universal language]. In C. Bullerjahn & W. Löfler (Eds.), *Musikermythen: Alltagstheorien, Legenden und Medieninszenierungen* (pp. 49–94). Hildesheim, Germany: Olms.

Kopiez, R., Langner, J., & Steinhagen, P. (1999). Afrikanische Trommler (Ghana) bewerten und spielen europäische Rythmen [Cross-cultural study of the evaluation and performance of rhythm]. *Musicae Scientiae, 3*(2), 139–160.

Kratus, J. (1993). A developmental study of children's interpretation of emotion in music. *Psychology of Music, 21*(1), 3–19.

Kraut, R. (1992). On the possibility of a determinate semantics for music. In M. Riess-Jones & S. Holleran (Eds.), *Cognitive bases of musical communication* (pp. 11–22). Washington, DC: American Psychological Association Books.

Krumhansl, C. L. (1997). Musical tension: Cognitive, motional, and emotional aspects. In A. Gabrielsson (Ed.), *Proceedings of the Third Triennial ESCOM Conference Uppsala* (pp. 3–12). Uppsala, Sweden: Uppsala University.

Krumhansl, C. L., & Keil, F. C. (1982). Acquisition of the hierarchy of tonal functions of music. *Memory and Cognition, 10,* 243–251.

Krumhansl, C. L., Toivanen, P., Eerola, T., Toiviainen, P., Järvinen, T., & Louhivuori, J. (2000). Cross-cultural music cognition: Cognitive methodology applied to North Sami yoiks. *Cognition, 76,* 13–58.

Kurth, E. (1931). *Musikpsychologie* [Music psychology]. Berlin, Germany: Hesse.

Langer, S. (1942). *Philosophy in a new key.* Cambridge, MA: Harvard University Press.

Langer, S. (1953). *Feeling and form.* London: Routledge & Kegan Paul.

Langner, J. (2000). Rhythm, periodicity and oscillation. In C. Woods, G. Luck, R. Brochard, F. Seddon, & J. A. Sloboda (Eds.), *Proceedings of the 6th International Conference on Music Perception and Cognition* (pp. 574–578). Keele, UK: Keele University.

Langner, J. (2002). *Musikalischer Rhythmus und Oszillation: Eine theoretische und empirische Erkundung* [Musical rhythm and oscillation: A theoretical and empirical investigation] Frankfurt, Germany: Peter Lang.

Langner, J., & Kopiez, R. (1995). Oscillations triggered by Schumann's "Träumerei": Towards a new method of performance analysis based on a "Theory of oscillating systems" (TOS). In A. Friberg & J. Sundberg (Eds.), *Proceedings of the KTH symposium on grammars for music performance* (pp. 45–58), Stockholm.

Langner, J., Kopiez, R., & Feiten, B. (1998). Perception and representation of multiple tempo hierarchies in musical performance and composition: Perspectives from a new theoretical approach. In R. Kopiez & W. Auhagen (Eds.), *Controlling creative processes in music* (pp. 13–36). Frankfurt, Germany: Peter Lang.

LeDoux, J. E. (1996). *The emotional brain: The mysterious underpinnings of emotional life.* New York: Simon & Schuster.

Lerdahl, F., & Jackendoff, R. (1983). *A generative theory of tonal music.* Cambridge, MA: MIT Press.

Lindström, E. (2000). Interplay and effects of melodic structure and performance on emotional expression. In C. Woods, G. Luck, R. Brochard, F. Seddon, & J. A. Sloboda (Eds.), *Proceedings of the 6th International Conference on Music Perception and Cognition*, (p. 825). Keele, UK: Keele University.

Lussy, M. (1882). *Musical expression: Accents, nuances, and tempo in vocal and instrumental music.* London: Novello. (Original work published 1873 as *Traité de l'expression musicale: Accents, nuances et mouvements dans la musique vocale et instrumentale* [Paris: Heugel])

Madison, G. (2000). Interaction between melodic structure and performance variability on the expressive dimensions perceived by listeners. In C. Woods, G. Luck, R. Brochard, F. Seddon, & J. A. Sloboda (Eds.), *Proceedings of the 6th International Conference on Music Perception and Cognition* (pp. 817–824). Keele, UK: Keele University.

Mazzola, G., & Beran, J. (1998). Rational composition of performance. In R. Kopiez & W. Auhagen (Eds.), *Controlling creative processes in music* (pp. 37–67). Frankfurt, Germany: Peter Lang.

Mazzola, G. (1995). Inverse performance theory. In *Proceedings of the International Computer Music Conference* (pp. 533–540). San Francisco: International Computer Music Association.

Mazzola, G. (2002). *The topos of music: Geometric logic of concepts, theory, and performance.* Basel, Switzerland: Birkhäuser.

Merker, B. (2000a). Synchronous chorusing and human origins. In N. L. Wallin, B. Merker, & S. Brown (Eds.), *The origins of music* (pp. 315–327). Cambridge, MA: MIT Press.

Merker, B. (2000b). Synchronous chorusing and the origins of music [Special issue]. *Musicae Scientiae*, 59–74.

Meumann, E. (1894). Untersuchungen zur Psychologie und Aesthetik des Rhythmus [Investigations into the psychology and aesthetic of rhythm]. *Philosophische Studien, 10*, 249–322, 393–430.

Meyer, L. B. (1956). *Emotion and meaning in music.* Chicago: University of Chicago Press.

Miklaszewski, K. (1989). A case study of a pianist preparing a musical performance. *Psychology of Music, 17*(2), 95–109.

Moore, S. F. (1992). *The writings of Emile Jaques-Dalcroze: Toward a theory for the performance of musical rhythm.* Unpublished doctoral dissertation, School of Music, Indiana University, Bloomington.

Nakamura, T. (1987). The communication of dynamics between musicians and listeners through musical performance. *Perception and Psychophysics, 41*, 525–533.

Narmour, E. (1990). *The analysis and cognition of basic melodic structures: The implication-realization model.* Chicago: University of Chicago Press.

Nyklicek, T., & Doornen, V. (1997). Cardiorespiratory differentiation of musically-induced emotions. *Journal of Psychophysiology, 11*, 304–321.

Oosten, P. van (1993). Critical study of Sundberg's rules for expression in the performance of melodies. *Contemporary Music Review, 9*, 267–274.

Palmer, C. (1992). The role of interpretive preferences in music performance. In M. Riess Jones & S. Holleran (Eds.), *Cognitive bases of musical communication* (pp. 249–262). Washington, DC: American Psychological Association Books.

Palmer, C. (1989). Mapping musical thought to musical performance. *Journal* of *Experimental Psychology: Human Perception and Performance, 15,* 301–315.

Palmer, C. (1997). Music performance. *Annual Review of Psychology, 48,* 115–138.

Patterson, B. (1974). Musical dynamics. *Scientific American, 231(5),* 78–95.

Peretz, I., Gagnon, L., & Bouchard, B. (1998). Music and emotion: Perceptual determinants, immediacy, and isolation after brain damage. *Cognition, 68,* 111–141.

Porter, D., & Neuringer, A. (1984). Music discrimination by pigeons. *Journal of Experimental Psychology: Animal Behavior Process, 10,* 138–148.

Quantz, J. J. (1966). *On playing the flute* (E. R. Reilly, Trans. and Ed.). London: Faber. (Original work published 1752 as *Versuch einer Anweisung die Flöte traversiere zu spielen.*)

Rehding, A. (1995). *(Mis)Interpreting Ernst Kurth.* Unpublished master's thesis, University of Cambridge, 1995.

Repp, B. H. (1989). Further tests on composers' pulses in computer performance of piano music from the Classical period. *Journal of the Acoustical Society of America, 85,* 66.

Repp, B. H. (1990). Patterns of expressive timing in performances of a Beethoven minuet by 19 famous pianists. *Journal of the Acoustical Society of America, 88,* 622–641.

Repp, B. H. (1992a). Diversity and commonality in music performance: An analysis of timing microstructure in Schumann's "Träumerei." *Journal of the Acoustical Society of America, 92,* 2546–2568.

Repp, B. H. (1992b). A constraint on the expressive timing of a melodic gesture: Evidence from performance and aesthetic judgment. *Music Perception, 10(2),* 221–242.

Repp, B. H. (1993). Music as motion: A synopsis of Alexander Truslit's (1938) "Gestaltung und Bewegung in der Musik." *Psychology of Music, 21(1),* 48–72.

Repp, B. H. (1997a). The aesthetic quality of a quantitatively average music performance: Two preliminary experiments. *Music Perception, 14(4),* 419–444.

Repp, B. H. (1997b). Expressive timing in a Debussy prelude: A comparison of student and expert pianists. *Musicae Scientiae, 1(2),* 257–268.

Repp, B. H. (1998). Individual differences in shaping a musical phrase: The opening of Chopin's Etude in E Major. In S. W. Yi (Ed.), *Proceedings of the 5th International Conference on Music Perception and Cognition* (pp. 27–34). Seoul, Korea: Seoul National University.

Rodriguez, C. X. (1998). Children's perception, production, and description of musical expression. *Journal of Research in Music Education, 46(1),* 48–61.

Rothfarb, L. A. (1988). *Ernst Kurth as theorist and analyst.* Philadelphia: University of Pennsylvania Press.

Rothfarb, L. A. (1989). Ernst Kurth's *Die Voraussetzungen der theoretischen Harmonik* and the beginnings of music psychology. *Theoria: Historical Aspects of Music Theory, 4,* 10–33.

Ruiter, J. de (1989). *Der Charakterbegriff in der Musik: Studien zur deutschen Ästhetik der Instrumentalmusik, 1740–1850* [The idea of character in music: German studies on the aesthetics of instrumental music, 1740–1850]. Stuttgart, Germany: F. Steiner.

Scherer, K. R., & Oshinsky, J. S. (1977). Cue utilization in emotion attribution from auditory stimuli. *Motivation and Emotion, 1,* 331–346.

Seashore, C. E. (Ed.) (1936) *Studies in the psychology of music: Vol. 4. Objective analysis of musical performance.* Iowa City, IA: University of Iowa Press.

Senju, M., & Ohgushi, K. (1987). How are the player's ideas conveyed to the audience? *Music Perception, 4*(4), 311–324.

Shaffer, L. H. (1989). Cognition and affect in musical performance. *Contemporary Music Review, 4,* 381–389.

Shaffer, L. H. (1992). How to interpret music. In M. Riess-Jones & S. Holleran (Eds.), *Cognitive bases of musical communication* (pp. 263–278). Washington, DC: American Psychological Association Books.

Shaffer, L. H. (1995). Musical performance as interpretation. *Psychology of Music, 23*(1), 17–38.

Skinner, K. (1932). *Some temporal aspects of piano playing.* Unpublished doctoral dissertation, University of Iowa, Iowa City.

Sloboda, J. A. (1985). *The musical mind: The cognitive psychology of music.* Oxford: Oxford University Press.

Sloboda, J. A. (1998). Does music mean anything? *Musicae Scientiae, 2*(1), 21–31.

Sundberg, J., Frydén, L., & Askenfelt, A. (1983). What tells you the player is musical? An analysis-by-synthesis study of music performance. In J. Sundberg (Ed.), *Studies of music performance* (Publications issued by the Royal Swedish Academy of Music, No. 39) (pp. 61–75). Stockholm: Adebe Reklam.

Tarasti, E. (1994). *A theory of musical semiotics.* Bloomington: Indiana University Press.

Terwogt, M. M., & Grinsven, F. van (1991). Musical expression of mood states. *Psychology of Music, 19*(2), 99–109.

Thompson, W. F., & Robitaille, B. (1992). Can composers express emotions through music? *Empirical Studies of the Arts, 10*(1), 79–89.

Thompson, W. F., Sundberg, J., Friberg, A., & Frydén, L. (1989). The use of rules for expression in the performance of melodies. *Psychology of Music, 17*(1), 63–82.

Tillman, B., & Bigand, E. (1996). Does formal musical structure affect perception of musical expressiveness? *Psychology of Music, 24*(1), 3–17.

Todd, N. P. M. (1985). A model of expressive timing in tonal music. *Music Perception, 3*(1), 33–58.

Truslit, A. (1938). *Gestaltung und Bewegung in der Musik.* Berlin, Germany: Vieweg.

Wallin, N. L., Merker, B., & Brown, S. (Eds.). (2000). *The origins of music.* Cambridge: MIT Press.

Watt, R. J., & Ash, R. L. (1998). A psychological investigation of meaning in music. *Musicae Scientiae, 2,* 33–54.

Woody, R. H. (1999). The relationship between advanced musicians' explicit planning and their expressive performance of dynamic variations in an aural modeling task. *Journal of Research in Music Education, 47,* 331–342.

Taking an Acquired Skills Perspective on Music Performance

7

ANDREAS C. LEHMANN

JANE W. DAVIDSON

Psychologists seem to agree that musical skills share many common features with skill-related phenomena in other areas outside of music, such as language, games, sports, science, and other domains. Music making entails perceptual skills (e.g., apprehending structural information as well as social information, including nonverbal cues exchanged between performer and audience), cognitive skills (e.g., memory, decision making, pattern recognition), and of course motor skills. These skills function, interact, and evolve in complex ways that we are slowly starting to understand. However, since each performer, be it the professional orchestra musician who earns his or her living playing an instrument or the amateur who plays solely for enjoyment, is a unique individual with his or her individual biography, there is no such thing as "the musical skill." Instead, the ways in which the skill was developed as well as the final skill structure will necessarily differ from person to person as a result of individual learning histories.

Each performer has artistic intentions, that is, a message to be conveyed. Some of these intentions are related to communicating information about the musical structure and expressive embellishments to it for aesthetically driven goals. For instance, slowing at a cadence point has become recognized generally in Western music as sounding "better" than not slowing. Other intentions are more emotionally directed, such as playing a piece "sorrowfully" or "happily." Of course, music making does not happen in a vacuum; it most always involves other people, be they coperformers or members of the audience with whom the performer communicates.

As a socially and culturally embedded skill, music making is one of the most important activities in all cultures. Attempting to understand musical skill is one way of paying tribute to the tremendous achievements of past and present musicians. At the same time, we may be able ultimately to derive suggestions for the improvement of music teaching and learning.

The integrative metaphor for this chapter—which will connect the different aspects that regard musical skills and their acquisition—is the image of a Western classical performer who has just stepped onto the stage to perform in front of an audience. Most of what we say would also apply to musicians in other musical traditions and cultures. We will first consider the performer's current skills that are about to be displayed in some form; we will then discuss the "hidden" side of these skills, namely, their acquisition in the course of the musician's biography; and finally, we will address issues that surround the display of skills, more specifically the interaction between audience and performer and the interaction among performers. This section addresses issues that pertain to socially situated cognition and sociocultural influences on cognitive processing. A brief concluding section will address educational consequences of research discussed in this chapter. Throughout the chapter, we will address the qualitative and quantitative aspects that may distinguish different levels of performance and comment on research methodologies that are employed to assess these issues. We will attempt to answer the following questions: What does the performer bring to the task of performing; what does skill acquisition entail; and finally, what happens during performance? When we talk about performers, we do not refer to expert or elite performers only but rather to any person who steps out on stage with the intention to perform in front of other people.

What the Performer Brings to the Task: Skills and Skill Components

General Introduction to Skill Research

Research into skill and skill acquisition has been conducted since the late 1800s, but we have seen a dramatic upsurge in recent years in many areas of human endeavor (see Proctor & Dutta, 1995, for an introduction to human skill and performance). There is hardly any area (domain) of human performance that has not been investigated: reading and writing, flying airplanes, reading X-rays, almost every athletic skill, typing, stockbroking, music making, and, foremost, chess playing (Ericsson & Charness, 1994; Ericsson & Lehmann, 1996; also, see Palmer, 1997, for a review of research on music performance). The common denominator of all these activities is the requirement for "coordinated processes of perception, cognition, and action" (Proctor & Dutta, 1995, p. 1). However, there are many methodological venues for the study of human performance.

The complexity of the skill under investigation varies widely: While some researchers are more interested in basic processes, restricting themselves to the study of relatively simple skills in well controlled laboratory situations (e.g., reaching motions, tapping, solving simple logic problems), other researchers try to tackle more complex skills in realistic settings inside and outside of the laboratory (e.g., memorizing a song, acquiring a new piece of music, judging music performance). The sophistication or expertise of the participant is also a factor to consider: We can expose participants to tasks they have never seen before and track their learning curves, or we can study established experts who are performing tasks that are highly familiar to them. Furthermore, tasks can be performed in different types of environments, which require various degrees of flexibility or transfer. Some so-called closed environments offer stable conditions under which to perform the task (e.g., chess, swimming), while other environments are open, forcing the participant to operate under unpredictable conditions (e.g., mountain climbing). In music, we could maybe classify the performance of rehearsed solo repertoire as a closed skill while improvisation (especially in an ensemble) could be classified as an open one.

What emerges as a finding from the literature is that "a skill is a skill is a skill," meaning that the findings are consistent across domains regardless of the stimulus onto which we direct our perception, cognition, or action. Skill researchers assume that human beings by and large cope with the problems they are facing in any domain by applying roughly similar perceptual, cognitive, and psychomotor solutions. Thus by studying one area of skill, such as musical skill acquisition and expertise, we learn some things about other domains and vice versa. The ultimate goal is to apply the results to education and benefit future generations of learners and their teachers.

Obviously, acquiring one skill does not allow us to perform all skills but only those with similar task characteristics; in other words, the transfer of skills from one domain to another is rather limited (see Tunks, 1992, for a more detailed discussion of transfer of learning). For example, the transfer of knowledge and skills (if we want to make this distinction and not assume that knowledge is an essential part of the skill) from one musical instrument to another depends on how similar the two instruments are. Pianists can easily adapt to playing on a harpsichord and saxophone players may experience few difficulties learning the flute, but switching to a string instrument would be difficult for them both. As obvious as it seems, this fact is not trivial, because it demonstrates a touchstone in skill research: namely, the domain-specificity of skills. This finding suggests that even high-level experts may experience problems if the stimulus material does not completely match typical requirements. For example, if an outstanding trumpet player with extensive experience in playing band music attempts to sight-read or memorize atonal music, he or she might be confronted with unexpected limitations. In the worst case, our brave trumpeter may not outperform a good band student. This finding is sometimes called the structure-by-skill (or expertise) interaction, because it means that skilled individuals only perform at superior levels when the stimuli are representative of the structural properties for which the cognitive mechanisms were developed. Furthermore, transfer may vary from one skill level to the next as

Palmer and Meyer (2000) showed. In their experiment, beginning and advanced pianists learned melodies and later were asked to perform them with a different hand, a different clef, or different notes (retaining the original fingering). The results showed virtually no transfer for the novices while the experts demonstrated reasonable transfer in expected ways, and the authors suggest that "as skill increases, mental representations for performance become dissociated from the movements required to produce a musical sequence" (pp. 66–67).

The issue of specificity leads us to a related characteristic of skilled or expert performance, namely, that skilled performers become maximally adapted to the task demands under which they usually operate. For this, performers undergo extensive adaptations with regard to physiological, psychomotor, and cognitive factors that allow them to be suited optimally for the task at hand. For example, athletes show a number of physiological adaptations, such as enlarged hearts or altered angles of rotation of their limbs or even neurophysiological changes that distinguish them from nonexperts. On musicians, the angle of forearm rotation of pianists is altered in comparison to violinists, and both differ from the normal population (Wagner, 1988). These changes reflect habitual usage and movement demands of different instrumentalists. Also, the coordination of sensory input and motor responses is enhanced: Tennis players, for instance, can respond to advance visual cues of their opponents in lieu of having to react merely to the quickly approaching ball, which would leave no time to select a response and perform the corresponding movement. In music sight-reading, better readers perform very different eye movements from less skilled readers, allowing the better readers to make "intelligent" use of the limited viewing time by looking ahead (Goolsby, 1994). Probably the most pronounced changes occur at the cognitive level that involves problem-solving and memory skills that are tailored to the experts' needs. Over time, experts have built up what are referred to as retrieval structures, which allow them to encode quickly and meaningfully what they see or hear and manipulate the information in desirable ways (Ericsson & Kintsch, 1995). This enables fast access to information stored in long-term memory, whereas novices often have problems storing and subsequently retrieving the information. For example, chess experts have stored large numbers of chess positions in long-term memory and are able to plan several moves in advance. Concert pianists have to memorize copious amounts of material and do so by practicing cues or prompt points at which they could continue should they have memory lapses (Chaffin & Imreh, 1997, Chaffin, Imreh & Crawford, 2002), and actors work hard at understanding the character and his or her motives they are portraying (Noice & Noice, 1997).

Why Study High-Level Performers?

The term *expert* is frequently used in the context of skill research, and many studies have investigated proficient performers rather than so called novices, that is, beginners or amateurs. But why bother talking about experts when we may be interested in studying how school-age children learn to perform music? There are several answers to this question:

1. Experts already show those cognitive and psychomotor adaptations that nonexperts are still trying to acquire, and therefore looking at experts might lead us to better understand where the novice's development is heading.

2. Experts are usually more able to verbalize and explain what happened in the course of performance, while novices can be quite surprised that they could do a given task at all; often they cannot report anything about their performance (e.g., Hargreaves, Cork, & Setton 1991). This is possibly the reason why many musicians like reading biographies of and books by famous musicians: These books usually contain deep and informative (and sometimes controversial) insights into musical processes not readily available to the lesser expert.

3. The performance of experts has been demonstrated to be less variable and less affected by extraneous conditions than that of novices, which is an important methodological consideration for laboratory studies (Ericsson & Smith, 1991). Several researchers have demonstrated that pianists can reproduce their own performance with extreme accuracy, which allows us to study reliable timing mechanisms in performance (see Kopiez, in this volume). Conversely, trying to study the same timing mechanisms in a group of band students would be more difficult since it is known that mood, motivation, and variability in skill can create large amounts of variance "noise" in the performance data (Proctor & Dutta, 1995).

Therefore, while studying experts has its merits, it also has its drawbacks, in that we do not know exactly how well our results generalize from one population to the other. It is necessary to undertake studies that involve various levels of performance (e.g., Drake & Palmer, 2000; Palmer & Meyer, 2000) and even study people who drop out of music studies (e.g., Sloboda, Davidson, Howe, & Moore, 1996) to ensure the validity and applicability of research findings.

What Is a Musical Skill and Are Different Musical Skills Related?

Having taken a more general survey of skill research, we can now apply some of these terms and principles to musical skills. What constitutes a skill in music depends on the cultural settings and historical time under consideration (see Gembris, 1997, for a similar argument regarding music aptitude). For example, the musical skills required for the performance of music in the Western European art music tradition are different from those of Gamelan performance in Bali or from the skills required to produce computer music or any form of popular music. Focusing on the Western classical tradition, we shall consider performances with or without a score of rehearsed music and the activities of sight-reading and improvisation. Of course, a marching band member, a musical actor, or an opera singer will have to also perform extramusical tasks concurrently with his or her main musical task.

In general, a skill can only be characterized by the task constraints or requirements that it imposes. For example, sight-reading requires the on-line matching of visual input to patterns in long-term memory, with subsequent programming and execution of a motor program. When the matching does not occur fluently due to real-time demands, the reader has to engage in problem solving and internally reconstruct the score by guessing, omitting, and improvising note sequences. Finally, sight-reading entails the strategic use of head and eye movements when it comes to coordinating the reading of the score with the playing of the instrument, especially when displacement of the limbs is required that would ordinarily warrant visual monitoring (e.g., on the piano, harp, double bass). Hence, sight-reading will consist of various subcomponents that together make up a culturally useful skill (Lehmann & McArthur, 2001). A similar analysis could be done for any other musical activity. In sum, a (musical) skill defines itself by the task demands it imposes (Ericsson & Lehmann, 1996) and hence by a specific constellation of accompanying cognition, perception, and actions (L. Davidson & Scripp, 1992; see also chapter 2 by Gruhn and Rauscher in this volume for how some of this constellation is neurophysiologically implemented).

A significant question for educators is whether all musical skills, such as reading, memorizing, and playing by ear, have a common mediating cognitive mechanism or are all isolated subskills. The domain of music has borrowed these ideas from research in intelligence, where researchers long assumed that a general factor (g) influences many cognitive skills. Not only would such a unified musical mechanism facilitate learning different musical skills because training one skill would suffice to training them all, but it would also show up in studies as a positive correlation between different musical performance measures. A major study that involved several musical skills was undertaken by McPherson (1995), who designed some new performance measures and investigated 101 children of two different age groups with regard to a variety of musical skills, including playing by ear, playing from memory, sight-reading, performing rehearsed music, and improvising. The published results of the entire sample of trumpet and clarinet players showed strong positive correlations among all subskills. For example, the better they played by ear, the better they tended to play rehearsed music.

It is difficult to say if McPherson's results would be the same for other instrument categories, but if we assume some similarities, the correlations suggest a very close association of different musical skills. This flies in the face of everyday experience, for many of us "know" that good performers of rehearsed music are often poor or just passable improvisers. How then can we explain McPherson's results? "Even if the correlations were somewhat lower after correcting for possible methodological concerns they remain relatively high for the older children." This high correlation in the older group could be caused by large skill differences within the group. Or it may be that better performers are more likely to seek out improvisational activities and try to learn to improvise. Why are musical skills related at all? Two alternative accounts are possible: It is possible that some skills transfer such that learning to play an instrument might foster musical reading as well as memory and musical imagery as a by-product, or there is indeed some underlying common factor or mechanism consistent with the idea of a musical intelligence (Gardner, 1983; see also Kopiez and Gembris, chaps. 6, 4 this volume). The decision for or against one account (or a combined version) remains speculative until further empirical evidence is available.

However, the educational consequences of the view that musical skills are rather specific is clear, namely, that each requires its own specialized training. For example, if you want your students to be able to improvise, you have to offer activities that would promote this skill, such as creating melodies, copying improvisations by ear, and listening to other people improvise. Unfortunately, at this point we do not know much about expressive skills and their acquisition, but it is likely that also here imitation of idiomatic patterns and listening experience plays an important role (Woody, 2003).

Key Component of Musical Skills: Mental Representation

Mental representations form a central concept in skill and expertise research, as they do in other areas of cognitive psychology, where they basically denote the "memory of an object or event, which is used to gauge whether a perception is a representation of the object or event in question" (Stuart-Hamilton, 1996, p. 74). It is the internal representation in memory that the performer produces while trying to encode or manipulate a relevant stimulus in a given situation. A common everyday term is *mental image* (e.g., Trusheim, 1991), although this description unduly favors only one form of representation, namely, the visual one, which may not be the only and most appropriate one. It is more consistent with contemporary psychological theory to argue that different phenomenological experiences of memory content (aural, visual, kinesthetic, etc.) are simply different modes of representing the same thing, which can be demonstrated by asking people to switch between modes (from visual to aural). For example: "Think the melody of 'Happy Birthday,' now imagine playing it on your instrument, now imagine its notated version." However, it is also apparent from research in learning styles that individuals prefer one mode to the other, which can become a problem in teaching if this preference differs between student and teacher.

The ability to generate and use mental representations efficiently is presumably one of the hallmarks of expert performers, and some music teachers even postulate that music making happens in your head, with the motor execution being of secondary importance only. L. Davidson and Scripp (1992, p. 405) report an anecdote that involves the cellist Pablo Casals and demonstrates the incredible flexibility afforded to performers by efficient mental representation. The master, after teaching a piece of music to a student with one set of fingerings and bowings, completely changed both a few weeks later, to the great astonishment of the student. Obviously, the mental representation will depend on the musical task at hand (e.g., improvisation, rehearsed performance, memorization) and vary from performer to performer. Also, the study by Palmer and Meyer (2000) mentioned earlier in the context of transfer of skills provides evidence for how representations may change from one skill level to the next. The following example will make this claim more tangible: A beginning trumpet student's mental representation of a piece of music might consist of simply a sequence of valve combinations, while a more advanced student might also represent the underlying chord progression along with some expressive information, some aural image of the sounds, and maybe a visual representation of how the score looks.

Strangely enough, performance can emerge with or without appropriate underlying representations, and music educators know that intuitively, if not explicitly. We generally presume that the goal of music education is to enable the student to form the mental representations necessary to enjoy and produce meaningful musical material. Yet most educators would agree that it is also possible to learn a given piece by mindless drilling and be able to produce it even when no understanding of the task and the material is present. A nonmusical example for this distinction would be the learning of a few useful phrases in a foreign language just prior to taking a trip to a different country. We might be able to say "good morning" or "thank you," but we would be unable to converse in the language or change the memorized phrases. The simplest musical example that comes to mind is playing "Chopsticks" (or the German equivalent, "Flohwalzer"), a piece that many people can play on the piano even without training. It requires mere visual orientation and hitting black or white keys and counting up to six. Useful mental representations are involved when musicians can learn new pieces based on what was learned previously and when the learned musical material can be manipulated in various ways (e.g., through transposing, changing of speed or dynamics, adapting to a different performance style, changing fingerings to accommodate speed).

In an experiment on musical memory, Lehmann (1997a) asked pianists to memorize short pieces of music by repeatedly presenting them with the score and then having them perform the piece from memory. Once the piece was learned, the pianists were asked to perform it under changed conditions, such as performing with only one hand or transposing the piece to a nearby key. Those pianists who had memorized the piece the fastest were more accurate in reproducing it under changed performance conditions. In the transposition task, for instance, faster memorizers immediately chose a new fingering that differed from that previously employed during memorization. Also, the results suggested that there was a common mediating mechanism to encoding (memorizing) and problem solving during recall. It is somewhat counterintuitive that faster memorization would actually enable better performance on subsequent performance under changed task demands. We believe, though, that better memorizers are likely to construct and use mental representations of the music, which would facilitate memorization as well as the subsequent manipulation of the memorized music. This account would substantiate the anecdote mentioned earlier about Pablo Casals, and it would help explain why musical skills correlate (see earlier section).

The fact that music performance is mediated by mental representation does not preclude some degree of automaticity. The performer cannot at all times be aware of every performance aspect—this would overload human information-processing capacity. However, the mental representation of the piece should be such that the performer can switch between levels of consciousness, going from an unfocused and quasi-automatic "letting the music flow" to a conscious attention to specific expression or note sequences. Being able to step back but also zoom in on detail if necessary is a desired state of mastery that differs from the novice's possibilities.

In sum, experts have been shown to possess sophisticated mental representations for information in their respective domains (see Ericsson, 1996; Ericsson & Lehmann, 1996, for reviews). For example, chess players seem to have some kind of generic mental template in which chess pieces are placed; the input can be either written, aurally presented, or visually presented positions. Some musicians may develop similar templates that allow them a more flexible performance. The next section elaborates on this point by looking at two cognitive models of musical skill that implicate those mental representations.

Matrix of Cognitive Skills.   In their excellent chapter on the coordinates of cognitive skills in music, L. Davidson and Scripp (1992) describe their own model for cognitive music processing, the Matrix of Cognitive Skills in Music (p. 395). The purpose of our brief review of Davidson and Scripp's model (see figure 7.1) is to show how cognitive processes can be classified and mapped to a given task (in this case, making music) and how plausible models are derived despite the fact that the exact functioning and structural nature of the model's component is hidden from the observer. In principle, each aspect of the model would be amenable to empirical testing and validation that used appropriate experimental methods. This model draws heavily on the insights gained from Harvard's famous Project Zero (in which the authors were involved) and provides a tool for a comprehensive and integrative understanding of how musicians think. *Thinking* in this context is interpreted as creating a *network of understanding*, an idea that the authors borrowed from Perkins (1989).

The whole of cognitive musical skills is divided into six categories, labeled *ways of knowing*, which can be traced in musical production, perception, and reflection on music. Those processes may be situated outside the musical performance situation or during performance, thus constituting different *conditions of knowledge*. The musician's ways of knowing outside the performance situation exist in fixed or declarative form (knowing what), while

COGNITIVE SKILLS MATRIX

Ways of knowing

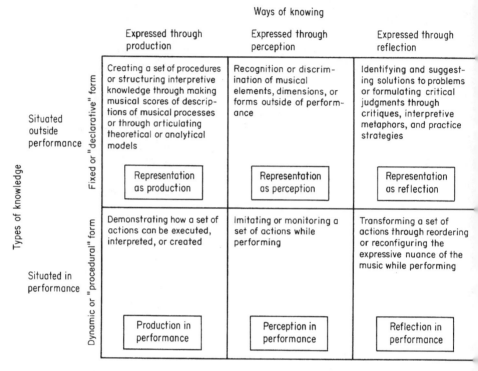

Figure 7.1. Davidson and Scripp's (1992) Matrix of Cognitive Skills in Music: Two conditions of knowledge crossed with three ways of knowing.

the ways of knowing during performance are of a more dynamic or procedural nature (knowing how). Each way of knowing captures a necessary and distinctly different set of cognitive skills. Thus *production* encompasses composing as well as interpretive performance (and presumably also sight-reading and improvisation); *perception* covers those aspects of thinking that support discrimination and judgment; *reflection* acknowledges the importance of reenvisioning, reconceptualizing, and reviewing a performance. These three ways of knowing are crossed with the two conditions of knowledge.

The authors present evidence for the development of some of these representations of knowledge and posit that the different parts of their matrix are sometimes formed in the individual musician independently from one another. For example, a musician might be a star performer but unable to notate a simple tune correctly (L. Davidson & Scripp, 1992, p. 401). This last point is most interesting for music educators, since it documents a common classroom observation. At the same time, it reinforces the educator's goal to promote not only individual skills but also the interaction and interconnectedness among them.

The model itself does not make any claims about underlying processes and the exact nature of the representations involved. The authors clearly state that the different ways of knowing are learned and trained and that they can be practiced through use of "cognitive tools" (p. 404), better known to educators as teaching methods, such as modeling and the utilization of metaphors. Accordingly, we can analyze teaching situations, as do L. Davidson and Scripp (pp. 404–406), with regard to the types of representations they are likely to produce. The idea that teaching results in representation is shared with the next model to be described, in which certain representations are seen as central to music making and hence constitute the ultimate goal of teaching and practice.

Triangular Model of Mental Representation in Music Performance.   The claim for the model described in the following is that instruction could be tailored to result in the postulated representations (Ericsson, 1997; Lehmann & Ericsson, 1997). Whereas the Davidson and Scripp model was rather descriptive in nature, applying a general psychological model of skills to musical skills in declarative and procedural instances, the following model aims at providing musicians with a framework for their daily work. The triangular model of musical performance skills assumes that musicians need at least three different types of mental representations. Those representations correspond to (1) a goal representation, (2) a production representation, and (3) a representation of the current performance. (Woody, 1999a renames those representations to goal imaging, motor production, and self-monitoring.) It is appropriate to conceive of these representations as answers to questions that teacher and student can ask, namely, "what should the music sound like?" "how is the sound achieved?" and "what is coming out right now?" Consequently, the goal representation captures whatever the performer does internally to represent the desired auditory outcome (including decisions about how to interpret the piece); the production representation entails the procedural knowledge of the performer of how to execute the music on the instrument; the representation of the current performance is the internal description of what is being produced at the moment (see figure 7.2).

There is empirical and everyday evidence for the existence of the proposed mental representations. Although they are not directly observable, indicators for their existence and functioning can be found in task performance and through the use of verbal reports (think-aloud protocols). Task performance under changed or stressful conditions often reveals flaws in the functioning of our representations and deficient interactions among the three components. The following are examples of flawed representations:

- The player knows that a crescendo is coming up and thinks he or she is playing it, but the teacher or audience does not hear anything. The singer

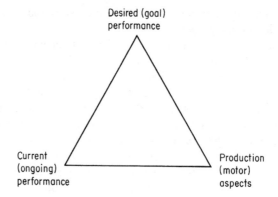

Figure 7.2. Triangular model of mental representations in music performance.

is out of tune with the piano but is satisfied with the performance (problem with motor and current performance representation but correct goal imaging).

- A player is not sure how a piece continues, yet the right notes still come out of his or her musical instrument (motor representation and memory function, but the goal representation is deficient).
- The performer knows how it should sound but realizes that what is being produced is not correct (problem with establishing a motor representation but correct goal imaging and monitoring of ongoing performance).

Some researchers have analyzed performance errors in experiments with the explicit aim to uncover underlying representations (e.g., Palmer, 1992; Repp, 1996; Lehmann, 1997a). Another useful research method is for participants to report their thoughts retrospectively, so that performance errors can be matched to cognitive processes. These reports can follow a fixed scientific method (e.g., Ericsson & Simon, 1993), but they can also be used as teaching tools (Woody, 1999a).

The following example stems from a controlled study that shows that representations play a role in musical expression. Woody (1999b) investigated pianists' ability to imitate short expressive model performances played to them from a computer. In between hearing the model and playing their imitations, subjects verbalized their thoughts about the expressive features they had heard in the aural model. Interestingly, those features that were explicitly identified were performed differently from those not reported: (a) Regarding musical features that were not familiar, participants who were able to identify them performed them more accurately (the performances of the other participants generally excluded these types of unusual features!); (b) musically appropriate (idiomatic) features of models were reproduced by almost all participants, but those who explicitly identified them performed at more pronounced overall levels (e.g., louder crescendos, softer descrescendos). This is somewhat surprising, because contrary to the results described earlier, musicians tend to think that expressive performance emerges "by intuition" or from the quasi-automatic (subconscious) imitation of expressive performances heard during the lesson or on a recording.

Experts have tried at all times to construct certain representations (even though they do not use this term) by employing or teaching specific practice strategies. For example, playing a memorized piece while watching television (probable effect: forces motor representation to act independently from goal representation), thinking through the piece note by note or playing on a muted instrument (probable effect: goal imaging independent of motor representation), playing louder than necessary or audio-taping performance (probable effect: strengthens representation of current performance, "listening to oneself").

As with sports, methods to improve training in music are becoming more sophisticated. For example, Edlund (2000) presented a method by which musicians were able to listen to themselves from a distance, similar to how the audience would hear them in a larger room. This was done by recording the music through use of a microphone positioned some distance away from the sound source and immediately transmitting the sound back to the player into a special headphone. First testing suggested that this method was greatly appreciated by musicians because it gave them otherwise unavailable and richer feedback on their current performance. Knowledge of results (KR), as it is called in psychology, is a potent factor in learning.

In short, mental representations form the core of any skill and constitute the result of practice (see next section), and musicians require specific types of representations to allow them to cope successfully with the performance demands. Functional problems with the representations and their enactment during performance may lead to errors and breakdowns in performance. Such problems can be remedied by designing practice activities that carefully isolate aspects of performance and make them accessible to conscious cognitive processing, which, in turn, gives rise to a smooth, flexible performance.

Hidden From the Audience: Skill Acquisition and Development

It is fair to say that nobody is born with the skills necessary to go onstage to perform and that skills do not accrue overnight but take a long time to develop. Granted, there are individual differences in personality, speed of development, and motivation, but even the most "gifted" individuals require large amounts of training and practice to develop noteworthy levels of performance. This development or skill acquisition phase is especially of interest once the level of performance exceeds the average adult level prevalent in the population, a level that is almost passively acquired through acculturation. For example, most people can sing the national anthem or whistle popular tunes; however, in Western classical music, we are concerned with levels of performance that come about as a result of deliberate and time-consuming instruction and training (which could include expert singers and whistlers). In this part of the chapter, we will discuss the development of expertise in music, introduce the concept of deliberate practice, and address issues that surround practice, such as the preparation of a specific piece and practice efficiency (see J. W. Davidson, Howe, & Sloboda, 1997; Lehmann, 1997b; Jørgensen, 2004, for reviews).

Life-Span View on Skill Development

Skills develop over long periods of time, and most researchers divide this time into distinct phases with more or less clear boundaries (Bloom, 1985; Ericsson, Krampe, & Tesch-Römer, 1993; Manturzewska, 1990). During the initial, preinstruction phase, the individual comes in contact with the domain through the immediate home environment. Playful interactions with music seem to be the rule rather than guided instruction, which sets in during the second phase. This early instruction continues until the student makes a full-time commitment to the domain, thereby entering a third phase. Most music students never make this transition unless they want to become musicians. A later phase is reached when the by-now-professional musician has risen to the peak of his or her career and is trying to make a lasting contribution to the field. One could postulate yet another phase, namely, that of maintaining the skill against a decline due to age with a possible shift of occupation from stage performance to teaching, as is the case in many musicians' lives (Krampe & Ericsson, 1996; Manturzewska, 1990).

The people and circumstances that contribute to the individual's skill acquisition as he or she progresses vary from one phase to the next. While the first teacher is often a warmhearted and friendly person who knows the child well, later teachers may be far more demanding and less amiable or pedagogically able. Not only the teachers but also the home environment play a role in the development of expertise. Being supportive parents does not simply mean allowing children to take lessons and paying for them. A truly supportive environment encompasses parents who go to the lessons, who monitor practice at home by making sure the students practice regularly or even assist and supervise practice more closely, and who create a generally positive value system concerning music learning (Bloom, 1985; J. W. Davidson, Howe, Moore, & Sloboda, 1996; Lehmann, 1997b; Manturzewska, 1995; Persson, 1996; Sloboda & Howe, 1991; Zdzinski, 1996).

Individual Differences in Musical Skills as a Result of One's Biography

The level of performance reached after years of training and practice is an amalgam of different subskills developed over time and influenced by the

individual's biography. This biography also entails a cultural and even historical dimension. For example, unlike today piano teaching and training in
the 19th century not only promoted the playing of rehearsed material but
also fostered the acquisition of improvisational skills (Gellrich & Sundin,
1993). Furthermore, teaching methods and materials became available and
evolved over time, as was the case for jazz music. But also at the level of
the individual, skill acquisition is a unique experience that results in a unique
set of skills. Take, for example, an average music student who starts playing
a musical instrument in school and practices very little at home and contrast
this situation with that of a musical prodigy who has been privately tutored
since early childhood. This ensures not only unique musical biographies (and
hence skill trajectories) but also a distinctive artistic voice. Given that practice is the most common activity musicians engage in during skill acquisition,
we will look at it more closely now (see Hallam, 1997; Jørgensen, 2004 for
references regarding practice).

Scientific Approach to Practice: Deliberate (Formal) Practice

In 1993, a seminal article by Ericsson, Krampe, and Tesch-Römer appeared
titled "The Role of Deliberate Practice in the Acquisition of Expert Performance," which has since spawned a wide variety of research in music. The
authors propose the concept of deliberate practice (other authors employ the
term *formal practice*), which basically posits that the amount of practice,
that is, goal-directed, not always enjoyable, deliberate, and effortful training
activities, is positively correlated with the attained level of performance.
More deliberate practice thus leads to higher levels of performance. This
idea was inspired by two complementing facts:

1. A claim was made by Simon and Chase (1973) that even high-level
experts need around 10 years of preparation to attain an international level
of skills; this finding has been corroborated by results from other domains,
among them music (Bloom, 1985) and sports (Starkes, Deakin, Allard,
Hodges, Hayes, 1996). Obviously, time spent is only one indicator of effort
invested in meaningful training activities.

2. Before Simon and Chase, Fitts and Posner (1967) had made their
"monotonic benefits assumption," stating that repetition leads to increased
speed—on simple motor tasks! This Power-Law-of-Practice (it might be exponential; see Heathcote, Brown, & Mewhort, 2000) has been applied successfully also to music and offers a simple argument in favor of a "do a lot
of the same thing" approach to music learning. Ericsson et al. (1993) argue
to the contrary, namely, that just a lot of the same is unproductive (a view
supported by many musicians, e.g., Wynton Marsalis, 1995). Instead, there
are certain constraints on practice that determine its success.

The stated constraints of practice are resources, effort, and motivation.
First of all, teachers, exercises, instruments, and practice environments need
to be available to the learner. Second, deliberate practice requires attentional

resources, that is, mental effort, and it can therefore only be sustained over many months and years without symptoms of physical and psychological burnout when applied in moderation. Around 4 or 5 hours a day seems to be the optimal amount for adults—less, of course, for children. Finally, the person needs to be motivated. Although Ericsson et al. make no assumption about how this motivation comes about or how it is maintained, other authors view motivation as a direct result of talent (e.g., Winner, 1996, especially for prodigious children) or as a by-product of expert teaching (e.g., Gholson, 1998, for a detailed analysis of Dorothy DeLay's teaching). Motivational differences, which may be personality-related, seem to play a decisive role in being successful at the beginning of instruction (Duke, 1999; O'Neill & Sloboda, 1997).

In Ericsson et al.'s original studies, three groups of adult violinists were compared with regard to the amount of time they had spent practicing over their life span. Two groups were made up of the "best" and "good" students as rated by their academy teachers, and the last group consisted of aspiring music teachers. To ascertain whether the "best" students were comparable to current professionals, the authors also surveyed members of professional orchestras. Results showed that experts had practiced more, even at younger ages (see figure 7.3a). Adversely, even at advanced ages, amateurs only accumulated a fraction of the time that full-timers accrued. The results are generally consistent with a later study by Sloboda, Davidson, Howe, and Moore (1996), who investigated a large sample of teenage music students at five different levels of achievement: from the highest level of achievement (Group One in figure 7.3b) to students who had abandoned playing altogether (reported as Group Five in the figure). The better students had practiced more, even in the beginning stages of learning.

Since correlations do not necessarily imply causation, it cannot be ruled out that other variables might have caused better performers to practice more. For example, one could argue that more talented people tend to be more motivated and therefore practice more and thus the difference between the groups was really due to differences in innate dispositions (for an extensive coverage of this and other aspects of the nature–nurture debate see Howe, Davidson & Sloboda, 1998, and some 30 commentaries published along with the target article).

Assessing deliberate practice is usually done by interviewing the subjects and obtaining retrospective estimates of practice for every year since the start of practice. Critics have suggested that these estimates may be unreliable and that time practicing alone may not be a good indicator for deliberate practice. Although this criticism is viable, there are also arguments in favor of this method of assessing practice. First, errors in estimates will likely affect all subjects of a given study similarly and therefore not influence the pattern of results, only the absolute magnitude of the estimates. This magnitude varies considerably among instruments anyway, with string and keyboard players topping the list of instrumentalists (Jørgensen, 1997). Second, if we

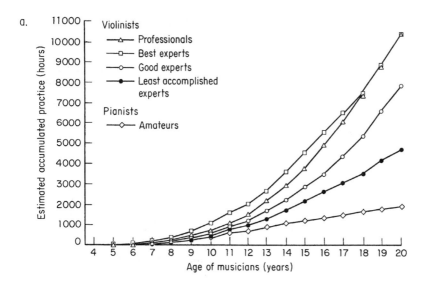

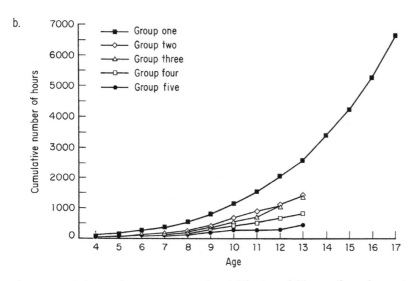

Figure 7.3. Relation between accumulated life-time deliberate/formal practice and attainment in instrumental music performance. Figure 7.3a: Study with experts by Ericsson, Krampe, & Tesch-Römer, 1993. Figure 7.3b: Study with novices by Sloboda, Davidson, Howe, & Moore, 1996.

find significant effects such as those described earlier, we are probably un-
derestimating the real effect size, since the estimates will include amounts of
time with nonoptimized practice. Third, the type of training activity assessed
with estimates depends on the goal of the study: Time at the instrument may
be a suitable indicator for classical music training but not so for skill acquisition in jazz (although good jazz musicians practice by themselves, too).
To use the retrospective estimates method in chess you might need to assess
the time spent studying published games (Charness, Krampe, & Mayr,
1996), in sight-reading you might need to assess time spent accompanying
(Lehmann & Ericsson, 1996), and in wrestling, time on the mat (Starkes et
al., 1996).

What we learn from these studies is that the amount of optimized practice
is related to the attained performance. Contrary to some criticisms of the
expertise view, this approach does not rule out possible individual differences
in aptitude; it merely focuses our view on those aspects of skill acquisition
that we can influence as educators. The criticism that this approach neglects
the quality of practice has already been mentioned and will be discussed in
the next section.

Aspects That Surround Practice

Practice Efficiency.   Practice is a fickle thing. Despite our best intentions to
work effectively (whatever this means at a given time), our goals escape us,
we fail to listen to our results, we simply do not know how to practice a
certain trouble spot, or we are simply too tired to muster up the necessary
attention. A number of factors influence the effectiveness of practice, including person-related aspects and task-related aspects. Among the person-
related aspects we can list age and maturational factors, motivation, socio-
economic background and education, current psychophysiological states
(e.g., being tired, hungry, unhappy, having mental presets), and musical self-
concepts. Other aspects pertain more to the practice activity itself, such as
length of practice time, distribution of practice across time (especially over
longer periods of time), practice strategies, and supervision (Barry & Hallam, 2001; Harnischmacher, 1997; Lehmann, 1997b; Rideout, 1992). When
conditions are unfavorable, we are not actually engaging in deliberate practice anymore but simply wasting time. Therefore, a student's apparent lack
of progress in spite of reported adequate amounts of practice might actually
be related to suboptimal quality of practice.

Practicing as a Skill.   In light of the many factors that play a role in making
practice efficient, it comes as no surprise that experts and novices differ in
the way they practice. What emerges as a consistent finding from studies
that looked at the preparation of a specific piece or performance (Chaffin
& Imreh, 2000; Gruson, 1988; Hallam, 1995; Jørgensen, 1997; Lehmann
& Ericsson, 1998; Miklaszewski, 1989; Nielsen, 1997; Williamon & Val-

entine, 2000) is that deliberate practice is allocated in response to encountered problems. Since this requires metacognitive or monitoring skills on the
part of the musician, learning to practice is in itself a skill that needs to be
acquired. Therefore, teachers should take great care to teach their students
how to practice correctly (Barry & McArthur, 1994; McPherson, 2005).

The Performance, the Performer, Audience, and Co-performers

In the Course of a Performance

A multitude of subskills acquired and the concert piece rehearsed, the performer comes to the stage with a mental representation of the music that
will allow smooth execution and some degree of flexibility to cope with
problems. As mentioned earlier, once the piece is well practiced, multiple
performances demonstrate great consistency, even when long time intervals
between performances occur (Clynes & Walker, 1982). The consistency does
not only apply to factors like reproducing similar overall timing profiles, but
many very particular moments within a piece can be systematically reproduced as well. For example, it is well known that slowing will always occur
at certain structural moments in a piece, like phrase boundaries, and an
individual performer will tend to give proportionally similar amounts of
slowing at a given musical feature (Todd, 1985; see chap. 6 by Kopiez in
this volume for a review). Gabrielsson and Juslin (1996) demonstrated that
when musicians have an explicit emotional intention their interpretations of
a particular musical feature will be consistently produced. For instance, playing in a happy manner encourages performances that are up-tempo and
played in a detached or bouncy style. Sad interpretations are slower and
much more legato (also Juslin, 2001). It can be assumed that though there
may be some error variability from one performance to the next, the emotional intention along with the musical structure will create a specific set of
constraints on how the music is performed. Through practice, the interpretative aspects have become an integrated part of the motor programming in
the mental representation of the piece and enable an accurate, fluent, and
highly automatized interpretation of the music.

It would be naive, of course, to say that once a representation of a piece
has been established through rehearsal it will not be subject to *some* variability or manipulation in the performance process. Performers can and want
to remain flexible. A detailed example clarifies this point. Clarke and Davidson (1998) studied two performances of Chopin's Prelude op. 28, no. 4,
given by a professional pianist who was asked to vary his interpretations of
the piece. After each rendition he was encouraged to disclose his interpretative intentions. Although there were similarities between the performances
(timing extensions occurring at similar locations in both performances, for

instance), there were also some striking differences, with the first rendition beginning much louder than the second. A structural analysis of this Chopin prelude reveals that it can be viewed either in a binary AA' structure or in a more unified manner. The researchers concluded that the pianist varied the two interpretations by highlighting each of the two possible structural frameworks. The pianist offered little precise knowledge of what he did to create differences between the two performances, other than saying that in the first interpretation he was preoccupied with knowing whether or not one of the researchers had children and so saw a scene with children and claiming that in the second interpretation he imagined the piece within a rugged moorland landscape. This use of visual imagery is commonly reported by many creative and performing artists as a means of focusing their expressive intentions. Experts often lack declarative knowledge about how they achieve certain moment-by-moment changes, and our example illustrates that performers often do not have a full awareness of what they do during a performance. Instead, they monitor and influence the lower level processes from higher and more abstract levels—such as a guiding idea or atmosphere.

From the general psychology literature it is known that arousal, with all its associated physiological traits (increased heart rate and thus heightened oxygen supply), can facilitate mental operations and can often result in performance task improvements in many domains (Gleitman, 1991). Musical performance is no different, for when circumstances produce optimal arousal, highly focused, energized, and inspired performances are often reported (Evans, 1994). Cziksentmihalyi (1990) has referred to the intense experience of optimal performance as "flow." Given the overwhelmingly positive reports of the enhanced quality of "flow-driven" or "inspired-feeling" performances, it seems important that the performer should aim to optimize his or her arousal level to become focused on the task. This implies arousal management, which, in turn, is also a characteristic of high-level performers (Wilson, 1997). The key point is, of course, that one cannot produce an "inspired" performance without having extensive and easily operationalized knowledge. The relevant task-related physical and mental skills are achieved in often arduous and time-consuming rehearsal and practice sessions.

Obviously, excessive arousal is undesirable, as it leads to performance anxiety or stage fright (see Wilson, 1997, for a concise coverage), and thus reducing the potential for being creative moment by moment. If, for example, the anxiety leads to an increase in heart rate that causes palpitations, the performance may be impaired. Indeed, violinists often report the dire consequences of palpitations on their ability to control their bowing arm, with the racing heart leading to an arm tremor.

So far, we have looked at individual performance. But musical performance is a social act, and whether it is real or virtual (in the recording studio, for example), the audience is critical in shaping the actual performance event. Also, coperformers influence how the performance is negotiated and presented to an audience (J. W. Davidson, 1997).

Social Facilitation Effects

Social facilitation has been reported in psychological research since the 19th century. For example, Triplett noted in 1897 that racing cyclists achieved faster times when they were racing against one another rather than the clock (cited in Zajonc, 1965). Subsequently, many experiments have shown the facilitating effects of coaction on human performance. In part this effect is accounted for by the *mere presence* of another person eliciting an arousal response (Zajonc, 1965), but it is Cottrell's (1972) *learned evaluation hypothesis* that provides an account representative of current belief. It suggests that facilitation depends upon a positive cognitive appraisal and concomitant physiological features, such as increased heart rate and visual acuity. In Western art music performance situations, it is typically an evaluative audience that is perceived as being most highly "threatening," but appraisal can vary depending on the performer's mood state at a given point in time and on the perceived trustworthiness of the coperformers. Indeed, the adage "a trouble shared is a trouble halved" is of salience here.

Social Display and the Cueing of Codes:
Etiquette and Context

Like any social interaction, coperformer and performer-audience behaviors are dependent on the communication of information. Of course, the music itself is usually the primary medium to be communicated, and performers and audience need to be able to "share" in the musical code. A strong corpus of research now indicates this to be the case, with coperformers adapting to one another's musical intentions to create a coordinated musical whole (Williamon & Davidson, 2000), audiences being able to detect even small expressive changes to the music (e.g., Sloboda & Lehmann, 2001), and both performers and audience having similar ideas about what the musical material is communicating (e.g., Sundberg, Frydén, & Friberg, 1995).

But the music itself is not the only communicative force, for rules of social etiquette determine other standards, from how the performers and audiences should dress to how they behave toward each other. For example, pop musicians are far more obviously interactive with their audiences than classical musicians and often engage in activities to involve the audience directly— singing the chorus and dancing to an instrumental interlude (J. W. Davidson, 1997). Due to these sociocultural influences on cognitive processing, it seems necessary to explore the ways in which the moment-by-moment cues between performer and audience are perceived and processed in the performance context.

Nonverbal Communication

It is well known that vision is the dominant perceptual sense, with at least 75% of all information being communicated through this channel; hearing only covers 13% and touch 6% (Long, 1997). It comes as no surprise, therefore, that an increasing amount of research reports the critical role that body movements have in the communication of musical performance information. For example, J. W. Davidson (1993, 1994) found that audiences detect finely grained information about musical expression and intention from musicians' body movements as well as their sounds. This is not surprising, of course, since the body produces the musical sounds and is driven by and itself cues the mental representations of the music. But in a climate where different and contradictory teaching philosophies about how to train musicians to play their instruments abound, it is worth critically evaluating the role of nonverbal aspects of performance communication in detail.

The first major point is that nonmusicians tend to be more reliant on the visual cues than the musical cues to discern whether a performer is playing with or without expression (J. W. Davidson, 1995). The visual cues that differentiate between performances range from varying quantities of movement (varying from stillness to rapid actions like cyclical body swaying) to the use of specific gestures that seem to form a movement repertoire (Davidson, 2002). In terms of musical expression, it has been reported that the varying degrees of movement and the employment of gestural cues are inevitable and largely desirable performance actions. Indeed, J. W. Davidson and Dawson (1995) showed that when performers were only able to make restricted movements in the music-learning process both sound and movement aspects of their final performances were much more constrained and less aesthetically appealing than when musicians were encouraged to use their bodies in a natural manner. The more obviously culturally determined gestures, such as an illustrative lifting of the saxophone bell to highlight the effort involved in playing while also creating an impression of playing with more intensity, are also reported as being desirable but need to be presented at an optimal level: Too many and the performance seems overly exaggerated; too few and the performance seems stilted (Clarke & Davidson, 1998).

The second point of emphasis is that many performance movements have clear roles:

- to communicate the expressive intention (for instance, a sudden surge forward to facilitate the execution of a loud musical passage or a high curving hand gesture to link sections of the music during a pause);
- to communicate directly with the audience or coperformers about issues of coordination or participation (for example, nodding the head to indicate "now" for the audience to join in a chorus of a song or exchanging glances for the coperformer to take over a solo in a jazz piece);
- to draw attention or signal virtuosity (for example, a singer's outstretched

arm gesture as he or she sings a high sustained note in order to demonstrate this achievement);

- to signal extramusical concerns (for example, gesturing to the audience to remain quiet);
- to present information about the performer's personality, with his or her individualized characteristics providing important cues (muted contained gestures or large extravagant gestures, for example).

Other performance movements offer no specific value to the audience as interpretative cues but are the by-products of psychophysical or educational practices that surround performance. For example, singers often stand characteristically "rooted" on both feet in order to facilitate breath support. Although the audience may not read such cues in their assessment of the performance, such movements add to the overall style and content of the performance.

Taken together, the facts about performance movement suggest that it is necessary for musicians to be able to use the full potentiality of their movements in their preparation and performance to make their music optimally communicable. Of course, performance traditions have roles to play, with some types of movement being inappropriate to some contexts (for instance, gesturing for audience participation in a classical concert) or meaningless for the uninitiated onlooker (for example, some emblematic movements in non-Western dance traditions). Observations by musicologists and psychologists indicate that for a truly effective visual communication with audience and coperformers a balance in the articulation of musical expression, coordination, and virtuosic display within the social convention needs to be attained (Cook, 1998; J. W. Davidson, 1997).

Coordination

Performers in ensembles have been found to share characteristics in timing, which indicate that the entire group has to be considered as one body with different parts to it and with some sort of unifying performance plan (Gabrielsson, 1999). For example, in Baroque music performance the melody instruments lead, while in jazz music the rhythm sections lead. By *leading*, we mean that the onsets of new notes or harmonic changes came earlier for some instruments than for others. Whether instrumentalists are aware of this or not at any given time is a secondary concern. More important is the notion that asynchronies must be coordinated by having specific ideas about how the end result should sound and by being able to time individual performance within the time frame of the other musicians. If it were the case that the melody instruments tried to get ahead all the time, we should observe a steady increase in tempo (which we do not, at least not in professional performances). Thus performance in an ensemble requires a common idea of what the piece should sound like. Unfortunately, in most classrooms only one person, namely, the band or choral director, knows what the result should be. Therefore, successful ensemble performance has to rely partly on a shared mental representation, which has to be communicated to one another either during performance via the conductor or through congruent body movements of the different members of the ensemble. This is demonstrated in figure 7.4.

Williamon and Davidson (2002) suggest that the balance between individual and shared representation emerges during rehearsal and by the time of performance coperformers are far more focused on shared rather than individual musical goals. For instance, in a case study (which obviously has

Figure 7.4. Two panels showing at the top a group of musicians with individual mental representations (desired performance or goal images) and at the bottom a group with a shared mental representation.

only limited generalizability) the researchers traced two pianists who worked on and then presented piano duo and duet repertoire in a concert. Initially, issues such as when to place a chord and who should lead at a certain point were central to their preparation concerns, but as a joint plan emerged, two interesting phenomena occurred: (1) both began to move in a similar manner (a rhythmic swaying that demonstrated some link to the musical pulse) to facilitate the coordination of the music; (2) by the performance, they were looking at each other constantly to negotiate subtle and more creative timing variations than those structured in the rehearsals. Thus there was a critical shift to a joint plan and action. Given the limited scope of the study, it is unclear at this point how these coordinative and communicative skills emerge and what types of training would facilitate their development, but it is evident that teachers should note these kinds of changes in behavior and attempt to find strategies to promote their development.

The Audience's Account

Appeal and Gender.   As noted when considering the critical role of nonverbal behavior in music performances, audiences are generally sensitive to musical cues of various types; however, there are all kinds of factors that influence observer judgment. For instance, Wapnick, Darrow, Kovacs, and Dalrymple (1997) carried out a brief study of university entrance auditions for singers and discovered that those who were more animated, smiled more often, and established more eye contact with their audience were rated more highly and thought to be more attractive. In addition, J. W. Davidson and Coimbra (2001) found that musical quality was only one of a number of audience concerns with singers. Critical additional factors included whether or not the performer looked tense and how verbal introductions were delivered. Indeed, the "display" that surrounded the music was of equal salience. Like Wapnick et al., Davidson and Coimbra discovered that first written comments by the audience tended to be about attractiveness, with phrases like "odd-looking chap" and "pretty girl, pretty voice."

In a series of experiments that used video recordings of female or male performers playing either a jazz or a classical piece of music, subjects were asked to rate the performances and the performers (experiments reported in Behne, 1994). The subjects were not aware that the sound tracks for a given piece were always identical, only the performers had been substituted. The results revealed a strong influence of the visual attributes on the evaluation of the performance, and gender stereotypes, such as female: expressive/dramatic and male: technical/precise, emerged. Consistent with results by J. W. Davidson (see earlier), musicians tended to extract more information from the visual display about the underlying musical interpretation than did non-musicians.

Gender stereotypes also exist at the level of choice of instrument. For example, O'Neill and Boulton (1996) reported peer pressure for children to learn only instruments appropriate to their gender: Flutes were deemed most appropriate for girls, drums for boys! An interview by Johnsen (1992) with Rebecca Bower (an American trombonist and one of the first successful female section leaders in a professional orchestra in the United States) showed that gender biases are rife in music. Bower said that at auditions she was refused jobs on grounds of being a woman in a man's world (trombonists are male, after all!) and that audiences tended to be shocked to see that someone "so frail and feminine" could play such a loud "male instrument." Not surprisingly, the switch to "blind" auditions, that is, auditions that use a screen, has led to a considerable increase of women in professional orchestras since the 1970s (Goldin & Rouse, 1997).

Race and Gender.   Of course, men and women behave and dress differently, and so audiences react to performers differently, too. Indeed, anyone who has attended various religious services will attest that African-American gospel singers and their audiences are far less inhibited than their Anglo-Saxon counterparts. Racial issues, like those having to do with gender or any other kind of social bias, are complicated and mostly undesirable. In Europe at least, there is not an established tradition of black classical musicians. When J. W. Davidson (2003) asked audiences to evaluate men and women musicians of black and white origin, they discovered that both black and white male and female audience members preferred the performances by black women. Objectively, the women were no better than the other performers (indeed, the video sound track they were apparently performing was made by another performer and was the same as that used for the other performers). The researchers interpreted this result as an illustration of positive discrimination in favor of black women, who are not usually associated with classical music. Elliott (1995), however, found many more typical and negative race and gender biases when black and white flute and trumpet students were viewed and evaluated: Whites were rated higher than blacks, and black women were rated much worse than black men on their abilities to play a stereotypical male instrument—the trumpet.

To summarize, the display of skill takes place in a social setting and is therefore influenced (biased) in much the same way by social perceptions as are all nonmusical social situations. More important, musicians have to acquire nonverbal means of underlining their musical "messages," and they have to learn how to coordinate their performances with other musicians—musically and physically.

The Acquired Skills Perspective in Music Education

Research in the acquisition of complex everyday skills has favored expert performance as an object of study—If we disregard the laboratory research on basic cognitive functioning for a moment. Although a number of reasons outlined earlier certainly justify this bias, many results are not immediately applicable to the classroom. Similarly, the focus on extremely gifted children and musical prodigies is less interesting to educators who are not commonly confronted with these rare children. However, experts as well as prodigious children are interesting in that they are living proof that education can facilitate the attainment of high levels of performance. If we assume that experts and prodigies operate on similar physiological mechanisms and constraints as do ordinary people, we can try to adapt insights from this research to teaching methods for individual and group instruction (Lehmann & Ericsson, 1997b). In this respect, skill research offers a promising perspective for music educators.

Other educationally important aspects of skill acquisition and display that await further investigation are musical creativity (improvisation, composition) and performance (body movements and communication among performers). It is particularly disturbing that these aspects have not been investigated thoroughly, since they are essential for our aesthetic experience, which sets musical activities apart from other human behaviors. We sometimes tend to think that creative skills (e.g., improvisation) and highly adaptive skills (e.g., sight-reading) are difficult to teach because their goals are to produce something new or react to something unfamiliar. However, this is not necessarily the case. For example, over the years jazz teachers have already prepared the grounds for skill research in their area by developing ample methods and materials for teaching an art that appeared difficult, if not impossible, to teach before.

Mainly because music also relates to emotion and expression, musicians consider their field something special compared to other areas of human performance—and in many ways it certainly is. Yet people outside music, such as biology teachers, actors, and athletes, would probably object to this view and claim that their fields also relate to emotions. It is correct that music encompasses mental, physical, affective, and social cognitions or actions, while other activities focus on a single aspect (e.g., cognition in chess). Music is becoming an increasingly popular playing field for many empirical researchers most likely because it involves the whole person. This research, undertaken by large numbers of researchers outside music education in an attempt to understand human behavior, is likely to ultimately benefit music education and its quest for understanding musical cognition and action. So, rather than viewing ourselves as endowed with a unique, unexplainable skill, we should allow others to show us how our abilities fit into the bigger picture.

The perspective on musical behavior outlined in this chapter may suggest to some readers an oddly strong emphasis on the environment (nurture) at a time when neurophysiology and behavioral genetics are showing convincingly how strong the influences of nature can be. Although leading researchers, including Maccoby (2000), do agree that behavioral genetics has solidly documented the influence of genetics on behavior, she argues on the basis of her review that "when genetic factors are strong, this does not mean that environmental ones, including parenting, must be weak. The relation between the two is not a zero-sum game, and the additive assumption [i.e., that heritability indices are subtracted from 100 to yield the variance explained by the environment] is untenable" (p. 22). What applies to parenting could easily be said for other social learning situations, such as those provided by music education.

Many research methodologies employed in skill research—which by definition is research in teaching, learning, and performance—could be turned into educational tools by clever practitioners. Take, for instance, the verbal protocol methodology mentioned earlier. If researchers can ask their subjects to think aloud in order to find out what cognitive processes play a role during performance, why should teachers not use similar strategies to get into their students' heads (Woody, 1999a)? Such attempts would also serve to bridge the gap between research and teaching, which is sometimes regrettably large.

The most important characteristic of research in skill acquisition and human performance is that this research opens up an optimistic view for educators because it does not focus on innate abilities (see Howe, 1999, for supporting arguments). A common misconception is that skill researchers deny or ignore individual differences that arise from factors beyond training and practice; this is certainly not the case. But if we can explain some individual differences in performance by taking recourse to acquired cognitive mechanisms, such as mental representations or aspects of practice, rather than by attributing individual differences to (almost) immutable genetic or dispositional factors, educators have a chance to consider those explanations in designing future education. High performance is certainly not the be-all and end-all of music education, but the need to achieve satisfactory levels of performance (however one defines them) will always be part of successful music teaching and learning.

STUDY QUESTIONS

1. (a) What are the general characteristics of skills and why are scientists interested in skilled or expert performance? (b) Explain the nature and role of mental representations.

2. Discuss the relation between practice and performance, taking into account quality and quantity of practice. When is quantity of practice a good predictor of outcome and when not?

3. The assessment of music performance is supposed to be objective and unbiased. Is this true, and if not, what influences the audiences' judgment? (Include examples from your own experience).

REFERENCES

Barry, N., & Hallam, S. (2001). Practice. In R. Parncutt & G. McPherson (Eds.), *Science and Psychology of Music Performance* (pp. 151–166). Oxford: Oxford University Press.

Barry, N. H., & McArthur, V. H. (1994). Teaching practice strategies in the music studio: A survey of applied music teachers. *Psychology of Music, 22,* 44–55.

Behne, K. E. (1994). *Gehört, gedacht, gesehen: Zehn Aufsätze zum visuellen, kreativen und theoretischen Umgang mit Musik* [Ten papers on the visual, creative and theoretical approach to the musical experience]. Regensburg, Germany: Con Brio.

Bloom, B. S. (Ed.). (1985). *Developing talent in young people.* New York: Ballantine.

Chaffin, R., & Imreh, G. (1997). "Pulling teeth and torture": Musical memory and problem solving. *Thinking and Reasoning, 3,* 315–336.

Chaffin, R., Imreh, G., & Crawford, M. (2002). *Practicing Perfection: Memory and Piano Performance.* Mahwah, NJ: Lawrence Erlbaum Associates.

Charness, N., Krampe, R. T., & Mayr, U. (1996). The role of practice and coaching in entrepreneurial skill domains. In K. A. Ericsson (Ed.), *The road to excellence* (pp. 51–80). Mahwah, NJ: Erlbaum.

Clarke, E. F., & Davidson, J. W. (1998). The body in performance. In W. Thomas (Ed.), *Composition-performance-reception* (pp. 74–92). Aldershot, UK: Ashgate.

Clynes, M., & Walker, J. (1982). Neurobiological functions of rhythm, time and pulse in music. In M. Clynes (Ed.), *Music, mind, and brain* (pp. 171–216). New York: Plenum.

Cook, N. (1998) *Analysing musical multimedia.* Oxford: Clarendon Press.

Cottrell, N. B. (1972). Social facilitation. In C. G. McClintock (Ed.), *Experimental social psychology* (pp. 131–169). New York: Holt, Rinehart & Winston.

Cziksentmihalyi, M. (1990). *Flow: The psychology of optimal experience.* New York: Harper & Row.

Davidson, J. W. (1993). Visual perception of performance manner in the movements of solo musicians. *Psychology of Music, 21,* 103–113.

Davidson, J. W. (1994). What type of information is conveyed in the body movements of solo musician performers? *Journal of Human Movement Studies, 6,* 279–301.

Davidson, J. W. (1995). What does the visual information contained in music performances offer the observer? Some preliminary thoughts. In R. Steinberg (Ed.), *The music machine: Psychophysiology and psychopathology of the sense of music* (pp. 105–113). Heidelberg, Germany: Springer.

Davidson, J. W. (1997). The social in music performance. In D. Hargreaves & A. North (Eds.), *The social psychology of music* (pp. 209–248). Oxford: Oxford University Press.

Davidson, J. W. (2002). Understanding the expressive movements of a solo pianist. *Musikpsychologie, 16,* 7–29.

Davidson, J. W., & Coimbra, D. C. (2001). Investigating performance evaluation by assessors of singers in a music college setting. *Musicae Scientiae, 5,* 33–54.

Davidson, J. W., & Dawson, J. C. (1995). The development of expression in body movement during learning in piano performance. *Conference Proceedings of Music Perception and Cognition Conference* (p. 31). Berkeley: University of California.

Davidson, J. W., & Edgar, R. (2003). Gender and race bias in the judgment of Western art music performance. *Music Education Research, 5* 169–182.

Davidson, J. W., Howe, M. J. A., Moore, D. M., & Sloboda, J. A. (1996). The role of parental influences in the development of musical ability. *British Journal of Developmental Psychology, 14,* 399–412.

Davidson, J. W., Howe, M. J. A., & Sloboda, J. A. (1997). Environmental factors in the development of musical performance skill in the first twenty years of life. In D. J. Hargreaves & A. C. North (Eds.), *The social psychology of music* (pp. 188–203). Oxford: Oxford University Press.

Davidson, L., & Scripp, L. (1992). Surveying the coordinates of cognitive skills in music. In R. Colwell (Ed.), *Handbook of research on music teaching and learning* (pp. 392–413). New York: Schirmer Books.

Drake, C., & Palmer, C. (2000). Skill acquisition in music performance: Relations between planning and temporal control. *Cognition, 74,* 1–32.

Duke, R. A. (1999). Teacher and student behavior in Suzuki string lessons: Results from the international research symposium on talent education. *Journal of Research in Music Education, 47,* 293–307.

Edlund, B. (2000). Listening to oneself at a distance. In C. Woods, G. B. Luck, R. Brochard, S. A. O'Neill, & J. A. Sloboda (Eds.), *Proceedings of the Sixth International Conference on Music Perception and Cognition* [CD-ROM]. Keele, UK: Department of Psychology, Keele University.

Elliott, D. C. A. (1995). Race and gender as factors in the judgment of musical performance. *Bulletin of the Council for Research in Music Education, 127,* 50–56.

Ericsson, K. A. (1996). The acquisition of expert performance: An introduction to some of the issues. In K. A. Ericsson (Ed.), *The road to excellence* (pp. 1–50). Mahwah, NJ: Erlbaum.

Ericsson, K. A. (1997). Deliberate practice and the acquisition of expert performance: An overview. In H. Jørgensen & A. C. Lehmann (Eds.), *Does practice make perfect? Current theory and research on instrumental music practice* (pp. 9–51). Oslo, Norway: Norges musikkhogskole.

Ericsson, K. A., & Charness, N. (1994). Expert performance: Its structure and acquisition. *American Psychologist, 49,* 725–747.

Ericsson, K. A., & Kintsch, W. (1995). Long-term working memory. *Psychological Review, 102,* 211–245.

Ericsson, K. A., Krampe, R. T., & Tesch-Römer, C. (1993). The role of deliberate practice in the acquisition of expert performance. *Psychological Review, 100,* 363–406.

Ericsson, K. A., & Lehmann, A. C. (1996). Expert and exceptional performance: Evidence for maximal adaptations to task constraints. *Annual Review of Psychology, 47,* 273–305.

Ericsson, K. A., & Simon, H. (1993). *Protocol analysis: Verbal reports as data.* Cambridge: MIT Press.

Ericsson, K. A., & Smith, J. (1991). Prospects and limits in the empirical study of expertise. In K. A. Ericsson & J. Smith (Eds.), *Toward a general theory of expertise: Prospects and limits* (pp. 1–38). Cambridge: Cambridge University Press.

Evans, A. (1994). *The secrets of musical confidence.* London: Thornsons.

Fitts, P., & Posner, M. I. (1967). *Human performance,* Belmont, CA: Brooks & Cole.

Gabrielsson, A. (1999). The performance of music. In D. Deutsch (Ed.), *The psychology of music* (2nd ed., pp. 501–602). San Diego, CA: Academic Press.

Gabrielsson, A., & Juslin, P. N. (1996). Emotional expression in music performance: Between the performer's intention and the listener's experience. *Psychology of Music, 24,* 68–91.

Gardner, H. (1983). *Frames of mind: The theory of multiple intelligences.* New York: Basic Books.

Gellrich, M., & Sundin, B. (1993). Instrumental practice in the 18th and 19th centuries. *Bulletin of Council for Research in Music Education, 119,* 137–145.

Gembris, H. (1997). Historical phases in the definition of musicality. *Psychomusicology, 16,* 40–58.

Gholson, S. A. (1998). Proximal positioning: A strategy of practice in violin pedagogy. *Journal of Research in Music Education, 46,* 535–545.

Gleitman, H. (1991). *Psychology,* New York: W. W. Norton.

Goldin, C., & Rouse, C. (1997). *Orchestrating impartiality: The impact of "blind" auditions on female musicians.* (Working Papers, No. 5903). Cambridge: National Bureau of Economic Research (NBER).

Goolsby, T. W. (1994). Profiles of processing: Eye movements during sightreading. *Music Perception, 12,* 97–123.

Gruson, L. M. (1988). Rehearsal skill and musical competence: Does practice make perfect? In J. A. Sloboda (Ed.), *Generative processes in music: The psychology of performance, improvisation and composition* (pp. 91–112). London: Oxford University Press.

Hallam, S. (1995). Professional musicians' approaches to the learning and interpretation of music. *Psychology of Music, 23,* 111–128.

Hallam, S. (1997). What do we know about practicing? Toward a model synthesizing the research literature. In H. Jørgensen & A. C. Lehmann (Eds.), *Does practice make perfect? Current theory and research on instrumental music practice* (pp. 179–231). Oslo, Norway: Norges musikkhogskole.

Hargreaves, D., Cork, C. A., & Setton, T. (1991). Cognitive strategies in jazz improvisation: An exploratory study. *Canadian Journal of Research in Music Education, 33,* 47–54.

Harnischmacher, C. (1997). The effects of individual differences in motivation, volition, and maturational processes on practice behavior of young instrumentalists. In H. Jørgensen & A. C. Lehmann (Eds.), *Does practice make perfect? Current theory and research on instrumental music practice* (pp. 71–88). Oslo, Norway: Norges musikkhogskole.

Heathcote, A., Brown, S., & Mewhort, D. J. K. (2000). The power law repealed: The case for an exponential law of practice. *Psychonomic Bulletin and Review, 7,* 185–207.

Howe, M. J. A. (1999). *The psychology of high abilities.* New York: New York University Press.

Howe, M. J. A., Davidson, J., & Sloboda, J. A. (1998). Innate talent: Reality or myth? *Behavioral and Brain Sciences, 21*(3), 419–421.

Johnsen, G. (1992). An interview with Rebecca Bower. *Music Educator's Journal, 78*(7), 39–41.

Jørgensen, H. (2004). Strategies for individual practice. In A. Williamon (Ed.), *Musical excellence: Strategies and techniques to enhance performance* (pp. 85–104). Oxford: Oxford University Press.

Jørgensen, H. (1997). Time for practicing? Higher level music students' use of time for instrumental practicing. In H. Jørgensen & A. C. Lehmann (Eds.), *Does practice make perfect? Current theory and research on instrumental music practice* (pp. 123–140). Oslo, Norway: Norges musikkhogskole.

Juslin, P. N. (2001). Communication of emotion in music performance: A review and a theoretical framework. In P. N. Juslin & J. A. Sloboda (Eds.), *Music and emotion: Theory and research* (pp. 309–337). Oxford: Oxford University Press.

Krampe, R. T., & Ericsson, K. A. (1996). Maintaining excellence: Deliberate practice and elite performance in young and older pianists. *Journal of Experimental Psychology: General, 125,* 331–359.

Lehmann, A. C. (1997a). Acquired mental representations in music performance: Anecdotal and preliminary empirical evidence. In H. Jørgensen & A. C. Lehmann (Eds.), *Does practice make perfect? Current theory and research on instrumental music practice* (pp. 141–164). Oslo, Norway: Norges musikkhogskole.

Lehmann, A. C. (1997b). Acquisition of expertise in music: Efficiency of deliberate practice as a moderating variable in accounting for sub-expert performance. In I. Deliege & J. Sloboda (Eds.), *Perception and cognition of music* (pp. 165–191). London: Erlbaum, Taylor & Francis.

Lehmann, A. C., & Ericsson, K. A. (1996). Structure and acquisition of expert accompanying and sight-reading performance. *Psychomusicology, 15,* 1–29.

Lehmann, A. C., & Ericsson, K. A. (1997). Research on expert performance and deliberate practice: Implications for the education of amateur musicians and music students. *Psychomusicology, 16,* 40–58.

Lehmann, A. C., & Ericsson, K. A. (1998). Preparation of a public piano performance: The relation between practice and performance. *Musicae Scientiae, 2,* 69–94.

Lehmann, A. C., & McArthur, V. (2002). Sight-Reading. In R. Parncutt & G. McPherson (Eds.), *Science and Psychogy of Music Performance* (pp. 135–150). Oxford: Oxford University Press.

Long, K. (1997). Visual-aids and learning. Retrieved September 2000, from University of Portsmouth, Department of Mechanical and Manufacturing Engineering. Web site: http://www.mech.port.ac.uk/av/AVALearn.htm.

Maccoby, E. E. (2000). Parenting and its effects on children: On reading and misreading behavior genetics. *Annual Review of Psychology, 51,* 1–28.

Manturzewska, M. (1990). A biographical study of the life-span development of professional musicians. *Psychology of Music, 18,* 112–139.

Manturzewska, M. (1995). Das elterliche Umfeld herausragender Musiker. In H. Gembris, R. D. Kraemer, & G. Maas (Eds.), *Musikpädagogische Forschungsberichte 1994* (pp. 11–22). Augsburg, Germany: Wissner.

Marsalis, W. (1995). *Tackling the monster: Marsalis on practice* [VHS tape 66312]. New York: Sony Classical Film and Video.

McPherson, G. E. (2005). From child to musician: skill development during the beginning stages of learning and instrument. *Psychology of Music, 33, 5 35.*

McPherson, G. (1995). The assessment of musical performance: Development and validation of five new measures. *Psychology of Music, 23,* 142–161.

Miklaszewski, K. (1989). A case study of a pianist preparing a musical performance. *Psychology of Music, 17,* 95–109.

Nielsen, S. G. (1997). Self-regulation of learning strategies during practice: A case study of a church organ student preparing a musical work for performance. In H. Jørgensen & A. C. Lehmann (Eds.), *Does practice make perfect? Current theory and research on instrumental music practice* (pp. 109–122). Oslo, Norway: Norges musikkhogskole.

Noice, T., & Noice, H. (1997). *The nature of expertise in professional acting: A cognitive view.* Mahwah, NJ: Erlbaum.

O'Neill, S. A., & Boulton, M. J. (1996). Boys' and girls' preferences for musical instruments: A function of gender. *Psychology of Music, 24,* 171–183.

O'Neill, S., & Sloboda, J. (1997). Effects of failure on children's ability to perform a musical test. *Psychology of Music, 25,* 18–34.

Palmer, C. (1992). The role of interpretive preferences in music performance. In M. Riess-Jones & S. Holleran (Eds.), *Cognitive bases of musical communication* (pp. 249–262). Washington, DC: American Psychological Association.

Palmer, C. (1997). Music performance. *Annual Review of Psychology, 48,* 115–138.

Palmer, C., & Meyer, R. (2000). Conceptual and motor learning in music performance. *Psychological Science, 11,* 63–68.

Perkins, D. (1989). Art as understanding. In H. Gardner & D. Perkins (Eds.), *Art, mind, and education: Research from Project Zero* (pp. 111–131). Urbana: University of Illinois Press.

Persson, R. S. (1996). Brilliant performers as teachers: A case study of commonsense teaching in a conservatory setting. *International Journal of Music Education, 28,* 25–36.

Proctor, R. W., & Dutta, A. (1995). *Skill acquisition and human performance.* Thousand Oaks, CA: Sage.

Repp, B. H. (1996). The art of inaccuracy: Why pianists' errors are difficult to hear. *Music Perception, 14,* 161–184.

Rideout, R. R. (1992). The role of mental presets in skill acquisition. In R. Colwell (Ed.), *Handbook of research on music teaching and learning* (pp. 472–479). New York: Schirmer Books.

Simon, H. A., & Chase, W. G. (1973). Skill in chess. *American Scientist, 61,* 394–403.

Sloboda, J. A., & Lehmann, A. C. (2001). Performance correlates of perceived emotionality in different interpretations of a Chopin Piano Prelude. *Music Perception, 19,* 87–120.

Sloboda, J. A., Davidson, J. W., Howe, M. J. A., & Moore, D. M. (1996). The role of practice in the development of expert musical performance. *British Journal of Psychology, 87,* 287–309.

Sloboda, J. A., & Howe, M. J. A. (1991). Biographical precursors of musical excellence: An interview study. *Psychology of Music, 19,* 3–21.

Starkes, J. L., Deakin, J., Allard, F., Hodges, N. J., & Hayes, A. (1996). Deliberate practice in sports: What is it anyway? In K. A. Ericsson (Ed.), *The road to excellence* (pp. 81–106). Mahwah, NJ: Erlbaum.

Stuart-Hamilton, I. (1996). *Dictionary of cognitive psychology.* London: Jessica Kingsley.

Sundberg, J., Frydén, L., & Friberg, A. (1995). Expressive aspects of instrumental and vocal performance. In R. Steinberg (Ed.), *Music and the mind machine: The psychophysiology and psychopathology of the sense of music* (pp. 49–62). New York: Springer.

Todd, N. P. M. (1985). A model of expressive timing in tonal music. *Music Perception, 3,* 33–58.

Trusheim, W. H. (1991). Audiation and mental imagery: Implications for artistic performance. *Quarterly Journal of Music Teaching and Learning, 2,* 138–147.

Tunks, T. W. (1992). The transfer of music learning. In R. Colwell (Ed.), *Handbook of research on music teaching and learning* (pp. 437–447). New York: Schirmer Books.

Wagner, C. (1988). The pianist's hand: Anthropometry and biomechanics. *Ergonomics, 31,* 97–131.

Wapnick, J., Darrow, A. A., Kovacs, J., & Dalrymple, L. (1997). Effects of physical attractiveness on evaluation of vocal performance. *Journal of Research in Music Education, 45,* 470–479.

Williamon, R.A. & Davidson, J.W. (2002) Exploring co-performer communication. *Musicae Scientiae, 6,* 1–17.

Williamon, A., & Valentine, E. (2000). Quantity and quality of musical practice as predictors of performance quality. *British Journal of Psychology, 91,* 353–376.

Wilson, G. D. (1997). Performance anxiety. In D. Hargreaves & A. North (Eds.), *The social psychology of music* (pp. 229–248). Oxford: Oxford University Press.

Winner, E. (1996). The rage to master: The decisive role of talent in the visual arts. In K. A. Ericsson (Ed.), *The road to excellence* (pp. 271–302). Mahwah, NJ: Erlbaum.

Woody, R. H. (1999a). Getting into their heads. *American Music Teacher, 49*(3), 24–27.

Woody, R. H. (1999b). The relationship between advanced musicians' explicit planning and their expressive performance of dynamic variations in an aural modeling task. *Journal of Research in Music Education, 47,* 331–342.

Woody, R. H. (2003). Explaining expressive performance: Component cognitive skills in an aural modeling task. *Journal of Research in Music Education, 51(1),* 51–63.

Zajonc, R. B. (1965). Social facilitation. *Science, 149,* 269–274.

Zdzinski, S. F. (1996). Parental involvement, selected student attributes, and learning outcomes in instrumental music. *Journal of Research in Music Education, 44,* 34–48.

Index

Fourier analysis, 76
frequency(ies)
  critical band, 77, 114
  fundamental, pitch and, 76–77
  timbre and, 110–111
  in tonal hierarchy, 101
  in voice harmony perception, 105
functional magnetic resonance
      imaging (fMRI)
  in affective research, 16
  of formal mental representations,
      48
  in neuromusical research, 13, 15
functions/functionality
  biological perspectives of, 9
  in musical ability development, 145–
      146, 152

gender
  audience's appeal based on, 249–
      250
  musical ability development and,
      144–145
  race and, 250
  stereotypes of, 249–250
general intelligence theory, of human
      ability, 166–167, 172, 175
genetics
  behavioral, 251–252
  of brain development, 17
  of human ability, 167, 178–179
  molecular, 50
  role of, 3, 127
  of Williams syndrome, 3
giftedness, 129, 237, 251
glial cells, development of, 18–19
global information processing
  in music learning, 52, 62
  in performance individuality, 201–
      202, 207–208
glucose, brain consumption of, 46
goal representation, in music
      performance, 235–237
grammar, rule-based, for
      performance, 198–199, 208
graphic representations
  musical ability development and,
      138
  of nonmusical meanings, 137–138
grouping
  in rhythm perception, 106–107
  tasks, in timbre perception, 111

habituation theory, 23
harmonic progression, "rules" of,
      102–106
harmonic series, 76
harmonicity, of periodic sounds, 104–
      105
harmonics, 76
harmony, 98
  implied, 99–100
  listening to, 74, 98–106
  in musical ability development, 134
  perceiving voices in, 102–106
  timbre and, 110–111, 113–114
  tonal hierarchy and, 100–102
  Western, 98–99
Hawthorne effect, 56
Hebb synapse, 45
height, pitch, 79–82
helical model, of pitch, 80–81
hemispheric asymmetry
  modularity and connectionism of,
      24–26
  music learning and, 52, 62
  neuromusical research on, 8, 12–13
  research directions for, 29
hierarchy
  metric, 106–108
  tonal, 101
hippocampus, postnatal development
      of, 49
holistic strategy, for performance
      plan, 194–195
hormone(s), brain regulation of, 8,
      24
human ability theory, 165–183
  cognitive processes range and, 172–
      176
  cognitive revolution of, 165–166
  conceptual model of, 174
  contextualization of, 168–172, 180
  developmental challenges in, 176–
      178
  disjunctures concept, 178–180
  domain mapping for, 174–175
  educational implications of, 167,
      180–183
  integration of, 176, 182–183
  interconnectedness of, 172–176,
      181–182
  psychology of (see psychology)
  review of past, 166–168
  sociocultural dimensions of, 171